Film as Philosophy

FILM AS PHILOSOPHY

Bernd Herzogenrath

EDITOR

University of Minnesota Press

Minneapolis • London

Published by the University of Minnesota Press
111 Third Avenue South, Suite 290
Minneapolis, MN 55401–2520
http://www.upress.umn.edu

Printed in the United States of America on acid-free paper

The University of Minnesota is an equal-opportunity educator and employer.

23 22 21 20 19 18 17   10 9 8 7 6 5 4 3 2 1

Library of Congress Cataloging-in-Publication Data
Herzogenrath, Bernd, editor.
Film as philosophy / Bernd Herzogenrath, editor.
Minneapolis : University of Minnesota Press, 2017. | Includes bibliographical references and index.
Identifiers: LCCN 2016015354 | ISBN 978-1-5179-0050-2 (hc) | ISBN 978-1-5179-0051-9 (pb)
Subjects: LCSH: Motion picture—Philosophy.
Classification: LCC PN1995 .F457545 2016 | DDC 791.4301—dc23
LC record available at https://lccn.loc.gov/2016015354

Contents

Introduction. Film and/as Philosophy: An Elective Affinity?   vii
   BERND HERZOGENRATH

1. Striking Poses: Gesture, Image, and Remake in the   1
   Cinematic Bergson
   JOHN Ó MAOILEARCA

2. Hugo Münsterberg, Film, and Philosophy   23
   ROBERT SINNERBRINK

3. Different, Even Wholly Irrational Arguments: 45
   The Film Philosophy of Béla Balázs
   ADRIAN MARTIN

4. This Is Your Brain on Cinema: Antonin Artaud   66
   GREGORY FLAXMAN

5. From Lyrosophy to Antiphilosophy: The Thought   90
   of Cinema in Jean Epstein
   CHRISTOPHE WALL-ROMANA

6. Montage Eisenstein: Mind the Gap   111
   JULIA VASSILIEVA

7. André Bazin's Film Theory and the History of Ideas   132
   ANGELA DALLE VACCHE

8. Strange Topologics: Deleuze Takes a Ride down   161
   David Lynch's *Lost Highway*
   BERND HERZOGENRATH

9. Hurray for Hollywood: Philosophy and Cinema   180
   According to Stanley Cavell
   ELISABETH BRONFEN

10. Thinking Cinema with Alain Badiou   200
    ALEX LING

11. Thinking as Feast: Raymonde Carasco   219
    NICOLE BRENEZ

12. Rancière's Film Theory as Deviation   241
    TOM CONLEY

13. Movie-Made Philosophy   265
    NOËL CARROLL

14. "Not Time's Fool": Marriage as an Ethical Relationship   286
    in Michael Haneke's *Amour*
    THOMAS E. WARTENBERG

15. Experience and Explanation in the Cinema   306
    MURRAY SMITH

Acknowledgments   331

Contributors   333

Index   337

Film and/as Philosophy

AN ELECTIVE AFFINITY?

Bernd Herzogenrath

Media and thinking are intimately related. Our memory, perception, and cognition are not just a given, as weightless, immaterial processes taking place purely mentally behind the walls of our skull, but also always already rest on a medial basis. As Nietzsche claims, "Our writing equipment takes part in the forming of our thoughts" (Unser Schreibzeug arbeitet mit an unseren Gedanken).[1] From here we can derive the media-philosophical insight that a new medium makes us think differently. Media thus reveal themselves as the body or, better, the different bodies of thought. It is important to note these bodies are not retroactive to those thoughts that they materialize, just as the microscope is not retroactive to the discovery of bacteria: media are *coextensive* to the thoughts they allow. Media generate potentialities of thought, make things "thinkable" in different, medium-specific ways. Thinking thus cannot be said to be taking place within the confines of our skull, only—thinking is noncentered, taking place on multiple levels and in feedback loops. Thus, media philosophy in general and film philosophy in particular are events, even praxes, rooted in the horizon of media themselves. They take place *through* and *within* the media in question and can be "put into words" only by translating them into the master medium: writing-thinking.

During the past ten to fifteen years, the convergence of film studies and philosophy has become the "next big thing" in (not only) the field of media studies. For a long time, academic discourse had considered film as the (or an) Other of philosophical reflections—as a dissipation and pastime, maybe as an aesthetical illustration of certain ideas. In an alternative "line of tradition," however, philosophy takes film as a serious field of scholarly engagement: beginning with Henri Bergson and Maurice Merleau-Ponty, this tradition culminated in recent decades in the approaches of cognitive film studies (in the tradition of analytical philosophy as represented by David Bordwell, Noël Carroll, Murray Smith, etc.), perspectives rooted in academic philosophy (e.g., Thomas E. Wartenberg and Martin Seel), and the film philosophies (in the wake) of Stanley Cavell and Gilles Deleuze, who argued for an appreciation of film *as* philosophy. How can this relationship between film and philosophy be thought anew? Can philosophy renew our concepts of film as a piece of art and/or as a medium? And vice versa, can film change our understanding of philosophy as a scholarly practice and endeavor? Or should the concepts *film* and *philosophy* be reconsidered (or revised) in their entirety once we dare their encounter? With the recent ubiquity of neuroscience in the humanities, which has found its way into film studies and philosophy as well, a new perspective has opened, one that puts a focus on the process of thinking itself, asking, what is thought and where does it occur? Questioning the philosophical status of film is thus situated within a grander context: Is there something like cinematic thought, thinking-with-images? How does it relate to philosophical thoughts and inquiries or to scientific analyses of this process? Can those disciplines benefit from each other? Once the disciplines of film studies and philosophy become mutually exposed to these conceptual extensions, they might allow for new contributions that benefit them both.

This volume argues the questions, what is film? (as a slight rephrasing of Bazin's *What Is Cinema?*), and, what is philosophy? (as Deleuze and Guattari have asked), are intimately intertwined—in a very pragmatic and institutional way. When Roger Odin, one of the pioneers of "institutionalized" film studies in France, was called to office in the early 1980s, he was faced with the fact that film studies as a discipline did not (yet) exist. Far from despairing, Odin felt confirmed, rather, in his belief that film and cinema were not suitable objects for an academic discipline. By that he did not mean to discredit cinema as an object worthy of academic analysis—on the contrary, Odin's firm belief was that cinema opened up a whole field of research, with a whole range of disciplines contributing. While Odin was taking Gilbert Cohen-Séat's Institut de filmologie as a model, which was an interdisciplinary institute par excellence, he found his own institute was still miles away from that ideal. Nevertheless, the number of film scholars worldwide who have a degree in another subject (Odin himself is a linguist by training)—be it one of the national philologies, art history, musicology, or philosophy—is overwhelming. So also institution-wise, an interdisciplinary approach to film (including philosophical expertise) is not only desired but fact.[2]

In the 1980s cognitive film studies discovered the brain for the analysis of film. Against the Grand Theories of psychoanalytic and (post)structuralist theory, they employed the findings of cognitive psychology for explaining the processes in the spectator's mind to "make meaning," seeing the understanding of film as a rational and cognitive endeavor that applied scientific "theories of perception, information processing, hypothesis-building, and interpretation"[3] At that time, the dominant strand in neuroscience was the field of computation, which took the computer as its model: the brain here was seen essentially as an input/output machine of representation.

Approximately at the same time, Gilles Deleuze, in the "new image of thought" he developed (among others) in his two *Cinema* books, also used the concept of the brain, with implicit and explicit references, on the one hand, to Henri Bergson and, on the other hand, to a more constructivist brand of neurosciences in the wake of Maturana, Varela, and Changeux, seeing both film and brain as agencies of the "creation of worlds": "The brain is the screen."[4] Certainly, the brain that cognitive film studies, neuroscience, and Deleuze talk about is not the same object/concept in these discourses. Recent developments in cognitive neuroscience into 4EA cognitivism, which considers the brain as embodied, enacted, extended, embedded, and affective, might create new insights, however, into the encounters of brains and screens. Here, in contrast to classical computation and, even, to connectionism, which is more advanced than computation insofar as it involves a more complex (and acentered) dynamics, thinking finally takes place not inside our skulls (only) but "out of our heads" (to quote the title of Alva Noë's book).

Yet one of the main difficulties that impede a smooth and simple marriage of film studies, (Deleuzian) philosophy, and the neurosciences is the fact that the brain in question is in fact many brains. Not only do the concepts of the brain among these various disciplines differ, but Deleuze himself uses the brain in different guises. First, on a very general level, he traces the motif or metaphor of the brain in movies by Alain Resnais and Stanley Kubrick. Far more important in the context of our interest, however, are Deleuze's references to the philosophy of Henri Bergson and his "new conception" of the brain: Bergson "introduced a profound element of transformation: the brain was now only an interval [*écart*], a void, nothing but a void, between a stimulation and a response."[5] In a universe that consists, as Bergson has it, of images in motion that all react on one another, the subject (and the brain) functions as "centers of indetermination," in which the direct cause/effect or stimulus/response reaction is slowed down.[6] This idea of the brain as a center of indetermination is supported by findings in neurosciences that focus on the brain as "an uncertain system,"[7] as rhizomatic neural networks. Deleuze is here referring to Jean-Pierre Changeux's *Neuronal Man: The Biology of Mind* and Steven Rose's *The Conscious Brain* (which also refers to Delisle Burns's *The Uncertain Nervous System*). For Deleuze it boils down to the following:

> We can consider the brain as a relatively undifferentiated mass and ask what circuits, what kinds of circuit, the movement-image or time-image traces out, or invent, because the circuits aren't there to begin with . . . the brain's the hidden side of all circuits, and these can allow the most basic conditioned reflexes to prevail, as well as leaving room for more creative tracings, less "probable" links. The brain's a spatio-temporal volume: it's up to art to trace through it the new paths open to us today. You might see continuities and false continuities as cinematic synapses—you get different links, and different circuits, in Godard and Resnais, for example. The overall importance or significance of cinema seems to me to depend on this sort of problem.[8]

One of the most decisive questions that emerges in the wake of thinking the interrelation between media—and here, more specifically, film—and thought is related to the respective status of "philosophy." As we have seen, there seems to be a great divide between analytic and continental "schools of thought."[9] However, there are also different "formats" that count as "film philosophy," one way or the other. To a degree, one can distinguish between (at least) four types:

Films about Philosophers

Here, film (documentary films but also some feature films) is basically a "mouthpiece" for either philosophical theories or the biographies of Great Thinkers—basically, the film version of a philosophical monologue or dialogue. Examples include *Derrida* (Kirby Dick and Amy Ziering Kofman, 2002), *Zizek!* (Astra Taylor, 2005), *Examined Life* (Astra Taylor, 2008), *The Ister* (David Barison and Daniel Ross, 2004), and *Being in the World* (Tao Ruspoli, 2010) in the documentary section and *Blaise Pascal* (Roberto Rossellini, 1971), *Socrates* (Rossellini, 1972), *Augustine of Hippo* (Rossellini, 1972), *Al di là del bene e del male* (Beyond good and evil) (Liliana Cavani, 1977), and *Wittgenstein* (Derek Jarman, 1993) as examples of feature films.

Films as Illustrations of Philosophical Propositions

This approach relates film to philosophical questions and axioms (ethics, justice, aesthetics, anthropology, etc.) but leaves the disciplinary boundaries intact: film may illustrate philosophical problems, but these problems "belong" to the field of (academic) philosophy proper. Film (unwittingly?) responds to or illustrates problems of a field external to it. Examples include *The Man Who Shot Liberty Valance* (John Ford, 1962) and *The Life of David Gale* (Alan Parker, 2003). Both this and the first type could be put under the heading "Philosophy in Film."

Philosophy of Film

This field comprises two approaches—analytic and continental, respectively—sketched at the beginning of this introduction. In both of their reactions against the Grand Theories, they nevertheless revise some of the fundamental questions of "classical film theory" and thus are connected to some of the key figures in the long genealogy of film and philosophy that this book aims to present.

Philosophy as Film (Film as Philosophy)

This approach, which I see as a continuation and radicalization of the ideas of Cavell and Deleuze, sometimes in a crossover with cognitivist theories (see, for example, the work of Robert Sinnerbrink, Patricia Pisters, and William Brown), is best summarized by the Cavell-inspired words of Stephen Mulhall: "I do not look at these films as handy or

popular illustrations of views and arguments properly developed by
philosophers; I see them rather as themselves reflecting on and evaluat-
ing such views and arguments, as thinking seriously and systematically
about them in just the ways that philosophers do. Such films are not
philosophy's raw material, nor a source for its ornamentation; they are
philosophical exercises, philosophy in action–film as philosophizing."[10]

In this claim, films themselves are seen as capable of doing a
unique kind of philosophical work (even though Mulhall's characterization of films philosophizing "in just the ways that philosophers
do" might still be in need of some qualification). Thus, the question
is, What kind of knowledge (affects and percepts themselves giving
rise to concepts) does the medium film generate qua medium?

Ultimately, the question, what is film philosophy? might better be
restated as, where is film philosophy? Does it reside in the institutionalized version of (academic) philosophy ("proper"), or might it also
be said to be inherent to film itself? An important qualification has to
be made here: the question, what is philosophy? has to be addressed
again at this point because the different relations of film and philosophy also owe a lot to the definition of the philosophical. If the rubric
of film as philosophy claims films or cinema can do philosophy, then
it is not the institutionalized version of academic philosophy (i.e., the
production of propositional knowledge) but rather what Deleuze and
Guattari call the "creation of concepts."[11] This entails a definition of
philosophy that goes beyond its traditional territorialization, one that
is extensional, forming assemblages rather than propositions, what—
again—Deleuze has called "the new image of thought."[12]

Following this approach, "philosophy" and "thinking" do not
necessarily refer to rational propositions and/or a purely neural activity, though. Thinking is not just a representation of the world as "it
is"—as Deleuze puts it, "*Something in this world* enforces thought.
This something is the base of a fundamental encounter, and not of
a recognition."[13] While the idea of "thinking as (re-)cognition" is
based on the verification of ideologies, of precollected knowledge,
customs, and articles of faith, the notion of "thinking as an encounter" shatters our epistemological and experiential habits, producing a
break in our "normal," habitual perspective of the world and enabling

the possibility of approaching alternative points of view and means of thought and of questioning our common practices. Thus film-thought is philosophical, since it offers its own genuine cinematic reflections about the world. According to Deleuze these are especially new looks at concepts of images, time, space, and movement (concepts grounded in the peculiarity of the medium as a stream of "moving images").

In an interview with Raymond Bellour and François Ewald, Deleuze stated, "I've never been worried about going beyond metaphysics or any death of philosophy. The function of philosophy, still thoroughly relevant, is to create concepts."[14] This affirmative function of philosophy is also a call to transdisciplinarity, so that even when Deleuze was working on "painting and cinema: images, on the face of it . . . [he] was writing philosophy books."[15] In defense of Deleuze against Sokal/Bricmont's attempt to control and regulate the limits of the disciplinary fields, Paul Harris points out that Deleuze's work shows, in contrast, "how productive it is to work with and think through material from others and other fields . . . , working with ideas cooked up in geology and geography, zoology and ornithology, archeology and paleontology, and even mathematics and physics."[16] The philosophical practice of "creating concepts," as a creation of "newness" as well, necessitates, according to Deleuze, that philosophy enter into manifold relations with arts and sciences, since philosophy "creates and expounds its concepts only in relation to what it can grasp of scientific functions and artistic constructions. . . . Philosophy cannot be undertaken independently of science or art."[17] These resonances and exchanges among philosophy, science, and art make philosophy "creative," not reflective. These relations— from the perspective of philosophy—are vital for reasons internal to philosophy itself—that is, vital for the creation of "concepts" and, from the perspective of film philosophy, for a resonance with the percepts and affective logics and modalities of art, in general, and film, in particular.

This book attempts to bring film studies and philosophy into a productive dialogue without assigning the role of a dominant and all-encompassing referee to one of these disciplines. Rather, it is about relating the diverse entry points—the many colors of the spectrum—

toward each other in a fertile manner in order to establish, ultimately, a media philosophy that puts the status, the role, and the function of the medium—here, film—into a new perspective: no longer are the representational techniques of the medium at the center of inquiry but rather its ability to "think" and to assume an active role in the process of thought, in finding alternative and differentiating point(s) of view (and thoughts). With such an approach, the medium film is shown as possessing "agency," and the dialogue between film and philosophy (and even neuroscience) is negotiated anew. The following sections provide a road map to this book and highlight the key figures in the history of film and/as cinema.

Henri Bergson (1859–1941)

Deleuze's film philosophy makes much of the notion of virtual images in Henri Bergson's *Matter and Memory,* but in doing so it transforms a psycho-meta-physical thesis into a (very) un-Bergsonian ontological one. In his essay, John Ó Maoilearca offers a corrective by exploring Bergson's *own* explanation of the image as an "attitude of the body"—something that projects an *actual,* corporeal, and postural approach *not only to cinema but also to philosophy.* As Renoir famously claimed, "A director makes only one movie in his life. Then he breaks it into pieces and makes it again." So, too, Bergson wrote each philosopher makes only one "single point" throughout his or her whole career. This one point, he then declared, was like a "vanishing image," one best understood only as an attitude of the body. Embodied image underlies an alternative Bergsonian cinema of the *actual* and the *body,* one Ó Maoilearca examines through Bergson's thoughts about "attitude," "gesture," and "mime" and also looks at through a gestural concept enacted by a film—to be precise, the five remakes comprised by Lars von Trier and Jørgen Leth's *The Five Obstructions* (2003). This brings Ó Maoilearca back to the idea of what it is that is being remade, both by directors and by philosophers, in Renoir's "one film" and Bergson's singular "vanishing image," respectively. Is the "one" being remade an image understood as a representation? Or is it a gesture understood as a bodily movement? The latter stance provides a new and alternative view of Bergson's philosophy of cinema.

Hugo Münsterberg (1863–1916)

Hugo Münsterberg was the first psychologist and philosopher to undertake a serious study of cinema; his recently revived text, *The Photoplay: A Psychological Study* (1916), is widely regarded as the first work of film theory. Robert Sinnerbrink discusses some of the key elements of Münsterberg's theorization of film, focusing on the philosophical dimensions of *The Photoplay*: its combination of neo-Kantian (and Schopenhauerian) aesthetic theory, empirical psychology, and an ontological-aesthetic concern with the medium—in particular, the question of film as art. On the one hand, Münsterberg was a pioneer in the empirical-psychological study of cinema, anticipating elements of contemporary cognitive theory; on the other, his pioneering philosophy of film remained wedded to "classical" theories of aesthetics and sought to synthesize the analysis of cinematic experience within the prevailing system of the fine arts. Nonetheless, he recognized the aesthetic distinctiveness of the medium, exploring its aesthetic and cultural possibilities as an art capable of communicating the "free and joyful play of the mind." In this regard, Münsterberg canvassed some of the central problems of classical film theory while struggling to articulate a coherent theory of cinema capable of synthesizing its psychological-cognitive and aesthetic-cultural dimensions.

Béla Balázs (1884–1949)

Among those we now consider classical film theorists, Béla Balázs offers a unique case. His first and most philosophically oriented book on film, *Visible Man or the Culture of Film* (1924), constituted an "originary" text on which each subsequent contribution, *The Spirit of Film* (1930) and *Theory of the Film* (1948), was built. Adrian Martin's essay passes from the passion of the early work to the pedagogy of his final years. This essay concentrates on the philosophical ideas and possibilities announced in Balázs's writing of the 1920s, taking up Anton Kaes's questioning of his retroactive status as a classical aesthetician. For Balázs cinema was not just *another* art to join the established pantheon but an altogether *new* art. Balázs was open to cultural experiences that both promised and threatened to overthrow and, thus, radically redefine what the aesthetic categories of the truthful, the beautiful, and the dramatically expressive could mean in the filmic medium. To fully grasp this crucial dimension, one needs to connect Balázs's writing to two bodies of work: first, the many contemporaneous writings, in the 1920s and 1930s, on the burgeoning of modernity and its radically changing social conditions and, second, Maurice Maeterlinck's theories of "new drama," which greatly influenced him.

Antonin Artaud (1896–1948)

Gregory Flaxman returns to Antonin Artaud's cinematic writings, in particular his fragmentary body of film criticism, in order to recover the constituents of a remarkable philosophy of cinema. Compared with his work on theater, poetry, language, and performance, Artaud's engagement with the cinema has inspired far less enthusiasm, and it is impossible not to read this response in light of Artaud's ultimate renunciation of cinema. Nevertheless, in this essay Flaxman argues that Artaud renounced the seventh art for the same reasons he had formerly embraced it—namely, the capacity of the moving image to affect the spectator, to move the senses, and finally, to inhabit the brain itself. Over the span of almost a decade, Artaud wrestled with the psychomechanics of the cinema, which he defined at various points as a drug, a waking dream, a trance, a spell, and a delusion. In each case, he described the moving image as if it consisted in a power to overtake consciousness. In line with this idea, Flaxman's essay poses the idea of a "cinematic automaton" on the basis of a concept borrowed from Spinoza and Leibniz, the "spiritual automaton." In light of this turn to classical philosophy, Flaxman contends that Artaud envisioned the cinema as a brain within the brain.

Jean Epstein (1897–1953)

Jean Epstein was a poet, filmmaker, theoretician, and philosopher of the cinema. Christophe Wall-Romana's chapter presents key facets of Epstein's holistic philosophy of the cinema, beginning with early concepts—lyrosophy and *photogénie*—that demonstrate his intermedial aesthetics at the intersection of philosophy, poetry, and cinema. What subtends this intermediality is, on the one hand, Epstein's focus on "coenasthesis"—that is, inner bodily sensations and their link with affects—and, on the other, the relations of similarity and dissimilarity between cinema and language. The intermedial holism of Epstein is expressed by his notion of the "unified intellectual plane," which is akin to (and inflected by) Deleuze's "plane of immanence" as directly related to the screen. Epstein's embodied philosophy devolved in important ways from his homosexuality, which lead him to develop a view of queerness and cinema as sharing an antinatural naturalism. Wall-Romana concludes with a reading of Epstein's philosophical summa, *The Intelligence of a Machine* (1946), an exploration of the cinema apparatus as presenting us with an autonomous cognitive agency. Epstein was the first to consider cinema not just as worthy of philosophical reflection but as generating a new understanding of time, space, and causality beyond the limits of our human scope and scale. Now that digital imaging has bracketed the issue of indexicality as the essence of cinema, his thought can be better understood, since he viewed cinema not as an inert tool confirming our ideas of realism but as an active prosthesis challenging and expanding them.

Sergei Eisenstein (1898–1948)

Over the past quarter century, as Sergei Eisenstein's previously unpublished major works, including his magnum opus, *Method,* have come to light, it has become possible to construct a richer, more nuanced understanding of Eisenstein and his legacy. As Julia Vassilieva argues, however, within this emerging reconsideration of Eisenstein, his engagement with philosophy is arguably the one aspect in most need of revision. On the one hand, dialogue with Eisenstein's heritage defined some key philosophical issues in film studies—such as André Bazin's discussion of realism, Noël Burch's analysis of formal dialectics in cinematic expression, Gilles Deleuze's theorization of movement-image, and Vivian Sobchack's embodied account of cinematic experience. On the other hand, analysis of Eisenstein's philosophy in its own right remains fixed on Marxist influence on Eisenstein and on the contextualization of his work in relation to the project of construction of socialism in Russia. In her essay Vassilieva argues there are now compelling reasons to rethink Eisenstein's philosophical position—beyond the ideological debates of the twentieth century. Drawing on recently published texts by Eisenstein in Russia and Vassilieva's own research on still unpublished writings by Eisenstein, her essay proposes new ways of understanding Eisenstein's philosophy of film.

André Bazin (1918–58)

Usually associated with French existentialism, André Bazin's film theory was in touch with Jean Paul Sartre's literary essays but rejected the philosopher's nihilism in favor of Emmanuel Mounier's personalist thought. The founder of the journal *Esprit* in 1932, Mounier was critical of American individualism, Soviet collectivism, and French capitalism. Although Sartre is usually credited for having invented the figure of the "engaged intellectual," this role was first conceptualized by Mounier. For the personalist thinker, the Other was a Neighbor, whereas for Sartre, the Other was "hell." In addition, Angela Dalle Vacche argues why and how Saint Augustine's focus on ambiguity and resurrection, Blaise Pascal's work on science and religion, Henri Bergson's duration and intuition, and Maurice Merleau-Ponty's phenomenology are relevant to Bazin's film theory.

Gilles Deleuze (1925–95) and David Lynch (1946–)

How do we make sense of a film? And how do we make sense of a film if this film does not follow the expected trajectories of Hollywood filmmaking? Using the example of David Lynch's *Lost Highway,* my essay argues for and makes useful Gilles Deleuze's film philosophy, particularly in connection with Bergson's conceptions of time and Deleuze's notion of "the encounter," calling for an approach that makes the "object in question" provide its own terms and conditions for a more affective mode of "making sense." This essay aims at showing Lynch's movie "doing philosophy," as thinking in/with images.

Stanley Cavell (1926–)

Elisabeth Bronfen discusses how throughout his career Stanley Cavell has explored the interface between moral philosophy and Hollywood in order to claim a specifically American way of engaging philosophically in the world. Given a play with visibility and invisibility, with presence and absence, the projected world we view on screen offers an explanation of our ability to know others as well as our own unknowability. How the specific issues of skepticism and moral perfection seminal to Cavell's work have been brought to bear on classic Hollywood is shown in two close readings: one of *The Philadelphia Story* in relation to the comedy of remarriage and the other of *Stella Dallas* in relation to the melodrama of the unknown woman. Both readings discuss not only the autobiographical interest inscribed in Cavell's writings on cinema but also the cultural moment in American history encoded in both films.

Alain Badiou (1937–)

Alain Badiou has held that philosophy is obliged to engage with cinema because it presents a unique "philosophical situation." Alex Ling accordingly provides an overview of Badiou's understanding of cinema itself—taken in the generic sense as an art almost entirely defined by its relation to other arts (as well as nonart)—while drawing out some of the more interesting artistic and philosophical consequences of his position. Following a brief examination of Badiou's "inaesthetic" conception of art and its relation to truth and philosophy, Ling's essay unpacks Badiou's (implicit) conception of cinema as an "inessential" art by isolating two central complications film presents to his inaesthetic program—specifically, the crucial concepts of "singularity" and "immanence." Ling then moves on to discuss cinema's peculiar position among the arts before finally addressing some of the paradoxes Badiou's understanding of cinema gives rise to, as well as some of the challenges it presents to his philosophical system as a whole.

Raymonde Carasco (1939–2009)

In her literary and cinematic work, French philosopher and filmmaker Raymonde Carasco has built a thorough study of the theoretical and practical forms of intersection and interchange between verbal and audiovisual thinking. Author of sixty articles, two books published during her lifetime, and one posthumous book; codirector

with her husband, Regis Hébraud, of sixteen films shot in 16 mm
and 35 mm; and director of two collective publications, Raymonde
Carasco is perhaps the only professional philosopher to have simultaneously led a scriptural and a cinematic work. As Nicole Brenez
argues, Raymonde Carasco offers a rare example, perhaps comparable
only with that of Alexander Kluge, of a creator who as a philosopher
and a filmmaker shed disciplinary partitions to merge the speculative resources for a large poetic project. How can such an endeavor
be defined? And how does it intertwine the respective dynamics of
philosophy and film? Raymonde Carasco's project was to invent descriptive forms faithful to the event of encountering the world, seen
at every moment in the depth of its infinite physical and mental
movements. This meeting does not stem, however, from an ego that
will be affected by some otherness but by a Carasquian encounter
that requires a recasting of identities. To be true to life implies an
experimental ethos.

Jacques Rancière (1940–)

A philosophy of cinema emerged from Jacques Rancière's varied
writings—on historiography, on the aesthetic regime of the arts, on
Flaubert and the French literary canon after 1789, on the politics of
dissensus—in which he instrumentalized the theory and practice
of *events*. According to Tom Conley, treating the latter as experience
of uncommon or heightened sensation calling into question the position an individual occupies in the world, Rancière showed the cinema
was of political mettle when events allowed spectators to "do" or
"make" with cinema what they wished. His work followed a trajectory from what he called a politics of the *amateur* (deviating from
that of the *auteur*) who related to film in a sensorial and impassioned
register, be it in classical or contemporary film, to that of deviation
and difference.

Noël Carroll (1947–)

Noël Carroll explores the prospects for doing philosophy by means
of the moving image. He examines and attempts to refute skeptical
denials of the possibility of movie-made philosophy by a number of

scholars, including Paisley Livingston, Murray Smith, Bruce Russell, and Deborah Knight. Instead, he sides with philosophers such as Thomas E. Wartenberg and argues it is possible to convey original philosophy through the moving image, though he concedes to the skeptics this is not as common as it is often assumed.

Thomas E. Wartenberg (1949–)

Thomas E. Wartenberg examines Michael Haneke's Academy Award–winning *Amour* in order to show the film makes a significant contribution to the ethics of assisted suicide, or euthanasia. The essay demonstrates that through the film's portrait of the dilemma facing an elderly husband confronted with the gradual degeneration of his wife's physical condition and his own mounting infirmity, there are circumstances in which killing one's spouse is an ethically justifiable act—indeed, even one that is morally required. His argument focuses on a claim made originally by Kant in his ethical philosophy: that dignity is the central value in human life. The wife in the film's central couple is threatened with a loss of dignity as a result of her growing incapacity, forcing her husband to find ways to counter this threat. When the only way to maintain a person's dignity is to end their life, then it is the moral thing to do, according to the film and the argument of this essay.

Murray Smith (1962–)

Murray Smith explores naturalism as a philosophical stance and the extent to which a naturalistic approach to film and film theory has been, could be, or should be adopted. Naturalism as a philosophical stance entails a commitment to understanding the world in the light of scientific knowledge and methods. While naturalism in this sense has emerged as arguably the dominant philosophical stance in the contemporary analytic tradition, it is not nearly so prominent in other philosophical traditions and is rarely explicitly recognized in film theory. An assessment of naturalism from the viewpoint of film theory and the philosophy of film thus seems overdue. Smith begins by looking at the history and aims of philosophical naturalism before turning to its manifestation in film theory under the guise of xxii •• BERND HERZOGENRATH

cognitive film theory. He examines this body of theory and the prospects of naturalism via four key problems: our apprehension of depth and movement in motion pictures, our failure to perceive certain kinds of edits, our recognition and attribution of states of mind to characters, and our emotional responses to such characters. In each case Smith first lays an emphasis on the subpersonal dimensions of mind that play a role in explaining these phenomena, such as the phi phenomenon, change blindness, and human facial perception. Scientific research sheds considerable light on all of these phenomena. Nonetheless, our apprehension and appreciation of films encompasses higher-order cognition as well, including that most abstract and refined form of cognition, which we think of as "philosophical reflection." Naturalism must be able to accommodate such cognition as well as the lower-level cognition that a focus on the subpersonal illuminates. Taking *District 9* as a case study, Smith aims to show how the lower- and higher-level forms of cognition come together in our experience through the film's play with facial and bodily expression and its exploration of personhood and social oppression. Smith thereby seeks to demonstrate, via an exercise in philosophical naturalism, that films may themselves be vehicles of sophisticated reflection on some philosophical problems.

As the editor of this collection, I am by no means entertaining the illusion of completeness. In a much humbler gesture, the essays presented here attempt to draw some light on the various connections between film and philosophy, sometimes even film *as* philosophy, as *doing* philosophy with other means, in another realm. They present this connection in a wide range—historically, thematically, and methodologically. The fundamental question, however, is not whether film actually *is* (indistinguishable from) philosophy but how these two "disciplines" can get into a dialogue, a fruitful encounter— how far they entertain (or can enter into) some kinds of "elective affinities." The field these essays chart is one of multiple logics, approaches, and perspectives that are by necessity sometimes incompatible. This should by all means not be seen as something negative but as something operative, provocative, and ultimately useful. It is our hope the reader will see for herself.

NOTES

1. Kittler, *Gramaphone, Film, Typewriter*, 204 (translation altered).
2. I am very grateful to Vinzenz Hediger for this information.
3. Currie, "Cognitivisim," 106.
4. See Flaxman, *The Brain Is the Screen.*
5. Deleuze, *Cinema 2*, 211.
6. Bergson, *Matter and Memory*, 36.
7. Deleuze, *Cinema 2*, 211.
8. Deleuze, *Negotiations*, 60–61.
9. For a brilliant overview of these "battles," see Sinnerbrink, *New Philosophies of Film.*
10. Mulhall, *On Film*, 4.
11. Deleuze and Guattari, *What Is Philosophy?*, 4.
12. With a nod to Arthur Danto, Robert Sinnerbrink has shown this tightrope act as an oscillation between the philosophical "disenfranchisement" of film and its "re-enfranchising." See Sinnerbrink, "Disenfranchising Film?"; and Sinnerbrink, "Re-enfranchising Film."
13. Deleuze, *Difference and Repetition*, 182.
14. Deleuze, *Negotiations*, 136.
15. Ibid., 137.
16. Harris, "Using Knowledge," 24–25.
17. Deleuze, *Difference and Repetition*, xvi.

BIBLIOGRAPHY

Bergson, Henri. *Matter and Memory.* New York: Zone Books, 1991.
Bordwell, David. "A Case for Cognitivism." *Iris* 9 (Spring 1989): 11–40.
———. "A Case for Cognitivism: Further Reflections." *Iris* 11 (Summer 1990): 107–12.
Bordwell, David, and Noël Carroll, eds. *Post-theory: Reconstructing Film Studies.* Madison: University of Wisconsin Press, 1996.
Brown, William. "Cognitive Deleuze: Conference Report on SCSMI Conference, Roanoke, Virginia, 2–5 June 2010, and Deleuze Studies Conference, Amsterdam, 12–14 July 2010." *Cinema: Journal for Philosophy and Moving Image* 1, no. 1(2010): 134–42, http://cjpmi.ifilnova.pt/1-contents.
———. *Supercinema: Film-Philosophy for the Digital Age.* Oxford: Berghahn Books, 2013.
Carroll, Noël. *Interpreting the Moving Image.* Cambridge: Cambridge University Press, 1998.
———. *Philosophical Problems of Classical Film Theory.* Princeton, N.J.: Princeton University Press, 1988.

XXIV •• BERND HERZOGENRATH

———. *The Philosophy of Motion Pictures.* Oxford: Blackwell, 2008.
———. *Theorizing the Moving Image.* Cambridge: Cambridge University Press, 1996.
Carroll, Noël, and Jinhee Choi, eds. *The Philosophy of Film and Motion Pictures: An Anthology.* Oxford: Blackwell, 2006.
Cavell, Stanley. *Contesting Tears: The Melodrama of the Unknown Woman.* Chicago: University of Chicago Press, 1996.
———. *Pursuits of Happiness: The Hollywood Comedy of Remarriage.* Cambridge, Mass.: Harvard University Press, 1981.
———. *The World Viewed: Reflections on the Ontology of Film.* Enlarged ed. Cambridge, Mass.: Harvard University Press, 1979.
Currie, Gregory. "Cognitivism." In *A Companion to Film Theory,* edited by Toby Miller and Robert Stam. Malden, Mass.: Blackwell, 2004.
Deleuze, Gilles. *Cinema 1: The Movement-Image.* Translated by Hugh Tomlinson and Barbara Habberjam. Minneapolis: University of Minnesota Press, 1986.
———. *Cinema 2. The Time-Image.* Translated by Hugh Tomlinson and R. Galeta. London: Athlone 2000 Press, 1989.
———. *Difference and Repetition.* New York: Columbia University Press, 1994.
———. *Negotiations, 1972–1990.* Translated by M. Joughin. New York: Columbia University Press, 1995.
Deleuze, Gilles, and Félix Guattari. *What Is Philosophy?* Translated by Hugh Tomlinson and Graham Burchell. New York: Columbia University Press, 1994.
Flaxman, Gregory, ed. *The Brain Is the Screen. Deleuze and the Philosophy of Cinema.* Minneapolis: University of Minnesota Press, 2000.
Harris, Paul A. "Using Knowledge: Denuding the Deluded, Including the Excluded." *Amerikastudien/American Studies* 45, no.1 (2000): 23–32.
Kittler, Friedrich A. *Gramophone, Film, Typewriter.* Translated with an introduction by Geoffrey Winthrop-Young and Michael Wutz. Stanford, Calif.: Stanford University Press, 1999.
Mulhall, Stephen. *On Film.* 2nd ed. New York: Routledge, 2008.
Noë, Alva. *Out of Our Heads. Why You Are Not Your Brain, and Other Lessons from the Biology of Consciousness.* New York: Hill and Wang, 2009.
Odin, Roger. "A propos de la mise en place de l'enseignement du cinéma en France: Retour sur une expèrience." In *Can We Learn Cinema?/Il Cinema si impara?,* edited by Anna Bertolli, Andrea Mariani, and Martina Panelli, 93–102. Udine, Italy: Forum, 2013.
Pisters, Patricia. *The Matrix of Visual Culture: Working with Deleuze in Film Theory.* Stanford, Calif.: Stanford University Press, 2003.
———. *The Neuro-Image.* Stanford, Calif.: Stanford University Press, 2012.
Seel, Martin. *Die Künste des Kinos.* Frankfurt am Main: Verlag S. Fischer, 2013.
Sinnerbrink, Robert. "Disenfranchising Film? On the Analytic-Cognitivist Turn

in Film Theory." In *Postanalytic and Metacontinental: Crossing Philosophical Divides,* edited by Jack Reynolds et al., 173–89. London: Continuum, 2010.

———. *New Philosophies of Film: Thinking Images.* London: Continuum, 2011.

———. "Re-enfranchising Film: Towards a Romantic Film-Philosophy." In *New Takes in Film-Philosophy,* edited by Havi Carel and Greg Tuck, 25–47. New York: Palgrave MacMillan, 2011.

Wartenberg, Thomas E. *Unlikely Couples: Movie Romance as Social Criticism.* Boulder, Colo.: Westview Press, 1999.

Wartenberg, Thomas E., and Angela Curran, eds. *The Philosophy of Film: Introductory Text and Readings.* Oxford: Blackwell, 2005.

Wartenberg, Thomas E., and Cynthia Freeland, eds. *Philosophy and Film.* New York: Routledge, 1995.

Wartenberg, Thomas E., and Murray Smith, eds. *Thinking Through Cinema: Film as Philosophy.* Oxford: Blackwell, 2007.

Striking Poses

GESTURE, IMAGE, AND REMAKE
IN THE CINEMATIC BERGSON

John Ó Maoilearca

According to Gilles Deleuze, "Cinema is Bergsonian."[1] Despite the
fact that Henri Bergson critiques the cinematographic mechanism
in his magnum opus, *Creative Evolution* (on account of its movement being one *applied* to still images rather than being immanent
to them), Deleuze correctly realizes how central the moving image
nonetheless is to Bergson's philosophy. Yet this is clear in Bergson's
own testimonies: "When I first saw the cinematograph I realized it
could offer something new to philosophy. Indeed we could almost say
that cinema is a model of consciousness itself. Going to the cinema
turns out to be a philosophical experience."[2] If Bergson's relationship
with the cinematic apparatus is ambivalent, then (being a model of
consciousness, but only in how it distorts the real) it remains to be
seen in what manner his affirmative stance toward film should be
understood. In his positive account, Deleuze emphasizes the virtual
image from Bergson's earlier work *Matter and Memory* in order to
show how movement is indeed immanent to the image, but only by
virtue of its *incorporeality*. Such "virtualism" has been criticized elsewhere for its un-Bergsonian tenets.[3] In what follows I show how the
cinematic body offers another way of rendering cinema Bergsonian.
This more actualist Bergsonism is pursued not in order to be more
faithful to Bergson but to show how his ideas dovetail with modern
corporeal, gestural readings of the film image. When Dominique
Chateau writes in *Cinéma et philosophie* that Bergson was the first
major philosopher to take cinema as a model for philosophy, this is
not only a historical thesis: his ideas remain pertinent to a range of

contemporary approaches in film theory and place further weight on the role of the body, not only for the experience of the spectator but also in the very nature of the moving image.[4]

Among Jean Renoir's various maxims concerning the creative process, probably the most renowned touches on a *lack* at the heart of such creativity: "A director makes only one movie in his life. Then he breaks it into pieces and makes it again." Yet such repetition within creation need not lead us to doubt the possibility of novelty. This becomes clear when we look at another, cognate observation from Renoir's fellow Frenchman Henri Bergson, only this time regarding philosophy. Discussing the "single point" each philosopher makes throughout his or her career, he writes:

> In this point is something simple, infinitely simple, so extraordinarily simple that the philosopher has never succeeded in saying it. And that is why he went on talking all his life. He could not formulate what he had in mind without feeling himself obliged to correct his formula, then to correct his correction: thus, from theory to theory, correcting when he thought he was completing, what he has accomplished, by a complication which provoked more complication, by developments heaped upon developments, has been to convey with an increasing approximation the simplicity of his original intuition. All the complexity of his doctrine, which would go on *ad infinitum,* is therefore only the incommensurability between his simple intuition and the means at his disposal for expressing it. What is this intuition?[5]

Coming from Bergson's essay "Philosophical Intuition," the first answer to his question, "What is this intuition?" arrives in the form of the philosophical "image," a "mediating" image that is "almost matter in that it still allows itself to be seen, and almost mind in that it no longer allows itself to be touched."[6] Yet it is not, he assures us, to be confused with the virtual images discussed in his earlier work *Matter and Memory* but is something far more actual, more embodied (and yet still not a spatial, fixed body). It is

> a receding and vanishing image, which haunts, unperceived perhaps, the mind of the philosopher, which follows him like his shadow through

the ins and outs of his thought and which, if it is not the intuition itself, approaches it much more closely than the conceptual expression, of necessity symbolical, to which the intuition must have recourse in order to furnish "explanation." Let us look closely at this shadow: by doing so we shall divine the attitude of the body which projects it. And if we try to imitate this attitude, or better still to assume it ourselves, we shall see as far as it is possible what the philosopher saw.[7]

Deleuze, we know, makes much of the virtual images of *Matter and Memory* in his two *Cinema* books, transforming a psychometaphysical thesis into an ontological one (thereby disregarding Bergson's own *antiontological* stance) while distorting Bergson's negative view of the cinematic *apparatus* (in *Creative Evolution*) into a positive view of cinema *editing*. In this essay I instead pursue this "attitude of the body" that projects the vanishing but singular image of philosophical intuition. I do so through an analogy with the idea of "one" (image or idea) that underpins a film. This is an attempt, therefore, to generate or project a film of intuition—to assume (or suggest) the (film) image of (philosophical) intuition (rather than simply one more philosophy of film). After all, even in *Matter and Memory* the image is described ardently as something that is *not* a picture ("to picture is not to remember"), and the brain is portrayed as an organ of mime: it does not represent (an idea or a picture); rather, it *performs* its images through its own equivalent of an actor's "gestures and attitudes."[8] I examine this performed, bodily cinema both through what Bergson has to say about gesture and through a gestural concept enacted by a film—to be precise, Lars von Trier's *The Five Obstructions* (2003).

This brings us to what is being remade, by both directors and philosophers, in Renoir's "one film" and Bergson's singular "vanishing image." *The Five Obstructions* comprises five remakes of an original work by another filmmaker, Jørgen Leth. Leth, a mentor of Von Trier, is instructed by Von Trier to remake five sequences from his own 1967 short film *The Perfect Human* (a pseudoanthropological study of human behavior). Each remake comes with an obstruction, or "creative constraint." The constraints are as follows: (1) that it be remade with no shot longer than twelve frames, (2) that it be remade in the most miserable place on earth, (3) that it be remade with *no* constraint at all (a form of metaobstruction of *total* freedom), (4) that it be remade as a cartoon (*the* definition of a nonfilm for both Von Trier and Leth), and finally, (5) that *Von Trier* makes the fifth remake, though it must be both credited to and narrated by Leth.

As such, one way of reading *The Five Obstructions* is as a precise enactment of Renoir's adage that each filmmaker makes only one film again and again, with Von Trier forcing Leth to recompose *The Perfect Human* repeatedly following certain constraints. Such forms of experimentation in film are not unique, however. In 1998 Gus Van Sant directed a shot-by-shot remake of Alfred Hitchcock's 1960 classic horror film *Psycho*. While the new film is in color rather than the original's black and white and is set in a contemporary era with a new cast, it otherwise retains nearly all of the first film's audiovisual structure—including Bernard Hermann's score.[9] Indeed, such is its fidelity to the 1960 film that some critics have dubbed it a (rather pointless) "duplicate" rather than a remake.[10] A duplicate like this, presumably, would lie somewhere between a mere remastered print of the original and a true remake. But if a remake is to be more than a duplicate, then *what* exactly is being remade (if it is *not* an audiovisual structure)? In answer to why Van Sant's audiovisual replica of the structure of *Psycho* is deemed such a failure, I propose the sheer repetition of such structures is never invention. Rather, what is remade—*but with novelty*—is never a fixed image or sound, a propositional state or story. And this is the (Bergsonian) conjecture I pursue: that what is remade (by philosopher or director) is not a picture but a posture—a bodily stance or "attitude." It is this gestural re-creation that allows novelty and repetition to coexist.

Bergsonian Reorientations

One basis for Bergson's reorientation (from picturing to posturing) in *Matter and Memory* and beyond can be gleaned from the description of intuition offered in his 1903 essay "Introduction to Metaphysics." Here, Bergson outlines the famous contrast between creative intuition and the "ready-made" concepts of "analysis":

> To try a concept on an object is to ask of the object what we have to do with it, what it can do for us. To label an object with a concept is to tell in precise terms the kind of action or attitude the object is to suggest to us.[11]

Bergson's corporealist stance is already indicated in this use of terms such as "attitude" and its ability to "suggest": *attitudine*, "fitness, posture"; and *suggerere*, "bring from below," from "gesture" or *gerere*, to "bear, wield, perform." And both are linked to Bergson's most renowned formulation of intuition, which comes from the same essay: thinking in duration means "to reverse the normal direction of the workings of thought."[12] Few philosophers have argued anything so heretical as found in Bergson's approach to metaphysics here: a radical reversal of what we think metaphysics (and philosophy) to be and how we think it operates (in an "anti-Kantian" metaphysics of immanence, as Quentin Meillassoux describes Bergson's method).[13] More than this, it leads us to a redirection of where thinking is supposed to take place: *thinking changes source and direction, passing from things to concepts, not from concepts to things.* Bergson's idea is not that we merely change the "direction" of our thought *about* things (whatever that might mean) but that metaphysical thinking somehow *starts with the object,* too, at least as an orientation, posture, or attitude. This is his call to reorient or reverse our stance: the inversion of the work of the mind is not intellectualist but behavioral in attitude.

At an even more most abstract level, this postural aspect of Bergson's thought engages with the theory of images in *Matter and Memory.* Let us recall the basics of the imagology in its first chapter, where what we perceive is only what interests us (and our bodies) at any moment:

> To the degree that my horizon widens, the images which surround me seem to be painted upon a more uniform *background* and become to me more indifferent. The more I narrow this horizon, the more the objects which it circumscribes space themselves out distinctly according to the greater or lesser ease with which my body can touch and move them. They send back [*renvoient,* "return"], then, to my body, as would a mirror, its eventual influence; they take rank in an order corresponding to the growing or decreasing powers of my body. *The objects which surround my body reflect its possible action upon them.*[14]

There is a "background" that returns to my body only what interests it so that even "distance" itself takes on an axiological form, representing, "above all, the measure in which surrounding bodies are insured, in some way, against the immediate action of my body."[15] My body is simply "an object," but one capable of performing a "new action" upon surrounding objects, and this ability to act anew is what marks out its "privileged position" in regard to other, background objects. Hence, to undo what the body instigates, to reverse this "narrow" attitude, is to look again in detail (in higher definition) and in close-up at this background: it requires a reversal of orientation.

Indeed, in *Matter and Memory* even memory, apparently the most *virtual* element of Bergson's thought, is tied to bodily stance:

> Whenever we are trying to recover a recollection, to call up some period of our history, we become conscious of an act *sui generis* by which we detach ourselves from the present in order to replace ourselves, first, in the past in general, then, in a certain region of the past—a work of adjustment, something like the focusing of a camera. But our recollection still remains virtual; we simply prepare ourselves to receive it *by adopting the appropriate attitude.*[16]

If this seems to go too far—especially given Bergson's purportedly disembodied "spiritualist" tendencies—then the following description of education from the introduction to *The Creative Mind* may help to confirm this revision of his work. Here he argues that to understand a text a student

> must fall into step with him [the author] by adopting his gestures, his attitudes, his gait, by which I mean learning to read the text aloud with the proper intonation and inflection. The intelligence will later add shades of meaning. Before intellection properly so-called, there is the perception of structure and movement; there is, on the page one reads, punctuation and rhythm. Now it is in indicating this structure and rhythm, in taking into consideration the temporal relations between the various sentences of the paragraph and the various parts of each sentence, in following uninterruptedly the *crescendo* of thought and feeling to the point musically indicated as the culminating point that the art of diction consists. . . . One knows, one understands only what one can in some measure reinvent.[17]

Reinvention is not the repetition of fixed structures but "structure and rhythm"—movement or gesture. In the note that follows this passage, Bergson goes even further in this gestural comprehension of comprehension, arguing that "rhythm roughly outlines the meaning of the sentence truly *written,* that it can give us direct communication with the writer's thought before study of the words has given them color and shading." In one lecture at the Collège de France on Descartes's *Discours de la méthode,* he tells us that he took some pages of the text as an example "to show how the comings and goings of thought, each in a particular direction, pass from the mind of Descartes to our own solely by the effect of the rhythm as indicated by the punctuation, and especially as brought out by reading it aloud correctly."[18] This note then refers the reader to Bergson's 1912 lecture "The Soul and the Body," where thinking is vectorized in a clearly behaviorist manner, albeit also being internalized as a tendency, "nascent" and "performed in the brain":

Consider thinking itself; you will find directions rather than states, and you will see that thinking is essentially a continual and continuous change of inward direction, incessantly tending to translate itself by changes of outward direction, I mean by actions and gestures capable of outlining in space and of expressing metaphorically, as it were, the comings and goings of the mind. Of these movements, sketched out or even simply prepared, we are most often unaware, because we have no interest in knowing them; but we have to notice them when we try to seize hold of our thought in order to grasp it all living and make it pass, still living, into the soul of another. The words may then have been well chosen, but they will not convey the whole of what we wish to make them say if we do not succeed by the rhythm, by the punctuation, by the relative lengths of the sentences and part of the sentences, by a particular dancing of the sentence, in making the reader's mind, continually guided by a series of nascent movements, describe a curve of thought and feeling analogous to that we ourselves described. . . . The rhythm speech has here, then, no other object than that of choosing the rhythm of the thought: and what can the rhythm of the thought be but the rhythm of the scarcely conscious nascent movements which accompany it? These movements, by which thought continually tends to externalize itself in actions, are clearly prepared and, as it were, performed in the brain.[19]

Here, we have a kind of microbehaviorism of the brain—as well as a macrobehaviorism of bodies in relation—one that would shortcut the traditional disputes between "central state" materialists and logical behaviorists by rendering behavior neurological while upgrading cerebral motor mechanisms to something more than just mechanical movements. If the brain does "control" behavior, then it is because it too *is* behavior.

Gestural Cinema

Of course, explicitly behavioral analyses in cinema theory are not unusual, either, though few can be as radical as that of Giorgio Agamben, for whom gesture rather than the image is the fundamental filmic property. His short essay "The Six Most Beautiful Minutes in the History of Cinema," for example, discusses a sequence from Orson Welles's unfinished *Don Quixote* in terms of gesture:

> Sancho Panza enters a cinema in a provincial city. He is looking for
> Don Quixote and finds him sitting off to the side, staring at the
> screen. The theater is almost full; the balcony—which is a sort of giant
> terrace—is packed with raucous children. After several unsuccessful
> attempts to reach Don Quixote, Sancho reluctantly sits down in one
> of the lower seats, next to a little girl (Dulcinea?), who offers him a
> lollipop. The screening has begun; it is a costume film: on the screen,
> knights in armor are riding along. Suddenly, a woman appears; she is
> in danger. Don Quixote abruptly rises, unsheathes his sword, rushes
> toward the screen, and, with several lunges, begins to shred the cloth.
> The woman and the knights are still visible on the screen, but the black
> slash opened by Don Quixote's sword grows ever larger, implacably
> devouring the images. In the end, nothing is left of the screen, and
> only the wooden structure supporting it remains visible.[20]

Quixote's gesture destroys the cinema image, and likewise, Agamben claims gesture is the quintessential cinematic element, replacing the photograph as its fundamental unit:

The mythical rigidity of the image has been broken and . . . here, properly speaking, there are no images but only gestures. Every image, in fact, is animated by an antinomic polarity: on the one hand, images are the reification and obliteration of a gesture (it is the imago as death mask or as symbol); on the other hand, they preserve the *dynamis* intact.[21]

Agamben's analyses of cinema indicate a nostalgia for "the homeland of gesture."[22] But they are also a political and an ethical call for a future cinema that reconfigures the relationship between image and gesture. For him the moving image as gesture has the power to liberate the cinematic from the last traces of a static image.

Despite his focus upon gesture, I will not follow Agamben any further here even if, in one respect, I stay true to his line (which itself follows Foucault) that what we call "gesture" is only "what remains unexpressed in each expressive act" and "*the exhibition of a mediality: it is the process of making a means visible as such.*"[23] Indeed, one of Bergson's most notorious demands for philosophy is that it should seek a means to know the Real "without any expression, translation or symbolic representation." And for Bergson intuitive "metaphysics is that means. *Metaphysics, then, is the science which claims to do without symbols.*"[24] And yet we know when Bergson describes a metaphysics that would dispense with symbols, the question is what *type* of symbolism is at stake—fluid or fixed, suggestive or direct, bespoke or ready-made—not the symbolic *tout court*. A philosophy-without-symbols is a philosophy-without-standard-symbols, therefore, and is practiced without *fixed* representations (be they linguistic, conceptual, or photographic). It begins, he says, with images that gesture toward (suggest) an intuition. Images *direct* us toward intuitions; they do not stand for (represent) intuitions.

Unconstrained Style

Behaviorism in *The Five Obstructions*

Von Trier's *The Five Obstructions* is a work whose very form explores a number of issues concerning aesthetic creativity and generative constraint. The third of the five constraints is also a metalevel one, involving no constraint at all—complete artistic freedom. For a filmmaker in the realist tradition like Leth, however, this is a definite imposition. The perversity arises because Leth initially asks for an alternative constraint whereby Von Trier would provide a new set of obstructions for him to endure: as he says, "I prefer you to make the decisions." Yet precisely because that would be *Leth's* preference, Von Trier decrees *Leth* must make *all the decisions* in absolute freedom for this third remake. So why is such total freedom an imposition for Leth (beyond the usual psychoanalytic/existential responses concerning the intolerable burden of personal responsibility)? It is simply because Von Trier shares with Leth the idea that constraints are crucial for creativity in filmmaking, such that imposing a freestyle film on his former teacher can only be—as Mette Hjort puts it—"a straightforward negation of Leth's characteristic approach."[25]

Note here that Leth's model of optical film realism involves patience—that is, a certain kind of passivity:

> I normally find places and then isolate something I want to examine. That's the method. And then I frame it very precisely and wait for the right moment. I believe very strongly in waiting and observing.[26]

Leth allows the moment to be captured to present *itself*—to let the randomness of the Real take *its* course. Admittedly, it is he who selects the "decisive moment" to record (to borrow one of Cartier-Bresson's terms), but its emergence is spontaneous. Let us say that it belongs to the Real (or Real Time, as Bergson would call it). Ordering Leth to make any film he wishes in the third obstruction is actually an imposition of sorts: less the burden of responsibility than the burden of creativity. Leth's natural preference is to let the Real offer up the "concrete instants" that he will passively record rather than that he conduct all affairs (a very Bazinian realism at first glance). Forcing all of the decision-making process onto Leth removes his artistic freedom, oddly enough. Naturally, Leth is free to escape from his freedom, in this third film at least, by reverting to his usual long-take realist aesthetic. And yet this is not what he does. Instead, he offers up a highly stylized, rather formal piece, using split screens, cryptic monologues, and clichéd "art house" imagery (a mysterious man and woman, sexual encounters in expensive hotel rooms, a sense of political or criminal intrigue, slow-moving limousines, clandestine meetings in rainy, desolate locations, and so on).

Earlier, I alluded to the pseudoanthropological approach in *The Perfect Human* in its original form. The narration of the third remake (in English), compounds this impression even further:

> *Here's the man. Here he is. What's he want?*
> *Here's the woman. Here she is. What does she want?*
> *Here's a man. We don't know him. I don't know what to say about him.*
> *We love that he is special, unreasonable. A distant look, a loss of soul, a distant look.*
> *I would like to know something more about him. I can see that he is here, and that he works. I have seen him smoke a cigarette. I didn't see him write. Is he good at describing death? Does he think about fucking? He is alone, preparing himself. He goes out and takes care of things. He's the perfect man.*

In this and other sequences, the question of what the man is thinking is reiterated but never answered. All we are given are external details, visuals of movement—of smoking, of shaving, of waiting. Alongside this unanswered inquiry comes the peculiar mannerism of this version, with a certain "type" of art house cinema (du Look) being replicated throughout. Paramount in this, however, is the acting role of the male protagonist. Leth casts Patrick Bauchau to play "the man" (Claus Nissen's role in the original) almost entirely because of his presence and style. Murray Smith remarks:

> The casting of Patrick Bauchau in *#3: Brussels,* for example, [was] inspired by Leth's admiration for his performance as the protagonist of Eric Rohmer's *La collectionneuse.* Intriguingly, Rohmer's film was, like *The Perfect Human,* released in 1967; it is as if Leth has chosen a better-known counterpart to Claus Nissen—an equally handsome actor from the same generation, both born in 1938—in order to stress the effects of time and experience on the model-like "perfection" of the figures in his original film (Leth notes the importance of Bauchau's "well-bruised" quality to his casting in *#3: Brussels*).[27]

Nonetheless, Bauchau is not given much to do by Leth in this film, for he mostly poses in rooms and has little dialogue and even less interaction with other actors. He is there because of his "look." Leth is obviously delighted with his casting, stating he is "really pleased with him. He looks great. . . . He is well . . . well bruised as a person. He has experience of life. He has lived a life. His story is fantastic." Bauchau, then, stands for a certain type and remakes the Claus Nissen protagonist through a distinctive acting style, almost bordering on nonacting: he is a man who "takes care of things" just by looking like such a man. Indeed, of all six films, the original and the third versions of *The Perfect Human* place the most emphasis on acting style (as opposed to editing in the first, location in the second, animation in the fourth, and performativity in the fifth).[28] Smith once more finds the right idea on this front, when describing the original *The Perfect Human*:

> *The Perfect Human* is an enigmatic, spare narrative film, depicting a man and a woman engaged in various generic activities—eating, dancing, undressing, shaving—mostly in isolation from one another. . . . The setting of the film is abstract in the extreme: the performers are afforded certain minimal props (a razor, a bed, a dining table) but the space behind them is so overexposed as to lead the eye into a white void. The man and the woman are beautiful, young, chic; much of the time they are doing little more than *striking poses* in the featureless zone that they occupy.[29]

I mention earlier one could read *The Five Obstructions* as a reflection on difference and repetition in filmmaking, with Von Trier forcing Leth to recompose *The Perfect Human* repeatedly following certain constraints. But the obstructions to each remake nonetheless ensure a creative reproduction rather than a faithful replica. This has been accounted for partly through the use of *constant stylistic innovation.* As Von Trier writes of his own work:

> You can become so good at producing things that they become nauseatingly boring to look at. That might have happened had I continued to make the same film again and again, as some people do.[30]

Von Trier is known for not repeating himself, *at least stylistically.* Yet Von Trier insists on a partial repetition in each task given to Leth, although the added obstructions guarantee a certain creativity in style. Mette Hjort comments on this, saying, "The commitment [to renewing styles] throughout, it transpires, is to a form of self-provocation that involves *abandoning* the cinematic techniques as they are mastered in favor of new challenges."³¹ Hence, we should interpret the qualification "at least stylistically" in such a way that the issue of style becomes a highly significant approach. As Smith also writes:

> In *The Five Obstructions* the game of style is narrativised; the variations in style have an overt motivation in the narrative contest recounted by the film. Even so, the variations are not motivated in the traditional manner as apt stylistic expressions of theme.³²

In the opening obstruction, set in Cuba, a certain behavioral attitude is also assumed. Adopting the same pseudoanthropological pose as its original, this *The Perfect Human* also asks questions such as, What is the perfect human thinking? Is he thinking about happiness? Death? Love? Yet the answers eventually provided to these and other questions often appear to be pseudoanswers, at least for those who are looking for sufficient reasons. Paisley Livingston describes the situation thusly:

> The response to the question: "Why does he move this way?" is a comical flaunting of Trier's injunction to answer the questions raised by the narrator of *The Perfect Human*; the proposed answer ("Because women like it") does not really answer the question, while seeming to do so in a blunt way; all the other questions remain willfully unanswered in the remake, which reinforces the thought that Leth has cleverly slipped past this obstruction.³³

I would respond to Livingston, however, that questions such as, what is he thinking? or those concerning the character's motivations are indeed *answered*, only through external behavior or style of movement. Hjort adds to this point about acting and style by referring to Arthur Danto's claim in *The Transfiguration of the Commonplace* that "style is a gift" (it cannot be directed) and expresses individual "ways of seeing the world."³⁴ Danto himself goes even further, arguing, "Style is the man." When someone paints in the style of Rembrandt, for example, "*he* has adopted a manner, and to at least that degree he is not immanent in the painting in the way Rembrandt is." All the same, the language of immanence is made licit by the identity of the man himself and his style—he is his style—and by transitivity of identity Rembrandt *is* his paintings considered in the perspective of style. . . . What, really, is "the man himself"? I have argued a theory to the effect that we are systems of representations, ways of seeing the world, representations incarnate.[35]

In Leth's films of *The Perfect Human*, consequently, we could say the human—who may be an actor *or* the director in the strict sense but always a performer in the broad sense—is these "representations incarnate," this way of seeing. It is also a way of answering, a way of reasoning without identifiably *philosophical* forms of rationality. One might say they are behavioral and cinematic explanations.

All in all, then, be it through this externalization of ideas, the behaviorist and anthropological approach adopted, or the role of the actor/director as a *type* of performer, this third version of *The Perfect Human* partly enacts the question of just what a remake, replica, or repetition is on a number of different levels. For the most peculiar thing is that having been given the utmost freedom to make this version, Leth's third film is probably the least like the original when compared with the others.

Crux Scenica, or Remaking the Gesture Cinematically

In conclusion I should say a little more about acting and Bergson's most sustained engagement with theatrical performance and gesture—his work *Le rire,* on laughter and the meaning of the comical. To begin with acting, according to Karen Jürs-Munby:

> The disciplined art of acting which corresponds to this aim is elaborated in instructional texts as late as Franciscus Lang's *Dissertatio de Actione Scenica* (1727). As here illustrated, the actor is taught to assume the basic posture, the so-called *"crux scenica,"* in which the feet were placed at a ninety-degree angle, while performing strictly prescribed physical representations of the emotions. By thus controlling his body according to the rules, the hero proves that he is also in control of the affects that storm in on him. . . . The comic figure—Pickelhering, Hanswurst, or Harlequin—similarly violates all the rules of this highly

regimented acting: rather than keeping his body taut and controlled, he bends his knees and upper body, shows his naked behind, and gestures obscenely below the waist.[36]

Earlier, I noted that the actor playing the perfect human for the third remake in *The Five Obstructions,* Patrick Bauchau, was cast in part for his "well-bruised" quality. He performs the "Man in Brussels" in a set of poses, his world-weary face doing a good deal of the acting for him, mute. Early cinema acting, following its theatrical forebear, was hugely influenced by the tradition of mime and gesture. And as Jürs-Munby on the *crux scenica* indicates, there were standard (heroic) and nonstandard (comical) postures in such acting that were characterized as deviations from the relaxed, erect, symmetrical pose. David Mayer explains this in more detail:

> To convey such an individual, the actor's stance is the prescribed *crux scenica*: the relaxed body upright, arms similarly relaxed to gesture easily, knees slightly flexed, heels together, toes apart at a ninety-degree angle. This posture, which coincides with the development of ballet positions, we recognize as First Position. In any departure from a posture in which the body is always in control, denying or subduing all unruly and anti-social impulses, the actor begins to define character. Should the actor assume another stance, the audience, reading these signs, may make inferences about the character depicted. The *crux scenica* identified the man or woman of intellect and self-discipline. Self-control—a few key gestures and a virtual absence of multiple histrionic gestures—allowed an admirable person to survive intrigues without needing to reach for his sword or break her fan.[37]

In the 1830s the Parisian elocutionist François Delsarte codified a "gestural vocabulary" for the stage. Delsarte kept to this early eighteenth-century notion that any stance that deviated from the *crux scenica* could be read as a sign of (bad) character. This gestural acting, while not realistic by present-day standards, was nonetheless regarded at the time as verisimilar performance. Crucially, because absolute reality was deemed unknowable, acting *Truth* was more highly valued than a putative *acting realism.* As James Naremore relates, this is what theater historians "now call the mimetic or 'pantomime' tradition—a performance technique that relies on conventionalized poses to help the actor indicate 'fear,' 'sorrow,' 'hope,' 'confusion,' and so forth." This is opposed to the position of "psychological realism" found in naturalism and later Method acting.[38]

Jean-Claude Schmitt has written about how the concept of attitude (*modus habendi*) is closely associated with that of *figuratio*. It results from the pausing of the movement that forms an ideal figure.[39] Similarly, Elisabeth Engberg-Pedersen tells us, "Differences in body posture link with emotionally different facial expressions to signal sequences of discourse with shifted attribution of expressive elements; this signals the intended character, but is not indexical, as changes in body posture do not indicate a locus."[40] In many respects, then, from what we have already seen, Bergson also belongs to this tradition of physicalized attitude, only now displaced onto philosophy. When writing on attention, he shows how "stage by stage we shall be led on to define attention as an adaptation of the body rather than of the mind and to see in this attitude of consciousness mainly the consciousness of an attitude."[41] It is even arguable that this rich behaviorism renders the problem of propositional attitudes (of beliefs) bodily, a matter of physical posture (*attitudine*). *Thinking* itself is equally vectorized in a clearly behaviorist manner, albeit internalized as a tendency "performed in the brain." Here, we have the aforementioned microbehaviors of the brain alongside the macrobehaviors of bodies. Any causal reduction (of brain by world or vice versa) would not be entailed, for the macroposture would simply be the "externalized" translation of many micropostures, none of which are determining, because each domain is equally real.

Deviations from the *crux scenica,* we were told, often bear the physical weight of comedy, the clownish, animal distortions of the perfectly human posture: erect and in control. The comical both imitates and distorts what is deemed the norm. In the kinds of cinematic aping seen in *The Five Obstructions,* each remake repeats and distorts the original (sometimes with comical results). As Livingstone notes, some of the remakes not only mimic their original (Leth's *The Perfect Human*) but also create "a comical flaunting of Trier's injunction"—cocking a snook at Von Trier's own attempts to "control" Leth's artistic work. Such gestural derision resonates with Bergson's theory of comedy in *Le rire*. Here, he points to the comic potential in the connection between gesture and repetition:

> In a public speaker, for instance, we find that gesture vies with speech. Jealous of the latter, gesture closely dogs the speaker's thought, demanding also to act as interpreter. . . . But I find that a certain movement of head or arm, a movement always the same, seems to return at regular intervals. If I notice it and it succeeds in diverting my attention, if I wait for it to occur and it occurs when I expect it, then involuntarily I laugh. Why? Because I now have before me a machine that works automatically.

This admonition in laughter is part of the social caution that Bergson finds operating at the heart of humor—the need to control those who deviate from life's proper function (to create, to be novel)—those who allow the mechanical to encrust itself upon the living (through habit, distraction, interference): "This is no longer life, it is automatism established in life and imitating it. It belongs to the comic." Yet what is notable here is that the perception of repetition, through gesture, results in "involuntary" laughter among those condemning it. The automatism is infectious.

Yet not only repetition but an *excess* of similarity leads to further humor. Bergson links this notion to a related problem found in Blaise Pascal's *Pensées*:

> This seems to me the solution of the little riddle propounded by Pascal in one passage of his *Thoughts*: "Two faces that are alike, although neither of them excites laughter by itself, make us laugh when together, on account of their likeness." It might just as well be said: "The gestures of a public speaker, no one of which is laughable by itself, excite laughter by their repetition." The truth is that a really living life should never repeat itself. Wherever there is repetition or complete similarity, we always suspect some mechanism at work behind the living. Analyse the impression you get from two faces that are too much alike, and you will find that you are thinking of two copies cast in the same mould, or two impressions of the same seal, or two reproductions of the same

negative—in a word, of some manufacturing process or other. This deflection of life towards the mechanical is here the real cause of laughter.[42]

This *excess* of similarity creates a comical monstrosity. Hence, perhaps, one answer to the negative reception of Gus Van Sant's replica of *Psycho* is that the excess similarity is not only a repetition of crude audiovisual structure and story but a monstrous, mechanical one lacking in the minimal vitality that would make a remake *more than simply a repetition of form* but the regeneration, or reinvention, of an idea. *The Five Obstructions* document how one might repeat the gestures of a short film, but doing so without this becoming a *mechanical* gesture—and this occurs through Leth's creative responses to Von Trier's obstructions. Each remake "reinvents"—to use Bergson's term—the original and thereby remakes neither a story component nor a visual but what was gestured, suggested, or directed in the original. In true Bergsonian fashion, it is a movement—actual and bodily—rather than an ideal (Deleuzian virtual) that is realized. Van Sant takes full control of his film by molding it on a fixed ideal (Hitchcock's 1960 original) and yet in doing so makes his work only all the more mechanical—or rather, exposes his own art to the accusation of being an automatism, a predictable cliché. Even when Leth is given full "control" of the third remake, he does not revert to (his) "type" by using his normal long-take realist aesthetic—he invents a new style, itself composed of others' clichés—those of the Cinéma du Look. By reinventing them for himself, however, he removes them from being simple formulae, just as his remakes on *The Perfect Human* are never predictable.

Bergson's philosophy was once described as "an analysis against analysis," and as such it could only *suggest* rather than *demonstrate* its truth.[43] Accordingly, it is entirely true, as Bernard Gilson writes, that each of Bergson's books was "conceived at once as a scientific work and as a work of art."[44] Writing in 1965, Paul de Man put the nature of Bergson's aesthetic in an even clearer light:

> The poetic image . . . becomes a close verbal approximation to what perception and sensation are actually like, much closer, at any rate, than the purely intellectual representation of reality found in the

scientific concept. Poetics thus becomes a vital source for theoretical psychology, rather than a minor part of it.[45]

The poetic image is not an ornament but an *aisthesis,* which we see now as a matter of "attitude," of "approximation," and of "direction": an imagery that embodies (gestures) suggestion, at least when it comes to communicating an intuition to another mind. Such posturing or "posing" is as much cinematic, however, as it is philosophical.

Despite Bergson's ambivalent relationship with the cinematic apparatus (as a device of capture and projection), we need not turn to Deleuze's monstrous reading to redeem it. That rendering inflates the virtual into (un-Bergsonian) ontology and so pays too high a price (while replacing a critique of capture with a commendation of editing): we can instead retain the processual and anti-Platonist dimension of Bergson's thought *and render it cinematic,* but only by focusing on the important place of the actual body—of gesture, attitude, and suggestion—in Bergsonism. Indeed, it is the cinematic Bergson who exposes the postural aspect of cinema and shows how one "idea" can be remade again and again and yet also be novel— through reinvention.

NOTES

1. Deleuze, *Cinema 1,* 109.
2. Douglass, "Bergson and Cinema," 218.
3. On Deleuze's ontologization of Bergson's virtual, see Mullarkey, "Forget the Virtual"; on Deleuze's distortion of Bergson's attitude to cinema, see Mullarkey, *Philosophy and the Moving Image,* 97–100.
4. Chateau, *Cinéma et philosophie,* 7.
5. Bergson, *The Creative Mind,* 108–9.
6. Ibid., 118.
7. Ibid., 109.
8. Bergson, *Matter and Memory,* 135, 14; Bergson, *Mind-Energy,* 53.
9. Apart from artifacts (both visual and auditory) stemming from the new contemporary setting of the story and its recasting, the most startling intentional differences come in the two murder scenes, which have surreal/subjective inserts.
10. See Cheshire, "Psycho—'Psycho' Analysis"; and Lien, review of *Psycho.*
11. Bergson, *The Creative Mind,* 177.
12. Ibid., 190.

13. Meillassoux, "Subtraction and Contraction," 70–71.
14. Bergson, *Matter and Memory,* 21 (first italics mine).
15. Ibid., 20–21.
16. Ibid., 133–34 (italics mine).
17. Bergson, *The Creative Mind,* 86–87.
18. Ibid, 304n14.
19. Bergson, *Mind-Energy,* 56–59. Bergson approved this translation.
20. Agamben, "The Six Most Beautiful Minutes in the History of Cinema," 93.
21. Agamben, "Notes on Gesture," 55.
22. Ibid., 56.
23. Agamben, "Author as Gesture," 66; Agamben, "Notes on Gesture," 58.
24. Bergson, *The Creative Mind,* 162 (translation modified).
25. Hjort, "Style and Creativity in *The Five Obstructions,*" 33.
26. Schepelern, "To Calculate the Moment," 98.
27. Smith "Funny Games," 130.
28. The rest of these remakes are analyzed—in the context of posthuman thought and François Laruelle's nonphilosophy—in Ó Maoilearca, *All Thoughts Are Equal.*
29. Ibid., 118.
30. Cited in Hjort, "Style and Creativity in *The Five Obstructions,*" 21.
31. Ibid.
32. Smith, "Funny Games," 135.
33. Livingston, "Artistic Nesting in *The Five Obstructions,*" 65.
34. Hjort, "Style and Creativity in *The Five Obstructions,*" 22, 23.
35. Danto, *The Transfiguration of the Commonplace,* 204.
36. Jürs-Munby, "*Hanswurst* and *Herr Ich,*" 129, 130.
37. Mayer, "Acting in Silent Film," 13.
38. Naremore, *Acting in the Cinema,* 51, 52.
39. Schmitt, *La raison des gestes,* 41, 177ff. My thanks to Sven Läwen for this reference.
40. Engberg-Pedersen, "From Pointing to Reference and Predication," 287.
41. Bergson, *Matter and Memory,* 100.
42. Bergson, *Laughter,* 12–13.
43. Delbos, "*Matière et mémoire,*" cited in Heidsieck, *Henri Bergson et la notion d'espace,* 90.
44. Gilson, *L'individualité dans la philosophie de Bergson,* 64.
45. De Man, "Modern Poetics in France and Germany," 154.

BIBLIOGRAPHY

Agamben, Giorgio. "Author as Gesture." In *Profanations,* translated by Jeff Fort, 61–72. New York: Zone Books, 2007.

———. "Notes on Gesture." In *Means without End: Notes on Politics,* translated by Vincenzo Binetti and Cesare Casarino, 49–60. Minneapolis: University of Minnesota Press, 2000.

———. "The Six Most Beautiful Minutes in the History of Cinema." In *Profanations,* translated by Jeff Fort, 93–94. New York: Zone Books, 2007.

Bergson, Henri. *Creative Evolution.* Translated by Arthur Mitchell. London: Macmillan, 1911.

———. *The Creative Mind: An Introduction to Metaphysics.* Translated by Mabelle L. Andison. New York: Philosophical Library, 1946.

———. *Laughter: An Essay on the Meaning of the Comic Laughter.* Translated by Cloudesley Brereton and Fred Rothwell. Seattle: CreateSpace, 2011.

———. *Matter and Memory.* Translated by Nancy Margaret Paul and W. Scott Palmer. New York: Zone Books, 1988.

———. *Mind-Energy: Lectures and Essays.* Translated by H. Wilson Carr. Westport, Conn.: Greenwood Press, 1975.

Chateau, Dominique. *Cinéma et philosophie.* Paris: Armand Colin, 2005.

Cheshire, Godfrey. "Psycho—'Psycho' Analysis: Van Sant's Remake Slavish but Sluggish," *Variety,* December 6, 1998.

Danto, Arthur. *The Transfiguration of the Commonplace: A Philosophy of Art.* Cambridge, Mass.: Harvard University Press, 1981.

de Man, Paul. "Modern Poetics in France and Germany." In *Critical Writings 1953–1978,* edited with an introduction by Lindsay Waters. Minneapolis: University of Minnesota Press, 1989.

Douglass, Paul. "Bergson and Cinema: Friends or Foes?" In *The New Bergson,* edited by John Mullarkey, 209–27. Manchester, U.K.: Manchester University Press, 1999.

Engberg-Pedersen, Elisabeth. "From Pointing to Reference and Predication: Pointing Signs, Eyegaze, and Head and Body Orientation in Danish Sign Language." In *Pointing: Where Language, Culture, and Cognition Meet,* edited by Sotaro Kita, 269–92. Mahwah, N.J.: Lawrence Erlbaum Associates, 2003.

Georges-Michel, Michel. "Henri Bergson nous parle du cinema." *Le journal,* February 20, 1914.

Gilson, Bernard. *L'individualité dans la philosophie de Bergson.* Paris: Librairie philosophique J. Vrin, 1978.

Heidsieck, François. *Henri Bergson et la notion d'espace.* Paris: Le circle du livre, 1957.

Hjort, Mette. "Style and Creativity in *The Five Obstructions.*" In *Dekalog 01: The Five Obstructions Notes,* edited by Mette Hjort, 15–37. London: Wallflower Press, 2008.

Jürs-Munby, Karen. "*Hanswurst* and *Herr Ich*: Subjection and Abjection in Enlightenment Censorship of the Comic Figure." *New Theatre Quarterly* 23, no. 2 (2007): 124–35.

Lien, Fontaine. Review of *Psycho*. IMDB archive for the rec.arts.movies .reviews newsgroup. Originally posted December 1998. www.imdb.com/ reviews/188/18868.html.

Livingston, Paisley. "Artistic Nesting in *The Five Obstructions*." In *Dekalog 01*, edited by Hjort, 57–77.

Mayer, David. "Acting in Silent Film: Which Legacy of the Theatre?" In *Screen Acting*, edited by Alan Lovell and Peter Krämer, 10–30. London: Routledge, 1999.

Meillassoux, Quentin. "Subtraction and Contraction: Deleuze, Immanence, and *Matter and Memory*." *Collapse* 3 (2007): 63–107.

Mullarkey, John. "Forget the Virtual: Bergson, Actualism, and the Refraction of Reality." *Continental Philosophy Review* 37 (2004): 469–493.

———. *Philosophy and the Moving Image*. Basingstoke, U.K.: Palgrave-Macmillan, 2010.

Naremore, James. *Acting in the Cinema*. Berkeley: University of California Press, 1988.

Ó Maoilearca, John. *All Thoughts Are Equal: Laruelle and Nonhuman Philosophy*. Minneapolis: University of Minnesota Press, 2015.

Schepelern, Peter. "To Calculate the Moment: Leth's Life as Art." In *Dekalog 01*, edited by Hjort, 95–116.

Schmitt, Jean-Claude. *La raison des gestes dans l'Occident medieval*. Paris: Gallimard, 1990.

Smith, Murray. "Funny Games." In *Dekalog 01*, edited by Hjort, 117–140.

2

Hugo Münsterberg, Film, and Philosophy

Robert Sinnerbrink

> Yes, it is a new art—and this is why it has such fascination for the
> psychologist who in a world of ready-made arts, each with a history
> of many centuries, suddenly finds a new form still undeveloped and
> hardly understood. For the first time the psychologist can observe the
> starting of an entirely new aesthetic development, a new form of true
> beauty in the turmoil of a technical age, created by its very technique
> and yet more than any other art destined to overcome outer nature by
> the free and joyful play of the mind.
>
> Hugo Münsterberg, *The Photoplay*

> How could we not have known him all these years? In 1916 this man
> understood cinema about as well as anyone ever will.
>
> Jean Mitry[1]

It is ironic that Hugo Münsterberg, one of the pioneering intellectual
figures in the history of film theory and the philosophy of film, was
ignored for the best part of a century, a period during which cinema
developed into the defining art form of modern times. Even more
striking is that his approach to film theory, already a century ago, was
thoroughly steeped in philosophical reflection on the psychological,
aesthetic, and cultural significance of the new medium. As a Harvard
professor of psychology and philosophy, Münsterberg published *The
Photoplay: A Psychological Study* (1916), a book widely regarded as the
first work of film theory proper.[2] Münsterberg was not only a psychologist and philosopher of the cinema but also an enthusiastic advocate
for it, publishing newspaper articles and magazine interviews, using

film in psychological experiments, and even dabbling in filmmaking himself. Despite his impressive stature as a public intellectual, Münsterberg's groundbreaking book soon went out of print after World War I and remained so until it was reissued as a Dover reprint in 1970. Indeed, only with the publication of *Hugo Münsterberg on Film* in 2002, edited by Allan Langdale, did Münsterberg's contribution to film theory and philosophy begin to gain the recognition it deserved. Although hard to imagine today, Münsterberg was one of the leading intellectual figures of his day, a prominent founder of applied and industrial psychology, and a noted philosopher who counted William James, George Santayana, and Josiah Royce among his peers.[3] He was a tireless proselytizer for the movies, promoting them as a promising new art form capable of synthesizing photography, drama, literature, and music. Like many early film theorists, moreover, Münsterberg was quick to articulate and defend the artistic specificities of the new medium, championing the validity of cinema as a novel art form distinct from and, in ways, superior to theater and literature. More originally, he articulated the distinctively *psychological* dimensions of cinematic experience, presenting one of the earliest—and most striking—instances of what Noël Carroll has called the "film/mind analogy": the suggestive parallel between cinematic techniques and perceptual experience.[4] On the one hand, he cautioned against the moral effects of the movies, pointing out their visual fascination and capacity for emotional engagement meant they could have a powerful psychological and social influence on audiences. On the other, he claimed this same power of cinema had the potential to be harnessed pedagogically for educational purposes and used artistically to further the "aesthetic education" of the general public.

Unfortunately, however, this remarkably prescient and eloquent study—one that Jean Mitry was amazed to discover anticipated his own psychological aesthetics of film—soon fell out of favor with the public and consequently had little influence on the intellectual development of film studies. In large part this was probably due to Münsterberg's rather abrasive critiques of contemporary American culture, coupled with the strong anti-German sentiment pervading American society following World War I.[5] One might also mention the intriguing fact that Münsterberg was an industrial psychologist whose studies of the psychology of work were taken up in American industry and business as a way of maximizing worker efficiency. After a century of neglect, however, it is time to acknowledge the contribution of Münsterberg's work to philosophical film theory, the full impact of which, as J. Dudley Andrew remarks, is perhaps "still to come."[6] In this essay I discuss some of the key elements of Münsterberg's theorization of film, focusing on the philosophical dimensions of *The Photoplay*: its intriguing combination of neo-Kantian (and Schopenhauerian) aesthetic theory and empirical psychology and its ontological–aesthetic concern with the medium, in particular the question of film as art. On the one hand, Münsterberg was a pioneer in the empirical–psychological study of cinema, conducting experiments in the field of the visual perception of moving images and anticipating elements of contemporary cognitive theory.[7] On the other hand, like those of other early film thinkers, Münsterberg's pioneering efforts in forging a philosophy of film remained wedded to "classical" theories of aesthetics and sought to synthesize the analysis of cinematic experience within the prevailing system of the fine arts.[8] At the same time, he recognized and argued for the aesthetic distinctiveness of the medium, exploring its aesthetic and cultural possibilities as an art capable of communicating the "free and joyful play of the mind."[9] In this regard, Münsterberg canvassed some of the central problems of classical film theory, anticipating many of the questions that occupied philosophers of film over the coming century, while struggling to articulate a coherent theory of cinema capable of synthesizing its psychological–cognitive and aesthetic–cultural dimensions.

Münsterberg on Film as Art

Like many later theorists, Münsterberg was quick to recognize the interplay of technological developments and psychological verisimilitude that made the cinema a unique modern art form. At the same time, he quickly discerned the popular appeal of the new art form and was receptive to both its liberating and its "corrupting" potentials.[10] Trained as an experimental psychologist (as a student of Wilhelm Wundt) and regarded as one of the founders of applied psychology, Münsterberg was a relative latecomer to the new art form of film, which he called, in keeping with the theatrical parallel common in his day, "the photoplay" (literally a filmed play, although he argued

cinema could not be reduced to theater). Overcoming his professo-
rial disdain for the "vulgar" new art form, he described the day in
1914 when he and a friend "risked seeing *Neptune's Daughter*," an
experience that rapidly converted him to the "marvelous possibilities"
that film had to offer.[11] This conversion included immersing himself
in the history of the new technology, meeting well-known directors
and film stars of the day, and writing voluminously on film for newspapers and magazines. Yet he quickly discerned the psychological
power of film as well as its artistic possibilities and distilled all of these
insights into *The Photoplay*. It was both an argument for the artistic
validity of film in comparison with the theater and an original exploration of the analogy between film-compositional devices (close-up,
flashback, flash-forward) and acts of consciousness (attention, recollection, imagination, emotional states). As we shall see, however, the
novelty of his philosophical insights into the psychological aspects of
cinema—the suggestive aspects of the film/mind analogy—strained
somewhat against his more classically Kantian approach to cinema's
aesthetic possibilities.

Münsterberg's Psychology of Film

Münsterberg's most original contribution to the philosophy of film is
his fascinating examination of the parallel between cinematic devices
and acts of consciousness. We can understand film's aesthetic power,
Münsterberg observes, once we attend to the way it "influences the
mind of the spectator," which means analyzing "the mental processes
which this specific form of artistic endeavor produces in us."[12] He
commences with the important phenomenological point that, although we know we are watching "flat," two-dimensional images
while in the cinema, we nonetheless *experience* the strong impression of depth and movement on the screen.[13] Drawing on numerous
psychological experiments (including ones he conducted himself),
Münsterberg's claim endorses the idealist thesis that the experiences
of depth and movement are not objectively present in the image as
such but are "added on" by the psychological (or cognitive) operations of our own minds.[14] What is the difference, then, between our
perceptions of movement on stage and those on film? For Münsterberg the former is obviously a real movement in space, whereas the

latter is an impression of movement generated by the "inner mental activity" uniting separate phases of movement in "the idea of connected action."[15] Depth and movement on screen are a mixture of "objective" perception and the subjective investment of this perception, a mixture we do not even notice once perceptually and psychologically immersed in the complex visual world of the film.

Depth and movement, however, are only the elementary features of the film image. Münsterberg emphasizes the psychological act of *attention* as the key to understanding the film/mind analogy. "Attention" is taken broadly to refer to the intentional directing of consciousness that selects what is relevant or not in our field of conscious awareness. Such directing can be further distinguished into *voluntary* and *involuntary* acts of attention. Voluntary attention involves our focusing of consciousness through particular ideas or interests we bring to our impressions or observations, ignoring whatever does not serve our interests or desires (attending to a task at hand, making something, solving a problem). Involuntary attention, by contrast, refers to the way events or objects in our environment can provide the cue for the (unwilled) focusing of our perceptual awareness (an explosion, a flashing neon sign, a cry that commands our notice). Involuntary attention also spans emotional and affective responses to what is happening in ourselves or in our environment: "Everything which appeals to our natural instincts, everything which stirs up hope or fear, enthusiasm or indignation, or any strong emotional excitement, will get control of our attention."[16] Clearly, ordinary experience involves a complex interplay of voluntary and involuntary attention (as when I attend to a friend's injury prompted by my reaction to her cry of pain).

Münsterberg then turns to the question of affective and perceptual involvement in film and theatrical performance, exploring the kind of psychological and philosophical issues that would later become central to theories of cinematic identification. In theatrical performance as in film, *involuntary* attention must be elicited in order to ensure aesthetic and psychological involvement. In the case of film, voluntary attention may of course come into play in a distanced, reflective way (as when we muse on an actor's attire, consider how a shot was achieved, or notice an inconsistency in the editing). Genuine aesthetic engagement with the film, however, demands opening up to the capturing of our involuntary attention: "We must accept those cues for our attention which the playwright and the producers have prepared for us"—namely, the particular elements of script, performance, setting, visual framing, and cutting comprised by a cinematic shot.[17] Involuntary attention is captured by the careful preparation and aesthetic presentation of visual, cinematic cues—an idea that strongly suggests the cognitivist concepts of "criterial prefocusing" and "affective prefocusing" that Noël Carroll and Carl Plantinga have proposed in order to account for our shared affective and emotional responses to narrative film.[18]

As with the theater, film (and Münsterberg means of course *silent* film) relies upon the expressiveness of the human face, the gestures of the actors' bodies, and the movement and action of the characters to compose the images commanding our involuntary attention. Not only movement but what later theorists dubbed *mise-en-scène* (the specific arrangement of objects and figures composing the image) can elicit our rapt attention. Elements of the actor's physiognomy, costuming, setting, artifacts, and the visual composition of space can all contribute to the capturing of involuntary attention: "An unusual face, a queer dress, a gorgeous costume or a surprising lack of costume, a quaint piece of decoration, may attract our mind and even hold it spellbound for a while."[19] Finally, the power of landscape and setting opens up immensely powerful visual means of capturing audience attention and even of expressing emotional coloring or mood—ideas that one can find developed further in theorists such as Béla Balázs and Gilles Deleuze.[20]

To this extent film parallels or extends the possibilities of theater. But film truly comes into its own through its capacity to emulate elements of acts of attention: intensification of attentive focus to what is most arresting and the withdrawal of attentive focus from what is not; the adjustment of the body toward that which captures our attention and the clustering of meanings—"ideas and feelings and impulses"[21]—around the object of our attention. In the theater, too, our attention is focused on that which is most relevant (the hand of the actor carrying the gun, the look of terror on his victim's face), but the theater has limits as to how vividly it can actually emulate these acts of attention (although my gaze is intent upon the killer's hand, I can see that man's hand only from a distance). Film can surpass theater in this respect, however, for it can visually elicit and direct our involuntary attention through cinematic devices of composition and montage in ways that theatrical performance would find difficult to match.

The close-up, for example, provides a visual analogue to the intensification of perception that attends attentive focus. Münsterberg is the first of many theorists to highlight the unique possibilities of the cinematic image—particularly the close-up—in drawing our attention to particular objects, gestures, or expressions. His originality lies in underlining the strong analogy between perceptual attention and cinematic devices, which cannot be emulated in live theatrical performance: "The close-up has objectified in our world of perception our mental act of attention and by it has furnished art with a means which far transcends the power of any theatre stage."[22] Not only does the close-up focus our immediate attention, but it quickly becomes part of the familiar grammar of narrative film. It provides a specifically visual means of prefocusing our attention; drawing our attention to particular objects, actions, or events; amplifying their affective power by extending or concentrating our visual scope; and using changes in scale and focus in ways that cannot be reproduced in the theater in quite the same way.

To the close-up, we must add the flashback and its rather striking suggestion of the operation of memory. Here again, a parallel can be found with the flashback and the use of montage, which is drawn out by contrast to the case of the theater. Understanding a theatrical performance, for example, relies on our remembering the sequence of scenes that preceded the one in front of us. A character can draw attention to an earlier scene, and stage props, lighting, and music can suggest one to us, but the scene itself cannot be "replayed" directly before our eyes. With film, however, the act of remembering can be screened, so to speak, before our very eyes thanks to the use of flashbacks. Here, Münsterberg claims the film can "screen" memory, whether the recollection of a character, which might be suggestive of the viewer's recollections, or the film's "own" recollection of an earlier scene or narrative sequence: "*The act which in the ordinary theatre would go on in our mind alone is here in the photography projected into the pictures themselves.*"[23] The film/mind analogy is thus most strongly drawn in the case of the flashback, which provides "an objectivation of our memory function" that parallels the "mental act of remembering."[24] Recollection-images are presented in movies in a manner that parallels the function of memory-images in our own conscious experience, even though the recollection-images depicted in cinema do not necessarily belong to an individual character or remain tied to a particular point of view.

So how do we make sense of the flashback? Münsterberg notes that not just our own recollection of past scenes can be represented on the screen; more typically, we are given privileged access to a character's recollection of past events (or a redramatization of those events). Münsterberg thus carefully anatomizes the varieties and conventions of the flashback as part of his strong claim for it being an "objectification" of memory.[25] In this sense Münsterberg suggests a parallel between the flashback and the memory: it is as though the outer world (of film images) were now shaped by our fleeting perceptions or imagined recollections, the narrative on screen thereby magically expressing "the inner movements of the mind."[26]

We might question, however, the grounds upon which Münsterberg draws such a strong parallel between the flashback and the memory. Although flashbacks are often connected with a particular character, it is unclear whether they belong to the character in question or, more strangely, are an "objectification" of his or her mental processes (most flashbacks are *about* rather than *of* a character). Nor is it obvious to what extent an analogy can be plausibly drawn between mental images and cinematic images: what mental images are remains a vexing question, and attempts to show that film directly screens mental images are at best controversial.[27] Cinematic images emulate, evoke, and in some cases, resemble "subjective" images belonging to conscious experience, but at the same time they are not reducible in any straightforward way to the "subjectivity" of any particular character or even to the implicit perspective of an (embodied) human observer. Indeed, many theorists have explored at length an impersonal, machinic aspect of moving images that overlaps with but also is distinct from lived perception: from Jean Epstein's "metallic brain"—cinema as a visual machine with the capacity to render thought in images—to cinema as a "spiritual automaton," as articulated by Antonin Artaud and taken up by Gilles Deleuze, in which images unfold in an automatic sequence to which viewers are subject as they enter the visual, cognitive, and temporal circuit of the film unfolding before them.[28]

What of the other aspects of this analogy? Emotional expression is clearly one of the most important dimensions of our experience of film. Indeed, the central aim of cinematic art, Münsterberg remarks, echoing many film theorists today, must be "to picture emotions."[29] This point is interesting given the absence of audible dialogue in silent film, which means actors have to rely on facial expression, physical gestures, and bodily comportment in order to communicate emotional meaning. Here again, the close-up reveals possibilities of emotional expression that theater would struggle to convey through strictly visual means. At the same time, silent film courts the risk of attempting to reproduce stage-like modes of performance, which may not be quite appropriate to the medium and indeed can quickly degenerate into caricature.[30]

In a lucid discussion of distinct forms of emotional identification, Münsterberg notes they can be divided into (1) identification with a character's emotional state and (2) our more independent emotional responses to a character's behavior. This distinction anticipates, without yet clearly articulating, Murray Smith's important distinction between visual, affective alignment with a character's point of view and emotional–moral allegiance with that character.[31] In Jonathan Demme's *The Silence of the Lambs* (1991), for example, we readily identify with the terror of FBI agent Clarice Starling (Jodie Foster) as she tries to find and shoot notorious serial killer Buffalo Bill in the darkened cellar of his house. To add to the horror of the scenario, we can see Clarice's terrified face and hear her panicky, shallow breathing from the perspective of Buffalo Bill himself, thanks to his unnerving night-vision goggles. We are not (one hopes) thereby disposed to identify with *his* murderous intent, though we do, disturbingly, see Clarice from his point of view. On the contrary, we are all the more able to sympathize with her terrifying plight while observing her from the killer's viewpoint, thereby realizing the awful proximity between them in the dark, Clarice's trembling hand and gun just inches from his face.[32] The scene enacts both forms of emotional response that Münsterberg describes: the sympathetic identification with Clarice's terrifying plight and the horror we feel in response to Buffalo Bill's hideous night-vision game of cat and mouse—not to mention the relief we experience once Clarice shoots him in the dark. It plays with the affect of *suspense*—will she slay the killer or become his victim?—which Münsterberg identifies as essential to successful cinematic drama.[33]

Of course, it is not only the emotional expression of characters to which we respond. As Münsterberg points out, film can elicit emotional investment in objects (the Rosebud sled in *Citizen Kane*) and landscape (in Malick's *Days of Heaven*), as well as through camera movements (Hitchcock's probing, roving, "thinking" camera in *Rear Window*; the "reality-effect" of handheld camera movements in Von Trier's *Breaking the Waves*; or the extraordinary continuous camera movement across time and history in Sokurov's *Russian Ark*). As though anticipating some of these examples, Münsterberg explicitly mentions how a filmmaker might wish to "produce the effect of trembling," such as we find in the use of handheld cameras today, and how mounting the camera on "a slightly rocking support," such that it would trace complex figures of movement with an "uncanny whirling character" and would result in "unusual sensations which produce a new shading of the emotional background."[34] All of these techniques are capable of generating powerful emotional and affective responses in distinctively cinematic ways. Münsterberg's analyses are remarkably prescient in their emphasis on the distinctive possibilities of the film image to generate affect when compared with theater and other visual arts.

Münsterberg's Aesthetics of Film

Film aesthetics has sometimes been taken as the "poor cousin" of film theory, an awkward amalgam of philosophical analysis and film criticism. Yet in this early film theory text, we find a rich vein of philosophical aesthetics brought to bear on the new art of the cinema. This is not really surprising, considering Münsterberg was a philosopher-psychologist who was able to bring classic motifs from neo-Kantian aesthetics into productive relationship with a strongly empiricist commitment to experimental psychology. It is worth remembering that much of the early debate over film concerned the question whether it qualified as a new art form or was merely a clever technical gadget, apt to record reality faithfully but devoid of real artistic merit. Like that of

Rudolph Arnheim, Münsterberg's aesthetic approach to film, in *The Photoplay*, strongly argues the case for film as art: a medium capable of artistically transfiguring rather than simply recording our visual and perceptual experience. Münsterberg combines, in novel fashion, a Kantian "aesthetic attitude" approach to film—that the aesthetic experience of film, like other arts, depends upon a detached, contemplative perspective in which our desires and "interests" are put out of play—with a Schopenhauerian account of art as enabling us, through the aesthetic experience of objects, to transcend our immediate spatiotemporal context and thereby experience "ideas" in sensuous form. He begins with the critical point that the traditional mimetic approach—art as an imitation of nature—is clearly inadequate as an account of art.[35] Art cannot simply be imitation, for imitation as such is not necessarily aesthetically pleasing (compare bird calls and wax dummies), while many of the most aesthetically striking arts are nonmimetic (architecture and music) or involve nonimitative aesthetic techniques or devices (for example, poetic speech in dramatic performance). Indeed, art is defined precisely by its *transcending* of the mere imitation of reality: "It is artistic just in so far as it does not imitate reality but changes the world, selects from it special features for new purposes, remodels the world, and is, through this, truly creative."[36] Art is about the transfiguration of our experience, transcending our immediate, "involved" cognition of the world, which will always trump mere imitation or decorative attractiveness.

The second point is that experiencing art aesthetically, according to Münsterberg's neo-Kantian perspective, requires that one adopt the appropriate *aesthetic attitude*: a detached, "disinterested" pleasure in the appearance of the object for its own sake. Echoing Kant and Schopenhauer, Münsterberg points out that the same object can be experienced differently depending upon the cognitive and practical interests we bring to bear upon it: the same landscape strikes the farmer, the scientist, and the photographer in quite different ways (as pasture, as geological stratum, or as aesthetic image). What Münsterberg adds to this familiar Kantian point is an interesting Schopenhauerian twist. The theorist (scientist or scholar) seeks to find the causal networks of which the object is a part, to situate it in the physical processes of the universe.[37] The artist, by contrast, presents the object independent of its causal relations or obedience to general laws; the artist creates an image of the singular object in splendid isolation, like a self-sufficient world we can nonetheless contemplate and enjoy.[38] Like Schopenhauer, Münsterberg claims art presents a part of our experience "liberated from all connection" with the world: an aspect of our experience temporarily emancipated from the purely instrumental, goal-driven, context-bound ways in which we ordinarily encounter objects in the world. It is the unified, harmonious, perfectly isolated work of art, free of the causal constraints and practical demands of ordinary experience, that procures genuine aesthetic pleasure for us as spectators. Why? Because it is only in art, to paraphrase Schopenhauer, that we can find temporary solace from the vicissitudes of desire, suffering, and frustration that attend our ceaseless striving. Works of art provide a transfigured image of unity—"complete in itself"—an idealized presentation of reality that transcends the practical world of our everyday concerns while satisfying our desires in a way that brings temporary aesthetic delight.[39]

How does this strongly Kantian and Schopenhauerian aesthetic approach relate to our experience of film? Münsterberg insists film has its own distinctive aesthetic features that cannot be imported or transposed from painting, literature, or theater. From both aesthetic and psychological perspectives, narrative film presents a human story that idealizes our "outer" experience of a world, transcending our immediate practical context of concerns while emulating our world of "inner experience"—that is, our subjective responsiveness to the world. Film works, in short, "by overcoming the forms of the outer world, namely, space, time, and causality, and by adjusting the events to the forms of the inner world, namely, attention, memory, imagination, and emotion."[40] In other words, the inherent abstraction of the film image (especially in silent film) takes the screen performance away from the physical realm and brings it closer to the mental dimensions of our experience. Cinema emulates subjectivity without being reducible to it. Movement can be presented in ways that extend or even defy the limits of our natural perception. Time can be "left behind" as we revert to the past; jump back to the present, now divided along different timelines; and imagine the future in different ways. The sheer fluidity of cinematic representation makes possible the *aesthetic transcending* of the ordinary constraints of time and space that order our lived experience—an imaginative transcending of our ordinary world in favor of an imaginative, idealized, alternative world that can be experienced directly.[41]

This is what Münsterberg means by contrasting the time- and space-bound character of theater and theatrical performance with the aesthetic liberation from time and space constraints opened up by the use of film narrative techniques (most vividly displayed, I would suggest, in the case of animation). As Münsterberg argues, film shows us narrative images that are "freed from the physical forms of space, time, and causality, are adjusted to the free play of our mental experiences, and which reach complete isolation from the practical world through the perfect unity of plot and pictorial appearance."[42] The aesthetic experience of moving images opens up a transfigured horizon of experience that allows us to "transcend" our ordinary, engaged forms of cognition and enter a virtual, visual, coherent narrative world that remains aesthetically "isolated" or independent of our everyday world of practical concerns.

Münsterberg's Film/Mind Analogy

What are we to make of this striking claim? Noël Carroll suggests Münsterberg construes the aesthetic "isolation" of film art to mean it *quite literally* attempts to "overcome outer forms of space, time and causality."[43] Carroll goes on to argue this is incoherent, since narrative film—even experimental film—is parasitic upon space, time, and causality in order to represent any kind of meaningful action (or to plot a narrative). Indeed, Carroll questions whether any art, particularly a narrative art like film, can ever "overcome" space, time, and causality, since narrative structure and meaning are dependent upon these fundamental conditions of cognitive experience. Carroll thus rejects Münsterberg's idea—taken from Schopenhauer's discussion of art in *The World as Will and Representation,* volume 1—that film art can "somehow release us from our ordinary experience of things with respect to space, time and causality."[44] Indeed, the only way of experiencing the world independently of space, time, and causality, Carroll argues, would be to imagine something like a "sheer bodily existent" living in a perpetual present, which is, no doubt, a fanciful form of "experience" that would always remain inaccessible to us as embodied knowers engaging with the world through practical action.[45] Hence, Münsterberg's claims about film's power to overcome space, time, and causality, Carroll concludes, cannot be sustained, since there is no meaningful contrast to be made between our own cognitive experience and something else that would transcend the very conditions of that experience.[46]

Carroll's critique rests, however, upon an overly literal interpretation of Münsterberg's claims concerning the aesthetic possibilities of cinema. It is neither a metaphysical nor an epistemological claim so much as a claim about the kind of *aesthetic experience* film makes possible in contrast to that of other art forms, like the theater. Cinematic performance is not bound to "space, time, and causality" in quite the same way as live stage performance, since the latter is always necessarily confined to the spatiotemporal present of the performers' speeches and actions. The screen performer's image, however, can be juxtaposed to any number of images from disparate spaces and times, even "defying" ordinary causality through the creative use of montage and special effects (especially today with the blurring of cinema and animation thanks to CGI and digital image technology).

To be sure, Münsterberg perhaps invited this confusion by his rather loose Schopenhauerian talk of "overcoming" space, time, and causality. What we should say, rather, is cinema has the power to *manipulate* outer forms of space, time, and causality in order to compose a particular cinematic world—an imaginative, idealized, fictional world depicted through moving images—that remains ontologically "independent" of our ordinary world of practical concerns and can even extend or augment our ordinary forms or perceptual experience. This would stress more clearly that we are not dealing with outlandishly metaphysical claims concerning the "literal" overcoming of the limits of time, space, and causality. Münsterberg's point, rather, is that the technical devices and the aesthetic techniques of the film medium make possible an aesthetic manipulation of space, time, and causality in ways often simply not available to theatrical performance. Once again, these claims are part of Münsterberg's broader agenda to defend the artistic specificity and aesthetic potentiality of the new medium. Carroll overlooks this key hermeneutic and aesthetic point—hence his rather sharp critique of Münsterberg's striking claim that film is an art that can "transcend" the conditions of our cognitive experience of the world.

What are we to make, then, of Münsterberg's intriguing but controversial analogy between film and the human mind? Mark Wicclair has argued it should be taken as a *phenomenological* correlation between film images and perceptual experience, a rendering of the first-person perspective that conveys the "what it is like" aspect of cognitive experience in a manner that emulates ordinary perception: the close-up resembles phenomenologically an act of attention; the flashback is a phenomenological analogue of memory; and so on.[47] As Wicclair points out, however, we do not actually perceive objects as a "close-up" image, nor do we recollect our own experiences from a third-person or "objective" point of view. As Wicclair, Carroll, and Daniel Frampton all rightly observe, a flashback that is phenomenologically accurate would show the persistence of my present perception along with the imaginary superimposition of my recollected image (seeing my absent partner's face as I stare at waves on the beach). For this reason Münsterberg's film/mind analogy, for Wicclair, fails to show any strict phenomenological correlation between film image and human perception.

How, then, should this analogy be taken? Wicclair suggests construing it *functionally* rather than phenomenologically: certain cinematic images or devices serve the same *functional role* as certain acts of perception or recollection.[48] This indeed avoids the difficulties afflicting the phenomenological version of the film/mind analogy (after all, we don't actually perceive the world in close-up, with zooms or via rapid cuts). In drawing a functional analogy between films and minds, we can better understand film's aesthetic power as well as the striking affinity between moving images and perceptual experience without reducing the former to the latter.

Here again, however, as Carroll argues, a serious problem emerges, one that afflicts *all* versions of the film/mind analogy.[49] The logic of analogy—I compare A to B in order to illuminate A—requires that we know more about the nature of B than of A, since that is the point of the analogy (to illuminate A). In Plato's *Republic*, for example, Socrates compared human beings to prisoners in a cave taking shadow-images for reality, who gradually discover the real world outside is illuminated by the sun (the Idea of the Good). We know from ordinary experience what that is like, so the cave analogy helps us understand the meaning of Platonic philosophical education.[50] The problem with film/mind analogies, Carroll argues, is they fail to follow this logic of analogy; we do not know enough about the mind, compared with what we know about film, in order to make the analogy theoretically illuminating. As Carroll notes, I can usefully compare the mind to a computer because we know how computers work, how they are programmed, and so on; hence, the cognitive science analogy between consciousness and artificial intelligence can be theoretically illuminating.[51] But to say that a computer is like the mind is not really illuminating in the right way, since we know very well how computers work but not really how our minds do, which is what the analogy is supposed to show. Hence, Carroll concludes, to say that *film is mind-like,* as Münsterberg does, is similarly un-helpful, because we do not really know enough about consciousness (memory, attention, imagination, and so on) to make the analogy theoretically useful.[52]

Does this render Münsterberg's film/mind analogy a theoretical dead end? Not necessarily, I would argue, for it depends on how we construe this analogy and what we are aiming to show. As Frampton observes, we can respond to Carroll's critique by making a familiar phenomenological point: "Münsterberg was obviously making a comparison with common 'experience,' and Carroll's critique seems better suited to those who propose that film can show mental states."[53] Carroll assumes the point of Münsterberg's film/mind analogy is strictly theoretical (epistemological and ontological): *knowledge* of what *film is,* pursued with reference to the mind, which implies we need to presuppose adequate knowledge of the nature of the mind (which we do not have). But what if the analogy is supposed to describe, rather, our aesthetic experience of film, of what Stanley Cavell describes as "the world viewed"?[54] After all, I do not need a theory of mind in order to perceive the world; likewise, I do not need a theory of mind in order to understand how images can have a functional role similar to ordinary states of consciousness, nor do I need one in order to engage aesthetically and cognitively with the complex cinematic world before me on screen. So contra Carroll, Münsterberg's film/mind analogy, construed in an appropriate way, can be illuminating because it draws on our *ordinary experience* of perception, attention, emotion, and imagination, which we must presuppose in understanding and enjoying any kind of film. The point of the analogy is to draw attention to the manner in which cinema can present an idealized world that remains independent of our own world yet shows this world in a manner that emulates different forms of perceptual or cognitive experience without being reducible to or identical with these.

Münsterberg and Contemporary Film Theory

From a contemporary perspective, however, there are some difficulties with Münsterberg's approach to philosophizing on film that invite further critical reflection. One significant problem concerns the tension that emerges between Münsterberg's commitment to a neo-Kantian account of aesthetic experience, as applied to cinema, and his investigation of the psychological–cognitive aspects of film viewing, which he applies to the aesthetic possibilities of filmmaking practice. How are we to reconcile Münsterberg's neo-Kantian "aesthetic attitude" approach to cinema with his protocognitivist account of the analogy between movie shots and cognitive operations like attention and memory? On the one hand, the Kantian aesthetic approach emphasizes the manner in which cinema opens up a self-contained world to "detached" perceptual contemplation in ways that transcend our ordinary, "interested" modes of engaging with the world; on the other, the psychological–cognitivist aspect of his theory of cinema underlines the analogies to be drawn between ordinary acts of cognition and the manner in which moving images elicit and direct both voluntary and involuntary attention. This aspect, however, is much more oriented toward the "interested" forms of cognition and dynamic emotional engagement at play in watching movies, which seems at odds with Münsterberg's emphasis elsewhere on a more "detached" point of view as characteristic of the aesthetic attitude toward works of art.

There is an unresolved tension here in Münsterberg's account of detached aesthetic contemplation and his recognition of cinema's capacity to elicit affective and emotional engagement, perceptual and imaginative immersion, or moral reflection. Indeed, Münsterberg struggled to reconcile his commitment to classical neo-Kantian aesthetics and his forward-looking psychological approach, which combined cognitivist insights with an inquiry into the aesthetic possibilities suggested by the film/mind analogy. Like other early film theorists, moreover, Münsterberg remained tethered to the aesthetic framework that cinema, perhaps more than any other modern art form, served to both undermine and transform (see Walter Benjamin on cinema's radical challenge and transformation of traditional conceptions of art and aesthetics).[55]

In this respect, Münsterberg is to be praised for his efforts at opening up the field of philosophical film theory, even though he was unable to develop a theoretical approach to cinema that could adapt itself to the philosophical potentialities of the new medium—namely, to the challenge that cinema itself posed to traditional aesthetic theory. Nonetheless, his heroic attempt to take film seriously, as a cultural phenomenon worthy of philosophical inquiry, aesthetic engagement, and psychological investigation, remains provocative and suggestive today—especially since phenomenological and cognitivist approaches to digital media are renewing the philosophical problems that animated classical film theory. From an early proselytizer, psychologist, and philosopher of the medium to an almost forgotten figure whose legacy has been all but ignored, Münsterberg can now take his rightful place among the founding thinkers of philosophical film theory, one whose philosophical and aesthetic insights remain pertinent and provocative. The enduring legacy of his pioneering work is to explore how we should think philosophically about moving images in ways that remain true to our aesthetic experience of them.

NOTES

An earlier version of this chapter appeared as "Hugo Münsterberg," in Sinnerbrink, *Film, Theory, and Philosophy*, 20–30. This chapter has since been expanded and revised for publication in the present volume.

1. J. Dudley Andrew attributes the remark in the epigraph to a "private conversation with the author"; see Andrew, *The Major Film Theories*, 255. As Colapietro notes in "Let's All Go to the Movies," Mitry's remark carries the authority of one of the great French film theorists "who devoted two volumes to the very topics to which Münsterberg devoted the two main parts of *The Photoplay*"—namely, *The Psychology of Film* and *The Aesthetics of Film* (495).

2. Langdale notes in "S(t)imulation of Mind" that Münsterberg's book was preceded by American poet Vachel Lindsay's *Art of the Moving Picture* (1915) but is "clearly more compelling" than Lindsay's lyrical work (27). *The Photoplay* anticipates Arnheim's better known and theoretically quite similar *Film as Art,* which has had an immense effect on film theory, whereas *The Photoplay* has been all but ignored.

3. Andrew, *The Major Film Theories,* 14–15; Colapietro, "Let's All Go to the Movies," 477.

4. As I discuss later in this essay, this "film/mind" analogy has been sharply criticized by Wicclair in "Film Theory and Hugo Münsterberg's *The Film*" and Carroll in "The Film/Mind Analogies." I offer an alternative account in the conclusion to this essay.

5. Langdale, "S(t)imulation of Mind," 5–6.

6. Andrew, *The Major Film Theories,* 26.

7. See Bruno, "Film, Aesthetics, Science," for a fascinating discussion of Münsterberg's psychological experiments and his empirically grounded scientific explorations of the parallels between consciousness, emotion, and moving images.

8. See Fredericksen, *The Aesthetic of Isolation in Film Theory,* for a discussion of the importance of neo-Kantian aesthetic theory in Münsterberg's philosophy of film. See also Fredericksen, "Hugo Münsterberg."

9. Münsterberg, *Hugo Münsterberg on Film,* 160.

10. See Münsterberg's cautionary essay "Peril to Childhood in the Movies," advocating censorship of depictions of immorality, in *Hugo Münsterberg on Film,* 191–200.

11. Münsterberg, *Hugo Münsterberg on Film,* 172. As Langdale notes in "S(t)imulation of Mind," *Neptune's Daughter* (1914) was a fantasy film directed by Herbert Brenon and starring Annette Kellerman, an Australian swimming star who founded synchronized swimming, invented the one-piece swimsuit, and pioneered "that rarefied genre of Hollywood films involving aquatic spectacles" (7–8).

12. Münsterberg, *Hugo Münsterberg on Film,* 65.

13. Arnheim's *Film as Art* makes just the same point. After noting how easily depth perception can be emulated by "the stereoscope" (the simultaneous projection of slightly different images for each eye) and noting the difference between natural depth perception and the "shallow" depth of the film image, Arnheim remarks that the "effect of film is neither absolutely two-dimensional nor absolutely three dimensional, but something between" (20). Münsterberg makes the same observations on depth perception, the stereoscope, and the "depth effect" of motion pictures over a decade and a half earlier: "We have reality with all its true dimensions; and yet it keeps the fleeting, passing surface suggestion without true depth and fullness, as different from a mere picture as from a stage performance." *Hugo Münsterberg on Film,* 71.

42 •• ROBERT SINNERBRINK

14. Münsterberg, *Hugo Münsterberg on Film*, 69–71.
15. Ibid., 78.
16. Ibid., 80.
17. Ibid., 82.
18. Carroll, "Art, Narrative, and Emotion"; Plantinga, *Moving Viewers*, 79.
19. Münsterberg, *Hugo Münsterberg on Film*, 84.
20. Balázs, *Early Film Theory*; Deleuze, *Cinema 1*.
21. Münsterberg, *Hugo Münsterberg on Film*, 86.
22. Ibid., 87.
23. Ibid., 90.
24. Ibid., 90.
25. Ibid., 90–96.
26. Ibid., 128.
27. See Frampton, *Filmosophy*, 15–26.
28. Epstein, *Jean Epstein*, 311–12; Deleuze, *Cinema 2*, 164–68.
29. Münsterberg, *Hugo Münsterberg on Film*, 99.
30. Ibid. 100–101.
31. Smith, *Engaging Characters*.
32. Parallels can be drawn here between cinematic spectatorship, voyeurism, and even sadism and masochism, as psychoanalytic film theory has explored at length.
33. Münsterberg, *Hugo Münsterberg on Film*, 21.
34. Münsterberg, *Hugo Münsterberg on Film*, 107. Münsterberg appears to have anticipated the kind of "whirling," "rocking" camera movement popular in some contemporary pop videos (e.g., the Cure's "In Between Days," directed by Tim Pope, 1985). See Gaspar Noé's even more remarkable "whirling," "rocking" camera movements in his controversial film *Irreversible* (2002).
35. Münsterberg, *Hugo Münsterberg on Film*, 113–17.
36. Ibid., 114.
37. Ibid., 116.
38. Ibid., 116–17.
39. Ibid., 121.
40. Ibid., 129.
41. In "Film Theory and Hugo Münsterberg's *The Film*," Wicclair argues what is "overcome" is not the spatiotemporal and causal structure of the outer world "but rather the physical constraints which govern an actual agent's direct observation of events in the 'outer world'" (44).
42. Münsterberg, *Hugo Münsterberg on Film*, 138.
43. Carroll, "Art, Narrative, and Emotion," 494.
44. Ibid., 496.
45. Ibid., 495–96.
46. Ibid., 496.

47. Wicclair, "Film Theory and Hugo Münsterberg's *The Film: A Psychological Study.*"
48. Ibid., 43.
49. Carroll, "Art, Narrative, and Emotion."
50. It is an analogy, incidentally, with a long history in philosophy of film.
51. Carroll, "Art, Narrative, and Emotion," 498.
52. By contrast, to say the mind is like a film—as philosophers such as Henri Bergson and Bernard Stiegler have done—can be highly illuminating.
53. Frampton, *Filmosophy*, 22.
54. Cavell, *The World Viewed.*
55. See Benjamin, *The Work of Art in the Age of Its Technical Reproducibility.*

BIBLIOGRAPHY

Andrew, J. Dudley. *The Major Film Theories: An Introduction.* Oxford: Oxford University Press, 1976.
Arnheim, Rudolf. *Film as Art.* 1933. London: Faber, 1958.
Balázs, Béla. *Early Film Theory: Visible Man and the Spirit of Film.* Edited by Erica Carter. Translated by R. Livingstone. New York: Berghahn Books, 2010.
Benjamin, Walter. *The Work of Art in the Age of Its Technical Reproducibility, and Other Writings on Media.* Edited by M. W. Jennings and T. Y. Levine. Cambridge, Mass.: Harvard University Press, 2008.
Bruno, Giuliana. "Film, Aesthetics, Science: Hugo Münsterberg's Laboratory of Moving Images." *Grey Room* 36 (Summer 2009): 88–113.
Carroll, Noël. "Art, Narrative, and Emotion." In *Emotion and the Arts,* edited by Mette Hjort and Sue Laver, 190–214. Oxford: Oxford University Press, 1997.
———. "Film/Mind Analogies: The Case of Hugo Münsterberg." *Journal of Aesthetics and Art Criticism* 46 no. 4 (Summer 1988): 489–99.
Cavell, Stanley. *The World Viewed: Reflections on the Ontology of Film,* enlarged ed. Cambridge, Mass.: Harvard University Press, 1979.
Colapietro, Vincent. "Let's All Go to the Movies: Two Thumbs Up for Hugo Münsterberg's *The Photoplay* (1916)." *Transactions of the Charles S. Peirce Society* 36, no. 4 (2000): 477–80.
Deleuze, Gilles. *Cinema 1: The Movement-Image.* Translated by Hugh Tomlinson and Barbara Habberjam. Minneapolis: University of Minnesota Press, 1986.
———. *Cinema 2: The Time-Image.* Translated by Hugh Tomlinson and Robert Galatea. Minnesota: University of Minneapolis Press, 1989.
Epstein, Jean. *Jean Epstein: Critical Essays and New Translations.* Edited by Sarah Keller and Jason N. Paul. Amsterdam: University of Amsterdam Press, 2012.
Frampton, Daniel. *Filmosophy.* London: BFI Books, 2006.
Fredericksen, Donald. *The Aesthetic of Isolation in Film Theory: Hugo Münsterberg.* New York: Arno Press, 1977.

————. "Hugo Münsterberg." In *The Routledge Companion to Philosophy and Film*, edited by Carl Plantinga and Paisley Livingston, 422–34. London: Routledge, 2009.

Langdale, Allan. "S(t)imulation of Mind: The Film Theory of Hugo Münsterberg." Introduction to *Hugo Münsterberg on Film*, by Hugo Münsterberg, 1–41.

Münsterberg, Hugo. *Hugo Münsterberg on Film. "The Photoplay": A Psychological Study and Other Writings.* Edited by Allan Langdale. London: Routledge, 2002.

Plantinga, Carl. *Moving Viewers: American Film and the Spectator's Experience.* Berkeley: University of California Press, 2009.

Sinnerbrink, Robert. "Hugo Münsterberg." In *Film, Theory, and Philosophy*, edited by Felicity Colman, 20–30. Durham, N.C.: Acumen Publishing, 2009.

Smith, Murray. *Engaging Characters: Fiction, Emotion, and the Cinema.* Oxford: Oxford University Press, 1995.

Wicclair, M. R. "Film Theory and Hugo Münsterberg's *The Film: A Psychological Study.*" *Journal of Aesthetic Education* 12, no. 3 (July 1978): 33–50.

Different, Even Wholly Irrational Arguments

THE FILM PHILOSOPHY OF BÉLA BALÁZS

Adrian Martin

> The passions and feelings of a modern poet must, in despite of
> himself, be entirely and exclusively modern.
>
> Maurice Maeterlinck, "The Modern Drama"

In a recent roundtable discussion organized and published by the
highbrow American art magazine *October* on the topic of a current
return to the archives of classical film theory, the scholar Anton Kaes
asks a good, provocative question:

> How do we actually define classical film theory? Is it really a unified,
> coherent body of texts that can be set against contemporary film the-
> ory? Are the theories of [Siegfried] Kracauer, [Walter] Benjamin, [Béla]
> Balázs, [Rudolf] Arnheim, and [André] Bazin "classical film theory"?[1]

Kaes cites Balázs's *Visible Man* from 1924 as a significant instance of
the lively disruption of the concept of classical film theory:

> In the preface to this book he defines "theory" not as a system but as a
> "road map" that indicates "pathways and opportunities," so that what
> appeared as "iron necessity" can be shown as just "one random route"
> among many others. In this sense, film theory for him reveals alterna-
> tives, possibilities, promises, "roads not taken." I believe the same is
> true for theorists like [Jean] Epstein and Bazin, who were also active
> film critics.[2]

Among those whom we now usually consider—sometimes quite erroneously—as classical film theorists (from the medium's inception to the early 1960s), Béla Balázs, born Herbert Bauer in 1884, offers a unique case in his trajectory as a writer. He did not silently labor, over decades, toward a single magnum opus to be unveiled in a single blow, as Siegfried Kracauer did with his *Theory of Film* in 1960. He did not attempt to order the scattered writings of his lifetime at its end into a coherent theoretical program, as André Bazin did when he sketched the contents for the three volumes of *Qu'est-ce que le cinéma?* in 1958. He did not change the direction of his ongoing reflection in large, radical ways, whether for reasons of restless, personal inclination or the malign pressure of the sociopolitical environment, as did Sergei Eisenstein.

Balázs was, in the manner of his output, closer to Jean Epstein (who deserves the retrospective "classical" label even less): he wrote many books of many kinds (fiction and nonfiction, essays and creative texts, covering diverse media and subjects) and pursued a reasonably consistent set of interests and obsessions across the biographical and social stages marked by these publications. In Balázs's particular instance, we see something special. His initial book on film, *Visible Man or the Culture of Film* (1924), constituted an originary text on which each subsequent tome by him was built: first in 1930, when *Visible Man*, composed in the era of silent cinema, was coupled with its "sequel" (he called it "a theoretical epilogue"), *The Spirit of Film*, and, second, through the successive versions and editions of what we know in English as *Theory of the Film (Character and Growth of a New Art)*, published in 1952, which crystallized itself in Hungarian as *Filmkultúra* in 1948.[3] Balázs himself, although he worked hard to clinch the international dissemination of this ultimate work on cinema, did not live to see all of its translated editions; he died in 1949 at the age of sixty-four.

The progression through these three books is intriguing. In 1924 Balázs set out to define what he saw as the flowering of an art that may well have "only just begun to emerge from the trashy products of the picture palace,"[4] but that—almost unnoticed or unremarked by the intelligentsia—had nonetheless already developed rapidly in its expressive "muteness" ("the art for the deaf," as he frequently called it in the 1920s).[5] By 1930 sound had entered cinema's technological equation, and it clearly shook up both Balázs and his philosophic–aesthetic system: as he gloomily saw it, the arrival of the talkies "put an end" to a "great opportunity."[6] Therefore, a "balance sheet" was required for this art and its industry—for what purposes, in his mind, we shall explore later on. Balázs spoke at this second pinnacle of his theorizing of wishing to "outline a kind of grammar of this language" of film, "a stylistics and a poetics, perhaps."[7] The tone was immediately less strident, more tentative than that in *Visible Man*.

Then there was a larger leap all at once in terms of geography, time, and intention: by the late 1940s cinema itself in many parts of the world (but particularly Hollywood) was entering the last golden decade of its studio-controlled classicism. Balázs had lived as an exile in the Soviet Union since 1931, and he had seen his own communist dream (if not entirely his theorized Marxist ideology) sour to a marked degree. But had cinema in general been accepted by this point as an art? Yes and no, in Balázs's view.

On the one hand, the record of its varied achievements was incontestable, and Balázs accordingly expanded the survey of its forms and genres he had started a quarter of a century previously. But the battle for the recognition of film—and the need to institute what he rightly and presciently called a *film culture*—remained an urgent necessity, as in fact it was to remain for a very long time and, in some places and levels of society, still today.

Visible Man, as many have commented, is an idealistic, even utopian book. It is a virtual fantasia on film's aesthetic possibilities—imaginatively, even fancifully, projected onto the page via Balázs's lively, engaging prose (which remains a pleasure to read and conjure with in a thought experiment). Cinema is what is *ahead* of the book in a shared, cultural, cosmopolitan future. *Theory of the Film* is by contrast far more sober stuff: it is keyed to retrospection and preservation and, more generally, to the task of *education*—a course with which Balázs had deeply involved himself in the 1930s and 1940s at Moscow's State Film Institute and later in Hungary, Poland, and Prague. In other words, cinema by 1949 incontrovertibly *existed*; it had become the author's stated mission to keep it on the rails, cultivate it, extend its most fruitful tracks and paths. But it was no longer such a wide-open space.

So we have passed in Balázs's work, not so imperceptibly, from the passion of the early 1920s to the pedagogy of the late 1940s—a seemingly inevitable fate or condition of growing older, some would say. It was a fate Epstein, as a point of comparison, managed to avoid largely by remaining outside institutions (such as the university) and pursuing his own highly individualistic, idiosyncratic mode of experimental documentary fiction as a filmmaker. In the period between his first and last film books, however, Balázs was tempted by the potential of official programs to help build a better culture in and for a socialist/communist world (an experience first fanned by his service within the short-lived and ill-fated Communist government in Hungary under Béla Kun's Soviet Republic in 1919), and this fed his drive to posit prescriptive rules for filmmaking, the type of rules that Epstein temperamentally loathed and evaded and that eventually made life difficult for Eisenstein.

In this transition from the 1920s to the 1940s, we have also passed from a Balázs who was openly fond of philosophizing and theorizing ("every profession should have a theory," he declares within the first pages of *Visible Man*'s preface) to one who, twenty-five years on, was more concerned with practicalities—whether concerning the methods of making films or procedures for disseminating them and instructing about them.[8] Thus, Balázs naturally seems more of a film philosopher at the start of his adventure than at its end—which means that, in this essay, I place more prominence on the earlier than on the later work.

It is hardly surprising, in the light of this general, supposedly maturing progression in Balázs's career, that *Visible Man* can strike us today as a typically youthful book in its spirit and expression. But Balázs was not literally so young when he wrote it; the relevant dates are worth scrutinizing. He embarked on a prodigious period of cultural journalism in 1922, at the age of thirty-eight, and his first film book appeared (carved in part from that journalistic material) when he was forty. By this time he had already lived since his teenage years a full and heady career as a writer, mixing in the Sunday Circle from 1915 with the likes of Georg Lukács, Béla Bartok, Zóltan Kodály, and Karl Mannheim and applying his skills diversely across a dizzying array of arts: literature, theater, opera, and ballet, as well as film, where he became well known as a scriptwriter and director during the 1920s. (In a 1930 review of *The Spirit of Film*, Kracauer tartly remarked: "I have seen bad films by him").[9] In this essay I have neither the scope nor the pretext to compare and contrast Balázs's theories with the many films he made or to which he contributed in his lifetime; that is work for a future historian.

Béla Takes a Train

Many lines of contact, affinity, and mutual influence can be (and have been) drawn between the popular journalism practices of Balázs, Kracauer, and Walter Benjamin during the 1920s and 1930s. But they were (mind the years again) not the same age: Balázs was older than Kracauer by five years and older than Benjamin by eight. The difference between someone of thirty and thirty-eight can be vast not only in terms of individual personality but even more so in terms of what I would call *cultural receptivity*, a feeling for and closeness to the sensations and transformations occurring in everyday life. And such receptivity enjoyed a very intense, intimate relation with the kind of writing we evaluate today as in some sense reflecting or registering the upheavals of twentieth-century modernity up until the onset of World War II.

Here, we find something truly admirable in Balázs's trajectory: his long-sustained open-mindedness and the consequent freshness of his on-the-spot reportorial observations and reflections during the 1920s. (As Kracauer pointed out, this is also, for the most part, the fertile period in Balázs's political development before he succumbed wholesale to the lures of Soviet ideology as a set of "doctrines" in which "he feels secure.")[10] I therefore begin this account of Balázs's philosophy of film by underlining the sharpness of his best writing in this essayistic mode, for as Kaes has pointed out, even the smallest piece of descriptive journalism by the likes of Balázs (or countless other figures from this period, as by Bazin twenty years later) can serve to focus and configure a great many things on the horizon of history and culture at a precise moment and in a precise place: intuitions relating to theory and philosophy, changing social and technological apparatuses, subjectively felt movements in the Zeitgeist, the cross-pollination and interplay of different artistic forms, and (last but not least) the methods of critique possible or imaginable in the mass media.[11] All of this feeds into *Visible Man*, helping to make it so vibrant both as a text and as a testament. As Kaes suggests:

> You see theory residing in these anecdotes, observations, reflections, meditations, and ruminations. That's where theory hides, where it lies dormant, waiting for us to awaken it and make it speak to us.[12]

In 1925 Béla Balázs took a train.[13] Or rather, he evoked (in scarcely six hundred words) the experience of modern train travel and the associations to which it gave rise—in him and, by extension, in many, the mass public for whom he presumed to speak by bringing to the surface what was only dimly known or intuited by them and even, as he put it, what could be "embarrassing" to them. There was a childish, archaic sensation that goes with such travel in the writer's view. He called upon "Freudian theory" to explain this but, whether through tact or unfamiliarity, avoided Freud's own account of train travel (as discussed by Peter Wollen) as generating a motion and excitation in passive passengers linked indelibly to masturbation.[14]

Balázs's supposedly Freudian explanation was, in fact, the sweet, sentimental, and obvious one: falling asleep on a train and then waking up amid a crowd of dozing strangers was an undeniably odd but absolutely comforting sensation—a reliving of the experience of being protected in your mother's lap. Yet he also regarded it as a modern phenomenon, not just a Proustian memory trigger but a thing in itself, a novel and hence small-scale but telling historic experience: the train allowed a tantalizing, ephemeral, almost perverse sense of intimacy (a woman murmured "good night" to her partner "as if she might even be including you").[15] And it involved a real, present-tense relation to a "caring, benevolent power" that was no longer a parental figure but an impersonal machine piloted by yet another stranger: this train was "doing its job, it is awake even though you sleep," and it protected us: "Nothing can happen to us."[16] This is a strange thing to read in 2014, when Bong Joon-ho's spectacular action film *Snowpiercer* (2013) allegorizes both seething class struggle and a malign society of control in the central figure of a train (from its front to tail compartments, each one completely different) carrying in an endless circle the last surviving members of the human race through a frozen landscape—and where "to control the engine is to control the world."

Balázs had gentler symbolic options in mind in 1925. His short, wonderful piece can serve as an intersection point for several strands of Balázs's writing across many fields, as well as for several different ways in which his work has been interpreted. Commentators including Johannes von Moltke and Izabella Füzi have stressed the ways in which Balázs's fiction—especially his identification with fairy tales—serves to indicate the type of phantasmatic wish fulfilments his film theory, on another register, also expresses.[17] As history has often shown us, it is the figure of the exile, facing the tearing fragmentations of his or her itinerant life, who can come to wish most desperately for mystical fusion, for an impossible ideal of "wholeness," wherever it can be found, imagined, or projected. In Balázs's case—recall his early film books were written once he had left Hungary for Germany, in exile—this yearning was channeled not into transcendental religion but into politics (the communist dream of class abolition), on the one hand, and into art, on the other hand. Searching for the most apt analogy to describe his sleepers on a moving train, Balázs evoked a great deal of collective, traumatic history (past and yet to come) with a deft, disarmingly light touch:

> We are like emigrants who carry something of the atmosphere of home and family with them on their journey. A melancholy sense of solidarity takes hold, as it always does among people sharing a similar fate. If we had managed to swim to an island after a shipwreck, who would be embarrassed? We lie down to sleep together in drowsy confidence, and the gloom of a common destiny blankets us weary children.[18]

So where did Balázs's recounted train ride take him? All at once, it led him back to a mother's embrace; it delivered him into the arms of a presently existing social, institutional mechanism (symbolized by the benevolent engine of the train, constant and on schedule) that he could trust; and it opened up a more fanciful, otherworldly realm of dreams. Balázs ended his brief but potent reflection with the specific sensation every modern traveler knows: dozing through a trip makes you feel as if you have not actually traveled anywhere at all; outside the window frame, the world has simply changed. Isn't this rather like the substitution of a reel or a shot change in the presentation/projection of a movie inside the frame of its screen—a link (between travel and cinema) that directors from Max Ophüls (*Letter from an Unknown Woman*, 1948) to Raúl Ruiz (*Time Regained*, 1999) have richly played upon in their work? But it was not directly to cinema that Balázs chose to manifestly appeal here, however much we might sense as his retrospective readers this latent connection. He reached elsewhere: "You have simply gone to sleep and awakened someplace else. Just as in a fairy tale."[19]

Yet Balázs was no fool, no simpleminded dreamer looking to trip off on transcendence. Fairy tales (he himself devised many) had a complex sense and a diverse set of uses for him; they could "convey the meaning of larger complexes, the meaning of reality."[20] *The Spirit of Film,* his riposte to Eisenstein (the two men jousted in public, across their texts, over key points of film theory, especially relating to montage), is as fine a piece of philosophical and logical deconstruction as any later poststructuralist could manage:

> Seven years ago, in *Visible Man,* I spoke only of visual culture which, sidelined by the invention of the printing press, of conceptual culture, would be reborn once again thanks to the film. Eisenstein harks back yet further, to primeval beliefs in magic, to discover an analogy for the unity of mental experience that he wishes to reinstate with film.
>
> The unity of speculative thinking and unconscious emotion? But such unity surely exists only at a stage, as in the age of magic, when these categories simply do not exist in a separate and distinct duality. This unity cannot be achieved by gluing or mixing. If the idea of a unity emerges only as the antithesis of a divided nature, it is impossible from the outset. Unity as an unproblematic, self-evident quality can hardly be capable of realization simply by the cinema. Nor indeed by art of any kind.[21]

Face Front

But let us return to that earlier euphoric dream of a reborn visual culture and its underpinnings. If Béla Balázs is known for anything today among a general film-literate public, it is his eulogy of the human face as the locus of cinema—and of an expressive (in his terms, visual or visible) culture in general. The testament he left on this idea has informed much recent work in film theory and the study of spectatorship, from Gilles Deleuze's philosophical categories (such as the affection-image) in his *Cinema* books to Therese Davis's *The Face on the Screen: Death, Recognition and Spectatorship,* which places our shared "face complex" within cultural contexts as diverse as Australian indigenous land rights campaigns, the death of Princess Diana, and the mourning over the events of September 11, 2001.

Let us note, at the outset, the theoretical and philosophical primacy—easy to overlook when dealing with a medium such as film—accorded by Balázs to visibility, to surfaces and spectacle. This emphasis had the same polemical charge in his time as, mutatis mutandis, Susan Sontag's famous opposition to interpretation and "reading for deep meaning" did in the the 1960s.[22] It also corresponds intimately with the film philosophy of a now little-cited figure, Guido Calogero, probably quite influenced by Balázs, who in his *Philosophy Lessons* of 1947 proposed:

> In the cinematograph, the substantial figuration, which is *asemantic,* utilizes means other than those of literary semanticity. . . . The actor is called upon to exhaust, thanks to the external technique of his living person, the entire asemantic vision of the author. . . . The mass public follows a film like a novel, but the film is an asemantic narrative, a texture of tableaux that face front and reflect life.[23]

So on a first level, Balázs found himself offside—as many film critics down the decades have also discovered themselves—of the predominantly thematic tenets and values of literary and dramatic criticism when applied to the movies. He regularly and enthusiastically encouraged the "stripping out" of what made a literary work profound so as to fully make it available for a radically different cinematic treatment. Meaning in film was neither a floating, insinuated essence nor a "hidden depth"; it was something to be directly *seen* and imbibed as a *mood,* a material atmosphere (many years later, V. F. Perkins would rephrase this argument in differently elaborated but closely related terms).[24]

On another and more decisive level, Balázs decried what he saw as a baleful tendency toward *abstraction* in all social realms—the abstraction guaranteed by rational intellectualism at any cost. As Noël Carroll has pointed out, Balázs implicitly formulated (in the manner of Hegel but contrary to Hegel's own conclusion) a world-historical role for cinema art as a redemptive force that would reconnect us with concrete, physical reality.[25] What differentiates Balázs from Kracauer along this "physically redemptive" path, however, is the relatively slight importance that the former attached to documentary and related modes of naturalistic (or neorealistic) filmmaking that claimed or presumed to depict "life as it is,"[26] which is in stark contrast to the latter. *Visible Man* goes so far as to speak the aesthetic heresy (still to claim its proper legacy in contemporary film theory) that "it is illusion alone that counts in a picture."[27]

In 1983 Deleuze declared: "The affection-image is the close-up, and the close-up is the face"—a very Balázsian formulation to any modern cinephile's ears.[28] In fact, there was already a slight *décalage* between the definition of these two closely related terms, *close-up* and *face*—and the investment placed in them by Balázs—between his books of 1924 and 1930. In the former he militated for what was veritably a new cult of face worship, holding general significance; in the latter it was the more circumscribed technical, filmmaking technique of the close-up that was emphasized (and carried over, more or less as is, into his final book). Why this immense significance of the face for Balázs in the 1920s—expressed with such passion and force that it still incites theoretical rhapsodies in its wake?[29] In a wide-ranging social analysis that anticipated Vilém Flusser's later distinction between a print-based culture and one based on techno-images,[30] Balázs kicked off the main thrust of *Visible Man* with the following affirmation:

> The discovery of printing has gradually rendered the human face illegible. . . . The thousands of books fragmented the single spirit of the cathedrals into a myriad different opinions. The printed word smashed the stone to smithereens and broke up the church into a thousand books. In the way, the *visual spirit* was transformed into a legible spirit, and a *visual culture* was changed into a conceptual one. It is universally acknowledged that this change has radically altered the face of life in general. But the degree of change to which the face of the individual human being has been subject—his brow, his eyes, his mouth—has been largely overlooked.[31]

The movement of analogy and metaphor in the rhetoric of the argument is masterful: the smashed stone of the cathedral is transformed into a thousand books (a hideous, Babel-like image for Balázs); the figure of speech "face of life" is instantly redirected into a consideration of the literal, human face. It is in and through this face, re-found, magnified, and in a sense reinvented or refigured by cinema (once again, the affinity with Epstein is palpable) that cinema will put us back in touch with soul, essence, spirituality, but in Balázs this is a very modern, secular kind of soulfulness, keyed more to the everyday possibility of ecstasy than to a transcendental, religious sublime. The rhapsody over the face soon grew into something larger, much debated by Balázs's many commentators since his time: *physiognomy.* This idea bore very little relation to eugenics or "breeding," despite the momentary lapse in 1924 (discreetly edited out of the iterations of these passages in his later books) that a "uniform ideal of beauty" as propagated on world screens by cinema would eventually help "produce a uniform type of the white race."[32] A growing Marxist consciousness put a swift end to that particular fantasy of its era—closely allied, in Balázs as in others, with the dream of silent cinema as a kind of visual Esperanto, a universal language to overcome the Babel of different tongues (which, for Balázs, the coming of talkies instantly annihilated). Physiognomy was, at once, both a soulful and a highly material, ecstatic property in *Visible Man*—a fusion of *appearance* and what he called *atmosphere.*

Recall the atmosphere of that real, everyday, but also fairy-tale train for the man-child Balázs, which offered transport in every sense but also was very much a thrill tied to sensuality and sexuality (that strange lady across the aisle who bids you goodnight and, as it were, "sleeps with" you). Atmospheric physiognomies in Balázs cover a far larger territory than merely the human: landscapes, objects, architecturally designed spaces, all possess character and mood. And while it is a little facile to categorize Balázs's philosophical theory as merely anthropomorphic in nature, there can be no doubt he placed the interplay of human *passions*—to the detriment, as we shall see, of narrative storytelling itself—at the absolute center of the cinematic medium. Again and again, he returned to this assertion or affirmation: "In the final analysis, it is only human beings that matter."[33]

But this human passion was itself a volatile and *transformative* element for him—something irreducibly dynamic. It was passion that, at its extreme, left the confines of the human individual and found concrete, eternal form elsewhere in art, such as the art of film: "a projected lyricism, a lyricism made objective."[34] And such ecstatic lyricism is also linked, once again, to those off-center states of being Balázs privileged in charged asides, such as when he celebrated the "world of film" as "simply more childlike"—tied intimately to "the closer perspective of little children"—and related this perspective, shared by both young people and Charlie Chaplin's vagabond, to a certain *dispossession* from the crippling adult mind-set of the "hot pursuit of distant goals" and consequent lack of "intimate experience" of things. The eye of film, however, merrily dispossesses us as spectators because we become these "children at play" who "gaze pensively at minor details."[35]

A New Art

In his perceptive and sympathetic evaluation of Balázs's early work on cinema, Noël Carroll suggests it follows the "very recognizable format" of what we now label, retrospectively, classical film theory. For my part, I echo Kaes's skeptical question about this assumption of a corpus, group, or designated era in writing about film. Carroll notes for his case that Balázs's first two film books are "designed primarily to answer two questions that taxed silent-film theorists: Can film be an art form? and, if it can, can it be a unique art form (and not merely theater in a can)? Balázs answers these questions affirmatively."[36] Indeed, Balázs—who was astutely praised by his friend and colleague Edwin Arnet for his "talent for formulation and definition"[37]—swiftly fulfilled the obligations of any film theory truly worthy of the name: he set out to determine both what is *specific* to cinema as a medium and what is *unique* to it.

To that extent, Carroll is perfectly correct in stating Balázs forms a familiar part of the scattered community of classically minded film theorists. But he misses or downplays an important aspect of Balázs's writing in the context of its time: namely, his insistence on cinema as not just *another* art to join the established pantheon of arts but an altogether *new* art. In this regard Balázs's film theory and his philosophy of art walked a tightrope: while wanting to claim cinema its rightful place in the artistic pantheon (the image of Parnassus returns often in his prose), thus adding it to an honorable and honored line of aesthetic *tradition,* he also seized the possibilities of this new art as a *challenge* to tradition and, in some sense, a complete *regeneration* of aesthetic givens and assumptions.

Like all the most interesting theorists of early cinema, Balázs was open to new aesthetic experiences—indeed, to experiences that threatened to completely overthrow and thus radically redefine what the aesthetic categories of the truthful, the beautiful, the dramatically expressive, and so on could mean. When, for example, he (like Adorno, Benjamin, Bazin, Eisenstein, Epstein, and the surrealists) celebrated Charlie Chaplin as a creator-performer, he did not hesitate to plunge into the type of aesthetical paradox that was no doubt confronting and provocative in its day: "His antics are not psychologically complex," but the "grotesquerie" that defined his comedy was, in fact, "lyrical."[38]

As both he and the cinema grew older, Balázs leaned (as *Theory of the Film* ultimately shows) more to the conservative position of ensconcing film within a respectable tradition; a quarter of a century earlier, however, he staked more on the value of radical newness for its own sake. As his readers today, we should heed Alain Badiou's recent admonition to an audience of philosophy students: "When you have become an old man, as I am, you must pay attention to not become too skeptical, because of so many failures, so many temptations. The temptation is to say that it is the illusion of youth and now [I am] in my wisdom. So don't become as Plato in the end; instead, be as Plato in the beginning."[39] We should, likewise, be as Balázs in the beginning.

To fully grasp this crucial dimension of Balázs, we need to connect his writing to two bodies of work: first, as already indicated, the many contemporaneous writings in the 1920s and 1930s on the burgeoning of modernity and its radically changing social conditions in that era and, second, the theories of new drama that formed part of a background that greatly influenced him. The first track has already received some close attention, as in texts by Gertrud Koch and Johannes von Moltke, as well as a remarkable essay by Eszter Polónyi on the "eye of the microscope" and its relevance to Balázs's theories (drawing upon the largely uncited scientific work of his brother, Ervin Bauer, who "retained an almost philosophical desire to find a pure expression of the physical mechanisms constituting life," something uncannily close to Balázs's film theory).[40] I will say a little more along the lines of this research before turning to the question of the new drama.

Is it really any wonder that Balázs wandered for a moment into a eugenic fantasy of the white race? It is somewhat excusable once we grasp that for him as for other cultural reporters in the midst of 1920s modernism, the very idea of the human being—the complex concatenation of body, mind, spirit, reflex, emotion, gesture, soul, and so on—was in flux. The human being was starting to be philosophically considered, even accepted, as a *machine,* and like any machine, it was open to transformation, retooling, and outright improvement (the notion was even more stridently advocated in the contemporaneous writings of Dziga Vertov on the "new Soviet man" to be created for a new society).[41] In particular, the idea that the human *perceptual apparatus*—including all forms of vision, mental processing, memory, and even dream—could be "fed" and hence altered by cinema appealed to Balázs in the 1920s.

In 1924, the year of *Visible Man,* his essay "Radio Drama" toyed with the idea that each art (such as radio or film) must "switch off certain senses" in order to address just *one* sense at a time because "the whole world is somehow too much for people, stretching their perception to the point of superficiality" and "one cannot enter the world through five senses simultaneously."[42] In this way, through media, we can speculate that Balázs imagined the human sensorium could be developed, cultivated, and refined.

In a remarkable 1925 text, drawn upon for a section of *The Spirit of Film,* Balázs speculated upon a particular, new type of *cinematic human* who had entered upon the world stage: the "compulsive cameramen" of documentary, who risked their own life in extreme conditions or, indeed, sometimes lost their lives while their camera recorded (and was destined to deliver to spectators around the world) the situation of their final moments. Balázs's speculation on a "new, objectified form of human self-awareness" anticipated Michel Foucault's historical philosophy of "technologies of the self" as constituting, quite precisely, a kind of modern laboratory or training ground of the human being—especially, when Balázs wrote of how, in the person of the cameraman, a "subjective mentality is transformed into a social one."[43]

Involved in the cameraman's decision to keep filming at all costs was "a new kind of self-examination," presumably in comparison to, for instance, previous religious and ethical codes of the self; "the interior process of accounting for themselves shifted to the outside."[44] Furthermore, this man became a machine: what was previously (in a striking formulation) the human "film of self-control" was now, literally, wound onto the camera's spool, and "one remains conscious as long as one films"—not the other, traditional way around.

In this piece Balázs admitted he must resort to "different, even wholly irrational arguments" in order to convince those skeptical of or revolted by these spectacular documents of death that provided, for him, a defining limit case (as it did, in the 1950s, for Bazin) of cinema as a new and sometimes shocking medium. He hesitated, as almost any thinker would, between old and new, residual and emergent frameworks of explanation. The "compulsive cameraman" was, after all, from one angle an old-fashioned (if extreme) kind of hero, an "extreme sports" adventurer (as we would say today), a Werner Herzog–style character whose "taking it to the limit" offered both the "moral force" of a "yardstick" and an intense fantasy of escape for those workaday citizens "yearning for the strenuous life that relegates the petty life of ordinary men to the shadows."[45]

That was Balázs's emotive, even "sublime" justification for what he beheld on screen. The *irrational* justification we can sense, however, has much more to do with the lineaments of a radically new art— and the type of philosophical and conceptual somersaults Balázs had to push himself to perform in order to be the equal of this newness.

The Modern Drama: Plot as Human Gesture

It can be surprising, looking back from at least seventy years of screenwriting manuals that preach supposedly proper, classical plot construction (John Howard Lawson's *Theory and Technique of Playwriting and Screenwriting*, in successive editions between 1936 and 1949, is a model example), to gauge how little store Balázs's early film theory placed in *narrative* as a resource for cinema. Although he must have regularly grappled with building plot structure in his own projects, he wrote little of the problems of narrative poetics (as Bordwell defines this field)—the construction of believable, flowing, coherent, tightly woven story lines—in *Visible Man*.[46] This is so despite the fact he was clearly providing craft insights directly from the production planning rooms of the film studios of the 1920s—rather than the canny intuitions of a more distant observer of the industry, such as Bazin—when he noted, for instance: "Modern directors mainly do not show the climax in close-up, since our attention focuses on this automatically and so it does not call for any special emphasis."[47]

Instead, to take an example from a rightly famous passage at the end of *Visible Man* (the second of "Two Portraits" that concludes a series of "Supplementary Fragments"), Balázs breathlessly celebrated the screen performance of Asta Nielsen in Leopold Jessner's *Erdgeist* (*Earth Spirit,* 1923):

> The film's only content is that Asta Nielsen ogles, flirts with, bewitches and seduces six men. The film's content is the erotic charisma of this woman who regales us with the great and complete dictionary of gestures of sensual love. (This may even be the classical form of the cinematic art, where gestures are not triggered by a "plot" with external purposes, but where every gesture has only reasons and hence points inwards.)[48]

To adapt Anton Kaes's remark: in this canny parenthesis staged by Balázs as a seeming afterthought, theory truly hides dormant, waiting to be awakened. For in a single stroke, so-called classical cinema is severed both from the exigencies of mere plot (or storytelling) and, especially, from what has long been assumed as a central mechanism of plot structure, i.e., the driving relation of cause and effect (those "external purposes" that "trigger" action). Balázs's conception of "pointing inwards" (or inner "reasons") allowed by the camera's close-up presentation of the human face involves a complex, intricate meshing of temporal and spatial properties peculiar to cinema. For the moment, let us concentrate on the relation between *drama* and *gesture* that Balázs posited—a central pylon of *Visible Man*'s argument.

Balázs's "secular mystery play" *Duke Bluebeard's Castle* (1912, written when the author was twenty-eight) was based on an 1899 text by the Belgian writer Maurice Maeterlinck (1862–1949). Erica Carter in her comprehensive and very useful introduction to the English translations of Balázs's early film theory notes in passing his debt to Maeterlinck as a central purveyor of "a mystical modernism rooted in Symbolism and the fin-de-siècle avant-garde," alongside poet Endre Ady and composer Claude Debussy.[49] I would add to this account by stressing the importance of Maeterlinck's own theoretical writing about drama, which has recently formed a central reference point in Jacques Rancière's historical account of the "aesthetic regime" of early twentieth-century culture—especially in relation to the crossover between a particular type of determinedly unclassical theater in that period and the "new art" of cinema.[50]

Maeterlinck's 1904 text "The Modern Drama" (published in his long-out-of-print 1920 collection *The Double Garden*) is a remarkable speculation on the dedramatized form of theater he saw as emerging as a positive force at the dawn of the twentieth century:

> The first thing that strikes us in the drama of the day is the decay, one might almost say the creeping paralysis, of external action. Next we note a very pronounced desire to penetrate deeper and deeper into human consciousness, and place moral problems upon a high pedestal; and finally the search, still very timid and halting, for a kind of new beauty, that shall be less abstract than was the old.[51]

There is both concordance and divergence between Maeterlinck's theater theory and Balázs's film theory. Because Maeterlinck's polemic was against external action—especially of the busy, melodramatic, adventure-filled type—he also necessarily railed against the purely "visible" element of dramatic presentation on the stage. Clichéd, purely externalized action was for him the most sclerotic aspect of the old theater. Action in a broader Zeitgeist-related sense was also what defined an entire old, lost world for Maeterlinck, a world that could no longer be depicted, dramatized, or narrated in the same way—an old world in which the "being and objects" arranged around an emotional event, the "environment" or "the circumstances, hour and place wherein it was given" constituted "every image that has helped it to visible form," for instance in the work of Shakespeare.[52]

For Maeterlinck, quite simply and definitively, the world that was both conjured and reflected by this classical form of drama had changed: "These conditions no longer exist,"[53] and "these adventures no longer correspond with a living and actual reality."[54] Maeterlinck abhorred—as Balázs in his way also did when he decried "theater on film" productions—compromised artistic formations or solutions, "the necessarily artificial poems that arise from the impossible marriage of past and present."[55] These compromise formations were inauthentic works that had "lost their faith" in the spirit of the contemporary world and the hope of capturing and embodying it in artistic form. One can hear echoes of Maeterlinck's sentiment eight decades later when the filmmaker Olivier Assayas constantly exhorted his colleagues to "film the present" in all its complexity or when Deleuze in *Cinema 2* asserted (in relation to films from Rossellini to Garrel) that "the point is to discover and restore belief in the world, before or beyond words"—another very Balázsian formulation.[56]

In Maeterlinck's vision it was the rendering of interior psychology, what he called the "invisible protagonists—the passions and ideas"— something of which in 1904 he could still find only glimmers in the work of Ibsen and a few others, that mattered most.[57]

> Let us consider what happens in Ibsen's plays. He often leads us far down into human consciousness, but the drama remains possible only because there goes with us a singular flame, a sort of red light, which somber, capricious—unhallowed, one almost might say—falls only on singular phantoms.[58]

Balázs, in short, produced an ingenious rearrangement of these ideas for the medium of cinema. Although he placed a high value on what he, too, called the "inner reasons" and the experience of passions in the new medium of film, he also rescued and redefined *action* as *gesture*—thus rehabilitating the regime of the visible (including visible *movement*) and resisting the drift to minimalistic stasis that Maeterlinck favored in modern theater.

At the same time, the injunction against visible action in Maeterlinck goes hand in hand with a suspicion about the importance and power invested in words, and this finds a clear and pungent echo in Balázs's following statement:

> Where we are to look, then, for the grandeur and beauty that we find no longer in visible action, or in words, stripped as these are of their attraction and glamour? For words are only a kind of mirror which reflects the beauty of all that surrounds it; and the beauty of the new world wherein we live does not seem as yet able to project its rays on these somewhat reluctant mirrors.[59]

To Maeterlinck's question, "Where we are to look for the grandeur and beauty that we find no longer in visible action?" Béla Balázs would no doubt have answered, not on the stage but on the screen. There, we would encounter "a new beauty, that shall be less abstract than the old"—a beauty that necessarily calls for different, even wholly irrational arguments.[60]

NOTES

1. Roundtable, "On the Return to Classical Film Theory," 8.
2. Ibid., 8.
3. Balázs, *Béla Balázs,* 93.
4. Ibid., 93.
5. Balázs, "Radio Drama," 48.
6. Balázs, *Béla Balázs,* 93.
7. Ibid., 97.
8. Balázs, *Béla Balázs,* 6.
9. Ibid., 231.
10. Ibid., 232.
11. Roundtable, "On the Return to Classical Film Theory."
12. Ibid., 12.
13. Balázs, "On the Train at Night."
14. Balázs, "On the Train at Night," 57; Wollen, "Freud as Adventurer."
15. Balázs, "On the Train at Night," 57.
16. Ibid., 58.
17. Von Moltke, "Theory of the Novel"; Füzi, "The Face of the Landscape in Béla Balázs' Film Theory."
18. Balázs, "On the Train at Night," 57.
19. Ibid., 58.
20. Balázs, *Béla Balázs,* 223.
21. Ibid., 150.
22. Sontag, *Against Interpretation and Other Essays.*
23. Quoted in Legrand, *Cinémanie,* 76–77.
24. See Balázs, *Béla Balázs,* 20; Perkins, "Must We Say What They Mean?"
25. Carroll, "Béla Balázs."
26. Balázs, *Béla Balázs,* 223.
27. Ibid., 42.
28. Deleuze, *Cinema 1,* 87.
29. See Szaloky, "Close-Up."
30. Flusser, *The Shape of Things.*
31. Balázs, *Béla Balázs,* 9.
32. Ibid., 14.
33. Ibid., 51.
34. Ibid., 44.

35. Ibid., 62.
36. Carroll, "Béla Balázs," 56.
37. Balázs, *Béla Balázs*, xv–xvi.
38. Balázs, "Chaplin, or the American Simpleton," 53, 54.
39. Badiou, *(Notes on) Badiou on Badiou.*
40. Koch, "Béla Balázs"; Von Moltke, "Theory of the Novel"; Polónyi, "Béla Balázs and the Eye of the Microscope."
41. Vertov, *Kino-Eye.*
42. Balázs, "Radio Drama," 48.
43. Foucault, *Technologies of the Self*; Balázs, "Compulsive Cameramen," 51.
44. Balázs, "Compulsive Cameramen," 51.
45. Ibid., 52.
46. Bordwell, *Poetics of Cinema.*
47. Balázs, *Béla Balázs*, 40.
48. Ibid., 87.
49. Ibid., xviii–xix.
50. Rancière, *Aisthesis.*
51. Maeterlinck 1920, 93–94.
52. Ibid., 96.
53. Ibid., 97.
54. Ibid., 95.
55. Ibid., 98.
56. Deleuze, *Cinema 2*, 167.
57. Maeterlinck, *The Double Garden*, 99.
58. Ibid., 108.
59. Ibid., 101.
60. Ibid., 94.

BIBLIOGRAPHY

Badiou, Alain. *(Notes on) Badiou on Badiou.* July 19, 2014. http://badiouonbadiou.wordpress.com.

Balázs, Béla. *Béla Balázs: Early Film Theory.* Edited by Erica Carter. Translated by Rodney Livingstone. New York: Berghahn Books, 2010.

———. "Chaplin, or the American Simpleton." *October*, no. 115 (2006): 53–54.

———. "Compulsive Cameramen." *October*, no. 115 (2006): 51–52.

———. "On the Train at Night." *October*, no. 115 (2006): 57–58.

———. "Radio Drama." *October*, no. 115 (2006): 47–48.

Bordwell, David. *Poetics of Cinema.* New York: Routledge, 2010.

Carroll, Noël. "Béla Balázs: The Face of Cinema." *October*, no. 148 (2014): 53–62.

Davis, Therese. *The Face on the Screen: Death, Recognition, and Spectatorship.* Portland, Ore.: Intellect, 2004.

Deleuze, Gilles. *Cinema 1: The Movement-Image.* Minneapolis: University of Minnesota Press, 1986.

———. *Cinema 2: The Time-Image.* Minneapolis: University of Minnesota Press, 1989.

Flusser, Vilém. *The Shape of Things: A Philosophy of Design.* London: Reaktion Press, 1999.

Foucault, Michel. *Technologies of the Self: A Seminar with Michel Foucault.* Amherst: University of Massachusetts Press, 1988.

Füzi, Izabella. "The Face of the Landscape in Béla Balázs' Film Theory." *Acta Universitatis Sapientiae: Film and Media Studies* 5 (2012): 73–86.

Koch, Gertrud. "Béla Balázs: The Physiognomy of Things." *New German Critique* 40 (1987): 167–77.

Legrand, Gérard. *Cinémanie.* Paris: Stock, 1979.

Maeterlinck, Maurice. *The Double Garden.* New York: Dodd, Mead, 1920.

Perkins, V. F. "Must We Say What They Mean? Film Criticism and Interpretation." *Movie* 34/35 (1990): 1–6.

Polónyi, Eszter. "Béla Balázs and the Eye of the Microscope." *Apertúra* 8 (2012). http://uj.apertura.hu/2012/osz/polonyi-bela-balazs-and-the-eye-of-the -microscope.

Rancière, Jacques. *Aisthesis: Scenes from the Aesthetic Regime of Art.* London: Verso, 2013.

Roundtable. "On the Return to Classical Film Theory." *October,* no. 148 (2014): 5–26.

Sontag, Susan. *Against Interpretation and Other Essays.* New York: Farrar, Straus and Giroux, 1966.

Szaloky, Melinda. "Close-Up." In *The Routledge Encyclopaedia of Film Theory,* edited by Edward Branigan and Warren Buckland, 92–97. New York: Routledge, 2013.

Vertov, Dziga. *Kino-Eye: The Writings of Dziga Vertov.* Berkeley: University of California Press, 1984.

Von Moltke, Johannes. "Theory of the Novel: The Literary Imagination of Classical Film Theory." *October,* no. 144 (2013): 49–72.

Wollen, Peter. "Freud as Adventurer." In *Endless Night: Cinema and Psychoanalysis, Parallel Histories,* edited by Janet Bergstrom, 153–70. Berkeley: University of California Press, 1999.

This Is Your Brain on Cinema

ANTONIN ARTAUD

Gregory Flaxman

> We are not yet able to attend as well as we should to the destiny of
> Antonin Artaud. Neither what he was, nor what happened to him in
> the domains of writing, of thought, and of existence—none of this,
> even if we knew it better, could provide us with signs that would be
> sufficiently clear.
>
> Maurice Blanchot, "Cruel Poetic Reason (the rapacious need for flight)"[1]
>
> In the cinema we are all . . . [text missing]—and cruel.
>
> Antonin Artaud, "Reply to a Questionnaire"[2]

Poet and critic, sometimes surrealist and sublime schizophrenic, Antonin Artaud has been the subject of vastly greater posthumous interest than he ever enjoyed during his relatively short life. His fame derives primarily from his poetry, plays, letters, and essays—above all,
from the revolutionary Theater of Cruelty he developed "to restore a
passionate and convulsive conception of life" to the stage.[3] Still, his
writings acquired a significant readership only after he died, alone in
a psychiatric clinic, in 1948.[4] Thus, Artaud was as much discovered as
rediscovered in the subsequent decades, when the initial publication
of the *Oeuvres complètes* introduced his writing to a new generation.
His ferocious vitality naturally inspired enthusiastic readers from a
growing critical counterculture, and it should be hardly surprising
that among the notable French intellectuals who sought a way out
of the doctrines of psychoanalysis and structuralism, so many found

their way back to Artaud's *crie de coeur*.[5] Even today, when we no longer speak of "Saint Artaud," his writings have been canonized in the history of literary, critical, and performing arts.[6]

By contrast, Artaud's film criticism remains an idiosyncrasy— superficially acknowledged, selectively anthologized, but largely neglected. Most of us have encountered the criticism, if at all, in the pages of collected volumes; we can scarcely suspect the scope of Artaud's writings on cinema or their significance for a philosophy of film.[7] For this reason, virtually every essay on the subject is bound to begin, as I do here, by underscoring the extent to which Artaud was devoted to cinema. For the better part of a decade, he expressed un- abashed enthusiasm for the medium, going so far as to insist that "cinema involves a total reversal of values, a complete revolution in optics, perspective, and logic."[8] Like the Theater of Cruelty, the promise of the cinema lay in revealing "those darker, slow-motion encounters with all that is concealed beneath things, the images— crushed, trampled, slackened, or dense—of all that swarm in the lower depths of the mind."[9] More than once, Artaud predicts that the moving image will inevitably surpass the experiential possibilities of the stage. When filmmakers finally develop aesthetic means com- mensurate to the "psychic ingredient" of movement, he writes, the medium "will go far beyond theater, which we will then relegate to the attic with our souvenirs."[10] Next to the moving image, the theater is destined to become a "betrayal."[11]

For this reason, Artaud looked to the development of methods, techniques, narratives, and concepts equal to the unique resources of the cinema: without them the moving image was likely to be re- duced to the conceits of the plastic and dramatic arts, when those same conceits ought to be discarded in light of the cinematic image. In his most exuberant moments, Artaud regarded the medium as revolutionary, but its power remained an article of faith more than an established fact. In truth, Artaud seldom discusses specific films at any length, preferring instead to disclose his taste for American com- edy (Sennett, Chaplin, Keaton, and the Marx Brothers), his respect for German production (of the kind found "around Ufa"[12]), and his reverence for Carl Dreyer (especially *Joan of Arc*). Far and away his most recurrent reference is *The Seashell and the Clergyman* (1928), Germain Dulac's landmark of the avant-garde and the only film to have been based on one of Artaud's own *scenarii*. More than once, he reminds his audience that the film, preceding *Le chien Andalou* by a year, was the first work of surrealist cinema.

But even here the reference is more abstract than it might otherwise appear. Artaud entertained deeply mixed feelings about Dulac's film: though he praised it in print, he had been effectively banned from the set, and he seems to have harbored serious reservations about the production (Artaud may well have been among those who, violently reacting to the film, were thrown out of its premier). Thus, even when Artaud speaks about *The Seashell and the Clergyman,* he gestures beyond the film itself—not merely to his own scenario but to the virtual and (as yet) obscure potentialities of the medium. *The Seashell and the Clergyman* constitutes "an attempt or an idea" that not even the film itself was capable of cashing out.[13] "I like any kind of film," Artaud once told an interviewer, only to admit that "the kinds of films [I like] have yet to be created."[14] Given this state of affairs, the discussion to follow returns to Artaud's criticism in order to stage a kind of prolepsis. Believing in the possibility of film equal to "Film," Artaud envisions a cinema to come, composed of "purely visual situations whose drama would come from a shock designed for the eyes, a shock drawn, so to speak, from the very substance of our vision."[15]

The Cinematic Automaton

Given Artaud's predilections, we're naturally inclined to regard his idea of cinema as a kind of idealization, if not idealism—but this conclusion misses the point. For Artaud the essence of cinema consists in a kind of movement that does not merely belong to what we see. "In cinema," he confesses, "I've always been aware of a virtue proper to the secret movement of images."[16] What is this secret? Artaud's theory of cinema, such as it is, begins by insisting on the *affective reality* of the moving image; the cinema unleashes vibrations, shocks, and even a kind of violence upon its viewers. *The moving image moves thought,* and it is on this basis that, I'll argue, Artaud suggests a new way forward for film and philosophy.

More to the point, the idea of cinema ventured by Artaud in the late 1920s and early 1930s unwittingly resumes a problem endemic to seventeenth-century philosophers. In the aftermath of Descartes, such classical philosophy was decidedly devoted to the (now familiar) dualism of mind and body, *res cogitans* and *res extensiva*. With the appearance of Spinoza and then Leibniz, however, the conditions and consequences of this dualism were extended to a kind of delirium that, I think, we rediscover in Artaud's film criticism. For the present, then, let us outline the philosophical context without which this claim would make little sense. For Spinoza and Leibniz, the distinction between material bodies and immaterial ideas is fundamentally irreducible, but while this contention defines the domains of dualism, broadly construed, both philosophers insist these discrete domains are necessarily—and, one could say, miraculously—*correlated*. The respective autonomy of mind and body does not prevent but rather *permits* the correspondence of mind and matter, thoughts and things. Thus, in the context of considering Spinoza's philosophy, Leibniz coined the term "parallelism" to designate the invisible alignment of domains that are undeniably separate and absolutely inseparable.[17] This brief summary may seem to carry us far afield from the cinema, but parallelism produces the remarkable eventuality whereby classical philosophy and film criticism improbably converge. How does this happen?

For Spinoza and Leibniz, the series of material bodies in space derives from and can be deduced back to the operation of divine mechanism (God, the prime mover, etc.), but inasmuch as this is the case, both philosophers suggest that the series of immaterial ideas entails a corresponding logic. In other words, the mechanism of bodies demands an automatism of thought qua soul (*spiritus*). Thus, in an early (and unfinished) essay, Spinoza introduces the concept of a "spiritual automaton" to describe the procedure whereby the mind unspools a sequence of ideas that, while autonomous, seems to have been "parallel processed" with materiality. In borrowing the concept, Leibniz explains that the spiritual automaton consists in a kind of "law of program" implanted so deeply inside the soul as to be virtually indiscernible and all but unconscious.[18] Hence, the spiritual automaton precipitates a problem familiar to baroque philosophy: If it is in fact subject to automatism, does the soul enjoy or express any measure of freedom? Does it qualify itself apart from nature? Does it even deserve to be called a soul? My point here is not to resolve the problems unleashed by baroque philosophy but to argue that they presage the problems one finds in Artaud—or, inversely, that Artaud unwittingly resumes the spiritual automaton in his film criticism. Having said this, we're obligated to approach this thesis with all due circumspection, lest we reduce the relationship between film and philosophy to mere analogy. So let me be clear: moving images do not unfold an order of ideas (pace Spinoza) that can be logically deduced all the way to God, nor do they unfold the successive modifications of the soul (pace Leibniz) that can be rationally ascribed to a preestablished harmony. Rather, the *déroulement* of moving images introduces an automatism that displaces the spectator's natural perception with a machinic perception.

This argument inevitably recalls Gilles Deleuze's philosophy of film ("the brain is the screen"), and in *Cinema 2* he goes so far as to render the spiritual automaton a definitive achievement of "modern" cinema, the emanation of a thinking image. For Deleuze the spiritual automaton interrupts the sensory-motor logic that stereotypically defines perception and action with its own affective logic of *inaction*. Notwithstanding the significance of this argument, it's no coincidence that at the point of reckoning with this *impuissance*, Deleuze recourses to Artaud's film criticism to grasp the automatism of images that takes hold of the brain. Indeed, Artaud likens the cinema to possession, delusion, vision, hypnotism, trance, hallucination, and narcosis because, in all of these experiences, we are inhabited by an "other" logic, our brains and bodies given over to a force that lies outside of us. With respect to the moving image, Artaud's question is not, What is the nature of thinking? but, What is this thing that thinks inside me?[19]

The *Pharmakino*

Despite its incredible vitality and originality, Artaud's writings on film have inspired surprisingly modest interest among scholars.[20] Especially today, when classical film theory has become the object of thoroughgoing critical recovery and revaluation, the comparative quietude surrounding Artaud's film criticism is noteworthy. No doubt, many reasons could help to explain this underwhelming reception history. Compared with his far more extensive writings on theater, Artaud's film criticism is bound to seem slender, marginal, even aberrant—and this impression isn't entirely inaccurate. Most of what he wrote about the cinema was "occasional," scattered among circumstances and genres, dispersed amid publications (until the record was compiled in Artaud's *Oeuvres complètes,* several pieces remained unpublished, having been tucked away in personal libraries and private correspondences).

First issued in 1961 (Gallimard subsequently published an expanded version), the third volume of the *Oeuvres complètes* brings together Artaud's numerous film treatments (*scenarii*), a trove of letters, two film-related interviews, several pieces related to his scenario for *The Seashell and the Clergyman,* stray commentaries, a savage review, and the draft of a production proposal. While the book doesn't entirely dissolve the impression of fragmentation or enigma, Artaud's luminous film criticism ought to dispel any suggestion this theory was incidental or paratextual.[21] Indeed, the aggregation of these pieces extends his apparent idiosyncrasy into the iterations of a surprisingly sustained, if also variable, reckoning with the cinema. Why, then, haven't these writings provoked greater interest?

Beyond the reasons to which I've alluded, I suspect the greatest dilemma posed by Artaud's film criticism lies in his own repudiation of the medium. In "The Premature Old Age of the Cinema" (1933), Artaud not only renounces the industry and art of cinema but (in so many words) disavows his own prior criticism, suggesting it was written under the influence of "the dark and subtle enchantment which the cinema exerted."[22] As he explained thereafter, no doubt with his own history in mind, the movies "have maintained us for ten years in an ineffectual torpor, in which all of our faculties appear to be foundering."[23] As the decade wore on, Artaud conceived of cinema in ever more cynical terms. Far from realizing the promise of moving images, the "old age" of the cinema suggested its lapse into the very "economic, utilitarian and technological state" against which, in his younger days, Artaud had upheld the medium.[24] Eventually, Artaud turned away from the cinema, and as to the Theater of Cruelty, he left no doubt as to his radical shift: we can no longer be content "to leave the task of distributing the Myths of man and modern life entirely to the movies."[25]

The reversal is so stark we cannot ignore it.[26] How is it possible to affirm Artaud's film criticism, much less construe it as a matter of philosophy, when he seems to have disowned the medium? This ineluctable problem lies at the heart of Artaud's idea of cinema. What arouses his fear and dread in "The Premature Old Age of the Cinema" is no less what had once fired his hope and enthusiasm—namely, the power of the moving image to affect perception, to take hold of the sensory-nervous system, and ultimately (if temporarily) to introduce an automaton into thought itself. For Artaud, we might say, *this is your brain on cinema*. Readers will likely recognize the phrase, the title of my essay, as an allusion to a notorious advertising campaign in the decades-long war on drugs. Produced by the Partnership for a Drug-Free America and launched in the final years of the Reagan administration, the iconic ads follow a simple formula: we see an egg ("this is your brain," the narrator says) and then the egg cracked onto a hot skillet ("and this is your brain on drugs"). This slogan has long since become a cliché, but in light of Artaud's film writings, the reference could not be more apt. Of course, Artaud was a drug addict, but beyond simply suggesting that, in so many words, he knew of what he spoke, I want to ask, in all seriousness, what does it mean to say the cinema is a drug?

Insofar as the cinema makes images move, it communicates movements (as affects, vibrations) directly to the brain. Merely the "rotation of images" produces "physical intoxication."[27] For Artaud "the cinema is a remarkable stimulant" capable of inducing fantastic visions and hallucinations: "The cinema has the power of a poison that is harmless and direct, a subcutaneous injection of morphine."[28] This is not (or not only) a metaphor, and Artaud means for us to take the *pharmakon* quite literally. Before moving images, we are always under the influence. Cinema is a drug: *pharmakino*. Thus, Artaud may well strike us as the relic of a bygone era in film criticism, when a kind of romantic enthusiasm for the transportations of moving images was still possible—when critics could still get high, so to speak, on the cinema. Nevertheless, I'd argue his ruminations are not so remote from contemporary concerns; the questions he addresses confront us with new, if still unsuspected, urgency today. Artaud's reflections anticipate problems that already loom over cinema in the midst of an increasingly and irremediably digital world. If the digital revolution entails a fundamental challenge to the "idea of cinema," that challenge does not refer to the "ontology" of moving images, as we're often told, so much as it does to the psychomechanics of cinema. Beyond taking and reproducing images, newer media possess processors (computers) capable of feedback, and it's no secret the prospect of an "interactive" user is frequently used to cast aspersions on the "passive" spectator of cinema. The progress of optical media and information technology seem to have so surpassed the communicative means of the cinema, or assimilated those means to more sophisticated machines, as to make its spectator seem submissive, outdated, and even suspicious.[29]

Surely this is why, in recent years, scholars have sought to envision cinema as an interactive medium. Far from endorsing this view, Artaud would have found it a betrayal of the cinema's intrinsic power to formulate an automatism of moving images to which we submit. This, and nothing less, is what he gleans at the heart of the Seventh Art, for the *dispositif* of cinematic spectatorship consists in arresting the body and relinquishing perception. Whatever we hope to say about the work of the spectator, however we want to cast the active mind of the viewer, the cinema consists in the experience of movement (in the image, of the image, between images) in the absence of our motor movement. Of course, we can close our eyes, leave the theater, or turn the channel, but inasmuch as we watch, we surrender our movement and submit perception to the unraveling of images that are not our own. "The form of the film is final and without appeal," Artaud writes: "although it allows a sifting and a choice of images before it presents them, it forbids the action of those images to change or to transcend itself."[30]

"True Cinema"

Having come to Paris in 1920 as a budding playwright, Artaud first became acquainted with cinema as an actor, playing "small parts in various films"—most notably, Gance's *Napolean*, Dreyer's *Joan of Arc*, Poirier's *Vedun*, and L'Herbier's *L'argent*.[31] At roughly the same time, he began to write for and, occasionally, about the cinema. His most conspicuous achievement was to have written *The Seashell and the Clergyman*, and whatever misgivings he harbored about the film, he fervently believed the scenario to be one of the few genuine attempts to realize "true cinema."[32] Artaud was well aware of the commercial obstacles that stood in the way of such truth—he witnessed the worst of it with the studio release of Dreyer's *Joan of Arc*—but he continued to believe in the cinema.[33] Buoyed by the appearance of *The Seashell and the Clergyman* and flush with enthusiasm for the seventh art, he proclaimed cinema was on the threshold of a "profound renewal of the plastic matter of images"; moreover, he sincerely believed he would play an integral part in this renewal.[34]

Nevertheless, Artaud's opportunities to act soon petered out, and his screenwriting career suffered an even worse fate: after *The Seashell and the Clergyman,* none of his subsequent *scenarii* were produced (he authored fifteen in total). To his profound disappointment, he was relegated to penning miscellaneous pieces about a medium for which he'd hoped to write, direct, and even produce. For this reason one can plot the course of Artaud's criticism according to his self-described "service record"[35] to the cinema: stoked by early success and then enduring on the basis of increasingly unrealistic plans, he eventually came to believe he had grossly overestimated the "truth" of the medium. Of the cinema, Artaud now wrote, "The idiot world of images trapped as if in birdlime in a myriad of retinas will never live up to the image that some persons have managed to form for it."[36] Surely, Artaud's circumstances, which began so hopefully and ended so inauspiciously, colored his critical reflections—but those reflections are too complex and nuanced to explain Artaud's change of heart, much less to dismiss it. In this spirit we might seek to grasp the power Artaud attributes to the moving image, for better or worse.

This power crystallizes when we consider the most conventional aspects of his film criticism. Almost all of Artaud's commentaries on cinema begin with the pretense of an alternative to which the medium seems consigned: abstraction/reality, purity/impurity, avant-garde/psychological, dramatic/documentary. "Two paths seem to be open to the cinema right now," he writes in "Cinema and Reality," and the same sentiment characterizes a number of his essays.[37] Rather than augur a dialectical resolution, Artaud's point is that the oppositions typically misconstrue the nature of cinema itself. Hence, when he evokes a pair of alternatives, he does so to expose what escapes the familiar terms within which we consider cinema. Take the opposition of pure (or abstract) and popular (or psychological) cinema with which several of his early pieces are ostensibly concerned. On the one hand, Artaud critiques the idea of "pure or absolute cinema,"[38] especially as a penchant of the avant-garde, because its pursuit dispenses with an "essential requirements of cinema"[39]—namely, "a peculiarly terrestrial principle that things can act on the mind only by way of a certain state of matter, a minimum of substantial forms."[40] The pursuit of abstraction, leading all the way to stark geometry, alienates the image from the material world when, for Artaud, the very fact of the moving image "exalts matter."[41] The cinema is literally mundane insofar as it consists in the materiality of the earth: "The foundation of cinematographic thought seems to be the *utilization of existing objects and forms*."[42] On the other hand, Artaud mercilessly critiques the dramatic predilections of popular cinema. Heavily plotted films represent a recrudescence of theatricality that, he says, misappropriates the cinema every bit as much as abstraction: "To use it [cinema] to tell stories, a superficial series of deeds, is to deprive it of the finest of its resources, to disavow its most profound purpose."[43] The poverty of the theatrical impulse lies in finding a visual "equivalent for written language" when, for Artaud, the cinema is gifted with the power to reveal the "essence of language," that to which language refers but which escapes language, the otherwise mute substance of the movement.[44] "One cannot go on indefinitely destroying its galvanizing power by the use of subjects that neutralize its effects, subjects that really belong to the theater."[45]

Thus, when Artaud says that "two paths seem to be open to the cinema right now," he is quick to add neither "is the right one."[46] Why, then, pose the alternatives? Rather than choosing one option, or reconciling both, Artaud stages the opposition in order to demonstrate the theoretical and practical miscarriage of the medium. In every case, the opposition derives from a crucial misunderstanding with respect to the intrinsic power of the medium—what the cinema can *do*.[47] Indeed, Artaud's critique of virtually every aesthetic category (abstraction, reality, purity, impurity, avant-garde, psychological, dramatic, documentary, etc.) is that it grafts the received wisdom of other arts and disciplines onto the cinematic image as opposed to beginning with the intrinsic power to make images move. Of course, thinking (about) movement is no easy task; the relationship between movement (not to mention time) and thought is notoriously fraught in the history of philosophy. But this is also the very reason why philosophy has so much to gain by looking to the cinema and why we have resolved to look to Artaud—not to find an analogue (or, worse still, an allegory) but to discover new problems, challenges, and opportunities with which to invigorate philosophy.

The Automation of the Image

What do we really mean by movement? Prior to the cinema, the plastic arts had been forced to abstract movement from immobile objects or to reconstitute movement on the part of a seeing subject. In other words, movement was largely restricted to representation—intimated, symbolized, extrapolated, but never given in itself. By contrast, a cinematic image is not an image of movement, nor the movement of so many discrete images; movement does not refer to particular objects, as if things moved against a stable background, or to successive instances, as if movement could be reduced to so many frames. Rather, movement is the modulation of the image in itself and in "all of its parts," and Artaud's contention is that the cinematic automaton communicates real movement directly into the brain. Once more, the moving image moves us.[48]

In this respect, we can define movement in the cinema as *automated, autonomous animation.* On the basis of a mechanism (automated), which is independent of my own perception (autonomous), a movement-image is projected into my perception (animation). No longer reduced to space qua extension, movement gives rise to a virtual or intensive dimension that pertains to the domain of thought. This is the very heart of Artaud's theory: the cinema is not a representational system but an expressive machine with the power to produce movement, to provoke affect, and even to make us think. Looking forward, he says cinema may one day be capable "of carrying the action onto a level where all translations would be unnecessary and *where action would operate almost intuitively on the brain.*"[49] Needless to say, Artaud was hardly the only early theorist to have ventured a psychomechanics of cinema. One finds variations on this theme in the effusions of early French critics who hailed the rush of cinematic affects (Jean Epstein, Elie Faure, various surrealists), in Soviet theorists of montage who dwelt on the physiology and psychology of cinematic stimuli (Dziga Vertov, Sergei Eisenstein), and in various other theorists who sought to describe the sensation of cinema (Ricciotto Canudo, Émile Vuillermoz, Jean Goudal, Walter Benjamin). Still, Artaud's modest collection of criticism remains unique, both then and now, in its ambition to affirm the potential of the moving image to move thought. By integrating art (*aesthesis*) and science (*technē*), cinema precipitates a kind of experience that is at once altogether novel, even futuristic, and strangely primitive: "The kind of virtual power images have goes rummaging in the depths of the mind for unused possibilities."[50]

The dark and occult arts of the cinema enjoy an expressive power that inherently outstrips the vulgar psychologism of the theater and, thereby, returns "original and profound barbarity" to motives.[51] Stripped of the need for traditional dramatic exposition or even symbolic enactment, the cinema potentially disperses motives into "pure visual situations" in which the drama derives from "a shock designed for the eyes, a shock drawn, so to speak, from the very substance of our vision and not from psychological circumlocution."[52] Though the cinema is a technical medium, Artaud suggests its "mystery" consists in having made possible unmediated, immediate, and immanent movement: "Nothing comes between the work [the film] and ourselves."[53] This is no doubt why he resists reducing images to representations, preferring to conceive of movement along the lines "neurophysiological vibrations" or "nerve-waves."[54] To watch a film is to surrender brain and body, to make ourselves the vehicles for moving images. As Deleuze declares, this passivity—this *impuissance*—is precisely "what Artaud makes into the dark glory and profundity of cinema."[55]

Gray Matters

Why then does cinema become the source of regret and renunciation? Having traced the arc of Artaud's criticism, we might recapitulate his film theory according to three "tenses" he brings to bear. Because he seldom refers to actual films, tense is a function of Artaud's idea (or ideal) of cinema, and over the course of his criticism, the conceptual tense devolves from the future to the present and, finally, to the *already* past.

In several of his early and most effusive essays, Artaud seems to presage "*a cinematographic quality which is yet to be found,*"[56] as if to suggest the medium is on the threshold of a "profound renewal of the plastic matter of images."[57] But while he looks to the future, Artaud increasingly formulates an indictment of the present. Hence, in his magnificent "Sorcery and the Cinema" (1927), Artaud confesses he does not understand the notion that "the cinema is in its infancy."[58] In fact, "cinema arrives at an already advanced stage of development,"[59] and though he expects technological and material advances, Artaud insists the medium already possesses everything necessary to produce a distinctly "*cinematographic quality.*" By the early 1930s, with growing misgivings, Artaud openly questioned the cinematic campaign in which he had served for the past decade. Despite his long-standing convictions, Artaud finally finds himself profoundly alienated from the enterprise of film and at odds with its apparent direction: the remarkable possibilities of cinema, which he understands as a matter of the brain itself, had lapsed into unremarkable and often idiotic representations. (The one film to which he devotes any real discussion, *The Polish Jew* [dir. Jean Kemm], Artaud calls a "masterpiece of imbecility" so profound as to offer proof of the "exhaustion of our epoch").[60] Beyond its promises (the future) and shortcomings (the present), then, he eventually consigns the cinema to history (the past).

Hence, in his aptly titled essay "The Premature Old Age of the Cinema," Artaud reflects on the medium as if its age were already over. Where the cinema once prophesized the future and prevailed upon the present, Artaud now relegates the cinema to the past tense: "The most striking virtues of the cinema *were* always, or almost always, the result of chance."[61] Thus, at the very point he would normally dispatch stereotypical oppositions in order to conceive of "cinema in itself,"[62] Artaud launches a blistering critique of the medium and aesthetics of film. Among other things, he argues that cinematic images are the substance of arbitrariness and contingency, that those images remain at the level of superficial "external habits of the memory and the mind," that the very world of cinema is "dead, illusory, and fragmented," that cinematic attempts to imbue images with poetry only demonstrate what eludes the screen, and finally, that all of this is only made worse by the introduction of the talkie.[63] As if to leave no doubt, he writes, "It is not to the cinema that we must look to restore the myths of man and of life today."[64]

As I've suggested, Artaud's critique is conditioned by a sense of disappointment, betrayal, and even complicity. In the bleakest of renderings, we could say Artaud aspired to reveal the esoterica of cinema only to discover, rather grimly, that what he'd taken to be an occult pursuit was a great deal more like having belonged to a cult. Ostensibly, this is what happens when one looks to the cinema "to restore the myths of man": one is entranced, hypnotized, brainwashed. While Artaud still leverages the lexicon of sorcery to characterize the moving image, his description now passes through cynicism rather than *cinéphilia*:

> To have one's nerves more or less pleasantly massaged by abrupt and unusual cavalcades of images whose sequence and whose mechanical appearance eluded the laws and even the structure of thought may have delighted a few aesthetes of the obscure and the unexpressed who were seeking out these sensations systematically but without ever being sure that they would appear.[65]

Naturally, the description recalls the practices and predilections of the surrealists, among whom Artaud was sometimes counted, but I suspect he is after something else in this passage—namely, what we have referred to as "the dark and subtle enchantment which the cinema exerted over certain minds."[66] The moving image casts a spell, and Artaud leaves no doubt that *he was among the spellbound*: "We all went" to the cinema, he writes, in search of a "mystery whose fatality we never managed to explain."[67] By all accounts, then, "The Premature Old Age of the Cinema" marks the end of Artaud's cinematic "enchantment"—as if he had suffered from a prolonged lapse of reason, a season of delusion, only to finally come to his senses.

I've already suggested this is the single-greatest problem with which Artaud's film criticism confronts us, since it seems not only to mark a profound change of heart but, in a sense, to imply a renunciation of his prior position. Should we discredit the previous essays and miscellany because they were written under its influence? How can we affirm Artaud's film criticism, much less its use for film philosophy, after this? Contrary to what one would expect, my answer is that we should understand "The Premature Old Age of the Cinema" as the perverse confirmation and consummation of those earlier essays. Beyond his litany of the cinema's shortcomings, Artaud finally rejects cinema for the very same reasons he once embraced the medium: it entrances, enthralls, and captivates thought itself. If anything, his bitter farewell to the cinema actually confirms the power of the moving image in terms of the powerlessness it imposes on the spectator. Any doubts one might have about the power of the moving image, any suggestion that cinematic affects are more rhetorical than real, are personally laid to rest in "The Premature Old Age of the Cinema." In truth, Artaud offers himself as an object lesson in cinematic experience: can anyone really doubt his was among the minds most affected by film?

Even in the midst of denigrating cinema, then, the brilliance of Artaud's criticism is to have disclosed the singularly passive and receptive experience of the moving image. Though he excoriates the limits and pretenses of the cinema, Artaud still bears witness to the psychomechanics unleashed by the moving image. The "dark enchantment" of the cinema means nothing less nor more than that film "acts directly on the gray matter of the brain."[68] Once again, I want to insist this is not a metaphor for Artaud, but perhaps we are now in a position to say what it is—namely, the presentiment of a cinema of cruelty ("films in which there is a pulverizing, a recombining of the things of the heart and the mind").[69] In Artaud's words, the "raw state" of cinema—*le cinéma brut*—"emits something of the atmosphere of trance conducive to certain revelations,"[70] and with this insight, I think we can grasp how his film theory revives and recasts the spiritual automaton of baroque philosophy.

The Prosthetic Brain

The spiritual automaton emerged in classical philosophy, but its derivation is more complicated than one might imagine and its reach greater than one might expect. While Spinoza is often credited with the term, its invention can be traced back to Descartes, and its popularization, traced forward to Leibniz.[71] For his part Spinoza uses the phrase only once in his entire corpus of writings, in an early and unfinished essay, "Treatise on the Emendation of the Intellect."

More enigmatically still, he introduces the spiritual automaton in the course of venturing what would otherwise appear an unoriginal and axiomatically Aristotelian distribution. At first glance, Spinoza admits, his philosophical account may seem "identical with the saying of the ancients that true science proceeds from cause to effect."[72] And yet, he adds, the ancients *never conceived the soul, as we are here doing, as acting according to fixed laws, a sort of spiritual automaton.*[73] This stipulation marks the tremendous originality and creativity of Spinoza's philosophy. As I have said, per Spinoza, the laws that determine ideas are irreducible to the laws that determine bodies: whereas bodies are modes of extension in space, ideas are modes of intension in thought, and there is no causality between these two domains. Nevertheless, Spinoza writes, "The order of action and passions of our body is, by nature, at one with the order of actions and passions of the mind."[74] In other words, the orders are independent and irreducible, but also synchronized.

What makes this parallelism so difficult to conceive is precisely that it seems to correlate entirely different orders. After all, the arrangement and movement of bodies (Nature) refers to the mind of God, in whom thought is immanently material and materialized. Both Spinoza and, thereafter, Leibniz insist that there must exist an analogous power, belonging to the subject, that renders ideas in relation to bodies and thereby unfurls these parallel lines. In relation to the divine power to unfold material bodies, there must also be an "internal force" capable of unfolding a sequence of ideas.[75] For both philosophers this proposition verges on preposterous: how can we envision a subjective "force" commensurate to the world, to nature, and even to God? But if one accepts that mind and matter, thoughts and things, are in fact synchronized, then the question might just as well be, How could we experience bodies, if not nature itself, *without* a corresponding logic of the soul qua mind? What Spinoza ventures, what the ancients "never conceived," is that an automaton "equal to a combinatorial world" God unfolds could be given to thought, gifted to the soul.[76] "Bodies do not know what happens in the soul, and the soul makes no impression on the body," Leibniz writes, "but God makes up for this"[77] by inscribing a "law"[78] in us that makes us equal to the incredible variety of nature. The spiritual automaton "makes man commensurate with God, and puts him in possession of a new logic," but it does so by virtue of mechanisms that scarcely seem our right to claim.[79] The soul qua soul is endowed with a kind of power we do not possess so much as it possesses us. Of course, as a matter of philosophy, this power preexists the cinema by several centuries, but my contention is that Artaud's criticism represents a remarkable instance whereby that philosophical suggestion is unwittingly resumed, mutatis mutandis, as a matter of cinematic experience.

Indeed, the cinema claims a power to co-opt perception by dint of its own automatism of moving images. Long before Deleuze articulated this idea of cinema—"producing a shock to thought, communicating vibrations to the cortex, touching the nervous and cerebral system directly"—Artaud gave voice to this automatism.[80] Because moving images are capable of hijacking perception by folding spatio-temporal sequences into the brain, the cinematic automaton insinuates a corresponding series of ideas, a train of thought, whereby films think in and through us. As Artaud explains, film

> does not tell a story but develops a series of states of mind which are derived from one another, just as one thought is derived from another without this thought reproducing the reasonable sequence of events. From a collision of objects and gestures are derived real psychic situations among which the cornered mind seeks some subtle means of escape.[81]

In this passage, one of his most remarkable evocations of a cinema, Artaud expresses a thoroughly Spinozistic insight: the impassive logic of moving images ("a collision of object and gestures" concretized as a "sequence of events") and the passive logic of a corresponding series of ideas ("states of mind which are derived from one another"). When we watch a film, Artaud suggests, we cede our perception to an "other" perception, to a *déroulement* of moving images whose durations, rhythms, and sensations take hold of us.[82] Film vehicularizes its viewer.

However dimly, Artaud conjures an idea of cinema that could well help to set film philosophy on a different path than it has heretofore staked out. The automatism of the moving image, delivered directly to perception, actually constitutes a kind of foreign brain, a technoaesthetic brain injected into the organic brain.[83] Surely, this is why cinema could become, for Artaud, the source of vastly disparate responses—of ecstatic optimism, awaiting liberation, and of profound antagonism, fearing despotism. In fact, the promise and danger of the cinema refer to the same ineluctable reality: the moving image affects our sensory perception, inhabits our brains, and even automatizes our thoughts. Why else would Artaud invoke so many altered states—narcosis and hallucination, hypnosis and possession, vision and revelation, dreaming and delusion—to describe cinematic experience? To varying degrees, all of these states entail a loss of control and a displacement of consciousness, and we need only refer to Georges Duhamel's famous (and nearly contemporaneous) complaint to express the possibilities and problems posed by cinema: "I can no longer think what I want, the moving images are substituted for my own thought."[84] Perhaps now we're in a position to see that, beyond all the alternatives he dismantles, Artaud leaves us facing the only one that could have mattered to him in the end. If we follow the cinematic automaton to its limits, we are left with the extremes that characterize his criticism, the promise and the danger—metempsychosis and psychosis.

For the Orphics metempsychosis described the transmigration of the immortal soul from one mortal body to another, one lifetime to the next, and in a sense Artaud regards the cinema as the modern (and technical) means to renew this mystical experience. Rather than incarnate the soul in a sequence of mortal bodies, the cinema projects sequences of moving image into the brain, a series of mobile perspectives we see and feel precisely because we are passive and immobile. Before a film, as far as Artaud describes it, we exist in a kind of suspended animation: the body is inert, and the brain is receptive. Relatively speaking, then, the moving images we experience are closed off to our own motor movement: our perceptions cannot extend into action, but for this reason they are prolonged and intensified as affection. In other words, moving images migrate through the nervous system, consolidating an automaton that though not our own displaces natural perception with its own approximation. In Artaud's earlier writings, as we know, the flights opened up by the cinema are the subject of uninhibited exuberance, but the prospect of this automaton also introduces the colonizing force of images into the brain, the delusory experience of visions and auditions. The lamentations of psychotics and schizophrenics ("there's a transmitter in my skull," "there's a computer chip in my brain," "there's an influencing machine inside my head") give voice to the very truth that Artaud discovers at the heart of cinema: there's a cinema inside my head, a cinematic automaton in my brain!

Still, it would be a mistake to reduce cinema to these alternate fates, metempsychosis or psychosis, when both express the very same invention—the same prosthetic brain.

NOTES

1. Blanchot, *The Infinite Conversation*, 293.
2. Artaud, *Antonin Artaud*, 181. While the third volume of Artaud's *Oeuvres complètes* brings together all of his film-related writings in French and English, the text is not widely available, and the translations are not entirely satisfying. Whenever possible, I refer to Sontag's anthology, which contains five major pieces devoted to film. References to Artaud's "Sorcery and Cinema" are taken from another widely available collection, *The Shadow and Its Shadow*, edited by Paul Hammond. These essays, a few other more obscure ones, Artaud's film *scenarii,* and related letters can be found in Artaud, *French Surrealism.*
3. Artaud, *The Theater and Its Double.*
4. Artaud was able to mount one of his plays, an adaptation of Shelley's *The Cenci,* in 1935, but it was a commercial failure and soon closed.
5. In France this radical change of fortune can be traced back, through the philosophers I've mentioned, to Maurice Blanchot. Indeed, the importance of Blanchot in the rediscovery and revaluation of Artaud cannot be underestimated. See Blanchot, *The Book to Come*, esp. ch. 4.
6. See Sollers, "Saint Artaud."
7. A great deal of the scholarship written about Artaud's film work revolves around his relationship to surrealism. For instance, see Williams, *Figures of Desire*; and Kuenzli, *Dada and Surrealist Film,* which contains Sandy Flitterman-Lewis's important essay "The Image and the Spark: Dulac and Artaud Reviewed."
8. Artaud, *Antonin Artaud*, 181.
9. Artaud, *Antonin Artaud*, 312. The phrase "cinema of cruelty" is the familiar title of André Bazin's book; in relation to Artaud's Theater of Cruelty, see Stoller, "Artaud, Rouch, and the Cinema of Cruelty."
10. Artaud, *Antonin Artaud*, 181–82.
11. Ibid., 182.
12. Artaud, *French Surrealism*, 88.
13. Ibid., 63.

14. Artaud, *Antonin Artaud*, 181.

15. Ibid., 151.

16. Artaud, "Sorcery and Cinema," 103.

17. Deleuze makes this point in *Spinoza*, 81–83. See also Leibniz, "Reflections on the Doctrine of a Universal Spirit," in *Philosophical Papers and Letters*, 554–60.

18. Artaud, "Sorcery and Cinema," 104.

19. See Deleuze, *Cinema 2*, ch. 7. In this context Heidegger plays a fleeting but important part; here and elsewhere, Deleuze refers primarily to Heidegger's *What Is Called Thinking?*

20. More recent work on Artaud's film theory include Barber, *Artaud*; and Jamieson, "The Lost Prophet of Cinema." The importance of Artaud's relationship to surrealism notwithstanding, he has not inspired a great deal of interest among film philosophers (apart from Deleuze).

21. Artaud refers to *The Seashell and the Clergymen* frequently, but I want to avoid the long-standing inclination to read his criticism on the basis of this scenario or any other. As Barber argues, Artaud's creative work, which panders to popular taste in some cases, is not so easily synthesized with his criticism, nor need it be. See the first section of Barber, *Artaud*.

22. Artaud, *Antonin Artaud*, 313.

23. Artaud, *The Theater and Its Double*, 84.

24. Ibid., 88.

25. Ibid., 122.

26. Artaud eventually turned against the cinema: "Movies in their turn, murdering us with second-hand reproductions which, filtered through machines, cannot unite with our sensibility." See Artaud, *The Theater and Its Double*, 84.

27. Artaud, "Sorcery and Cinema," 103.

28. Artaud, *Antonin Artaud*, 182.

29. In his lectures devoted to optical media, Kittler avers that the "endpoint" of his history consists in "the integration of optical media and the universal discrete machine known as the computer." See *Optical Media*, 26.

30. Artaud, *Antonin Artaud*, 312.

31. Ibid., 183.

32. Ibid., 151.

33. In an interview Artaud says, "The cinema is a terrible profession. Too many obstacles prevent one's expressing oneself or carrying out an idea. Too many commercial or financial contingencies hamper the directors I know. One defends too many people, too many things, too many blind necessities." Artaud, *Antonin Artaud*, 184.

34. Artaud, *French Surrealism*, 68.

35. Artaud, *Antonin Artaud*, 182.

36. Ibid., 314.

37. Artaud, *Antonin Artaud*, 150.
38. Ibid., 150.
39. Ibid., 150.
40. Ibid., 149.
41. Ibid., 151.
42. Ibid., 149 (italics mine).
43. Artaud, "Sorcery and Cinema," 104.
44. Artaud, *Antonin Artaud*, 151. This is the basis for a great deal of what Deleuze has to say about cinema in *Cinema 2*, esp. ch. 2, where he considers the relations between language qua semiotics and the "a-signifying and a-syntaxic material" of the image (29).
45. Artaud, *Antonin Artaud*, 181.
46. Ibid., 150.
47. "What is certain is that most forms of representation have had their day," Artaud writes, but insofar as "we begin to perceive that this over-familiar life, which has forgone all its symbols, is not life in its entirety," it is "the cinema [that] brings us closer to that substance." Precisely because ours is a "world exhausted to the point of collapse," the cinematic capacity to make movement suggests a kind of vitalism at Artaud. "Sorcery and Cinema," 104.
48. Deleuze, *Cinema 1*, 12–24.
49. Artaud, *Antonin Artaud*, 151 (italics mine).
50. Artaud, "Sorcery and Cinema," 103.
51. Artaud, *Antonin Artaud*, 150.
52. Ibid.
53. Ibid., 182.
54. Ibid., 165.
55. Ibid., 166.
56. Ibid., 181.
57. Artaud, *French Surrealism*, 68.
58. Artaud, "Sorcery and Cinema," 103.
59. Ibid.
60. Artaud, *French Surrealism*, 74.
61. Artaud, *Antonin Artaud*, 313 (italics mine).
62. Ibid., 311.
63. Ibid., 312.
64. Ibid., 314.
65. Ibid., 313.
66. Ibid.
67. Ibid.
68. Ibid., 182.
69. Ibid., 181.
70. Artaud, "Sorcery and Cinema," 104.
71. Spinoza seems to have lifted the spiritual automaton from Descartes.

See Descartes, *The Passions of the Soul,* part 1. Still, whereas Descartes maintains "ideal or occasional" causality between these series, Spinoza insists they are absolutely discrete and mutually autonomous, though also perfectly synchronous.

72. Spinoza, *The Complete Works,* 24.
73. Ibid. (italics mine).
74. Spinoza, *A Spinoza Reader,* 155.
75. Leibniz, *Leibniz's "New System,"* 18.
76. Deleuze, *Expressionism in Philosophy,* 322.
77. Leibniz, *Leibniz's "New System,"* 97.
78. Ibid., 104.
79. Deleuze, *Expressionism in Philosophy,* 322.
80. Deleuze, *Cinema 2,* 156.
81. Artaud, *Antonin Artaud,* 149.
82. The cinema is able to tap into the recesses of the brain, but it is no less capable of nurturing a sadomasochistic brain routed through the circuits of dark fantasies. We need only recall the brainwashing machine of *A Clockwork Orange* or the influencing machine of *The Parallax View* to envision the worst eventualities of the cinema or, at the very least, to understand the title of this essay cannot be merely ironic.
83. In addition to synchronizing the spectator to what happens on screen, the traditional theatrical showing synchronizes the individual brains of its spectators; a crowded theater is a cerebral network, the "parallel processing" of so many sensory-motor systems. The sequence of moving images constitutes a virtual system unfolding in each spectator's brain simultaneously as well as in all of them collectively.
84. Duhamel, *Scènes de la vie future,* 52. Among others, Walter Benjamin and Gilles Deleuze have dwelt on this line.

BIBLIOGRAPHY

Artaud, Antonin. *Antonin Artaud: Selected Writings.* Edited by Susan Sontag. Berkeley: University of California Press, 1988.
———. *French Surrealism: Collected Works.* Vol. 3, *Cinema.* Translated by Alastair Hamilton. London: Calder and Boyars, 1972.
———. *Oeuvres complètes.* Vol. 3. Paris: Gallimard, 1978.
———. "Sorcery and Cinema." In *The Shadow and its Shadow,* edited by Paul Hammond, 103–5. San Francisco: City Lights, 2001.
———. *The Theater and Its Double.* Translated by Mary Caroline Richards. New York: Grove Press, 1994.
Barber, Stephen. *Artaud: The Screaming Body.* London: Creation, 2004.
Bazin, André. *The Cinema of Cruelty: From Buñuel to Hitchcock.* New York: Arcade Publishing, 2013.

Benjamin, Walter. *Walter Benjamin: Selected Writings*. Vol. 3, *1935–1938*. Edited by Howard Eiland and Michael W. Jennings. Cambridge, Mass.: Belknap Press, 2006.

Blanchot, Maurice. *The Book to Come*. Translated by Charlotte Mandell. Stanford, Calif.: Stanford University Press, 2002.

———. *Infinite Conversation*. Translated by Susan Hanson. Minneapolis: University of Minnesota Press, 1992.

Bordwell, David. *On the History of Film Style*. Cambridge, Mass: Harvard University Press, 1998.

Deleuze, Gilles. *Cinema 1: The Movement-Image*. Translated by Hugh Tomlinson and Barbara Habberjam. Minneapolis: University of Minnesota Press, 1986.

———. *Cinema 2: The Time-Image*. Translated by Hugh Tomlinson and Robert Galeta. Minneapolis: University of Minnesota Press, 1989.

———. *Expressionism in Philosophy: Spinoza*. Translated by Martin Joughin. New York: Zone Books, 1992.

———. *Spinoza: Practical Philosophy*. Translated by Robert Hurley. San Francisco: City Lights, 2001.

Descartes, Rene. *The Passions of the Soul*. Translated by Stephen Voss. Indianapolis, Ind.: Hackett, 1989.

Duhamel, Georges. *Scenes de la vie future: Quatre-vingt-unieme edition*. Paris: Mercure de France.

Heidegger, Martin, and J. Glenn Gray. *What Is Called Thinking?* New York: Harper Perennial, 1976.

Jamieson, Lee. "The Lost Prophet of Cinema: The Film Theory of Antonin Artaud." *Senses of Cinema*, no. 44 (2007). http://sensesofcinema.com/2007/feature-articles/film-theory-antonin-artaud.

Kittler, Friedrich. *Optical Media*. Translated by Anthony Enns. Malden, Mass.: Polity, 2009.

Kovács, Steven. *From Enchantment to Rage: The Story of Surrealist Cinema*. Cranbury, N.J.: Associated University Presses, 1980.

Kuenzli, Rudolf E., ed. "The Image and the Spark: Dulac and Artaud Reviewed." In *Dada and Surrealist Film*, 110–27. Cambridge, Mass.: MIT Press, 1996.

Leibniz, Gottfried Wilhelm. *Discourse on Metaphysics and Other Writings*. Peterborough, Ontario: Broadview Press, 2012.

Leibniz, Gottfried Wilhelm, R. S. Woolhouse, and Richard Francks, eds. *Leibniz's "New System" and Associated Contemporary Texts*. Oxford: Oxford University Press, 2006.

Leibniz, Gottfried Wilhelm. *Philosophical Papers and Letters*. 2nd ed. Edited by Leroy E. Loemker. Dordrecht, Netherlands: D. Reidel Publishing, 1969.

Sollers, Phillippe. "'Saint Artaud.'" *Le nouvel observateur*, September 16–22, 2004, 57–58.

Spinoza, Baruch. *The Complete Works*. Edited by Michael L. Morgan. Translated by Samuel Shirley. London: Hackett Publishing, 2002.

———. *A Spinoza Reader: The Ethics and Other Works*. Edited by E. M. Curley. Princeton, N.J.: Princeton University Press, 1994.

Stoller, Paul. "Artaud, Rouch, and the Cinema of Cruelty." *Visual Anthropology Review* 8, no. 2 (1992): 50–57. doi: 10.1525/var.1992.8.2.50.

Williams, Linda. *Figures of Desire: A Theory and Analysis of Surrealist Film*. Berkeley: University of California Press, 1981.

From Lyrosophy to Antiphilosophy

THE THOUGHT OF CINEMA IN JEAN EPSTEIN

Christophe Wall-Romana

> The philosophy of cinema is yet to be made.
>
> Jean Epstein, *Bonjour cinéma*

Jean Epstein (Warsaw 1897 to Paris 1953) was a cinephile, poet, writer, filmmaker, and philosopher of the cinema. Not only was he among the few in the silent era to consider cinema as an object for thought—a daring position in those days—but he espoused the more radical view that it altered experience, thinking and philosophy, generating an original, nonhuman mode of thinking about the universe: an antiphilosophy. It is fair to say the questions of whether and how radically cinema might change our thought were first posed in earnest and depth by Epstein.

Arguably the most innovative director and theoretician of the first French film avant-garde in the 1920s, Epstein found few backers from the 1930s onward and increasingly turned his energies toward documentaries (during the Front populaire) and toward writing. He died in semiobscurity in 1953.[1] His work did not resonate with the concerns of the New Wave nor, in the 1970s, with the critical suspicions film studies began entertaining toward the cinema apparatus as a tool of doxa, illusion, and control. Still, in spite of the marginalization of his theoretical and filmic oeuvre, his thought has been consistently invoked by incisive thinkers of the cinema such as Siegfried Kracauer, Edgar Morin, Gilles Deleuze, and Jacques Rancière. There are good reasons to believe that this bipolar reception is now changing to a more sus-

tained appreciation. Our present media moment, where digital inter-
faces percolate through and alter every relation between humans and
the world, renders Epstein's prescient thought at last relevant for and
as media philosophy. Indeed, the enthusiasm of new critical studies
on him, together with the republications of his collected writings and
eighteen of his films, suggests Epstein is the phoenix of film philosophy.[2] Reborn from the ashes of celluloid after the purported death of
cinema, his work invites us to rethink moving images not as cultural
or mechanical epiphenomena but as a foundational first philosophy
for modernity. The thought *of* cinema ultimately reverses, as we shall
see, from our thinking it to it thinking beyond us.

The Core of Epstein's Thought

Born in Warsaw from a Jewish Polish father and a gentile French
mother, Jean and his sister, Marie—a brilliant director of her own
and a lifelong filmmaking and living partner—were schooled in Swit-
zerland and France. Epstein studied medicine in Lyon during World
War I (he was briefly the secretary of Auguste Lumière) until his passion for writing and cinema took over after the war, at the same time
he came out as gay. Before shooting his first film, the docudrama *Pasteur* (1923), he quickly published three books: *La poésie d'aujourd'hui:
Un nouvel état d'intelligence* (Today's poetry: A new state of mind)
(1921), *Bonjour cinéma* (1921), and *La lyrosophie* (1922).[3] These titles
evidence his threefold concern for poetry, cinema, and philosophy
and, more important, for their interrelation within an intermedia
conceptual framework. In *La poésie d'aujourd'hui*, Epstein explains
the new French poetry of the likes of Blaise Cendrars, Guillaume
Apollinaire, Louis Aragon and Max Jacob through their need to find
aesthetic correlates to the somatic regimes of modernity, particularly
sensorial and emotional fatigue. Epstein asserts that for these poets
the remedy to fatigue as well as a key source of poetic inspiration was
the movies. In *Bonjour cinéma,* a mixed-media work with poems,
prose, photomontage, posters, and graphics, he provides an artful
account of his cinephilia. Partly lyrical and partly philosophical, his
investigation centers on the notion of *photogeny* and its reliance on
affect and the close-up. The third book theorizes the first two by
arguing that knowledge derived from individual affects and the body

(*lyro-*) and from logic and the mind (*-sophy*) should be regarded as complementary in a new holistic construct: lyrosophy. The first consequence of cinema for Epstein is, then, that it transforms poetry and philosophy into equally valid ways of investigating embodied subjectivity within modernity. This remarkable triptych makes of Epstein a poet-philosopher of his times who, like Nietzsche, theorizes his own somatic and intellectual impulses rather than engaging with conventional philosophical debates. Epstein's medical training included philosophical readings pertaining to life sciences (Claude Bernard, Louis Pasteur), psychophysiology (Hermann Ebbinghaus, Joseph Babinski), and psychology (Théodule-Armand Ribot, Henri Bergson). To this he added eclectic readings of antidualist philosophers like Nietzsche and Spinoza. His friend the filmmaker Abel Gance called him "a young Spinoza with a curious and solid vision."[4] Two currents of thought should be adduced to Epstein's philosophical makeup: first, the Kabbalah, whose equation between letters and the cosmos informed his view of cinema as itself a form of writing directly connected to the world and, second, Greek philosophy, whose entwinement with homosexuality provided Epstein a joint origin for sexual toleration and antidualist views of mind–body relations. While writing his triptych between 1919 and 1922, Epstein indeed published several short overtly homoerotic texts. At the conclusion of *La poésie d'aujourd'hui,* he states, "Health in the singular does not exist; there are plural healths, successive healths, fragments of illnesses at the border of pathology."[5] This repudiation of normative embodiment, that is, hygiene and heterosexuality, suggests that what attracted Epstein to the cinema apparatus was its capacity to alter and expand the human through its own mechanical and sensorial "intelligence," in a manner parallel to how homosexuality had expanded pre-Socratic philosophy. From the 1920s to the early 1950s, this prosthetic embodiment remained at the core of Epstein's thought. In what follows, we will unpack this multifaceted antiphilosophy, its ramifications and evolution, beginning with the key term *photogeny*.

Photogeny as the Affect of Cinema

Invented together with photography in the late 1830s, the term *photogeny* denoted an object or scene lending itself to be photographed. This is far from a casual notion: it points to a now inherent epistemic precedence of the photographic apparatus over nature. Epstein reprised this term by redefining cinema's photogeny as "any aspect of things, beings and souls that enhances its moral quality through cinematographic reproduction."[6] He adds, "Only mobile and personal aspects of things, beings and souls can be photogenic."[7] Superficial readings have construed photogeny as either naïve or animistic: Epstein either grants cinema the mistaken faculty of enhancing reality or embraces the belief that cinema bestows something human on the nonhuman.[8] As I explain elsewhere, Epstein's texts expound a much more complex idea.[9] At base, photogeny focuses on the fact that cinema, far from merely offering simulacra or copies of the world— "reproduction" as pejorative—generates instead a new type of *relation* between embodied thinking viewers and a film shot or sequence and, by extension, a machine. Through close-ups, slow motion, and montage, the screen reveals a new "moral" dimension and "personal" value in both the inert and the human because it phenomenologically suspends what we take life to be. Here, Epstein also theorizes our experience at the movies, where we are moved not only by thoughts and plots but by the curious intimacy and potentiality we discover in a telephone, a piece of sky, the back of a hand, or a sequence telescoping several shots. But by what exactly, then, and why are we so moved?

Epstein's answer points in two directions. On the one hand, photogeny, he writes, "is to be conjugated in the future and imperative."[10] Viewing a film affects us at a tangent from its plot, tugging imperatively at us, fascinating us with a kind of futurality or promise. This echoes the idea that only cinema can reveal to us something inherent in the world but beyond our rational apprehension. On the other hand, he encapsulates photogeny as "sensorial logarithms," a quick crystallization of multiple experiences.[11] Rather than actual and representational, photogeny is then virtual and suggestive: a realm of experiential potentialities shadowing the moving images we watch yet nonetheless real.

For Epstein cinema has equally to do with vision and with an inner sense few thinkers of cinema have noted before or since: coenaesthesis. Referred to today as *enteroception,* coenasthesis is the general sense we have of our bodily functions: pulse, digestion, muscles, nervousness, kinesthesis, sex, pain, etc. It "summarizes the sensory state of an individual at any given time. . . . [It is] the physiological face of the subconscious."[12] While Freud's unconscious comprises repressed *thoughts* linked to our psychosexual biography, emerging through dreams, symptoms, parapraxis, and analysis, Epstein's subconscious is made of *affects*—that is, indistinct feelings, bodily impressions, and the sensorial ideas and memories we retain of them. Rejecting Freud's unconscious as too narrative and forensic (and probably too heteronormative), Epstein defines individuals by the way their coenasthetic sensibility interacts with their intellectual development, this intermittency between the two being heightened by modernity.[13] Moments of photogeny arise from the director proposing to the subconscious affects of viewers a shot or sequence that resonates with his own coenasthesis, resulting from a mysterious affinity between the director's embodiment and the camera:

> My eye gives me the idea of a form; the film strip also contains the idea of a form—an idea inscribed outside of my consciousness, an idea without consciousness, a latent, secret idea, yet marvelous. . . . The Bell-Howell [camera] is a metal brain. . . . The Bell-Howell is an artist.[14]

For Epstein the ideal device disclosing photogeny is the close-up, "the soul of cinema" and "the keystone of cinema."[15] The close-up facilitates sensorial and emotional immersion in the moving image, heightening proximity and intensity to the point of altering perception. He writes, "In fact, cinema creates a specific single-sense regime of consciousness," powerful enough to cause a craving Epstein expressly compares to addiction, or "a hunger for hypnosis."[16] Thus, while the photogeny of the close-up seems hyperoptical, it always involves embodiment as a whole, again via coenasthesis. Photogeny, in sum, names all at once a new potential within moving images, a new mode of experiencing them, and a new epistemological promiscuity between cinema and embodiment.

If Epstein's philosophy of the cinema develops its own concepts—photogeny and coenaesthesis—it is not out of idealistic or intellectual premises but as corollaries to the material effects of the apparatus on humans. In this sense Epstein is a materialist, sensationalist, and functionalist thinker whose affinities lay with philosophies of empiricism and immanence from Spinoza to Whitehead and Deleuze. As for Bergson, the main French philosopher in the early twentieth century, Epstein rejected him because of his technophobic bias against cinema.

Cinema as Language

As a reader and poet and as a gay man and medical student, Epstein focused at first on the interactions between language and the body. In 1919 he wrote, for instance, that modernity helps "man to develop a greater surface of contact with the world; it multiplies the paths of absorption."[17] This metaphor invokes the skin as a membrane for chemical and erotic reactions that is historically mutable. It also reveals a new surface of inscription or projection, a tremulous page or screen. Accordingly, Epstein's thought on cinema is interspersed with a critical theory of language. He was among the first to assert the now well-worn cliché: "Yet, without anyone's notice, the universal language was born in the basement of a French café," a reference to the 1895 *cinématographe* shows of the Lumières.[18] His opposition to the talkies, which "brutally brought back the reign of literary and theatrical imitation," has to do with their repressing "this truly universal language, this direct language from the gaze to the heart."[19] Epstein's disparate statements about language and cinema amount to three distinct arguments. First, he asserts that cinema must be considered a novel form of language; second, that a film is thought out, shot, and edited according to a nonlinguistic signifying system; and third, that cinema and aspects of natural language, including experimental writing, are intimately linked. In practice these arguments are often closely interrelated. When he writes, "Cinematographic language is prodigiously concrete, direct, brutal and alive," the implicit contrast is with a traditional view (that Jacques Derrida later deconstructed) of language as abstract, indirect, communicative, and dead.[20] It is also a critique of narrative and prose as overprioritized categories in our thinking about language. Thus, although his best films—*Coeur fidèle* (1923), *The Fall of the House of Usher* (1928), *Finis terrae* (1928), and *Le tempestaire* (1947)—are narrative fictions, Epstein warns early on that "cinema is true; a story is a lie," adding famously: "There are no stories. There never were stories. There are only situations."[21] If the plot dominates a movie, photogeny cannot arise, and the potential language of its medium is smothered:

> Stripped of story, hygiene, pedagogy—o, marvelous cinema, tell us
> about man, crumb by crumb. Just that, and care not about the rest. Do

away with plot twists and fancy repartees, in favor of the pure pleasure
of watching the agility of life. Browse the human. This sailor whose
collar is so blue and tenderly gapes on his tan, leaps on the foothold of
a bureaucratic tramway. Four seconds of muscular poetry. The run-up.
The jump. A foot lands. The other foot adds an airy and curvy sign.
Instantly I summon the acrobatic ropes and meditative profile of a ship
of indeterminate sex. It hardly lasts, but that's what matters, and that's
enough.[22]

This passage interweaves perception—notably, homoerotic impressions of the sailor and his zoomorphic ship—with allusions to language, at first conventional and trite—"story," "plot twist," "repartee"—but switching to creative and embodied: "browse," "poetry," "airy and curvy sign." While this shift rehearses the opposition between fiction film and experimental cinema, the latter often compared to poetry, Epstein points to film's alternative signifying system: browsing and gestural signing. Because such actions are visual, quick, and paralogical, they speak to our bodily subconscious rather than our mind, and we are perfectly capable of deciphering them within this new language of affect of the screen.

This language nonetheless maintains a reciprocal relation with experimental writing, as Epstein makes clear by proposing that "in order to reinforce each other this new literature and the cinema must superimpose [*superposer*] their mutual esthetics."[23] He indicates specific ways through which cinema has transformed poetry, such as schematization, proximity, immediacy, rhythmic variation, and metaphoricty. In this intermedial framework, we shouldn't fail to notice that the operative term comes from a film editing technique the cinema avant-garde privileged: the superimposition of shots. The new material grammar of cinema therefore emerges as both a complement to and an expansion of natural language and experimental literature.

Yet as Epstein indicates, "Cinema's grammar is its own grammar,"[24] and as such it provides us with a metalinguistic purview:

Because it is so complex, this language [of cinema] is also incredibly subtle. All the details simultaneously pronounced outside of words trigger words at their very root and, prior to words themselves, the feelings that precede them.[25]

In Saussure's semiology all signs, including words, arbitrarily link a material signifier and an abstract signified. For Epstein cinema discloses nonarbitrary bonds between the *referents* of words and the affective motivation behind their use. "Through the wire of interlocution unexpected emotional parasites disrupt us," he writes, likely in an oblique reference to Saussure's oft-used telephonic model of interlocution.[26] In any case, Epstein has a sharp awareness of the difference between the arbitrary nature of linguistic signs and the "motivated" signifying system of cinema that fuses signifiers and signifieds: "The cinematographic image is essentially a calligram, that is to say, its meaning is indissolubly tied to its form."[27] In this, he proves a pioneer in interart and intermedia aesthetic thinking, which hinges in fundamental ways on the qualitative distinction between word and image or, in the terms of Jean-François Lyotard's book title, *Discourse, Figure*. It is striking to me that Epstein's sophisticated meditation on language and cinema was thoroughly ignored by film thinkers after the so-called linguistic turn in the 1970s. Christian Metz, for one, chose not to refer to Epstein while theorizing the cinema as a new signifying system, although there are clear convergences in their approaches. Ironically, Metz invokes linguist Roman Jakobson's views on cinema, especially on the close-up and superimpositions, and these were likely shaped by Epstein's own ideas.[28]

The "Unified Intellectual Plane"

As we have seen, Epstein has a theory of the body, a theory of cinema's resonance with the body's inner sense, and a broad theory of cinema as a language complementing natural language and literature. If Epstein can be said to be the first philosopher of the cinema, it is foremost because he considers that philosophy can no longer afford to discount the phenomenon of cinema. In other words, cinema is not for Epstein merely an apparatus or a medium, nor just an art form or a mass industry, it is a world-changing object and event, a new agent within our subjectivity, and a new material source of philosophy.

This conviction presents Epstein with a unique conceptual challenge. As is clear by now, Epstein's thought is profoundly holistic and antidualistic, rejecting even the way philosophy seeks to differentiate itself as a quasi science from more artistic or subjective discourses and modes of inquiry. But the question for Epstein is how to formalize his own holism, given it encompasses a machine. Spinoza's monism has to do with only two traditional substances—mind and body—ultimately derived from one entity, God or Nature, dictating an absolute determinism. Of what substance, then, is the machine of cinema made? How can it partake of the same substance as nature and the human? And according to what ultimate rationale?

Epstein's answer from 1921 is what he calls "le plan intellectuel," "le plan unique," and "le plan intellectuel unique," which I will translate as "the unified intellectual plane."[29] At the conclusion of *La poésie* he summarizes his argument as follows: "[In these works of the new poetry], all images are projected [*se projettent*] on the same intellectual plane."[30] That the plane is indeed the screen and not a metaphor is confirmed by a commentary on a poem by Louis Aragon:

> Thus it appears clearly that modern literature comprises a single intellectual plane. Everything—thought and action, idea and sensation, today, tomorrow and yesterday—is projected together, side by side, upon the same square of screen.[31]

This, I believe, is one of Epstein's richest philosophical statements. Cinema in the post–World War I era acquires the status of an operative principle regulating poetic composition, but also thinking as such. Now, we might ask the difficult question, If it is not metaphorical, then what and where is this plane/screen? A first answer is that it is simply the page as the material plane of intellectual activity, remediated by the cinema apparatus, with all the implications for and ramifications within subjectivity. The fact that the word *plan* in French means a film shot explains Epstein's choice of this otherwise curious term. Perceptions, ideas, and poetic images are as if projected on a huge virtual, collective, and multifaceted new page qua film shot.

Yet there is another explanation, which involves Descartes and Bergson. Descartes, as we know, formalized geometrical coordinates— the Cartesian *plane*—but he also spent a good deal of mathematical thought on the arcane problem of conical sections: how to derive geometrical figures from a plane slicing a cone. As I have shown elsewhere, the realization images on screen represent but a section in two dimensions of the 3-D film projection cone was very much on the mind of cinepoets contemporary to Epstein, such as Jean Cocteau in particular.[32] It is Bergson, however, in his 1896 *Matter and Memory*, who refashioned the Cartesian conical section into a qualitative model of time and memory, defining various planes where "images," as he calls perceptions and memories, are located along the cone of time, such as "the shifting plane of experience," "the plane of action," and "the plane of memory."[33] Bergson's decision to use the image as a central term/concept and a cone of projection as linchpin for the organization of time in human memory is undoubtedly influenced by cinema's apparatus of projection being developed at that time. Nonetheless, Bergson infamously discarded the latter as a quantitative misrepresentation of time in complete opposition to human duration, itself a qualitative and true apprehension of temporality. For Epstein such a view is at the least biased and shortsighted and at worse a philosophical blind spot due to technophobia. Epstein's invocation of the term *plan* aims therefore at recuperating the Cartesian–Bergsonian model of conical section by adding to it the denotation of film shot, thereby revaluing cinema's central role in historically reshaping our perceptions of time, subjectivity, and memory.

Epstein's cinematic revaluation of the Bergsonian conical section wasn't lost on Gilles Deleuze. Kindred spirits in their lyrosophical approach, they both placed Spinoza's antidualism at the core of their philosophies. It appears likely that Epstein's unified intellectual plane played a key role in reorienting the thought of Deleuze toward cinema, once he understood that Epstein's concept was broadly synonymous with the plane of immanence Deleuze had crafted in his book on Spinoza and through his collaboration with Guattari in *A Thousand Plateaus*. Epstein and Deleuze (in his *Cinema* diptych) see remarkably eye to eye when it comes to their respective planes, so much so that their definitions are virtually interchangeable. In the chapter directly following his theorization of the French school of photogeny—where he mentions Epstein by name, citing the title *Lyrosophy*[34]—Deleuze reframes the plane of immanence as cinema:

> The infinite set of images constitutes a kind of plane of immanence.
> The image exists in itself, on this plane. . . . The plane of immanence
> is the movement (the facet of movement) which is established between
> the parts of each system and between one system and another, which

crosses them all, stirs them all together and subjects them all to the condition which prevents them from being absolutely closed. It is therefore a section. . . . Here Bergson is startlingly ahead of his time: it is the universe as cinema in itself, a metacinema. This implies a view of the cinema itself that is totally different from that which Bergson proposed in his explicit critique.[35]

Epstein would agree with this view of the universe as metacinema, which he makes explicit in his final opus, *The Intelligence of a Machine* (1946). This is not to say their philosophies morph into each other. Deleuze steadfastly eliminates Epstein's emphasis on affection and coenaesthesis in *Cinema 1* in order to delineate a "new cinema of the brain" not beholden to the corporeal aesthetics of silent film. Yet while Deleuze seeks thereby to craft an epistemic break with the lyrosophical plane of Epstein as a culmination of the silent era, he ends up closely replicating the radical cineprosthetics Epstein propounds in *The Intelligence of a Machine.*[36]

The unified intellectual plane represents the first time in the history of film thought that cinema figures not as an exterior appendage or medium but as an internalized metacognitive and sensorial technics reaching all the way down into what historically constitutes the human. Before moving on to *The Intelligence of a Machine,* which focuses on this paradoxical internalism of cinema, we need to turn to an unpublished manuscript that makes more explicit Epstein's overall views on nature and history.

Nature against Nature: Homosexuality and Cinema

After an early period of being out, Epstein recloseted in the 1920s, publishing nothing more that might reveal he was gay, although some plot elements and themes in his films lend themselves easily to queer decipherment.[37] Sometime in the late 1930s, he nonetheless wrote "Ganymède: Essai sur l'éthique homosexuelle masculine" (Ganymede: An essay on male homosexual ethics), an essay that was only recently published.[38] On the basis of his other unpublished homoerotic pieces, we can surmise that in "Ganymede" Epstein was compensating for being forcibly recloseted by social stigma by both imagining a gay

Arcadia and retheorizing philosophy as born from Greek thinkers who saw homosexuality as an epochal cultural progress. In "Ganymede" Epstein argues against the instinct for preservation—fighting death and procreating—since it represents the ultimate enslavement of humans to nature, man's true state of nature. Human culture therefore does not devolve from fire, walking, language, death rituals, etc.—since all of them are at the service of preservation—but from four "inventions" that precisely go *against* *nature*: suicide, birth control, homosexuality, and writing. All four reject the slavish veneration for life preservation through a radical negation that is properly human. Although Epstein scarcely cites Hegel in his writings, this idea extends the power of the negative to an extreme antivitalism. Let's be clear: Epstein loved life and was a pacifist, so here he opposes only the centrality of vitalism as a philosophical premise and origin stories relying on murder (the Bible or Hegel's deadly dialectics of master and slave). Epstein adduces two important correlates to his argument. On the one hand, he considers writing as counternatural, what Bataille calls at about the same time a nonproductive expenditure from the purview of society, indicating that the *cinématographe* is just such a form of writing. On the other hand, he views nature as polymorphous and perverse, producing any and all possible forms of life just to give it a try (pace Darwin), and this includes homosexuality. Epstein, logically but against all orthodoxy, thus heralds homosexuality as perfectly *natural*. Homosexuality, he insists, is innate, just one of the combinatory makeups of the human.

Hence, for Epstein Greek philosophy is not perchance the oeuvre of homosexuals—it is radically and epochally homosexual. Homosexuality exemplifies a view of culture as naturally antinaturalist by fostering affective unions between individuals that require thought and care, thereby favoring ethics and aesthetics in constituting a new type of society (within society) and in which reproduction is no longer the driving cattle mentality that nature imposed upon humanoids. Epstein's edifice has both huge problems—such as a gynophobia that is glaring and oddly inconsistent for someone who collaborated with his sister all his life—and striking affinities with ethical approaches to homosexuality, such as Foucault's *History of Sexuality*. This is certainly a work, now that it is finally available, that will evince passionate commentaries. With regard to film and philosophy, two conclusions are clear. First, from the angle of the history of human culture, cinema no longer figures as a mere machine begat by the chance encounter of disparate techniques and bricoleurs, nor as a dumb prosthesis to our innate senses. To the contrary, it reflects the deepest layer of the queer invention of a natural antinaturalism coeval with a philosophically enlightened humanity. Second, our humanistic veneration for life or élan vital is shown to be a kind of bad faith, since we fail to think through the dangers of what he calls "the dictature of procreation" that propels heteronormative civilizations by dint of repressing Greek foundational homophilosophy.[39]

In a final twist, Epstein brings these two rationales together by suggesting a bold teleological conclusion. Cinema, he claims, is the perfect robotic scion to homophilosophy because its mode of cinematic reproduction and ethical photogeny rectifies nature's brutal regime of sexual reproduction.[40] Cinema is the prosthetic fruit and future of a homophilosophically enlightened humanity. Whatever one thinks of this thesis—in equal parts lyrosophically original, actively progay, and resentment tinged—it expands considerably the narrow scope of debates about cinema's essence, origin, death, and medium specificity in that cinema figures as an integral part of and agent in the cultural becoming of our species.

The Intelligence of a Machine

Although human made, the cinema, unlike Frankenstein's creature, Gepetto's Pinocchio, or *Blade Runner*'s replicants, eschews the android envy complex for a fully human consciousness, since, after all, this envy reflects only our anthropocentric phobia. Indeed, what Epstein most reveres about cinema is that it displays a markedly original cognitive autonomy from the human, one from which we can and should learn. Already in 1926 he wrote:

> Why should we prevent ourselves from benefiting from one of the rarest qualities of the cinematographic eye—that of *being an eye outside of the eye,* that of *escaping from the tyrannical egocentrism* of our personal vision. Why force the sensitive/sensible [*sensible*] emulsion to only repeat the functions of our retina? Why not seize eagerly the almost

unique opportunity to organize a spectacle according to another center than that of our visual purview. The lens in itself [*L'objectif lui-même*].[41]

The original French of Epstein plays on the polysemy of *sensible* (both sensitive and sensible) and *objectif* (both objective and lens) to suggest that two key attributes of the robot brain of the cinema are its new sensibility and its posthuman objectivity. In ways that Deleuze will again closely echo, Epstein proposes that the cinema develops its own phenomenology of the world and the human, substituting itself for the hypothetical disincarnate subject-observer of humanism. In phenomenological terms (pace Husserl), Epstein argues that cinema offers a nonhuman *epokhê*, a new mode of suspension of our habitual view of the world, a transcendental prosthetic of intentionality.

Epstein develops this idea in his philosophical summa published in 1946, *The Intelligence of a Machine*. It begins where "Ganymede" leaves off, with the premise that cinema is an autonomous intentionality that revolutionizes our view of the cosmos:

> We know that the cinematograph inscribes its own character within its representations of the universe, with such originality that it makes this representation not simply a record or copy of the conceptions of its organic mastermind [*mentalité-mère*], but truly a differently individualized system, partly independent, and comprising the seed of the development of a philosophy that strays far enough from common opinions so as to be called an anti-philosophy.[42]

There are five crucial aspects that warrant Epstein's redefinition of cinema as antiphilosophy, that is, enacting a radical break with Western philosophy: it undoes the false distinction between continuity and discontinuity and between quality and quantity, and it changes our notions of space-time, causality, and the nature of life.

Epstein begins with the obvious character of the cinema: it projects a continuous movement out of frames that are separate on the filmstrip. Bergson and later critics have insisted on this basis that cinema provides merely the illusion of movement. Regardless of the fact that optical science has proven them wrong (Max Wertheimer and others have shown we perceive real and filmic movement through the same perceptual processes), Epstein argues that cinema, in combining the three dimensions of space with time, which it can manipulate equally through reverse motion and slow or accelerated motion, shows that only in our human (and post-Kantian) perspective are these dimensions considered separate. Nothing in the universe as seen by cinema shows human time, Bergson's duration, to be in any way privileged. "The cinematograph has destroyed this illusion: it shows time to be merely a perspective resulting from the succession of phenomena, the way space is merely a perspective of the coexistence of things."[43] For Epstein filmic frames and atoms, filmic projection and light or continuous matter are equally real, so that our insistence in opposing discontinuity and continuity, atoms and waves, beings and Being, or nature and artifice is the real illusion.

Epstein's book doesn't engage with previous thoughts on or theories of cinema—in fact, he mentions not a single film thinker. He endeavors to confront the cinema with physics from the ancients (Euclid, Lucretius, the Pythagoreans, and Aristotle) and with the moderns (Malebranche, Daniel Bernouilli, Max Plank, Louis De Broglie, Niels Bohr, and Werner Heisenberg).[44] Triangulating their theories with the capacities of cinema (reverse motion in particular), Epstein deconstructs causality and determinism as figments of our need for order rather than realities. Going a step further, he claims that accelerated motion and close-ups, by showing a germinating seed or a magnified hand with all the characteristics reserved for life-forms—animation and autonomy—undo our ideas of the distinction between the living and the inert. Through the cinema,

> horses hover above an obstacle; plants gesticulate; crystals couple, reproduce themselves and heal their wounds; lava slithers; water becomes oil, gum, pine pitch; man acquires the density of a cloud, the consistency of vapor; he has become a purely gaseous animal, with feline grace and ape-like dexterity. All the partitioned systems of nature are disarticulated. Only one realm remains: life.[45]

In "Quantity Mother of Quality," a chapter deliberately titled to counter Bergson's central hierarchy of quality over quantity, Epstein argues that whatever a quality appears to be, in the end it amounts only to a phase within a quantifiable continuum: what we call *life* is but an appearance within a certain window of phenomenological speed.

Epstein reserves to causality some of his most incisive critiques. He shows, first of all, that causality is so closely intertwined with succession in time as to be indistinguishable from it: reverse a film projection and it looks for all intents and purposes as if smoke causes fire and rain levitates to feed clouds. While reverse motion is associated with a comic effect, Epstein takes it as a philosophical device putting in jeopardy our faith in time's arrow and attendant categories:

> Causality appears to be little more than a mental coloration bestowed upon certain degrees of probability within a succession of phenomena, about which it is entirely indifferent, and often impossible, to know whether they are independent of or dependent on each other in another way.[46]

The cinema as a new form of philosophical intentionality serves to disclose and expand the limits of our prejudices about what we think we know of the universe.

Epstein invokes idiosyncratic corollaries to prosecute his thesis. For instance, he argues that machines have quirks akin to personality. He also claims dreams demonstrate that our brains confuse cause and effect, since an outside cause (an alarm clock ringing) triggers a dream (about time anxiety) that, paradoxically, garbs itself as a cause in order to obtain the ultimate effect of waking us up. By pretending we are all logical all the time, we simplify the deterministic chains in which our subjectivity, no less and no more than the cinema apparatus, is fully embroiled. That is why he calls the cinema an agent of "photo-electric psychoanalysis," not in a personal biographical sense but in a profoundly philosophical way of helping us figure out who we, humans, are.[47]

Altogether, the philosophy of *The Intelligence of a Machine* is strikingly Spinozist and pre-Deleuzian. Indeed, it is difficult not to read in the following passage another adumbration of Deleuze's plane of immanence:

> A time variation is enough to cause the unknown that we call reality to become continuous or discontinuous, inert or alive, brute matter or flesh endowed with instinct or an intelligent soul, determined or random, subject to logic or a contrary logic, or a logic that would not

fit into any reasonable order. All the semblances of everything that can
or cannot be perceived, and all that exists or does not, communicate
among themselves, more than likely transform into each other according
to particular laws, but also and above all according to an absolutely general law of correlation with the values that the time variable can adopt.[48]

Although Epstein doesn't appeal in his book to the virtuality versus
actuality opposition so crucial in Bergson and Deleuze, it is plain
that the lesson of the cinema apparatus is that reality is far more
complex yet also far more holistic than we know and that all things
must "communicate among themselves." A major difference from
Deleuze is that when the latter speaks of blocks of duration or of
the Aion, he remains within an eminently humanistic temporality in
which the flow of time or the instant are not subject to the quantitative self-difference of Epstein's "absolutely general law" concerning
time scales. The cinema thus reveals in the end the utter relativity of
our so-called laws and constants and teaches us that the mathematical
sublime undergirds the universe: "We must therefore presume the
universe to be devoid of all laws other than those of pure numbers,
that is, frightfully simple and scandalously monotonous laws hiding
beneath the vertiginous and shaky ideologies in which the human
mind wraps itself."[49]

We cannot fully do justice to *The Intelligence of a Machine* here: it
is a dense philosophical and lyrosophical mind experiment that attempts to be conducted through the mind of cinema. In the history of
film philosophy, it stands alone as the most original and provocative
work because it takes cinema utterly seriously as the most important
phenomenon—at once natural, mechanical, and metahistorical—for
modern humanity.

Rediscovering Epstein

In this essay I have tried to represent rather than assess Epstein's
thought on cinema, since it has been too often hastily considered
and thus misrepresented. We will soon be in a position of gauging
the quasi entirety of his writings (in French, at least), and when this
comes about also for his films, cinema studies will finally be able to
give him his due. Epstein should be considered among the finest

modern thinkers of time, so long as we understand the variety and multiplicity of time revealed through the cinema. Indeed, we should take Epstein's films and writings as primarily focusing on and documenting this temporal multiplicity. Coenaesthesis is ultimately the time of our bodies, which is why we feel such a peculiar malaise at seeing ourselves on film (as Epstein repeatedly points out), because we no longer recognize the time of our subjectivity. Photogeny is the time of cinema proper, the moment when the layering of temporal eddies around things, scenes, or faces renders them enigmatic and virtual, dereifying them and reenergizing us.

Epstein also focused on workers and work time in his documentaries shot during the French Front populaire, and he thought of himself as a humble worker in the cinema, taking each shooting as an intellectual and collective adventure in the difficulties and joys of work and world. On well-funded film projects, he insisted all members of the crew be paid the same as himself, and in his later films he trained nonprofessionals, especially in Brittany, so that they could represent themselves and their worldview on screen. Ahead of his time, Epstein was also a thinker of his own time, and when he points to how quickly our ways of experiencing filmic idioms change, we should take it as evidence of the living reciprocity between cinema and the present. Epstein's thought is for us exceptionally timely. It can guide us beyond increasingly ghettoized views of cinema—as art or culture or industry or entertainment or dead medium but too often nothing more—when cinema as a philosophical ally can open for us new ways of understanding the temporalities of our body and mind, that of others, and of our history that extends to the universe.

NOTES

1. For a recent biography, see Daire, *Jean Epstein*.
2. Keller and Paul, *The Cinema of Jean Epstein*; Wall-Romana, *Jean Epstein*; Epstein, *The Intelligence of a Machine*; Epstein, *Écrits complets*; Le Gall, *Coffret Jean Epstein*.
3. Epstein, *La poésie*; Epstein, *Bonjour cinema*; Epstein, *La lyrosophie*.
4. Gance, *Prisme*, 163.
5. Epstein, *La poésie*, 212.
6. Epstein, *Écrits sur le cinéma*, vol. 1, 137. I quote from this edition of his works, since the new edition has not been completed.

7. Ibid., 138.
8. See Turvey, *Doubting Vision*, 21–26, 59–66.
9. Wall-Romana, "Epstein's Photogénie as Corporeal Vision."
10. Epstein, *Bonjour cinéma*, 94–95.
11. Ibid., 96.
12. Epstein, *La poésie*, 83.
13. Ibid., 116, 193.
14. Epstein, *Bonjour cinema*, 38–39.
15. Ibid., 94, 96.
16. Ibid., 107.
17. Epstein, "Le phénomène littéraire," 43.
18. Epstein, *Écrits*, vol. 1, 359.
19. Ibid., 360.
20. Ibid., 127.
21. Epstein, *Bonjour cinéma*, 31–32.
22. Ibid., 111.
23. Epstein, *La poésie*, 170.
24. Epstein, *Écrits sur le cinéma*, vol. 1, 146.
25. Ibid., 143.
26. Epstein, *Écrits sur le cinéma*, vol. 1, 146. Epstein's book from which these comments are excerpted, *The Cinema Seen from Etna*, is from 1926; Ferdinand de Saussure's *Cours de linguistique générale* was published in 1916.
27. Epstein, *Écrits sur le cinéma*, vol. 2, 60.
28. Metz, *The Imaginary Signifier*, 194–95; For Epstein and Russian formalism, see Liebman, "Novelty and Poiesis in the Early Writings of Jean Epstein."
29. Epstein, *La poésie*, 86, 141.
30. Ibid., 209.
31. Ibid., 144–45.
32. Wall-Romana, *Cinepoetry*.
33. Bergson, *Matter and Memory*, 197, 225.
34. Deleuze, *Cinema 1*, 49.
35. Ibid., 59.
36. My critique of Deleuze's strategic deconstruction of Epstein's cinema philosophy is forthcoming in volume 2 of *Kinoptic Modernity*.
37. Wall-Romana, *Jean Epstein*, 67–89.
38. Epstein, "Ganymède."
39. See Wall-Romana, "L'homosexualité dans les écrits et les films de Jean Epstein."
40. Saint-Pol Roux, a symbolist poet and visionary, had also proposed in the late 1920s that filmic reproduction should replace sexual reproduction, in part because he lost his son in World War I. See Wall-Romana, *Cinepoetry*, 150–57.
41. Epstein, *Écrits sur le cinéma*, vol. 1, 129.
42. Epstein, *The Intelligence*, 65.

43. Ibid., 24.
44. Ibid., 34, 41, 43, 44, 55, 71, 82, 83, 97.
45. Ibid., 3.
46. Ibid., 48.
47. Ibid., 55.
48. Ibid., 89.
49. Ibid., 49.

BIBLIOGRAPHY

Bergson, Henri. *Matter and Memory.* Translated by N. M. Paul and W. S. Palmer. London: George Allen, 1911.
Daire, Joël. *Jean Epstein: Une vie pour le cinéma.* Grandvilliers, France: La tour verte, 2014.
Deleuze, Gilles. *Cinema 1: The Movement Image.* Translated by Hugh Tomlinson and Barbara Habberjam. Minneapolis: Minnesota University Press, 1986.
Epstein, Jean. *Bonjour cinéma.* Paris: La sirène, 1921.
———. *Coffret Jean Epstein.* DVD. Paris: Potemkine, 2014.
———. *Écrits complets.* Vol. 3. Edited by Nicole Brenez, Joël Daire, and Cyril Neyrat. Paris: Indepencia société, 2014.
———. *Écrits complets.* Vol. 5. Edited by Nicole Brenez, Joël Daire, and Cyril Neyrat. Paris: Indepencia société, 2014.
———. *Écrits sur le cinéma.* Vol. 1. Paris: Éditions Seghers, 1974.
———. *Écrits sur le cinéma.* Vol. 2. Paris: Éditions Seghers, 1975.
———. "Ganymède: Essai sur l'éthique homosexuelle masculine." In *Écrits complets,* vol. 3, edited by Brenez et al.
———. *The Intelligence of a Machine.* Translated by Christophe Wall-Romana. Minneapolis: Univocal Publishing, 2014.
———. *La lyrosophie.* Paris: La sirène, 1922.
———. *La poésie d'aujourd'hui: Un nouvel état d'intelligence.* Paris: La sirène, 1921.
———. "Le phénomène littéraire." In *Jean Epstein: Cinéaste, poète, philosophe,* edited by Jacques Aumont. Paris: La cinémathèque française, 1999.
Gance, Abel. *Prisme.* Paris: Gallimard, 1930.
Keller, Sarah, and Jason N. Paul, eds. *The Cinema of Jean Epstein: Critical Essays and New Translations.* Amsterdam: University of Amsterdam Press, 2012.
Le Gall, Mado. *Jean Epstein: Termaji.* DVD. Paris: La huit, 2014.
Liebman, Stuart. "Novelty and Poiesis in the Early Writings of Jean Epstein." In *Jean Epstein,* edited by Keller and Paul, 73–91.
Metz, Christian. *The Imaginary Signifier: Psychoanalysis and Cinema.* Translated by Celia Britton, Annwyl Williams, Ben Brewster, and Alfred Guzzetti. Bloomington: Indiana University Press, 1977.

Turvey, Malcolm. *Doubting Vision: Film and the Revelationist Tradition.* Oxford: Oxford University Press, 2008.

Wall-Romana, Christophe. *Cinepoetry: Imaginary Cinemas in French Poetry.* New York: Fordham University Press, 2013.

———. "Epstein's Photogénie as Corporeal Vision: Inner Sensation, Queer Embodiment, and Ethics." In *Jean Epstein,* edited by Keller and Paul, 51–71.

———. "L'homosexualité dans les écrits et les films de Jean Epstein." Introduction to *Écrits complets,* vol. 3, by Jean Epstein, 11–19. Paris: Independencia société, 2014.

———. *Jean Epstein: Corporeal Cinema and Film Philosophy.* Manchester, U.K.: Manchester University Press, 2013.

6

Montage Eisenstein

MIND THE GAP

Julia Vassilieva

"The artist may be known rather by what he omits," as Eisenstein
quotes Schiller in a diary entry dated June 20, 1947, almost exactly
six months before his death in February 1948.[1] The quotation might
strike us as incongruous, coming from the master who was never shy
to voice his opinion or illustrate his points—in both his directorial
work and his theoretical commentaries. Yet at this late stage of his
career, Eisenstein becomes preoccupied with the issue of what he
termed "great nothingness"—the opposite, the emptiness, the non-
identity against which we can define what is present and given. With
his characteristic insatiable appetite, Eisenstein plans to explore this
idea in relation to philosophy, physics, and art—he refers to Einstein's theory of relativity, which he sees as privileging becoming over
matter; becomes fascinated by the paradoxical nature of the number
zero as a mark of nothingness; and plans to explore the role of empty
spaces in a range of arts: blank spaces in Chinese drawings, ellipses
in Rilke, negative space in Rodin's sculptures. He makes a note to
himself: "And don't forget about history and aesthetic of lace as a victory of omissions over the strands of fabric!"[2]—as if anticipating the
late twentieth-century move toward deconstruction, which implies
an acknowledgment "that there is *play*—in all senses of the word—
there where one thinks one sees only the immovable, cut off from all
alterity and alteration."[3]

In these late, harried, fragmentary, and still unpublished notes,
Eisenstein's future plans to explore "nonindifferent emptiness" are in-
terspersed with reflections about the past—the logic of montage in
Strike and *Battleship Potemkin,* the reiteration of montage principle as

a collision of two elements, the emergence of the third "lacking" element from this collision—meaning. Thus, the emphasis on emptiness and omission can be seen as a logical development of the idea of gap that so powerfully encompasses Eisenstein's early research and practice. The idea of omission also starts to resonate poignantly with the personal circumstances of Eisenstein's life and work—with everything that had to be repressed or destroyed for political and ideological reasons in his practice (think about the destruction of *Bezhin Meadow*), with what had been obliterated or lost due to tragic circumstances (think about the lost footage of *Que viva Mexico!*), with the long history of the publication of his theoretical heritage (think about his magnum opus, *Method*, that saw the light only by 2002), and with all the gaps that mark almost a century of appropriation of Eisenstein's thought.

Over the last quarter of a century, as Eisenstein's unpublished manuscripts have become available in Russian and have then been translated gradually into other languages, it has become possible to construct a richer, more nuanced understanding of Eisenstein and his legacy.[4] Within this emerging reconsideration of Eisenstein, however, his engagement with philosophy is arguably the aspect in most need of revision. On the one hand, dialogue with Eisenstein's heritage defines some key philosophical issues in film studies—such as André Bazin's discussion of realism,[5] Noël Burch's analysis of formal dialectics in cinematic expression,[6] Gilles Deleuze's theorization of the movement-image,[7] and Vivian Sobchack's embodied account of cinematic experience.[8] On the other hand, analysis of Eisenstein's philosophy in its own right remains fixed on Marxist influence on Eisenstein and on the contextualization of his work in relation to the construction of socialism in Russia. In this essay I argue there are now compelling reasons to rethink Eisenstein's philosophical position—beyond the ideological debates of the twentieth century. In doing so, this essay responds to Miriam Hansen's imperative that our engagement with early film theory—and we might add practice—should not only reconstruct their historical horizon but also suggest constellations in which they raise questions relevant to current concerns.[9]

The Cinema of Event

Eisenstein made his first full-length film, *Strike,* in 1925. This film signaled Eisenstein's overriding focus on history as film's subject matter and relentless motivation to experiment with the expressive means of the new medium of cinema. Set in 1903, *Strike* was a commemoration of a series of strikes in Rostov-on-Don and drew on Eisenstein's earlier theatrical efforts, the principle of montage outlined previously by Lev Kuleshov, and aesthetics of constructivism. This tour de force, combining strikingly composed shots, visual metaphors, and rapid editing with a dense set of intertextual allusions, is rightly described in critical literature as the best example of Eisenstein's early method of "montage of attractions," in which "attractions" were defined by Eisenstein as any element of emotionally effective cinematic impact.[10] Opening with a scene of a worker's suicide, passing through almost vaudevillian scenes depicting dwarves and buffoonish spies, and concluding with a now famous parallel cutting that moves between the massacre of the striking workers and the slaughter of a bull in the abattoir, the emotional diapason of *Strike* ranged from humorous and carnivalesque to tragic and blood curling. Thematically, *Strike* announced Eisenstein's recurring concern with the pleas of the oppressed and the crushing of these by brutal dehumanizing force.

Strike was followed by *Battleship Potemkin* (1925), a dramatized account of the 1905 mutiny on the battleship *Prince Potemkin Tavrichesky*. The film was executed in a more controlled and calculated manner and harnessed the possibilities of montage for greater emotional and intellectual impact. The film's centerpiece—the massacre on the Odessa steps—has become the most widely referenced sequence in film history and demonstrated overlapping use of metric, rhythmic, and tonal montage that were key to Eisenstein's early directorial work and cinema theory.[11] It also delivered some of the most direct and unsettling images of the merciless killing and agony of human bodies, thus foregrounding the theme of history achieved through cruelty and violence—one of the central themes throughout Eisenstein's work.

Following *Potemkin*, Eisenstein began work on a film about the transformation of a Russian village after the revolution, initially titled *The General Line* and released in 1929 under the title *Old and New*. Eisenstein's interest in the project was inspired by Lenin's idea that in rural areas in Russia five different historical formations coexisted side by side, from various modes of agrarian production to capitalism to the emerging socialist way of life. The film revealed Eisenstein's interest in another aspect of history: what endured and revealed itself through coexisting layers and traces of previous epochs.

The work on *The General Line* was interrupted when Eisenstein was commissioned to make *October* in 1927 as part of the celebration of the tenth anniversary of the Bolshevik Revolution. Addressing the founding event of the then-brief Soviet history, Eisenstein took both his concept of historical film and his experiments with montage to a new level. *October* moved to explore the possibility of intellectual montage concerned with communicating abstract conceptual meaning through the juxtaposition of visual images.[12] To achieve this, *October* interrupted largely linear narrative development with quasi-diegetic montage sequences intended to provide commentary on the ideological, political, or social implications of the depicted events. One of the most frequently analyzed examples of intellectual montage in *October* is the sequence commenting on the patriotic slogan "For God and Country." The sequence comprised a progression of images of deities drawn from various religious traditions, ultimately substituting a baroque statue of Christ with a wooden pagan idol, which was intended to ridicule the idea of the existence of God. Another part of the sequence was supposed to demonstrate the hollowness of the idea of the nation by reducing it to a meaningless parade of purely ornamental military regalia.

The reaction to the film was divided. While some critics gave their qualified support to the idea of intellectual montage, others argued that Eisenstein's formal experimentation in *October* had become self-indulgent and that the result was largely unintelligible to the Soviet masses. Another contentious point was the issue of historical authenticity, highlighted by Esfir Shub in her verdict: "You must not stage a historical fact because staging distorts the fact."[13] This led to the protracted polemics between Eisenstein, Shub, and Vertov about the relationship between historical facts and representation. These debates anticipated what has emerged as one of the key philosophical issues in relation to Eisenstein's oeuvre: how cinema can understand, model, and intervene in history.

Controversy also swirled around Eisenstein's strategy of using typage by selecting the right physical type for the part, especially his decision to use a worker, Nikonorov, for the role of Lenin. Earlier, *Strike* and *Potemkin* also used a broad range of typage performed by nonactors and emphasized features of a group identity and social types. By doing so, Eisenstein created a mass protagonist, an apt device to construct an image of "the time when the masses entered into history and history entered into the masses."[14] Later on, the use of typage and a mass protagonist opened Eisenstein's treatment of character to critique with far-reaching philosophical implications regarding personal identity versus collective identity and the role of the individual in the making of history.

The dominant reading of Eisenstein's silent films and montage theory in film studies is well illustrated by David Bordwell's influential view. Bordwell maintains that "Eisenstein's films of the 1920s are, in both content and form, paradigms of Marxist art."[15] He further insists that while at the level of themes and issues, these films illustrate "the Bolshevik version of history, which places class struggle at the center of change," and at the microlevel they "exemplify a politicized conception of cinematic narrative" by subordinating actions of individual characters (represented through typage) to a larger dynamic of social struggle between opposing classes.[16]

With various qualifications and nods to the opaque, fragmentary, and contradictory character of Eisenstein's theoretical writings, such a view has achieved a widespread, nearly axiomatic status.[17] And yet another philosophical perspective on Eisenstein has emerged gradually through scattered writings of scholars like Raymonde Carasco,[18] Jacques Aumont,[19] Georges Didi-Huberman[20] and Jacques Rancière[21] that construes Eisenstein's theory and practice as "explosive force, as welling-up, as outpouring,"[22] which places Eisenstein closer to tendencies within continental philosophy that run from Martin Heidegger to Alain Badiou and Jean-Luc Nancy than to dialectical materialism. My further analysis builds on this emerging critique of the received ideas of film-theoretical establishment and also draws on the recent archival publications in Russia and some fresh perspectives on Eisenstein's work that have emerged in his homeland over the past twenty-five years.

Presiding over publication of Eisenstein's archival texts and restoration of his lost films, the leading authority on Eisenstein's heritage in Russia, Naum Kleiman, argues Eisenstein's early films conceived social change and political cinema in broader terms, far exceeding the confines of class struggle. In his article "What Modeled Eisenstein's Art?" Kleiman hypothesizes Eisenstein's revolutionary trilogy modeled a revolution and a strike *in general* and were concerned with broader themes of innocence, dignity, violence, and justice.[23] Kleiman demonstrates this on several levels: Eisenstein's understanding of the construction of historical film and of formal and compositional levels and his use of intertextual references. Kleiman highlights how Eisenstein developed and implemented a unique understanding of historical film: not only did what was normally presented as historical background for the actions of human protagonists come to the foreground in his films, but the internal logic of events, the general historical laws that revealed themselves in these developments, were scrutinized while the singularity of their occurrence was addressed through the formal composition of the film.

While *Potemkin* was more tightly linked to a particular historical event, at least at the level of narrative, *Strike* was designed explicitly by Eisenstein as a composite image of several historical strikes across Russia. Although the action was based on the 1903 strikes at Rostov-on-Don and the closing title referred to a number of strikes that took place in Russia between 1903 and 1915, the image was abstracted from any geographical or historical particularity. In his later reflections on *Strike,* Eisenstein described the method of the film as "a method of reconstruction under the sign of typical behavior in a typical situation," which was also the reason for figuring characters as generalizations rather than as individuals: "the factory owner," "the provocateur," "the committee."

Similar tendencies toward generalization can be detected in *October.* As many scholars note, Eisenstein's fascination with French revolutionary history led to numerous intertextual allusions that linked the events of 1917 in Russia with the French revolutions of 1789 and 1830. Among them were the little figure of Hugo Gavroche on the barricades; images of "two Napoleons"(the real Napoleon and Kerensky, the head of the failed provisional government between the February and October revolutions); and references to Zola's *Germinal.* Most important, however, was the fact that the climactic moment of the Revolution, the storming of the Winter Palace, was staged by Eisenstein along the lines of the storming the Bastille rather than as reflecting anything that happened in Petrograd.

At this point we might recall Marx's famous remark that the French Revolution itself appeared on the stage of history in a Roman costume. Hannah Arendt attributed enormous significance to this statement as one hinting at the common dynamics of revolutions in the modern age, which she saw as a symptom of and reaction to the decline of political foundations in the West. From her point of view, "the revolutions of the modern age appear like gigantic attempts to repair these foundations, to renew the broken thread of tradition, and to restore, through founding new political bodies, what for so many centuries had endowed the affairs of men with some measure of dignity and reason."[24] Arendt's approach detached the analysis of revolution from the dynamics of class struggle in one particular country and considered it within a larger historical and geographical framework. Such a politicophilosophical analysis seems to be consistent with Eisenstein's focus on enduring historical tendencies, on generalization, and on the underlying mechanics that can bring about revolution as such, beyond any historical particularity.

Within the context of contemporary continental philosophy, Eisenstein's position can be compared to Jacques Derrida's reinterpretation of Marxism undertaken in the wake of the collapse of the Soviet Union and in the context of the questioning of the revolutionary potential of leftist ideology. In *Spectres of Marx*, Derrida argues that Marxism can be taken up not only as a radical critique but also as a messianic promise: "this eschatological relation to the to-come of an event *and* of a singularity, of an alterity that cannot be anticipated."[25] While many scholars reduce Eisenstein's position to orthodox Soviet Marxism and interpret his films as focused on class struggle, Eisenstein's focus might well have been wider: taken as a whole, his opus can be described as one concerned with radical interruption and break, with discontinuity and contingency, and with the coming of something absolutely new in the world and the surprise of this coming.

As such, Eisenstein's work can be seen to be in tune with what Slavoj Žižek defines as the main trend of twentieth-century philosophy and science: the "shift from substantial Reality to (different forms of) Event," where Event "stands for historicity proper (the explosion of New) versus historicism."[26] Contrary to the famous remark by Bazin that "montage as used by Kuleshov, Eisenstein, or Gance did not give us the event; it alluded to it,"[27] from this perspective Eisenstein's efforts can be seen as an attempt to model Event, in the sense the term has acquired toward the end of the twentieth century, which has shifted its emphasis from representation to rupture. From this philosophical ground, Eisenstein's overriding goal can be seen as an attempt to capture this explosion of the new, to map forces that in their dynamics can create a possibility for a change, to juxtapose the repetitiveness of description (historicism) with the singularity of occurrence (historicity proper).

Eisenstein's Unfinished Business

After completing his "revolutionary tetralogy," Eisenstein had to wait almost ten years for a successful cinematic project. That was the period of unrealized plans and aborted enterprises. Admittedly, Eisenstein's unfinished film projects occupy a peculiar place in film history: they stand like ghosts on the threshold of materialization, yet even from this liminal position, they manage to exert a powerful influence. One of the most ambitious of these plans was the idea of filming Karl Marx's *Das Kapital*, which preoccupied Eisenstein between 1927 and 1929. Eisenstein believed films of the future would "have to do with philosophy"[28] and saw *Capital* as a new form of cinema—film treatise—that would use a new, discursive type of cinematic language.

Eisenstein's notes on the project demonstrate a logical progression from his exploration of montage in *October* to a new type of intellectual montage in *Capital*—capable of communicating abstract conceptual meaning and philosophical ideas. Importantly, this new type of cinema would provide not only new montage strategies but also "their rationalization which takes these strategies into account."[29] The film treatise therefore becomes reflexive in a very fundamental sense: it simultaneously "thinks" its theme (capital) and "thinks itself"— that is, reflects on the cinematic process.

While the project to film *Capital* has never been realized, the idea—as a limit case modeling cinema's capacity to express and articulate thought—has had a long echo in cinema history. The project acquired an interesting afterlife in the recent magisterial film essay by Alexander Kluge *News from Ideological Antiquity: Marx/Eisenstein/ Capital* (2008)—an eight-hour-long contemplation of Marx's and Eisenstein's heritages. Less directly, the legacy of the idea of cinema treatise can be seen in the current explosion of interest in the film essay, particularly as a form of film criticism.

With the idea to film *Capital*, Eisenstein's exploration of the possibilities of intellectual montage reached its peak and, probably, came to an impasse. Beginning in the early 1930s, Eisenstein expanded the scope of his analysis of the expressive means of film and turned to the broader exploration of how cinema engaged the senses and sensorium—all categories of perception, ranging from the cognitive and intellectual to the sensory and carnal. This agenda encompassed two other projects started in the 1930s: the film *Que viva Mexico!* and Eisenstein's formidable but unfinished study *Method,* on which he worked until his death in 1948.

Eisenstein started to work on a historical film about Mexico during his trip to Europe and North America that began in 1929. When he was ordered to come back to Russia in 1932, however, the work stopped. Eisenstein was separated from the film footage, and the project remained unfinished. Eisenstein conceived of *Que viva Mexico!* as "a big poem about life and death," covering three millennia of Mexican history. The scenario involved six episodes set in different regions and focused on different aspects of Mexican history and culture, ranging from the ancient Mayan civilization to the present day. Compared with Eisenstein's films of the earlier Soviet period, *Que viva Mexico!* demonstrated a new set of interests and concerns: in the bodily and erotic; in myth, ritual, and ethnography; and in the grotesque and carnivalesque. It also marked a shift to a different attitude toward religion, which Eisenstein here acknowledged and explored as a powerful cultural force.

But the key focus of the film was an exploration of the fascinating, paradoxical coexistence of various historical epochs and cultural formations that Eisenstein saw in Mexico. The film staged the temporal polyphony of Mexico in a variety of ways: from the juxtaposition of ruined Aztec monuments and stone sculptures to images of contemporary Mexican people to an exploration of how religious rituals introduced by Catholic priests reworked cults of ancient gods that predated colonization to memorable sequences depicting death masks, skulls, and skeletons interspersed with children's smiling faces and fairground merriments during a celebration of the Day of the Dead. But what was at stake for Eisenstein in creating this image of Mexico as a giant living palimpsest was a new vision of history itself—as a simultaneous presence of different historical stages and epochs through their material traces and embodied practices.

This new perspective can be seen in the major theoretical project Eisenstein started at the same time as his Mexican film: *Method,* a study dedicated to the formulation of a unified method of art. Unlike his earlier preoccupation with montage, which was often and legitimately aligned with structural analysis, *Method* signaled a departure from and critique of structuralism. The distinct feature of the approach adopted by Eisenstein in *Method* was his consistent and determinant historicism, with equal attention given to the synchronic and the diachronic aspects of works of art. At the core of *Method,* Eisenstein positioned what he called the *Grundproblem,* the German term by which he referred to the central problem of art, which he saw as a paradoxical coexistence of two dimensions in the work of art: logical and sensuous, cognitive and emotional, rational and irrational, conscious and unconscious. Eisenstein suggested the laws regulating the psychological operation of various evolutionary stages were crystallized in brain structures and mechanisms that remained present in later stages of development. The human mind operated on several evolutionary levels simultaneously. Eisenstein further hypothesized that, in general, a work of art was congruent with properties of the world and of human consciousness: "The basic structure of consciousness is exactly the same in its organization as my formula of two indissolubly united parts as a foundation for the dialectical organization of image [in art]."[30] Moreover, art was effective because the laws of form were determined by the laws of earlier forms of human psychological functioning, which Eisenstein variously defined as "archaic," "prelogical," and "magical":

> We translate each logical thesis into the language of sensuous speech, sensuous thought and as a result we get enhanced sensuous effect. And further—you can take for granted that the source of the language of the form is represented by the whole trove of prelogical sensuous thought and there is not a single manifestation of form in art which would not grow from this source—which would not be determined by it entirely. It is a fact, it is a necessity.[31]

The exploration of the *Grundproblem* became for Eisenstein an exploration of such archaic forms of thinking and operating. In uncovering the evolutionary sources of such operations, Eisenstein went back in time not only to earlier stages of human history but also into the evolution of Homo sapiens as a species and the very emergence of life as such. In *Method* he explored such mechanisms under the rubrics of the "ways of regress" and "shifts in time," which included inner speech, magical thinking, synesthesia (nondifferentiated multimodal perception), *MutterleibsVersenkung* (the urge to return to the womb), androgynies, and the rhythmic organization of biological processes.[32] In doing so, Eisenstein was searching for the ultimately plastic forms that stood at the beginning of the invention of expressive means.

Eisenstein presented the central ideas of *Method* at a major Soviet filmmakers' conference, the First All Union Creative Congress, in 1935. They were found to be incompatible with the newly adopted doctrine of socialist realism. Consequently, *Method* had to wait for more than fifty years for publication. In the same year, 1935, Eisenstein began working on his first sound feature, *Bezhin Meadow,* which he saw as a practical exploration of the issues addressed in *Method.* The Soviet authorities declared *Bezhin Meadow* a failure, however, and destroyed the film. The history of both the conception and the destruction of the film merits reexamination.

Bezhin Meadow was based on an actual episode in which a young boy, Pavlik Morozov, informed on his father, who was sabotaging the decisions of the Soviet authorities and was then murdered by his uncles. The story was quickly turned into a modern Soviet myth in popular culture and propaganda celebrating the victory of the new social order over blood ties. In cinema history Eisenstein's decision to make a film on the topic has been interpreted customarily as a propagandist act, a response to social and ideological orders by the authority in which mere formal experimentation went wrong and made the release of the film impossible. Close analysis of Eisenstein's notes allows, however, for another interpretation: by engaging with this new Soviet myth, Eisenstein may have been attempting to explore and understand what such a readiness to accept human sacrifice would mean to society. As Kleiman's reconstructive work with surviving stills demonstrates, the film was shot through with religious iconography, historical allusions, and intertextual references. Significantly, two central reference points in *Bezhin Meadow* were the Old Testament myth of Abraham being commanded to sacrifice his son, Isaac, and the key New Testament trope of God sacrificing his son to save humanity. The image of the central protagonist, the young boy Stepok, alluded to the image of Christ, whereas his father was modeled on Abraham.[33]

It can be argued, thus, that just as the story of Abraham and Isaac exposed the tension between the ethical and the religious, the story of Pavlik Morozov exposed the tension between the ethical and the ideological. Hence, the key question Eisenstein raised in *Bezhin Meadow* can be seen as the question of the ethics of sacrificing human lives—for ritual, religious, or ideological purposes. The centrality of such a question for the political development of the Soviet Union in the mid-1930s is obvious: this period marked the height of the Stalinist repressions, which sent millions into jails and camps and to outright executions. But there is a more fundamental issue at stake in the problematic of sacrifice within the *long durée* of the twentieth century. As Giorgio Agamben argues in *Homo Sacer,* the question of sacrifice is closely bound up with the emergence of sovereign power. For Agamben the definition of sovereignty rests on how we understand and define sacrifice and position it in relation to killing and to the operation of the law. "The sovereign sphere is the sphere in which [it] is permitted to kill without committing homicide and without celebrating a sacrifice," writes Agamben.[34] This becomes possible because sovereign decision "suspends law in the state of exception" and creates a dangerous zone of nondistinction between legal and illegal, the zone where sacrifice becomes irrelevant and killing acceptable. While the concentration camps of the twentieth century serve as a preeminent example of the state of exception, Agamben sees in them a limit case that exposes the central paradox of sovereign power—the key issue of contemporary political philosophy. Read in this context, *Bezhin Meadow* can be seen as an act of radical and far-reaching political and philosophical critique rather than as an act of radical propaganda.

Taking the Leap

Eisenstein's last two films took up the figure of the sovereign as their key locus of historical analysis. His interest in a strong personality—in contrast to the early focus on a mass protagonist—emerged gradually over the 1930s. While in the United States, Eisenstein considered several films exploring the rise and fall of strong protagonists: *Sutter's Gold*, about Captain Sutter, a key pioneer of the Californian Gold Rush who amassed and then lost enormous wealth, and *Black Majesty*, about Henri Christophe, a former slave and leader in the Haitian Revolution who turned into a dictator after its victory. The structure of these—unrealized—works was uniformly based on tragedy, ending with the death of the hero. What was of particular interest to Eisenstein in these scenarios was the notion of hubris and the limits of power, an issue that acquired heightened urgency in Russia in the mid-1930s. As noted earlier, during this time Stalin's ideology made a transition from emphasis on the global community of true believers to emphasis on the importance of state, leading to the emergence of a brutal totalitarian power structure presided over by a dictator. While Eisenstein's last films, *Alexander Nevsky* (1938) and *Ivan the Terrible, Part I* (1943), are customarily read in film history as delivering a proauthoritarian message and lending support to Stalin's cult of personality (hence, the success and the accolades earned by the director), the broader concept of their inception proves that the issue was far more complicated and that the charge of propaganda was a problematic one.

Alexander Nevsky focused on Prince Alexander (1220–1263) and his struggle for Russian territorial sovereignty—the patriotic theme that had an immediate relevance for Russia just three years prior to Hitler's invasion. It is worth noting, however, that the Russian Orthodox Church made Alexander Nevsky a saint in 1547, and through his figure Eisenstein was inevitably tapping into another theme—the preservation of Orthodoxy at the core of a national consciousness.

The film opened with Alexander facing multiple threats—the despotic rule of the Tartar khans from the East and persistent German campaigns from the West. Alexander decided to fight the invasion of the Teutonic knights and defeated them in the scene of the famous Ice Battle. The projected ending of the film was not celebratory, however, but tragic: Alexander died having been poisoned by lesser Russian princes who were jealous of his success and threatened by his growing power. Work on the film was closely supervised by another scriptwriter assigned to the production, Pyotr Pavlenko, and in addition controlled by Stalin himself. After reading Eisenstein's original script, Stalin drew a red line across the page before the scene of Alexander's death and wrote, "Such a good prince shouldn't die!"[35] Following Stalin's directives, Eisenstein turned *Nevsky* from tragedy into epic, a historical spectacle with a streamlined narrative and a simplified range of issues. *Nevsky* received a widely positive reception in Russia on its release, even though Eisenstein regarded this film as his least accomplished one.

Following the public success of *Nevsky*, Eisenstein was allowed to take on another project: in 1941, the year Nazi Germany invaded Russia, he started work on *Ivan the Terrible*. Part I was completed in 1943 and was received favorably by the Soviet authorities, whereas Part II, completed in 1946, became a disaster for Eisenstein. Stalin was furious, as the disturbing parallels between Ivan's atrocities and Stalin's own reign were unavoidable. Eisenstein was accused of misleading historical representation of Ivan, who was depicted not "as a progressive statesman, but as a maniac and a scoundrel who behaves in a crazy manner."[36] The film was shelved and not shown until 1958, and Part III was never completed. Eisenstein died of a heart attack in February 1948, just past his fiftieth birthday.

The film followed Ivan IV, a contemporary of Henry VIII and Elizabeth I, in his efforts to consolidate power in the hands of the tsar and create a strong state. Part I depicted Ivan's struggle with Boyars, the aristocracy who shared power with the tsar, his successful capture of the throne, and his achievements in territorial expansion and strengthening of Russia. Part II brought with it a tragic turn: Ivan was transformed from a strong ruler into a dictator; he placed himself above religious, legal, and human law; he became paranoid in his clinging to power; he created the notorious *oprichnina,* his secret police and bodyguard; his paranoia led to the killing of his friends and supporters; and he ended up in isolation, loneliness, and madness. The tragedy of Ivan is a tragedy of power turning on itself, of sovereignty drowning in violence, of taking on the right to kill and disregarding the value of human life. The centrality of the issue was underscored by Ivan's self-questioning in Part II. At the beginning of Part II, Ivan asked himself, "By what right do you set yourself up as judge, Tsar Ivan?" In his answer he tried to justify the means by the ends: "For the sake of the Great Russian State." However, Ivan's somber reflection at the end of Part II—"My hands are free"— betrayed his own fear of the forces he had unleashed. This tragedy was intended to culminate in the symbolic act of Ivan's killing of his son, whom Ivan perceived as a threat to his power. As Eisenstein explained in *Method*:

> The killing of his son can be understood as the destruction of everything that Ivan has struggled for—as the self-annihilation of Ivan. This is a correct assumption: precisely through the killing of the son (a reversed defeat by the son—because his death itself is first of all a blow to Ivan himself) the self-destruction of the patriarch takes place, and this is equal to the annihilation of absolute power, which will disintegrate with Ivan![37]

As Eisenstein stated in his analysis of Ivan, "In this picture [the basic theme] is *the theme of power.*"[38] But what the film achieved was perhaps more than an exploration of the formation of absolute power in Russia in the sixteenth century and its transformation into dictatorship or, even, the analogy between this process and the totalitarian nightmare of the Stalin years. It touched on the fundamental relationship between power, law, and life that is coming increasingly under focus in contemporary political philosophy. As Agamben suggests: "The paradox of sovereignty consists in the fact that the sovereign is, at the same time, outside and inside juridical order."[39] Developing this idea, Agamben argues that if the exception is the structure of sovereignty, then the "original relation of law to life is not application but Abandonment."[40] According to Agamben, for life to be abandoned does not mean for it simply to be outside the law but "to be exposed and threatened on the threshold."[41] This vulnerability of life to being killed is an inescapable condition of sovereignty. As a model of power, sovereignty thus faces an impasse, and it was this impasse that was staged in *Ivan*. The challenge of *Ivan* then is perhaps to think about power in a radically different way—beyond sovereignty, not unlike the demands for new ontology made by the current politicophilosophical scholarship that insists that it "will only be possible to think a constituting power wholly released from the sovereign ban" if we "think the relationship between potentiality and actuality differently" and "a new and coherent ontology of potentiality" is put in place.[42]

The film also engaged the issue of potentiality on the level of form. Following Kristin Thompson's neoformalist analysis of *Ivan*, it has become customary to see Eisenstein's stylistic experiments in the film as aimed at the creation of excess—all the elements that are not necessary for the articulation and progression of the story but that on the contrary destabilize and complicate narrative at every turn.[43] Indeed, they abounded in *Ivan*: the rich ornamental interiors, the biblical frescoes, and the religious symbolism as well as the more formal elements such as the shadows, the contrast between light and dark, the juxtaposition of close-ups and long plane, the tense, tight framing, and the contrapuntal use of sound. For Eisenstein himself, however, the key issue of style in relation to *Ivan* was not excess but *ekstasis,* the heightened and self-amplifying emotional effect of the work of art exemplified by the finale of Part II. This was most clearly captured in the famous scene of the macabre dance of the *oprichnina,* an explosive experiment in color, rhythm, movement, music, and song connoting in different ways the themes of blood and fire and depicting the *oprichnina* as a force that simultaneously brought with it and descended into hell.

In his theoretical work carried out at the same time as *Ivan, Nonindifferent Nature* (1939) and *Method,* Eisenstein posited *ekstasis* as a broad aesthetic principle encompassing any work of art that was supposed to make the subject "leave himself behind," "transcend himself," or "lose himself."[44] *Ekstasis* represented the final stage in Eisenstein's exploration of the problem of art's effectiveness, addressed previously through the notions of a "montage of attractions" and pathos. The genesis of these three categories is crucial for the discussion of not only the aesthetic but also, more important, the ethics of Eisenstein's art. Because of his early military rhetoric of hitting the spectator's psyche with the "Cine-Fist" and his uncritical use of the Pavlovian stimulus-response model as an analogy, Eisenstein is often charged with instrumentality and manipulation of viewers' emotions. The transition from montage of attractions to *ekstasis* shows, however, he increasingly came to understand the encounter between art and viewers as the creation of space for new forms of subjectivity rather than as manipulation. While working on *Battleship Potemkin,* he had already begun to figure effectiveness as pathos, which in his use not only retained the traditional highly positive, indeed heroic, Russian connotation but was loaded with the additional function of transformation of the viewer.[45] Taking this line of thought one step further, *ekstasis* allowed not only the reorientation of a viewer but also the transcendence of the limits of actuality: "The leap outside oneself (=ek-stasis, ecstasy) is necessarily the passage to something else, to something of a different quality, something contrary to what proceeds."[46]

Eisenstein's definition of *ekstasis* can be seen as preempting, yet again, the discussion of Event in contemporary continental philosophy. There is a striking resonance between Eisenstein's writings and Jean-Luc Nancy's words: "When there is an event, it is the 'already' that leaps up, along with the 'not yet.' It leaps [over] every presented or presentable present, and this leap is the coming, or the *pre-sence* or *prae-sens* itself without a presence."[47] Opening oneself to the ecstatic state by engaging with the work of art, in Eisenstein's view, was closer to participating in the act than to surrendering oneself to the state of trance, for which *ekstasis* is often taken to be a euphemism. Eisenstein insisted that "the leap outside oneself" was not the "leap into nothings."[48] Being overcome by *ekstasis* in Eisenstein's model can be equated with being part of, being surprised by, and leaping with an Event. This leap can also be thought of as an expression of ultimate freedom.

Eisenstein's philosophical trajectory has been described as a move from determinism to symbolism (Ian Aitken),[49] a transition from technicism to mysticism (Robert Stam),[50] and an evolution from mechanistic to organic theory (Dudley Andrew).[51] These earlier and later stages are sometimes understood as separated by an "epistemological shift"[52] but are always posited in relation to dialectical materialism as an unescapable horizon of Eisenstein's thought and are presented as moving toward ever greater synthesis. Though capturing some important dimensions of Eisenstein's philosophy, these accounts quickly lose their explanatory power as new Eisenstein texts become known and we come to realize the internal heterogeneity of Eisenstein's writings will always resist the imposition of a unified and coherent framework. In contrast to these readings, this essay does not provide an integration of Eisenstein's philosophical ideas. Rather, it honors the spirit of the late Eisenstein's theorizing, which emphasized the generative potential of negativity, interruption, and break. In doing so, I have demonstrated how Eisenstein's legacy can be connected with the perspective in contemporary continental philosophy that valorizes negativity as an analytical tool and insists on refusing the temptation to counteract its work: "Negativity cannot pose itself as itself (which would also suppose that it can be taken as something else, as another kind of thing): it can only open, it opens, it hollows out or punctures, it has no genre, not even its own. Unexposable, absolute exposer."[53] It might be most productive, then, to engage with Eisenstein's theory and practice under the sign of rupture, which is perhaps the common denominator of his intervention in aesthetics, ethics, and epistemology. This might finally do justice to the artist whose ultimate gesture in cinema was to rupture the screen with the frontal onslaught of *Potemkin*—on his audience, time, and history.

NOTES

1. Eisenstein, diary, June 20, 1947, fond 1923-2-1178, Russian Government Archive of Literature and Art (thereafter RGALI). The full quotation reads, "The artist may be known rather by what he omits, and in literature, too, the true artist may be best recognised by his tact of omission," and is most likely taken from *The Works of Walter Pater*, 18.
2. Ibid. (author's translation).
3. Neyrat, *Jean-Luc Nancy*, 25.
4. See Christie and Elliot, *Eisenstein at Ninety*; Christie and Taylor, *Eisenstein Rediscovered*; LaValley and Scherr, *Eisenstein at 100*.
5. See Bazin, *What Is Cinema?*
6. See Burch, *Theory of Film Practice*.
7. See Deleuze, *Cinema 1*.
8. See Sobchack, *Carnal Thoughts*.
9. See Hansen, " 'With Skin and Hair.' "
10. See Eisenstein, "The Montage of Attractions"; Eisenstein, "The Montage of Film Attractions."
11. See Eisenstein, "Methods of Montage."
12. See Eisenstein, "The Dramaturgy of Film Form."
13. Shub, "This Work Cries Out!," 217.
14. Rosenstone, "October as History," 262.
15. Bordwell, "Sergei Eisenstein," 379.
16. Ibid.
17. See Bordwell, *The Cinema of Eisenstein*; Taylor, *Film Propaganda*; Aitken, *European Film Theory and Cinema*; Stam, *Film Theory*.

18. See Carasco, *Hors-cadre Eisenstein.*
19. See Aumont, *Montage Eisenstein.*
20. See Didi-Huberman, *La resemblance informe.*
21. Jacques Rancière, Film Fables.
22. Michelson, "Eisenstein at 100," 72.
23. See Kleiman, *Formula finala.*
24. Arendt, *Between Past and Future,* 139–40.
25. Derrida, *Specters of Marx,* 81–82.
26. Žižek, *The Parallax View,* 167.
27. Bazin, *What Is Cinema?,* vol 1, 25.
28. Eisenstein, "Letter to Leon Moussinac," 35.
29. Eisenstein, "Notes for a Film of *Capital,*" 4.
30. Eisenstein, fond 1923-2-256, RGALI.
31. Eisenstein, "Psychology of Art," 195.
32. See Eisenstein, *Method.*
33. Kleiman, *Formula finala,* 123–53.
34. Agamben, *Homo Sacer,* 83.
35. Eisenstein, *Memoirs,* vol. 2, 289.
36. *Culture and Life,* special publication by the Department of Agitation and Propaganda of the Central Committee of the Communist Party, July 1946.
37. Eisenstein, *Method,* vol. 2, 365.
38. Eisenstein, *Nonindifferent Nature,* 324.
39. Agamben, *Homo Sacer,* 15.
40. Ibid., 29.
41. Ibid.
42. Ibid., 44.
43. Thompson, *Eisenstein's "Ivan the Terrible."*
44. Eisenstein, *Nonindifferent Nature,* 50–71.
45. Aumont, *Montage Eisenstein.*
46. Eisenstein, *Nonindifferent Nature,* 61.
47. Nancy, *Being Singular Plural,* 172.
48. Eisenstein, *Nonindifferent Nature,* 61.
49. Aitken, *European Film Theory and Cinema,* 27–46.
50. Stam, *Film Theory,* 37–47.
51. Andrew, *The Major Film Theories,* 42–76.
52. See Bordwell, "Eisenstein's Epistemological Shift."
53. See Nancy, "The Technique of the Present."

BIBLIOGRAPHY

Agamben, Giorgio. *Homo Sacer: Sovereign Power and Bare Life.* Stanford, Calif.: Stanford University Press, 1998.

Aitken, Ian. *European Film Theory and Cinema: A Critical Introduction*. Bloomington: Indiana University Press, 2001.

Andrew, Dudley. *The Major Film Theories: An Introduction*. Oxford: Oxford University Press, 1976.

Arendt, Hannah. *Between Past and Future*. London: Faber and Faber, 1961.

Aumont, Jacques. *Montage Eisenstein*. Translated by Lee Hildreth, Constance Penley, and Andrew Ross. London: BFI; Bloomington: Indiana University Press, 1987.

Bazin, André. *What Is Cinema?* 2 vols. Berkeley: University of California Press, 1967–1972.

Bordwell, David. *The Cinema of Eisenstein*. Cambridge, Mass.: Harvard University Press, 1993.

———. "Eisenstein's Epistemological Shift." *Screen* 15, no. 4 (1974): 29–46.

———. "Sergei Eisenstein." In *The Routledge Companion to Philosophy and Film,* edited by Paisley Livingston and Carl Platinga, 378–86. Hoboken, N.J.: Taylor and Francis, 2008.

Carasco, Raymonde. *Hors-cadre Eisenstein*. Paris: Macula, 1979.

Burch, Noël. *Theory of Film Practice*. London: Secker and Warburg, 1973.

Christie, Ian, and David Elliot, eds. *Eisenstein at Ninety*. Oxford: Museum of Modern Art. London: British Film Institute, 1988.

Christie, Ian, and David Elliot, eds. *Eisenstein Rediscovered*. London: Routledge, 1993.

Deleuze, Gilles. *Cinema 1: The Movement-Image*. Minneapolis: University of Minnesota Press, 1986.

Derrida, Jacques. *Specters of Marx: The State of the Debt, the Work of Mourning, and the New International*. Translated by Peggy Kamuf. London: Routledge, 2006.

Didi-Huberman, Georges. *La resemblance informe ou le gai savoir visuel selon Georges Bataille*. Paris: Macula, 1995.

Eisenstein, Sergei. "The Dramaturgy of Film Form." In *S. M. Eisenstein: Selected Works,* vol. 1, 161–81. Edited by R. Taylor. London: British Film Institute, 1988.

———. "Letter to Leon Moussinac." In *Eisenstein at Work,* edited by J. Leyda and Z. Voynov, 35. London: Methuen, 1982.

———. *Memoirs*. Vol. 2. Moscow: Museum of Cinema, 1997.

———. *Method*. Vol. 1. Moscow: Museum of Cinema, Eisenstein–Centre, 2002.

———. "Methods of Montage." In *Film Form*, 72–84. Edited by J. Leyda. London: Dennis Dobson, 1949.

———. "The Montage of Attractions." In *S. M. Eisenstein: Selected Works,* vol. 1, edited by Richard Taylor, 33–38. London: British Film Institute, 1988.

———. "The Montage of Film Attractions." In *S. M. Eisenstein,* vol. 1, edited by Taylor, 39–58.

————. *Nonindifferent Nature.* Translated by Herbert Marshall. Cambridge: Cambridge University Press, 1987.

————. "Notes for a Film of *Capital.*" *October,* no. 2 (1976): 3–26.

————. "Psychology of Art." In *Psychologia processov chudojestvennogo tvorchestva,* author's translation, 195. Moscow: Isskustvo, 1980.

————. *The Works of Walter Pater.* London: Macmillan, 1901.

Hansen, Miriam. "'With Skin and Hair': Kracauer's Theory of Film, Marseille 1940." *Critical Inquiry* 19, no. 3 (1993): 437–69.

Kleiman, Naum. *Formula finala: Stat'i, vystuplenija, besedy.* Moscow: Eisenstein-Centre, 2004.

LaValley, Albert J., and Barry P. Scherr, eds. *Eisenstein at 100: A Reconsideration.* New Brunswick, N.J.: Rutgers University Press, 2001.

Michelson, Annette. "Eisenstein at 100: Recent Reception and Coming Attractions," *October,* no. 88 (1999): 69–85.

Nancy, Jean-Luc. *Being Singular Plural.* Translated by Robert D. Richardson and Anne E. O'Byrne. Stanford, Calif.: Stanford University Press, 2000.

Nancy, Jean-Luc. "The Technique of the Present." Lecture given during *Whole and Parts, 1964–1995,* an exposition of On Kawara's works, Nouveau musée, Villeurbanne, France, January 1997, http://www.usc.edu/dept/comp-lit/tympanum/4/nancy.html.

Neyrat, Frédéric. "Jean-Luc Nancy: An Existential Communism." Translated by Arne De Boever. *Parrhesia* 17 (2013): 25–28.

Rancière, Jacques. *Film Fables.* Translated by Emiliano Battista. London: Bloomsbury, 2010.

Rosenstone, Robert A. "October as History." *Rethinking History* 5, no. 2 (2001): 255–74.

Shub, Esfir. "This Work Cries Out!" In *The Film Factory: Russian and Soviet Cinema in Documents, 1896–1939,* edited by Ian Christie and Richard Taylor, 217. Cambridge, Mass.: Harvard University Press, 1988.

Sobchack, Vivian. *Carnal Thoughts: Embodiment and Moving Image Culture.* Berkeley: University of California Press, 2004.

Stam, Robert. *Film Theory: An Introduction.* Malden, Mass.: Blackwell Publishing, 2000.

Taylor, Richard. *Film Propaganda: Soviet Russia and Nazi Germany.* London: I. B. Tauris, 1998.

Thompson, Kristin. *Eisenstein's "Ivan the Terrible": A Neoformalist Analysis.* Princeton, N.J.: Princeton University Press, 1981.

Žižek, Slavoj. *The Parallax View.* Cambridge: Cambridge University Press, 2006.

André Bazin's Film Theory and the History of Ideas

Angela Dalle Vacche

André Bazin was influenced by many philosophical figures. This range of influences was no gratuitous eclecticism. Rather, it stemmed from Bazin's need to develop a critical discourse that would address the impure ontology of the cinema. Because the medium involves nature and culture, it perforce requires insights into art, religion, science, and technology. Without a doubt, the history of philosophy helped Bazin bring together all these dimensions, even if he seldom identified his sources. As a critic he did not seek a perfect fit between his overall film theory and a single philosopher. Bazin never mentioned the names of Saint Augustine or Maurice Merleau-Ponty, while Blaise Pascal comes up in conjunction mostly with Jean Racine's tragedies. Bazin did signal the philosophers relevant to the cinema by using keywords or phrases such as "the embalming of duration" to bring in Henri Bergson; "paradox" to show his allegiance to Blaise Pascal; and in regard to acting styles, "incarnation" to point to the Catholic personalism of Emmanuel Mounier and Gabriel Marcel. Perhaps, Bazin kept his references to a minimum so as not to appear pretentious when writing about a popular art, most often for a popular, if intelligent, audience.

Dominique Chateau and Jean Ungaro: Bazin and Sartre

Since Bazin wrote from 1943 to 1958—the heyday of existentialism and phenomenology—it makes sense to start with the overlaps and differences between the film critic and Jean-Paul Sartre. Besides a reference to Bergson's *Time and Free Will* (1889),[1] Sartre is the only philosopher whose name repeatedly appears in Bazin's criticism, no doubt because Sartre maintained an active involvement with film culture throughout his life.[2] Sartre's relation to cinema was hardly exclusively philosophical. In his book *André Bazin: Généalogies d'une théorie* (2000), Jean Ungaro devotes three full chapters to the relation between Bazin and Sartre. Originally trained as a philosopher, Ungaro displays quite a knowledge of film theory and history. In contrast to Ungaro's focus on the film critic, in Dominique Chateau's short monograph *Sartre et le cinéma* (2005), the author concentrates on the history of Sartre's relationship with film culture, which became disappointing over time.

Chateau explains that Sartre's scenarios rarely became successful films, even if the philosopher was very eager to move beyond literature and theater. Sartre's involvement with the film world increased his notoriety and helped him financially, so that he could cease teaching and devote himself fully to writing. Sartre enjoyed the glamour of the movies; he attended the Cannes Film Festival in 1947 to be present for Jean Delannoy's adaptation of his play *Les jeux sont faits!* (The chips are down). In the pages of the *Parisien libéré*, Bazin comments on Sartre's "excellent" scenario for this film, which evidently called for a mise-en-scène filled with detail. The result disappointed the critic, however. He compared Delannoy's handling of Sartre to "a mayonnaise that wouldn't emulsify"[3]

Chateau treats Sartre as a *cinéphile*, as a writer, and as an intellectual who became immeasurably prominent during and after the war. Though the philosopher attended screenings at Bazin's *ciné-club*, with Simone de Beauvoir,[4] Bazin responded to Sartre's ideas and projects much more than Sartre engaged with Bazin's reviews. In 1947, however, Bazin published a rebuttal to Sartre's negative review of Orson Welles's *Citizen Kane* in the prestigious *Temps modernes,* a journal which Sartre founded with Maurice Merleau-Ponty in 1945.[5]

As a politically engaged intellectual on the left, Sartre did not hesitate to take a position on major American novels and films. In the pages of *L'écran Français* in 1945,[6] Sartre achieved a journalistic scoop by writing against *Citizen Kane*. According to Chateau, one reason for Sartre's resistance to *Citizen Kane* was that he saw the film without subtitles in the United States during a brief stay. More substantially, Welles's film struck the philosopher as an antiexistentialist text. The screenplay denied free will and an open future not just to the characters but to the viewers who received the film's conclusion in its first scene. Such fatalism went against the medium itself, as Sartre conceived it, in opposition to literature and theater. He quoted the title of his own recent play *Les jeux sont faits!* implying Welles's handling of temporality in reverse dictated an inevitable conclusion with no margin of free will concerning the development of the central character. Sartre went as far as to declare that the linear, teleological narratives of standard Hollywood films had a stronger existentialist thrust than *Citizen Kane.*

In Sartre's mind classical Hollywood emphasized individual freedom and striving toward a goal. Ungaro points out Sartre attacked Welles for both his pseudointellectualism and his baroque visual style. The philosopher did not understand that cinematographer Gregg Toland's deep-focus lens worked with the focal length of the wide angle and that this combination emphasized depth of field through a layered mise-en-scène. Sartre found America to be fascinating, but he despised its cultural ideology and economic system. He took on the role of the superior French intellectual in scolding Welles for pretending to be an innovative artist. Welles's reliance on depth of field to urge the spectators' interpretations was not the first example of a cinema breaking away from classical Hollywood's analytical editing. In fact, this synthetic and more intellectually challenging approach had been anticipated through reframing by Jean Renoir during the thirties.

Sartre's contempt for this flashpoint film did not intimidate Bazin in the least. He defended *Citizen Kane* as if it were a new species of life that had just emerged in the evolutionary chain of film history. Without hesitation Bazin appropriated ideas from the literary Sartre and turned them upside down in favor of Welles. Sartre's argument was that the novel should be open to the present tense and to the spontaneity of its characters, as happens in John Dos Passos's *1919* (1938).[7] This stance might seem to confirm the philosopher's negative reaction against the power of the past in *Citizen Kane.* Instead of attacking Sartre directly on *Citizen Kane,* Bazin singled out Welles's montage sequence in relation to Susan Alexander, Kane's second wife, who becomes an opera singer. This stylistic choice matched the philosopher's discussion of *la forme fréquentative anglaise,* or the so-called duration form, in his 1939 essay on Faulkner and temporality.[8]

Bazin wrote: "After the series of superimpositions encapsulating three years of torture for Susan and ending on a light going out, the screen thrusts us brutally into the drama of Susan's attempted suicide."[9] Bazin carried out a detailed analysis of Welles's use of deep focus when Kane becomes aware of Susan's suicide attempt:

> The screen opens up on Susan's bedroom seen from behind the night table. In close-up, wedged against the camera, is an enormous glass, taking up almost a quarter of the image, along with a little spoon and an open medicine bottle. The glass almost entirely conceals Susan's bed, enclosed in a shadowy zone from which only a faint sound of labored breathing escapes, like that of a drugged sleeper. The bedroom is empty; far away in the background of this private desert is the door, rendered even more distant by the lens' false perspectives, and behind the door a knocking. Without having seen anything but a glass and heard two noises, on two different sound planes, we have immediately grasped the situation: Susan has locked herself in her room to try to kill herself; Kane is trying to get in. The scene's dramatic structure is basically founded on the distinction between the two sound planes: close up, Susan's breathing, and from behind the door, her husband's knocking. A tension is established between these two poles, which are kept at a distance from each other by the deep focus. Now the knocks become louder; Kane is trying to force the door with his shoulder; he succeeds. We see him appear, tiny, framed in the doorway, and then rush towards us. The spark has been ignited between the two dramatic poles of the image.[10]

Thanks to Welles's use of the wide-angle lens, the powerful Kane looks "tiny," while the glass is "enormous." Deep focus with depth of field, or the synthetic approach of a sequence shot, replaces Hollywood prearranged, step-by-step editing, which minimizes the spectators' effort. At the same time, this approach ensures an antianthropocentric miniaturization of Welles's powerful protagonist. The deep focus in wide angle looks like a cross-section from Kane's glass sphere with falling snow. This object reminds Kane of his childhood sled, Rosebud. Instead of coming across as an admirable rescuer, Kane looks as helpless as a child about to be overwhelmed, once again, by a huge glass—or a set of emotional circumstances—beyond his control.

At the end of Welles's film, only the spectator knows the solution to the mystery of Rosebud. For Bazin this open question is a gesture of intellectual and moral empowerment. It is an invitation to evaluate the life of an imperfect individual whose enormous success and gigantic failures do not make him less or more human and imperfect than anyone else in the audience. And it is this coming to terms with how being human is riddled with weaknesses that made *Citizen Kane* valuable for Bazin: "Obliged to exercise his liberty and intelligence, the spectator perceives the ontological ambivalence of reality, in the very structure of its appearances."[11] Bazin here underlines that we see Kane as he really is, even if his public persona is based on power. Instead of indulging in baroque excess for its own sake, Welles's film explores the contradictory nature of Kane's personality: a giant with clay feet.

Totally undaunted by Sartre's dislike of the film, Bazin proposed to encapsulate Welles's achievement through Sartre's famous sentence: "Every novelistic technique necessarily relates back to a metaphysics."[12] Thus, the philosopher's accusation of a gap between Toland's deep focus and Welles's "*implicit* decoupage or editing,"[13] through depth of field in space, could not hold. Bazin argued that Welles's interlocking of form and content was just as admirable as the fit of literary style and metaphysics Sartre ascribed to Dos Passos and Faulkner. Yet Chateau reports it was De Beauvoir and not Sartre who, in the footsteps of Bazin's support for *Citizen Kane,* mentioned Welles's innovative use of crisp details in the background and foreground of his sequence shots in deep focus. Bazin trailed Sartre, and De Beauvoir trailed Bazin.

After the controversy around *Citizen Kane,* Chateau concludes the philosopher settled into an overall negative opinion about the cinema:

> The nature of the cinematographic medium is . . . [for Sartre] anti-existentialist and hardly phenomenological. In regard to *Joyless Street* by Pabst, Astruc observes, the philosopher notes that "the cinema, better than the other arts, is effective . . . in giving the image of destiny. . . . The latter means the key of destiny in opposition to the contingency of things in life—and this . . . [fatalistic orientation for Sartre] defines the specificity of the cinema."[14]

Unable to distinguish between the irreversible mechanical flow of the images at the level of recording and Bazin's interest in open interpretations through cinematography, Sartre claimed for cinema a situation of congenital inferiority in comparison to literature and theater. In the end, Sartre's inspirational role for Bazin's film criticism was limited to specific insights on temporality from the philosopher's literary essays.

Citizen Kane is a touchstone case that lets us peer into the possible rapport between these two thinkers. Jean Ungaro has looked into the coincidence and dissonance between Bazin's key ideas and Sartre's philosophical worldview. In discussing the role subjective perception plays in twentieth-century phenomenology against the objective knowledge of nineteenth-century positivism, Ungaro mentions Edmund Husserl's emphasis on intentionality and its impact on Sartre, for whom all consciousness is "consciousness of something in the world."[15] Because Sartre's individual is free to choose any one thing or another, consciousness by itself is no-thing, and hence, there is no essence to human nature. In opposition to Immanuel Kant's idealist metaphysics, for Sartre *being* means to live one's own life as a project, to exist by seeking authenticity. Our external actions define what we are internally. We are what we do. Sartre's essay "The Humanism of Existentialism" (1946)[16] spelled out that free will can potentially override patterns of behavior and genetic heritage. For Sartre life is worth living only when humankind confronts itself with itself. Man's only option is to achieve an existential identity that gives meaning to the unstable coexistence of facts and freedom in an otherwise indifferent and alienating world.

Though Bazin is often accused of being an idealist or essentialist thinker, for him, too, opaque reality exists as matter, while "existence precedes essence," in the sense that anything unstable or unpredictable, ranging from atmosphere to chance, can become creative instead of inducing nausea, the way it was for Sartre. Thus, contingency may push daily life to contribute to filmmaking, while the cinema draws energy from happenstance.[17] In other words, Bazin rejected Sartre's nihilism, even if he was well aware of social injustices and human suffering. Neither an optimist nor a pessimist, Bazin cherished an open approach that would not underplay human mediocrity but that always left room for hope. Bazin was a pioneering critic in

a new intellectual field of inquiry, whose spiritual or ethical impact
he deeply cared about. As a matter of fact, filmmaking can thrive
on spontaneity and improvisation because the cinema is an antianthropocentric medium that decenters free will and stable meanings
through motion, analogy, and contingency. At the same time, human
agency and technology can interrogate life on earth through a dialogue of their own. Nature, in turn, resonates with the fullness of an
elusive universe. When all this comes together, a film finds the energy
to make itself as a quasi-live being gifted with its own immanence
and complexity, whether or not a strong directorial ego is involved.[18]

Alternatively, cinema can oscillate between propaganda and escap-
ism, experiment and newsreel, art and science. Well aware of all these
options, Bazin advocated for a cinema of discovery, if not revelation,
about one's own unstable placement in culture and nature. Likewise,
Bazin discussed the evolution of film language as a medium-in-process
whose direction had been an increasing realism through sound, color,
cinemascope, and 3-D technology. Very different from Hollywood's
realist model based on causal logic, simultaneity, and verisimilitude,
Bazin's modern cinema, after 1945, was filled with nonlinear and open
narratives set in daily life, hovering between fiction and nonfiction.
A critic without a prescriptive agenda, Bazin was interested in any
aspect of film language or minor genre that would throw light on
changes in the perception of Otherness. This is the case because, on
the one hand, the camera lens brings everything down to the same
level on screen. On the other hand, cinema involves the embodied,
kinetic projection of a technological yet human-inflected way of
seeing.

In Sartre's anxious view of modernity, the concept of responsibility is the most important feature of consciousness. Yet in the philosopher's novel *Nausea* (1938),[19] lifeless objects and the uncontrollable
appearances of events are inevitable sources of loneliness and isolation. Bazin stands in contrast to Sartre here. For him the cinema
is a popular art that may address the individual but that appeals to
the masses and can potentially foster a sense of community and exchange. Thus, for the film critic the cinema is the equivalent of a
religious ritual that, through intelligence and intuition, community
and exchange, can mitigate, if not counteract, Sartrean alienation.
Moreover, because the lens of the camera can bring out the analogical

energy between people and objects, the cinema unites the viewers in a partially shared or shareable view of the world based on mutual dependency between Self and Other.

Ungaro makes clear that even if the cinema was a component of everybody's daily life in the forties and fifties, its potential as an art form or as a serious object of academic study was still unthinkable. In fact, for Sartre the magic and the mystery of the cinema belong to his childhood far more than to his adult years. His most heartfelt recollections about the cinema appear in *Les mots* (*The Words,* 1964), where he writes about his own young age being in synchrony with cinema's humble beginnings:

> Born in a den of thieves, officially classified as a travelling show, it
> had popular ways that shocked serious people. It is an amusement for
> women and children. My mother and I loved it, but we hardly gave it a
> thought and we never talked about it. . . . When we came to realize its
> existence, it had long since become our chief need.[20]

During rainy Parisian days, the spell of the screen at the Pantheon, a movie theater in Rue Soufflot, lures little Jean-Paul with his mother:

> The show had begun. We would stumblingly follow the usherette. I
> would feel I was doing something clandestine. Above our heads, a shaft
> of light crossed the hall; one could see dust and vapor dancing in it. A
> piano whinnied away.[21]

Chateau's study takes up Sartre's later relation to cinema through Simone de Beauvoir's writings to explain how she and Sartre navigated their contemporary film landscape in a state of intellectual confusion. For instance, they preferred American films to the Soviet ones, even though they were sympathetic to the French Communist Party, which they never officially joined. As far as the image of the Soviet Union in the West, it is important to remember the falling out between Sartre and Albert Camus in 1952. Once the Stalinist gulags became known through the French press, Camus argued that, after the Holocaust, it was crucial to confront the French Communist Party on this issue. In contrast to Camus's disappointment with Stalinism, Sartre felt his colleague's position was too demanding.

Within this context it is worth noting that in 1950 Bazin had already
discussed the shortcomings of Soviet sociorealism in "The Myth of
Stalin in the Soviet Cinema."[22]

The 1950s in France saw the continuation of the surrealist avant-
garde,[23] which Sartre wrote against but whose historical importance
Bazin was well aware of, even if neither the film critic nor the philosopher ever embraced psychoanalysis. The two thinkers shared a
cognitive approach. As Dudley Andrew explains, regarding Sartre's
1940 work:

> *The Psychology of the Imagination* is a crucial text because it links art
> to ontology. Sartre found it necessary to consider art as indispens-
> able in man's psychological effort to avoid or to go beyond his real
> conditions. . . .
>
> Sartre . . . conceives of art as an activity by which human beings
> try to remake the world and their situation in it. Art is just one way we
> deal with this impulse; it is comparable to daydreaming, to emotional
> release, and to certain acts of the imagination, which for Sartre would
> include . . . lovemaking, political activism, and suicide. All these modes
> show man trying to shape, in the emptiness of his consciousness, the
> fullness of a world he can call his own. . . . By means of the various
> modes of consciousness we term "imaginary" man overcomes the
> determinateness and inescapable solidity of an alien world. . . . Art is
> a privileged mode of the "imaginary," for it creates a human object
> alongside the world of alien objects.[24]

In other words, Sartre's art competes with alienation, while imagination makes life livable. Bazin valued creativity in nature and culture,
but he knew that cinema was not always art. Inasmuch as Bazin loved
literature and theater, he disliked painting's elitism. In contrast to
pictorial virtuosity, photography's natural and technological creativity thrives on traces made of light and on the absence of the human
hand in making an image. Furthermore, photography's automatism
aligns this technology with the creation of new life or the metaphorical birth of a child with a fresh attitude. Photography, like the
cinema, is cosmological because it is based on direct contact. Nature
is the artist. As Dudley Andrew observes:

The real force in Bazin's claim lies in his observation that the solution to the problem of psychology in the arts comes not as a *result* of increased realism but from a new way of *achieving* realism. . . .

In a psychological sense, realism then has to do not with the accuracy of the reproduction but with the spectator's belief about its origin. . . .

Bazin's crucial point, that realism stems more from the means of picture-taking than from its product, clearly stems from deep meditation on Sartre's discussion of the role of the image in art.

Sartre's ideas pose a great problem for the photographic arts because, in his view, all image-making must be an intentional act of consciousness.[25]

Sartre and Bazin alike associated creativity with art and human beings, but in the special case of photography, Bazin situated its creative force in nature's contingency and technology's automatism. Most important, the physiochemical traces of photography, in comparison with all the other images before and after this unique invention, have the irrational power to defy our disbelief. This is the case because a photograph activates the illusion of being in the momentous presence of something or someone absent. In contrast to Sartre, Bazin defined the photographic event in surrealist terms. This move did not come because Bazin embraced Freud's unconscious but because the film critic wanted to underline that any photograph is simultaneously an objective fact and a subjective hallucination. By drawing on his Catholic cultural background, Bazin had a Christological view of photography. It is the paradoxical incarnation of the earthly and the cosmological, the human and the nonhuman.

Sartre found surrealism to be infantile in its attachment to a vulgarized understanding of Freud's theories. In addition, for Sartre surrealism, despite its rhetoric of shock, eroticism, and transgression, was politically contradictory. The fact that Louis Aragon had become a dogmatic Communist and that André Breton took a stance against colonialism in Algeria was not enough.

The more Sartre became politicized and traveled internationally, the more Bazin emerged as an inclusive but totally free-spirited thinker more interested in ethics than in either aesthetic contemplation or political loyalty. His allegiances were neither to Saint Sulpice—namely, the most conservative wing of the Catholic Church—nor to Moscow through the French Communist Party. Bazin's refusal to join anyone's institutional camp enabled him to write more freely in the Parisian dailies and to change his mind if he wanted to, without having to uphold a party line or an institutional policy. He approved or disapproved of work by the very same director. He wrote in defense of Italian neorealism, but he also described the degeneration of this approach in several Italian films. He praised the Catholic Fipresci award during film festivals and had great respect for Peuple et culture, another Catholic activist cultural group. However, he chose to work, along with Chris Marker, for the Communist cultural organization Travail et culture. As far as developing *ciné-clubs,* giving lectures, running discussions, and screening films in factories, cinema always came first. In short, personal celebrity was not as important for Bazin as it was for the cosmopolitan Sartre.

Sartre's Nihilism and Christian Existentialism

Although he admired Sartre's literary criticism, Bazin was much more influenced by the personalist movement of the community activist Emmanuel Mounier (1905–50) and by the essays of the playwright Gabriel Marcel (1889–1973). An engaging thinker but not a professional philosopher, Marcel was close to Mounier, and both were much more polemical with Sartre than Bazin ever was.[26] In contrast to American individualism, Soviet collectivism, or French capitalism, personalism looked for a new model of social relations. Often confused with a so-called third way, the personalist model argued the constant interrogation of ethical values was more important than financial greed and economic power. In the footsteps of the utopian thinker Pierre-Joseph Proudhon, Mounier spoke against elitism, Adam Smith's free market, and anti-Semitism in conjunction with the release of Veit Harlan's *Jud Süß* (1940). Personalism advocated a dialectical definition of intersubjectivity, the constant growth of a person's moral sense, and self-interrogation through Otherness. Marcel, for example, coined the paradoxical concept *creative fidelity,* an open-ended, two-way street that would respect differences among people as well as media.[27] An advocate of adaptation as the flip side of adoption, Bazin's worldview was symbiotic because it was based on dynamic relationships. Inasmuch as he cherished freedom, action, responsibility, choice, eccentricity, and exception, it was not possible for him to identify with Sartre's egotistical definitions of these concepts. Sartre was a nihilist, and his brand of existentialism was influenced by Dostoevsky's cynical dictum: "God is dead, everything is permissible." Mounier, by contrast, did not even include Dostoevsky in his book on the history of different branches of existentialism.[28] Sartre described how someone's "look" could degrade the Other to an object. In his play *Huis clos* (*No Exit*, 1944),[29] Sartre went so far as to declare, "Hell is other people." Without relations with other people, we cannot define ourselves, yet these relations are so complex that they also alienate us.

In an ethical sense Bazin's famous question, What is cinema? also meant, What is a human? *Citizen Kane's* deep focus, for example, was of interest to the critic because it stood up against Hollywood's Manichean ideals of good and evil. With Welles, moral ambiguity and human limitations had moved center stage, with an unprecedented force, in American cinema. This development implied a new attitude toward humankind, which European critics had already encountered in Jean Renoir's *La règle du jeu* (*The Rules of the Game*, 1939). In this film nobody is a monster; each character—rich or poor—is unhappy, struggling, and caught up in their own misperceptions and biases. In the end, "everybody has his reasons." Renoir's questioning of individual mediocrity, selfishness, and delusions asks all of us to evaluate subjective perception in the guise of "personal reasons" at the end of his darkest film, released right before Germany's occupation of France. After World War II, during the trials to prosecute French collaboration with Nazism, the ethical debate on moral codes had reached a new level of urgency. Bazin called attention to "the need to recall, across the political divisions of the world, the reality of man."[30] Interestingly, political disagreements, for Bazin, could also stimulate the urgency for an antianthropocentric and post–World War II neohumanism. As Mounier had declared in the first issue of *Esprit* (1932), a new kind of Renaissance had been long overdue. After gestating throughout the thirties during a series of ups and downs, detours and dead ends, this new personalist humanism was supposed to rally against man's superiority on the basis of technology or money in order to deal with the moral weaknesses of humankind. Put another way, technology and money alone, without ethics or spirituality, could not bring about the postwar development of Mounier's "social person."

Man's reality involves how each of us handles living with oneself and with Others. Thus, Sartre's concept of good faith and his call for a project based on authenticity stroke the most powerful chord. Yet the humanist side of existentialism is not enough to explain Bazin's famous question, What is cinema? Hence, it is necessary to briefly address Bazin's theological position. A dissident Catholic on the left, Bazin was certainly a personalist. Well aware that by 1945 Christianity had become a corrupt religion, Bazin was interested in retailoring its ethos through the cinema, the mass medium that allowed everybody to be alone but not lonely, accountable but not absolute. Although Mounier had been quite critical of Sartre's existentialism,[31] his movement included individuals of multiple religious faiths–Catholic, Protestant, Jewish—as well as atheists. Likewise, Bazin made sure to be in a position that would allow him to dialogue with anyone genuinely interested in the future and the value of the cinema.

Sartre quickly became famous as a politically engaged intellectual who traveled all over the world. Yet he was not the one who invented the persona of the cosmopolitan intellectual. To be sure, a much less glamorous idea of social engagement was proposed, for the first time, by Mounier because he was extremely alarmed about the future of French education.[32] Personalism's attention to the development of character, the role of self-consciousness, and the ethics of social behavior did underpin Bazin's constant critical concern with the direction of actors and acting styles. These two most delicate aspects of filmmaking involve working with and against personal boundaries during film performance. Bazin's discussions of specific actors and actresses in relation to mise-en-scène muse on the egalitarian interrelation of elements—i.e., the staging of objects, animals, and landscape around the actor's body. Otherness is as important as the performer, so much so that the human element is not the center of filmmaking but only a component within an equalizing system comprising dialectical and potentially analogical terms of reference. For Bazin the cinema can offer a moving-picture gallery of behaviors to be freely evaluated by the audience. During a film the viewers constantly shift their terms of identification from the camera shots to the characters' point of view of each other and on the world. The cinema is such a kinetic experience of multiple and changing ways of seeing that it can decenter and recenter viewers, as happened in classical Hollywood cinema. In the postwar European art film, however, cinema's decentering of viewers into a modernist, non-Euclidean space of unstable or contradictory appearances marked an irreversible epistemological shift. In the wake of the Holocaust and Hiroshima, 1945 spelled out that confidence in human knowledge and control was no longer possible unless radically new models of living together could be found in touch with issues of difference and marginality within postcapitalist societies and the postcolonial world. Unfortunately, 1945 also paved the way for the Cold War's polarization, such that the personalist agenda stood out even more forcefully within Bazin's antianthropocentric, symbiotic, and cosmological film theory.

Cinema, for Bazin, was the medium where the arts of man and the sciences of the earth dialogue with each other by interrogating the cosmos through a screen that hides and reveals. By stating that "photography is a fragment of the universe,"[33] Bazin reminded us that a photograph is a natural image, a factual trace made of light and matter. He maintained that we need cinema to record our imperfect ways of being human and to learn how to relate to Others. The value of this photographic, antianthropocentric recording is to encounter, from the point of view of the future, the Otherness of the past. Bazin's interrogation of what is "human" in man called for a definition of the nonhuman, such as animals, plants, minerals. It is well known, for example, that Bazin loved animals and that he admired the free-spiritedness of Roberto Rossellini's *The Flowers of Saint Francis* (1950). Often considered to be "the Saint Francis of post-war film theory," Bazin was more of a cultural activist than an isolated mystic. While Bazin's love for animals anticipated our contemporary interest in biodiversity, his approval of Rossellini's Saint Francis was due to how the ruthless individualism of the Renaissance needed to temper itself with medieval spirituality.

Since Bazin's library is not available, it is possible to work with only one kind of written evidence: Bazin's published and unpublished writings, which call for the transfiguration of science into a lyrical style of writing. Both science and poetry are human endeavors, but science is based on repeatable and shareable experiments through predictable laws and quantifiable results. Science fights misperceptions and ignorance by challenging mistakes and superstitions. Poetry, by contrast, comes from inspiration or, in a physiological sense, from the breathing of life itself. The latter is as uncontrollable as the wind. Inspiration's *souffle vital* is comparable to an energizing connection. As a form of abstract language, poetry is the oxygen of human spirituality, which for Bazin was supposed to pave the way toward ethical self-interrogation. As lyrical as it was, Bazin's metaphorical prose is difficult to read and summarize unless one becomes familiar with his constant reliance on the history of science. For example, Bazin was keen on the science of meteorology and played on the French homophone *temps,* which means both "time" and "weather." Neither weather nor time is under human control; likewise, inspiration can prompt lyricism, sharing, and love. In contrast with his antianthropocentric transfiguration of science through poetry, Bazin acknowledged the "scientific tree of photography"[34] because the scientific tree of human knowledge leans more toward utilitarian goals than toward spiritual insights.

Besides supporting Mounier's legacy, Bazin was familiar with the ideas of Gabriel Marcel (1889–1973), a playwright and Christian existentialist who placed art above science, just as the film critic did in his film theory. In *The Mystery of Being* (1951), Marcel held that an elusive dimension exists within man and nature. For Marcel this mystery was

> something in which I am myself involved, whereas a problem, as the Greek literal meaning suggests, is "thrown" before us and can therefore be objectified. . . . Consequently a mystery is not thinkable except as a sphere in which the distinction of what is in me from what is before me loses its meaning and its initial value.[35]

In short, Bazin turned the cinema into his lay vocation because of the egalitarian impact of the cinematic lens over everything it sees. Sartre believed literature and left-wing political activism could change the world. Bazin believed in cinema's power to rejuvenate perception and bridge the divide between Self and Other during the Cold War and the space age of the fifties. For Sartre the world was absurd, lonely, but there was action and freedom. For Bazin, too, action was important, because Bergson had embraced William James's pragmatic view of action as an expression of belief. In addition, since man is only one component of a much larger, intricate, and unstable milieu, the world of nature is worthy of our respect, even if it knows no morality. Human society with its evils needs our forgiveness not for the sake of oblivion but in order to overcome revenge and be open to new models of behavior. In other words, suffering should promote spiritual growth instead of leading to deeper divisions. Due to their contrasting attitudes toward nature and culture, Bazin became more and more disappointed with the impact of nihilist existentialism on French life. Sartre had become a "fashion." In his film reviews Bazin openly decried the rebellious, pessimistic, and jaded attitudes of a 1950s youth culture hypnotized by the philosopher of Saint-Germain-des-Prés.[36]

The Philosophical Matrix of Bazin's Film Theory

In order to understand the overarching framework of Bazin's film theory, one needs to investigate the ways in which Saint Augustine, Blaise Pascal, Henri Bergson, and Maurice Merleau-Ponty are relevant to the critic. Saint Augustine (354–430) underlined the coexistence of good and evil within every individual. As a religious leader in a time of extreme divisions and bloodshed, Augustine was the first to understand how personal and collective histories become interrelated in the choices of daily life.[37] Bazin's cinema—a time machine—found in Saint Augustine its first visionary philosopher in terms of ethical consciousness and social justice. For Augustine, God's creation of the universe coincided with the creation of time. It was impossible to know whether God created time or if God was time itself. From a human standpoint, neither God's eternity nor human time fit parameters of rationality and control. As the Other to human beings, God's time—namely, eternity—is accessible only through religious faith. In the footsteps of Augustine's emphasis on resurrection, time is the true protagonist of Bazin's film theory.

In the wake of Augustine's asceticism, Jansenius (1585–1638) developed a movement calling for clarity and modesty that appealed to Blaise Pascal (1623–62). Centered in the Parisian convent of Port-Royal, a Jansenist group of Catholic philosophers, scientists, and theologians who opposed the Jesuits' tendency to attract as many

followers as possible without questioning sincerity of faith, moral lax-
ity, and political corruption. Pascal's insights on the contradictions of
human nature shed light on Bazin's antianthropocentric film theory.
Within this framework man is only one little yet morally responsible
element within an ultimately unknowable universe. For instance, in
his essay about theater, Bazin stated:

> The camera puts at the disposal of the director all the resources of the
> telescope and the microscope. The last strand of a rope about to snap
> or an entire army making an assault on a hill are within our reach.
> Dramatic causes and effects have no longer any material limits to the
> eye of the camera. Drama is freed by the camera from all contingencies
> of time and space.[38]

This statement implies objects or masses that are either very small
or very large—and therefore too difficult for the human eye to see
unaided—become perceivable through the nonhuman lens of the
camera. All of a sudden, it is the nonhuman scale and size of uncontrollable events that become the protagonists of the dramatic action,
thus displacing human superiority, centrality, and agency. According to Pascal, the physical proportions of our body alone prevent us
from exchanging our own placement in the world with the very far
and the very small.

The microscope and the telescope register two limit points, while
they can also refer to the close-up and the aerial view. Because photography is based on tracing that which existed, cinema's realist vocation does not lie with either the invisible subatomic or the impossible
supernatural. Even if it operates beyond gravity's constraints on the
screen, the nonhuman lens of cinema can suggest abstraction, through
a miniature or a gigantic scale, much more eloquently than through
special technological effects. Geared toward realism, cinema's technology matches human perception to elicit belief.

In a word, for Bazin cinema can make time visible, open space to
contingency, create by either design or chance, interconnect across the
living and the dead, link the external to the internal, show egalitarian
relations, and even reveal some potential analogies among objects,
plants, animals, machines, and human beings. These very same analo-

gies are valuable because they have the power to displace rigid meanings that often consolidate themselves into clichés.

In the case of the aerial view and the close-up, the interface between the nonhuman lens and the human eye may lead to nonfigurative yet still perceivable images. In Bazin's antianthropocentric cinema, the aerial view and the close-up can reposition normal sight on the margins of an incommensurable but still representable event. Even if humankind would like to control nature as well as culture, it is fully embroiled in a world of appearances. Without the nonhuman eye of the camera joining human perception in the cinema, we could not experience insights into the realities that we constantly try to grasp and that constantly baffle us. For Pascal this condition of incommensurability between subject and object, the human and the nonhuman is tragic and unavoidable. While using the term *grace* to speak about chance, Pascal argues that human beings are nothing in relation to the infinite but also everything in front of nothingness. What the Jansenist philosopher means is that man is inevitably imperfect in an existential sense. For the personalist Bazin the only way to bypass human incompleteness is through respect for the Other, even if the Other does not reciprocate or if it is so nonhuman it cannot do so at the same level. Love is a stronger action than hate. For Saint Augustine, Pascal, and Bazin, human nature is ambiguous, since man is neither an angel nor an animal but a being struggling between these two extremes. This means man is an impure yet unique mix of greatness and misery, of errors and consciousness.

As a mathematician, a physicist, and an inventor, Pascal's religious faith was nevertheless more important than his science. This is why after studying the void in physics, Pascal concluded irrational faith or spirituality could better sense the infinite than could the precise measurements of mathematical ingenuity. The unknowable is neither a number nor a formula. Pascal believed science could only partially explain where the human element fit within the universe. Thus, for him, science needs religion, logic needs prayer, hope needs example. The problem of God's existence prompted Pascal to formulate the famous wager out of his fascination with risk, probability, and gambling.[39] Whether or not God existed, Pascal's idea was to behave as if this were indeed the case.

Clearly, Bazin admired Pascal's clarity, simplicity, and depth—
and most of all, his use of paradoxes. In this regard, one final point
of contact between Pascal and Bazin's film theory has to do with
"the logic of the heart,"[40] or with how intuitive thinking (*esprit de
finesse*) can go further than geometrical reasoning (*esprit de géométrie*).
This anti-Cartesian recovery of intuition links Pascal's philosophy to
Henri Bergson's interest in process and becoming.

The turn-of-the-century philosopher had studied in depth many
kinds of mathematics, ranging from algebra and Euclidean geometry to differential calculus. By asking how the measuring time of
science differs from the streaming time of interiority, Henri Bergson
(1859–1941) formulated his concept of "duration." The latter involves
a psychological dimension or a stream of consciousness. As an in-
divisible, heterogeneous process, duration overflows into memories
from the past while pulling in the imagination of the future.

In the wake of Bergson's emphasis on the present tense of film
projection as duration, Bazin upheld the long take. In contrast to
Soviet montage, this technique would do justice to the integrity or
continuity of real space. In addition, by matching real time, the duration of the long take would also encourage the spectators to be
more in touch with their own sense of inner time. This is not to say
that Bazin disliked editing. Whereas the long take coincided with the
camera's exploration of the world, editing conveyed the operations of
human thought.

The crucial point was the equal importance of the human and
the nonhuman, because the world through camera movement was as
valuable as the thoughts of editing. The film critic was against a kind
of editing that simplified reality in the light of human superiority. It
eliminates analogical or ambiguous relations by dividing reality into
binary oppositions.

Closer to Bergson's creative evolution than to Darwin's natural
selection, Bazin's evolutionary model for the history of film language
depends on contingency, self-consciousness, free will, human creativity, and technological change. Bergson felt the human species was not
the climax of a teleological trajectory but only one of the many possible outcomes of an unpredictable process made of steps backward
and steps forward, hiatuses and leaps.

Bergson argued that life does not handle change out of intelligence and organization, the way an engineer would tackle and solve a problem. Even though he wrote his major works way before the popularization of quantum physics, the idea of contingency is intertwined with Bergson's élan vital, or perpetual motion. Bergson's élan vital is a wave that overcomes obstacles, although it can still remember them. It is a larger concept than Darwin's instinct for survival because regardless or beyond natural selection, this concept describes the uncontrollable and unpredictable resilience of life everywhere. Intelligence cannot explain life, but life depends on instinct for animals and on intelligence, together with intuition, for humankind. Intuition and intelligence are never opposite for Bergson, though these two resources are both incomplete. The first is too repetitive, and the second is too schematizing. Yet whenever intuition becomes the instinct of intelligence, it is possible to experience a moment of spiritual illumination in the intricacies of one's own embedding within reality.

By sharing these kinds of introspective and rare experiences through epiphanies, Bazin felt that a cinema of editing and camera movement could lay bare the interconnectedness of beings and things. By so doing, the cinema would underline the value of spirituality and mutual respect for the world to which humankind belongs. Bergson argued the technologically inclined Western world had made too much room for intelligence and logic alone. Thus, philosophy's task was to reestablish the unity of mental life by moving from intuition to intelligence, because the reverse shift from intelligence to intuition was not possible.

The relations between Maurice Merleau-Ponty (1908–61) and Bazin are intricate because they cut across painting and literature, science and cinema. While there is no evidence of an official encounter between the personalist film critic and the philosopher of phenomenology, they were inevitably conscious of their respective contributions. Well aware of Bergson's uneasiness with cinematic technology, Merleau-Ponty was interested in the cinema, although he was cautious in his statements. He corrected Bergson's dismissal of the cinématographe as an example of intellectual compartmentalizing and spatial thinking. Bergson's rejection of the cinema took place at a time when this newborn medium was used only as a scientific tool for motion studies.[41] At the end of "The Ontology of the Photographic Image," Bazin mentions Cézanne by saying: "So, when form, in the person of Cézanne, once more regains possession of the canvas there is no longer any question of the illusions of the geometry of perspective."[42] Thus, the film theorist sided with phenomenology, or with Merleau-Ponty's fascination with an emerging and alternative order—that is, any object in the act of appearing in a new, albeit subjective way. Bazin's "Ontology" was published in 1945, the same year as Merleau-Ponty's *Phenomenology of Perception*.

The phenomenologist's work on Cézanne is useful in distinguishing his brand of existentialism from Sartre's nihilism. Merleau-Ponty admired Cézanne because the painter's style grasped the ever-changing rhythms of Mont Sainte-Victoire. For Cézanne this mountain was alive, and he painted it multiple times, every time in a different way. Nothing was permanently set any longer. Thus, Cézanne was a painter in doubt because he was trying to represent the world's perpetual motion on a static canvas. Merleau-Ponty was keen on how landscape would register itself on Cézanne's nervous system and on how the artist would suggest the mountain's restless appearance through light, color, and quasi-abstract shapes. With Cézanne, Euclidean geometry breaks down once and for all, while the line of drawing and geometry becomes obsolete. Difficult to prove, however, is the argument that, in contrast to the conceptual pairing of Merleau-Ponty and Cézanne, Sartre's emphasis on alienation found his strongest spokesperson in Alberto Giacometti. Without a doubt, Sartre's rejection of any theological grounding resonated in Giacometti's thin and emaciated figurines. In "The Search for the Absolute" (1948), Sartre spoke of thoughts of stone haunting Giacometti, of his *horror vacui,* namely his fear of empty space and his sense of desolate sterility.[43]

Were we to move away from sculpture and return to the cinema, however, Giacometti's insights are much closer to Merleau-Ponty's phenomenology, which runs parallel to Bazin's film theory. For Giacometti the cinema destabilized his rigid ways of seeing:

> It happened after the war, around 1945, I think. Until then . . . there was a split between the way I saw the outside world and the way I saw what was going on on the screen. One was a continuation of the other. Until the day there was a real split: instead of seeing a person on screen I saw vague black blobs moving. I looked at the people around me and as a

result I saw them as I had never seen them. . . . I remember very clearly
coming out on the Boulevard du Montparnasse and seeing the Boulevard as I had never seen it before. Everything was different: depth, objects, colours and the silence. . . . Everything seemed different to me and
completely new. . . . It was, if you like, a kind of continual marveling at
whatever was there. . . . That day reality was completely revalued for me;
it became unknown, but at the same time a marvelous unknown.[44]

Besides encountering each other in Cézanne's quasi-abstract landscapes before cubism, Bazin and Merleau-Ponty shared an interest
in quantum physics. This openness toward contingency characterized
Mounier's personalist thought, since the founder of *Esprit* urged the
Vatican to accept Louis de Broglie's 1924 discovery of a wave/particle
duality in the depths of matter.[45]

According to Werner Heisenberg's principle of indeterminacy,
mathematics becomes fuzzy because at the subatomic level randomness and flux—namely, élan vital's perpetual motion—prevail
over exact measurements. Heisenberg stated that certain kinds of
knowledge—for example, a particle's position and its velocity—
cannot be calculated simultaneously. The more precisely one property is measured, the blurrier and more uncertain the other becomes.
Wave and particle do coexist, yet despite their consubstantial status,
they are mutually exclusive. This theme of indeterminacy reappears
in Bazin's argument that reality is opaque, obscure, and elusive.

Heisenberg belonged to the Danish school of modern physics,
which found a serious opponent in Albert Einstein. An advocate of
mathematical time, Einstein deeply disagreed with Henri Bergson's
defense of psychological time in *Duration and Simultaneity* (1922).
With this controversial book, the philosopher of élan vital failed to
defend his ideas against the famous physicist. Besides dismissing his
"spiritualism," Einstein kept pointing out how weird quantum physics really was. The problem was not just between wave and particle
but also with the paradox of their unpredictable locations in space
next to their inevitable entanglement. Einstein concluded that no
reasonable definition of reality could be expected to permit this.
More work needed to be done. The Danish school's arguments were
only transitional. There must be, he proposed, a deeper theory that
looked way behind or beyond the appearances of the quantum veil.

Besides updating the relationship between Bergson and cinematic technology, Merleau-Ponty should be credited for his loyalty to Bergson's duration. In contrast to Gaston Bachelard, who ridiculed the old philosopher, Merleau-Ponty upheld Bergson's stream of consciousness during the latter's controversial debate with Einstein. Bergson's stream of consciousness found its most diversified responses in the world of literature. In her famous review of *What Is Cinema?* volume I, Annette Michelson lined up Joyce and Eisenstein in opposition to Bazin and American realism: "We know that, for Eisenstein, the twentieth century was not, as for Bazin, 'The Age of the American Novel,' but that of Joyce." David Trotter, however, has recently demonstrated that even if Eisenstein thought of bringing *Ulysses* (1922) to the screen, the encounter between Joyce and the founder of intellectual montage was quite thin. Michelson's negative reduction of Bazin to a passive disciple of Sartre and to the middlebrow realism of Stephen Crane, Theodore Dreiser, Frank Norris, and Ernest Hemingway is odd. To be sure, Merleau-Ponty embraced a broadly defined perceptual model as flexible as the various kinds of films Bazin supported. Merleau-Ponty's literary framework accommodated utterly different writers, such as James Joyce, William Faulkner, and Fyodor Dostoyevsky because it placed all of them under the rubric of the *stream of consciousness.*[46]

Patrick Bourgeois, a historian of phenomenology, points out that Merleau-Ponty's heterogeneous literary horizon became possible because he believed in polymorphous time and living simultaneities. Needless to say, these two categories approximate the perception of the world in motion proposed by the cinema. They also ground editing and camera movement within the stream of consciousness of film viewing and projection. Bourgeois writes that Merleau-Ponty agrees with Bergson in affirming that when perceivers perceive one another, there is a "restitution of all duration to a unified whole."[47]

In other words, for Bazin and Merleau-Ponty, reality is ontologically ambiguous, in flux, amorphous, but it does amount to a dynamic whole or a current of energy, even if we tend to dissect its perpetual motion into separate parts to reassure ourselves that we are in control. Due to our arrogance, we like to think we know what is what, in contrast to how we just perceive the world through our prejudices. As a medium based on perception rather than on knowledge, the cinema can remind us of this state of affairs.

Thanks to Mauro Carbone's historical account of the philosopher's statements on the cinema,[48] we know that Merleau-Ponty gave a lecture at the Institut des hautes études cinématographiques in Paris in 1945. Again, the philosopher discussed filmic movement in his notes for the 1952–53 course "The Sensible World and the World of Expression." As far as engaging a popular audience comparable to the one Bazin was regularly addressing in a variety of newspapers, Merleau-Ponty explained the connection between modern art and Cézanne's non-Euclidean space on the radio during seven educational lectures, or *causeries,* for a program called the *French Culture Hour.*[49] This program also hosted Bazin's mentor, Emmanuel Mounier, who spoke on the psychology of character.

Merleau-Ponty's sixth lecture included an open-minded yet prudent statement on cinema's future potential. The phenomenologist's sentences possibly look back at Bergson's work on ever-shifting temporalities and spell out the latter's interest in musical rhythm:

> Cinema has yet to provide us with many films that are works of art from start to finish: its infatuation with stars, the sensationalism of the zoom, the twists and turns of plot and the intrusion of pretty pictures and witty dialogue, are all tempting pitfalls for films which chase success and, in so doing, eschew properly cinematic means of expression. . . . What matters is the selection of episodes to be represented and, in each one, the choice of shots that will be featured in the film, the length of time allotted to these elements, the order in which they are or are not to be accompanied. . . . All these factors contribute to form a particular overall cinematographical rhythm. . . . The way we experience works of cinema will be through perception.[50]

Significantly, Merleau-Ponty's broadcast happened one year after the presentation of Roberto Rossellini's *Paisà* in 1947 at the first Cannes Film Festival after the war. One wonders if and when Merleau-Ponty became aware of Bazin's celebration of Italian neorealism in the light of French phenomenology. Whatever the case may be, according to Carbone, in a course scheduled for 1960–61, Merleau-Ponty endorsed fully Bazin's film theory based on photographic ontology. Bazin had opened up a new horizon of intellectual inquiry for him. Merleau-Ponty's teaching notes suggest a much greater degree of enthusiasm for the cinema:

André Bazin ontologie du cinéma
    Dans les arts
    Cinéma ontologie du cinéma—Ex. La question du mouvement au
    cinéma.[51]

André Bazin and Maurice Merleau-Ponty were two wonderful minds interrogating human perception, the history of science, and the relationship between cinema and the other arts. In contrast to Bazin, who valued literature over painting, Merleau-Ponty thought the study of painting as a static, subjective universe of its own could help him explain his "priority of perception" over knowledge—namely, the interface between consciousness and the world. Despite their different views on the arts, the film critic and the philosopher did agree that humans, in life and in the cinema, can be seen only from the outside. It would seem, therefore, that Mounier's interest in Otherness became an indispensable source of ideas for Bazin, while his personalist orientation matched Merleau-Ponty's interest in animals' behavior and children's psychology.

NOTES

1. "As for the characters themselves, they exist and change only in reference to a purely internal time—which I cannot qualify even as Bergsonian, in so far as Bergson's theory of the *Données immédiates de la conscience* contains a strong element of psychologism. Let us avoid the vague terms of a 'spiritualizing' vocabulary. Let us not say that the transformation of the characters takes place at the level of the 'soul.' But it has at least to occur at that depth of their being into which consciousness only occasionally reaches down." Bazin, *What Is Cinema*, vol. 2, 85.

2. Fautrier, "Le cinéma de Sartre," 103–4.

3. "Une mayonnaise qui aurait refusée de prendre." Bazin, "Jean-Paul Sartre," 2. On the topic of Sartre and the cinema, see also Rohdie, "Jean-Paul Sartre, Hollywood, *Citizen Kane* and the Nouvelle Vague."

4. Andrew, *André Bazin*, 47.

5. Bazin, "La technique de *Citizen Kane*," 943–49. In 1950 Merleau-Ponty left *Temps modernes* because he could not identify with Sartre's Marxism. The title of this prestigious journal was inspired by Chaplin's *Modern Times* (1936).

6. Sartre's essay on Welles's *Citizen Kane* "Quand Hollywood veut faire penser," is reprinted in Leenhardt, *Chroniques du cinéma*, 113, 116.

7. See Sartre, "John Dos Passos et *1919*."

8. See Sartre, "À propos de *Le bruit et la fureur.*"

9. Bazin, *Orson Welles,* 81.

10. Ibid., 77–78.

11. Ibid., 80.

12. Ibid., 81.

13. Ibid., 78.

14. Chateau, *Sartre et le cinéma,* 66. "La nature même du médium cinématographique est . . . , pour lui, anti-existentialiste et aussi peu phénoménologique que possible. À propos de *La Rue sans joie* de Pabst, remarque Astruc, le philosophe montre que 'le cinéma, mieux que tout autres arts, est propre . . . à donner l'image du destin. . . . Cela veut seulement dire que la clef du destin tout à l'opposite de la contingence des choses de la vie—définissait, à ses yeux, la spécificité du cinéma.'"

15. See Ungaro, *André Bazin.*

16. See Sartre, "The Humanism of Existentialism."

17. Bazin, "In Defense of Mixed Cinema," vii.

18. On these issues, see Vacche, "The Difference of Cinema"; and Vacche, "Interstices and Impurities in the Cinema."

19. See Sartre, *Nausea.*

20. Sartre, *The Words,* 118–19.

21. Ibid., 119.

22. Bazin, "The Myth of Stalin in the Soviet Cinema," 23–40.

23. On postwar surrealism, see Vacche, "Surrealism in Art and Film"; Beaujour, "Sartre and Surrealism."

24. Andrew, *André Bazin,* 61–62.

25. Ibid., 66–67.

26. Mounier, *Introduction aux existentialismes.* See also Marcel, *The Philosophy of Existentialism.*

27. On personalism, see Sawchenko, "The Concept of the Person."

28. See Mounier, *Introduction aux Existentialismes.*

29. Bazin, "*Huis Clos,*" 6.

30. "Le besoin de retrouver, à travers les divisions politiques du monde, la réalité de l'homme." Bazin, "Le petit monde de Don Camillo," 2.

31. Mounier, *Introduction aux Existentialismes.*

32. Ibid., 79–92.

33. Bazin, "Le cinéma et la peinture," 116.

34. Bazin, "Un musée des ombres, magie blanche, magie noire."

35. Sawchenko, "The Concept of the Person," 23; see also Marcel, *The Mystery of Being,* vols. 1 and 2.

36. See Bazin, "Les mauvaises rencontres."

37. On God and the nature of time, see book 11 in Augustine, *The Confessions of St. Augustine,* 257–84.

38. Bazin, *What Is Cinema?,* vol. 1, 103.

39. "Blaise Pascal (1623–1662) offers a pragmatic reason for believing in God: even under the assumption that God's existence is unlikely, the potential benefits of believing are so vast as to make betting on theism rational." Saka, "Pascal's Wager about God," top of page.

40. See Peters, *Augustine, Pascal, and the Rationality of Faith*.

41. Bergson, *Creative Evolution*, 298–313. On Merleau-Ponty's rereading of Bergson and the cinema, see Carbone, "Merleau-Ponty and the Thinking of Cinema."

42. Bazin, *What Is Cinema?*, vol. 1, 15–16.

43. Satre, "La recherche de l'absolu," 153–63.

44. Peppiatt, *Alberto Giacometti in Postwar Paris*, 7.

45. Mounier, *Personalism*, 6. On the controversy between Bergson and Einstein, see also Canales, *The Physicist and the Philosopher*; on quantum physics, literature, and phenomenology, see Dolidze, "Phenomenology in Science and Literature."

46. See Michelson, Review of *What Is Cinema?*; see also Trotter, "James Joyce and the Automatism of the Photographic Image."

47. Bourgeois, "Maurice Merleau-Ponty," 355–56.

48. See Carbone, "Le Philosophe et le cinéaste."

49. On Maurice Merleau-Ponty, art, science, and psychology, see Baldwin, introduction to *The World of Perception*.

50. Ibid., 73.

51. See Carbone, "Le Philosophe et le cinéaste."

BIBLIOGRAPHY

Andrew, Dudley. *André Bazin*. New York: Oxford University Press, 2013.

Augustine, Saint. *The Confessions of St. Augustine*. Translated by Rex Warner. New York: New American Library, 1963.

Baldwin, Thomas. Introduction to *The World of Perception*, by Maurice Merleau-Ponty. London: Routledge, 2009.

Bazin, André. "*Huis clos:* Un film curieux." *Parisien libéré*, December 28, 1954, 6.

———. "Jean-Paul Sartre: Vedette du jour au festival de Cannes." *Parisien libéré*, September 18, 1947, 2.

———. "La technique de *Citizen Kane*." *Temps modernes*, February 17, 1947, 943–49.

———. "Le cinéma et la peinture." *La revue du cinéma* 19, no. 2 (Fall 1949): 116.

———. "Le petit monde de Don Camillo." *Parisien libéré*, June 9, 1952, 2.

———. "Les mauvaises rencontres . . . mais de bonnes ambitions." *Parisien libéré*, October 31, 1955.

———. "The Myth of Stalin in the Soviet Cinema." In *Bazin at Work*, edited by Bert Cardullo, 23–40. New York: Routledge, 1997.

————. *Orson Welles: A Critical View.* Los Angeles: Acrobat Books, 1991.

————. "Un musée des ombres, magie blanche, magie noire." *Écran Français,* December, 21 1948.

————. *What Is Cinema?* Vol. 1. Berkeley: University of California Press, 2005.

————. *What is Cinema?* Vol. 2. Berkeley: University of California Press, 2005.

Beaujour, Michel. 'Sartre and Surrealism. " *Yale French Studies* 30 (1963): 86–95.

Bergson, Henri. *Creative Evolution.* Translated by Arthur Mitchell. Mineola, N.Y.: Dover Publications, 1998.

Bourgeois, Patrick. "Maurice Merleau-Ponty: Philosophy as Phenomenology." In *Phenomenology World-Wide: Foundations, Expanding Dynamics, Life-Engagements,* edited by Anna-Teresa Tymieniecka, 355–56. New York: Springer, 2002.

Canales, Jimena. *The Physicist and the Philosopher: Einstein, Bergson, and the Debate That Changed Our Understanding of Time.* Princeton, N.J.: Princeton University Press, 2015.

Carbone, Mauro. "Le philosophe et le cinéaste: Merleau-Ponty et la pensée du cinema." In *La chair des images: Merleau-Ponty entre peinture et cinéma,* 85–127. Paris: VRIN, 2011.

————. "Merleau-Ponty and the Thinking of Cinema." *Chiasmi International: Philosophy and Moving Pictures,* no. 12 (2010): 47–70.

Chateau, Dominique. *Sartre et le cinema.* Biarritz, France: Atlantica-Seguier, 2005.

Contat, Michel. "Sartre et le cinéma." *Magazine littéraire,* September 1975, 103–4.

Dalle Vacche, Angela. "The Difference of Cinema in the System of the Arts." In *Opening Bazin: Postwar Film Theory and Its Afterlife,* edited by Dudley Andrew with Hervé Joubert-Laurencin. New York: Oxford University Press, 2011.

————. "Interstices and Impurities in the Cinema: Art and Science." *Alphaville: Journal of Film and Screen Media* 5 (Summer 2013). Web. ISSN: 2009-4078.

————. "Surrealism in Art and Film: Time and Face." In *Global Art Cinema,* edited by Rosalind Galt and Karl Schoonover, 181–97. New York: Oxford University Press, 2010.

Dolidze, Mamuka G. "Phenomenology in Science and Literature." In *Phenomenology World-Wide,* edited by Tymieniecka, 608–616.

Fautrier, Pascale. "Le cinéma de Sartre." *fabula-LhT* 2 (December 2006). http://www.fabula.org/lht/2/fautrier.html.

Leenhardt, Roger. *Chroniques du cinéma.* Paris: Éditions de l'étoile / Cahiers du cinéma, 1986.

Marcel, Gabriel. *The Mystery of Being.* Vol. 1, *Reflection and Mystery.* Translated by G. S. Fraser. London: Harvill Press, 1951.

————. *The Mystery of Being.* Vol. 2, *Faith and Reality.* Translated by René Hague. London: Harvill Press, 1951.

———. *The Philosophy of Existentialism*. New York: Citadel Press, 1970.

Michelson, Annette. Review of *What Is Cinema?* by André Bazin. *Artforum* 6, no. 10 (Summer 1968): 67–71.

Mounier, Emmanuel. *Introduction aux existentialismes*. Paris: Denoël, 1947.

———. *Personalism*. 1923. Notre Dame: University of Notre Dame Press, 1952.

Peppiatt, Michael. *Alberto Giacometti in Postwar Paris*. New Haven, Conn.: Yale University Press, 2002.

Peters, James R. *Augustine, Pascal, and the Rationality of Faith*. Grand Rapids, Mich.: Baker Publishing Group, 2009.

Rohdie, Sam. "Jean-Paul Sartre, Hollywood, *Citizen Kane*, and the Nouvelle Vague." Part 1. *Screening the Past* (2013). http://www.screeningthepast.com/2013/12/jean-paul-sartre-hollywood-citizen-kane-and-the-french-nouvelle-vague.

Saka, Paul. "Pascal's Wager about God." *Internet Encyclopedia of Philosophy*. http://www.iep.utm.edu/pasc-wag.

Sartre, Jean-Paul. "À propos de *Le bruit et la fureur*: La temporalité chez Faulkner." In *Critical Essays: Situations I*, translated by Chris Turner, 70–81. London: Seagull Books, 2010.

———. "The Humanism of Existentialism." In *Essays in Existentialism*, 31–62. New York: Citadel Press, 1993.

———. "John Dos Passos et *1919*." In *Critical Essays*, 18–31.

———. "La recherche de l'absolu." *Temps modernes*, no. 28 (1948): 153–63.

———. *Nausea*. Translated by Lloyd Alexander. New York: New Directions, 2013.

———. "Quand Hollywood veut faire penser . . . *Citizen Kane* Film d'Orson Welles." *Écran Français*, August 5, 1945.

———. *The Words*. Translated by Bernard Frechtman. New York: Vintage Books, 1981.

Sawchenko, Leslie Diane. "The Concept of the Person: The Contributions of Gabriel Marcel and Emmanuel Mounier to the Philosophy of Paul Ricoeur." Master's thesis, Department of Religious Studies, University of Calgary, Alberta, 2013.

Trotter, David. "James Joyce and the Automatism of the Photographic Image." In *Cinema and Modernism*, 87–123. Oxford: Wiley-Blackwell, 2007.

Ungaro, Jean. *André Bazin: Généalogies d'une théorie*. Paris: Harmattan, 2000.

8

Strange Topologics

DELEUZE TAKES A RIDE DOWN DAVID LYNCH'S
LOST HIGHWAY

Bernd Herzogenrath

Opening Credits:
You are wondering why so many people write about cinema. I ask
myself the same question. It seems to me because cinema contains
a lot of ideas. What I call Ideas are images that make one think. . . .
In each case, the thoughts are inseparable from the images; they are
completely immanent to the images. There are no abstract thoughts
realized indifferently in one image or another, but concrete [thoughts]
that only exist through these images and their means.

Deleuze, "Cinema-1, Premiere"

Cinema thinks. Film is a medium of philosophical investigation and
exploration. Propositions such as these distinguish Gilles Deleuze
from most other film philosophers, granting film an *immanent* power
of thinking much at odds with the idea that film and philosophy
are totally different (and sometimes opposed) disciplines, with one
(film) at best able to illustrate the ideas and doctrines of the other
(philosophy). Although this essay is not the place to fully zoom in
on Deleuze's two cinema books (*Cinema 1: The Movement-Image* and
Cinema 2: The Time-Image),[1] I would like to refer first to some basic
ideas of these two volumes while focusing on two crucial terms in the
chapter epigraph: *thinking/philosophy* and *film.*[2]

In the second volume of his cinema books, Deleuze refers to Eisenstein's notion that movies can present a *"shock to thought"*—that is,
cinema's capacity to "shock" the brain into thinking, *"communicating*

vibrations to the cortex, touching the nervous and cerebral system directly."[3] "Thinking" here, however, does not follow the preestablished path of already acquired knowledge. Thinking, for Deleuze, is first of all an encounter: "Something in the world forces us to think. This something is not an object of recognition, but a fundamental *encounter*," a contingent encounter "with that which forces thought to rise up and educate the absolute necessity of an act of thought or a passion to think."[4] Deleuze thus distinguishes between two strategies of knowing, of thinking. The one is what we might call (re)cognition, which simply relies on matching our experience with our culturally acquired knowledge, ideology, habits, and beliefs. The other strategy is what Deleuze calls an encounter. An encounter challenges our routines of experiencing and perceiving the world. It creates a fundamental break with our strategies of how to "make sense" of that world, and for Deleuze there is no way to "deny . . . that the cinema . . . has a role to play in the birth and formation of this new thought, this new way of thinking."[5] Movies can provide such encounters, such shocks (in)to thought, and here Deleuze builds up a parallel between the screen and the brain—epitomized in his famous motto "The brain is the screen": "Thought is molecular. Molecular speeds make up the slow beings that we are. . . . The circuits and linkages of the brain don't preexist the stimuli, corpuscles, and particles [*grains*] that trace them."[6]

"Creative tracings," "less probable links," "encounters"—according to Deleuze, these are what distinguish the thinking inherent to the cinema of the time-image from the less creative tracings, the more probable links, and the thinking-as-recognition of the cinema of the movement-image, based on the more or less linear cause-and-effect chain of the sensory-motor schema. This "newness" and unpredictability define "real thinking" and the powers of both film and philosophy.

Since its birth, cinema has entertained a complex relation with time. First of all, film was seen as a medium of *representing* time. Étienne-Jules Marey's chronophotography can be seen, here, clearly as one of the midwives of film. By creating ever smaller temporal equidistances in the measuring, fragmentation, and representation of time, Marey wanted to lift the veil of the mystery of "living machines." According to him, chronophotography proved once and for all that "motion was only the relation of time to space."[7] This puts Marey in direct opposition to Henri Bergson's philosophy of time—Bergson explicitly understood time *not* in its reduction to movement in space. It thus comes as no surprise that Bergson entertained a skeptical or at least ambivalent attitude toward the cinema. In his 1907 study, Bergson reveals what he calls the mechanistic "contrivance of the cinematograph"—it "calculates" movement out of "immobility set beside immobility, even endlessly."[8] If, as Marey had claimed, movement is only "the relation of time to space," then, Bergson argues, "time is made up of distinct parts immediately adjacent to one another. No doubt we still say that they follow one another, but in that case succession is similar to that of the images on a cinematographic film,"[9] and this completely misunderstands the fundamental difference between time as becoming, as continuous production of newness in the dynamics of an endless differentiation of life, and time as a "mechanic" succession of moments "cut out" of that very continuum. Bergson's *durée* has to be understood as a heterogeneous, qualitative duration completely at odds with Marey's quantitative, numeric, and linear conception of time as *temps* (t)—an opposition that finds its filmic equivalent in the tension between the succession of single images on the celluloid strip and the projected film.

The classic narrative film *represents* time *in* film with well-known narrative strategies such as suture, organic montage, rational cuts, continuity editing, and flashbacks and, hence, with the action–reaction model. Even in its connection with more complex *plots* (see *Back to the Future* or *Memento*), narrative film is ultimately based on the concept of an abstract and linear time—exactly what Marey had in mind. Deleuze's two cinema books are as much a testimony to and inquiry into "what the cinema can do" as they are a comment on Bergson's time philosophy—in fact, Deleuze's books "do philosophy" by focusing on cinema's affinity to the philosophy of time, to "think time" with and beyond Bergson.

Films based on the action–reaction schema (basically, classical Hollywood films) are films that in the Deleuzian taxonomy belong to the *movement-image*. Deleuze argues that when the reality of World War II and its aftermath exceeded our capacity for understanding, traditional forms of cinematic "cause-and-effect" strategies became irritatingly inappropriate, resulting in the "crisis of the action-image" and the breakdown of its corresponding "realist fundament," the "sensory-motor schema."[10] Through this pragmatic arrangement of space, the organic regime of classic cinema established a spatial continuity based on the movement of its protagonists. Action extends through rational intervals established by continuity editing so that the actor's translation of dramatic action into movement provides the primary vehicle by which a cohesive narrative space unfolds. Since the war, as Deleuze points out, dramatically "increased the situations which we no longer knew how to react to, in spaces which we no longer know how to describe," the "action-image of the old cinema" fell into crisis.[11]

As a result, the rational cuts and the continuity of the sensory-motor linkage loosen and collapse—the emerging interval marks the convergence of discontinuous durations and gives way to "false continuity and irrational cuts."[12] In the postwar climate of "any spaces whatever" (e.g., the deserted *Trümmer* wastelands of Italian neorealism), movement comes to take on *false* forms that delink and uncouple continuity, allowing "time in its pure state [to rise] up to the surface of the screen."[13] The resulting time-image emerges as something *beyond* movement, an image not defined as a succession of spatial segments, subverting the sensory-motor schema and not treating time as a simple derivative of space.[14] In fact, the privileged form of space in the films of the time-image is a rather disconnected space, with characters playing a passive role and the film concentrating more and more on "inner spaces" and traumatic psychic breakdowns, which goes along with a complex and nonlinear treatment of time itself.

According to Bergson, the present is the temporal aggregate state of matter, equating the present tense with the actualized and stating an absolute identity of movement, matter, and image. But the present at each moment splits into two trajectories, one that proceeds into the future and one that holds all the moments of the past and keeps them: for Bergson (and also Deleuze) it is "impossible . . . to imagine any way in which the recollection can arise if it is not created step by step with the perception itself. Either the present leaves no trace in memory, or it is twofold at every moment, its very up-rush being in two jets exactly symmetrical, one of which falls back towards the past whilst the other springs forward into the future."[15]

Bergson's concept of a past that emerges simultaneously with the present, that is coextensive with it, constitutes a kind of ontologi-

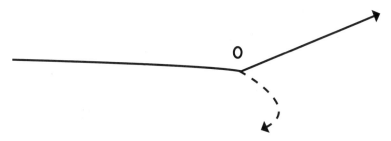

Figure 8.1. Taken from Deleuze, *Cinema 2*, 295.

cal past that consists of all the unlimited virtual potentialities and aggregate states not (or not yet) actualized, a dynamic past/memory, which is not a memory of a subject but a "generalized past/memory" that "comes" to the subject, which cannot be actively grasped. Thus, whereas the movement-image and its foregrounding of "the present" and time in/as movement are related to the realm of the actual, the time-image and its depicting of "time in its pure state" are related to the realm of the virtual. What we call "objective reality" is just the one possible version that has been actualized. For Deleuze the movement-image "constitutes time in its empirical form, the course of time: a successive present in an extrinsic relation of before and after, so that the past is a former present, and the future a present to come,"[16] whereas "time-images are nothing to do with before and after, with succession. . . . Time-images are not things happening in time, but new forms of coexistence, ordering, transformation."[17] This realm of the virtual, of a simultaneous past-present-future in all its endless, nonactualized potentialities, is something the cinema of the time-image is able to capture, to present, even to produce. In cinema it is particularly in what Deleuze calls the "crystals of time," where the present is shown to coexist with the past.

And that is a very rough sketch of Deleuze's two cinema books. In the following, I want to treat *Lost Highway* as an instance of the Deleuzian time-image,[18] and the question I focus on is, What conception of time, space, and memory drives *Lost Highway*? For more than forty years, Lynch has been changing the face of popular culture. When *Lost Highway* came out in 1996, it was received with both excited appraisal and unsympathetic disbelief. For some critics it was "the best movie David Lynch [had] ever made,"[19] whereas others "emerged from an early screening of *Lost Highway* with the cry 'Garbage!' "[20] So what was the excitement all about? Although I am aware any attempt to summarize *Lost Highway* would result ultimately in smoothening its complex structure into a linear narrative, I will nonetheless provide a short outline of its content.

Ostensibly, *Lost Highway* is the story of Fred Madison, a jazz musician. His wife, Renee, is a strangely withdrawn beauty. A disturbing study of contemporary marital hell, the first part of the movie concentrates on Fred's anxiety and insecurity, which escalates as he begins to realize Renee may be leading a double life. Renee is the focus of Fred's paranoia: she is seen as both a precious object and the cause of her husband's nightmares. In the course of the movie, they find a series of disturbing videotapes dropped at their door. The first merely shows their house. The second depicts the couple in bed, from an incredibly strange angle. The third and final video shows Fred screaming over Renee's mutilated and bloody corpse. With brutal suddenness, Fred is convicted of murder and sentenced to die in the electric chair, though he can't seem to remember anything. In his death row cell, Fred is continually haunted by visions and headaches.

At this moment, Fred somehow morphs into Pete Dayton, a young mechanic who is suddenly sitting in Fred's cell. Pete's life is situated in a typical Lynchian suburbia, an almost exact replica of the small town in *Blue Velvet*. Pete's life is overshadowed by his connections to the town's Mafia boss, Mr. Eddy. At some point, Pete meets Alice Wakefield, Mr. Eddy's babe. Within a few minutes Pete, although still dating his girlfriend, Sheila, finds himself entangled in a love affair with the local Godfather's moll—who looks like Renee *to a hair*: whereas Renee was brunette, Alice is a platinum blonde (if you're thinking of Hitchcock's *Vertigo* double, Kim Novak, you're right). Alice, like Renee, is leading a double life. A member of the porn underworld, Alice, in classic film noir femme fatale fashion, tempts Pete into betrayal and murder, and finally, a strange encounter at a cabin in the desert connects the movie's two story strands: Pete disappears, and Fred resurfaces.

Such is the rough plot. Already, it should be apparent the movie's structure is anything but simple. Thus, I approach my subject by way of digression.

Digression 1: On Suture/*Suture*

The enigmatic character of Lynch's *Lost Highway* confronts us with the questions: What are we doing when we watch a film? How do we read films? Does the reality "on screen" mimetically represent reality "out there," or is something different at stake? For critics that see film as representation, watching a movie turns into the task of "finding out what it is about," of a purely mental, detective-like strategy to make sense, to combine the clues into a coherent narrative, the film's *about-ness*.

The problem boils down to whether a movie is something that should necessarily be *about* something. Lynch himself has warned against attempts at an unequivocal reading of a filmic text, especially when asked for the "hidden meaning" of *Lost Highway*: "The beauty of a film that is more abstract is everybody has a different take. . . . When you are spoon-fed a film, people instantly know what it is. . . . I love things that leave room to dream."[21] Though vague to the question of meaning, Lynch does emphasize film as an art form in its own right: "It doesn't do any good . . . to say 'This is what it means.' Film is what it means."[22] It should be noted Lynch was trained as a painter. Accordingly, his movies excel in the purely visual, so much so critics have judged his work as devoid of characterization and plot. Yet such a criticism ignores the painterly, iconographic, and self-conscious use of motifs in his movies. The recurring velvet curtain, for example, suggests both surface and something beyond, the intrigue of what this curtain conceals provides an anticipation of revelation but does not necessarily establish meaning. Foregrounding the painterly and nonnarrative aspects of film as a medium—a medium that is *not* only a narrative, like a novel, and in which the visual and the atmospheric are two prime factors—a visually and affective-oriented mode of interpretation should be considered. We have learned to view abstract art in that way, but somehow, we still have not learned how to watch abstract/painterly movies.

I want to return to my initial question, What are we doing when we are watching a film? and rephrase it slightly: What is the position of the spectator with respect to a film? Traditionally, at least for films that belong to the movement-image, the spectator identifies with the central character in/of the film, which ultimately is an identification with a certain camera position. The position of the spectator is thus basically voyeuristic, a position that has been problematized in many films (*Psycho, Peeping Tom, Halloween*), a paradigmatic example being Lynch's own *Blue Velvet*. In film studies the relation of the spectator position to the film's narrative is called *suture*.[23] Suture is first of all a medical term—it refers to stitching up of a wound, producing a seam, a scar.

In Lacan *suture* refers to stitching the realm of images (the imaginary) to that of narrative (the symbolic), both of which make up a certain reality, with the seam closing off the unconscious (the real) from conscious subjectivity. This suture prevents the subject from losing its status as a subject, prevents it from falling into madness and psychosis. Thus, the subject's identification with the movie relies fundamentally on this conjunction of the imaginary and the symbolic levels within the cinematic discourse itself. Usually, that is. In most classical Hollywood movies, this junction is well balanced: the means of representation, the images shown on the screen, parallel the narrative itself, in a mutual and constant comment.

A good example of how suture functions—in a quite literal sense—can be seen in John Woo's *Face/Off* (1997). The suture that holds the movie together is quite literally the seam that stitches Nicholas Cage's face onto John Travolta's head (and vice versa) and functions in fact only if the spectator is willing to accept this improbability. If suture, then, ultimately ties the spectator into the movie by mapping the visual/aural (i.e., perceptual and, thus, imaginary) means of representation onto the narrative, the *ripping open* of that seam consequently results in a problematizing, if not complete undermining, of identification. A 1993 film by Scott McGehee and David Siegel provides a good example for such a *desuturing*.

"Our physical resemblance is striking," says Vincent to Clay, his twin brother. On the level of representation, the spectator is held constantly in the process of desuturing, since the movie repeatedly emphasizes the physical similarity of the two twin brothers, which is in fact a prerequisite for the film to function in the first place. However, the two twins could not be more different: Vincent is white, and Clay is black. This perverse logic is reflected in the title of the film, *Suture*, but ultimately withholds the comfort of suture, of a stable position within reality both on screen and off screen. If suture is, thus, an indispensable means of creating the movement-image and foregrounding the present, the actual, and cause-and-effect logic, then desuturing belongs to the realm of the time-image and its focus on the virtual. Suture is instrumental and paramount in the actualization of one reality. Desuturing thus foregrounds false continuities, irrational cuts, and the time-image "initiates the reign of 'incommensurables' or irrational cuts: this is to say that the cut no longer forms part of one or the other image, of one or the other sequence that it separates and divides. It is on this condition that the succession or sequence becomes a series. . . . The interval is set free, the interstice becomes irreducible and stands on its own."[24]

Lost Highway functions in a similar manner with respect to questions of time, space, and memory. In order to further approach this problem, I will comment on aspects I think are crucial for approaching the movie. First is the structure of the film. After the credit titles flicker over the screen—accompanied fittingly by David Bowie's "I'm Deranged," a track that sets the tone for what's to come—the movie begins with Fred Madison sitting alone in front of a window, smoking, his image mirrored in the glass, when a message comes suddenly through the intercom: "Dick Laurent is dead!" Fred does not—yet—know who this mysterious Dick Laurent is (or was) nor who has brought this message. Neither does the spectator. Shortly before the end of the movie, we witness a scene in which Fred himself delivers this same message through the intercom. Some reviewers fail to notice this strange structure, favoring a straightforward telling of the tale, but even the articles that *do* mention it fail to acknowledge its full impact: when Fred returns home to deliver the message that will set the whole narrative in motion again, a new element has entered the script that was not there the first time around, in the form of cop cars waiting outside the home. This illustrates well that repetition is never identical and that at the core of sameness is difference.[25]

Now, let us have a look at—or much more important, a careful *listen to*—the first scene again. Right after the "Dick Laurent is dead" message, we can hear sirens and a car speeding off. In fact, they're the same sirens (and car speeding off) that occur at the end of the movie. So the reviewer quoted before was right: it is about repetition with a difference. There is a new element, but it is not the cop cars: it is the position of *Fred*. It is not, however, that he has simply changed from receiver to sender: he is both sender *and* receiver and *at the same time* and *in the same space*. In order to approach this mystery, a different topology is needed, a topology accounting for a *time-space* that differs markedly from Euclidean space and teleological time concepts. A topological figure that makes such things possible is the Möbius strip, and both Lynch and Barry Gifford, with whom Lynch collaborated on the screenplay, have mentioned this figure in interviews.[26] So what is a Möbius strip?

Digression 2: How to Make a Möbius Strip

1. Take a strip of paper.
2. Make sure it has two sides.
3. Take one end of the strip, make a 180-degree twist, and place it over the other end.
4. Tape or, better with respect to suture, *stitch* the two ends together.
5. You now have a one-sided figure instead of a two-sided figure.

The Möbius strip subverts the normal (i.e., Euclidean) form of spatial (and ultimately, temporal) representation, seemingly having two sides while in fact having only one. At one point the two sides can be clearly distinguished, but when you traverse the strip as a whole, the two sides are experienced as continuous. Binary oppositions such as inside/outside, before/after, Fred/Pete, Renee/Alice, Dick Laurent/Mr. Eddy, etc., somehow *do not exist in such a topological space*.

This figure is an apt one for Lynch, whose movies emphasize the position where

> violence meets tenderness, waking meets dream, blond meets brunette, lipstick meets blood, where something very sweet and innocuous becomes something very sick and degrading, at the very border where opposites become both discrete and indistinguishable.[27]

In *Lost Highway* the merging of opposites is crucial, and the problematization of the inside/outside opposition is important. In fact,

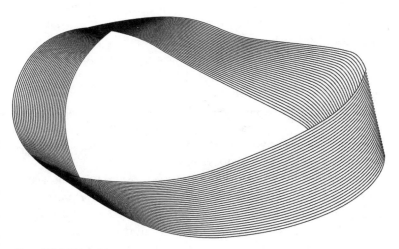

Figure 8.2. Möbius strip.

it is important to Lynch's oeuvre as a whole: recall the early scene in *Blue Velvet* where Jeffrey finds the ear and the camera zooms in tightly and the one at the end in which the camera seemingly zooms directly out of Jeffrey's ear. In *Lost Highway* the question of inside and outside and their conflation is repeatedly posed. On a general level, the diegetic reality of the movie—what we actually see on screen, *inside* the movie—is composed of bits and pieces from other movies: Lynch uses the different genres and classics of Hollywood as a kind of quarry—here most notably, Hitchcock's *Vertigo*. He not only uses Hollywood's genres but almost violently exploits his own wealth of images: almost every shot initiates the *shock of recognition*. One might call this repetitive, but after all, language in general—especially, a distinct film language such as Lynch's—relies on repetition to function.

Another example of the merging of inside and outside, apart from the frame tale of "Dick Laurent is dead," is the scene in which Fred meets the Mystery Man for the first time, at Andy's party. The Mystery Man—simultaneously inside and outside—can be read as the place where opposites meet: he is the twist in the Möbius strip. By suturing off the unconscious, *reality* remains for the subject a *coherent illusion*, so the subject does not fall into psychosis. No wonder the Mystery Man appears only when a change in personality is close at hand.

The Möbius strip, then, treats binaries not as oppositions but as places of transition. In contrast to traditional Hollywood movies, in which the narrative unfolds in a straightforward, teleological manner—even if strategies such as flashbacks and the film within a film are used—*Lost Highway* presents a multiple narrative. The more so, since both stories—of Fred and of Pete—are *not* simply related to each other as prequel and/or the solution of the other. Although definite anchoring points clearly connect the two stories, one does *not* subsume the other without remainder.

What, then, is the relationship between past and present, actual and virtual, perception and memory in Lynch's *Lost Highway*? The present passes, and the past does not—thus, this ontological past (which is not the immediate past, the present that passes) is not one of progressing nor of a succession of moments but one that perpetually expands and grows. Equally, "time-images are nothing to do with before and after, with succession . . . but with new forms of coexistence, ordering, transformation."[28] Bergson refers to this conserving expansion of the past, the virtual, memory as a "cone"—the "tip" of the subject being in direct communion with perception-action (but not memory) and the actual, the present—and the further the subject dives toward the cone's base, the more dreamlike and similar to contemplation and memory or virtuality it becomes. Subjectivity is, thus, in time, even is time: "Time is not the interior in us, but just the opposite, the interiority in which we are, in which we move, live and change. . . . Subjectivity is never ours, it is time, that is, the soul or the spirit, the virtual."[29]

Lynch translates Bergson's oscillation of the subject between the tip and the base of the cone into the one-sided fold of the Möbius strip. Here, the actual present perception (the one actualized version of the ontological past we call "reality," which—as memory—turns into the immediate past) folds into what might be called a "counter-actualization," another version of the ontological past that has not been actualized: "I like to remember things my own way. . . . How I remembered them. Not necessarily the way they happened," says Fred in *Lost Highway*. In fact, such a counteractualization or "creative fabulation has nothing to do with a memory, however exaggerated, or with fantasy. In fact, the artist, including the novelist, goes beyond the perceptual states and affective transitions of the lived. The artist is

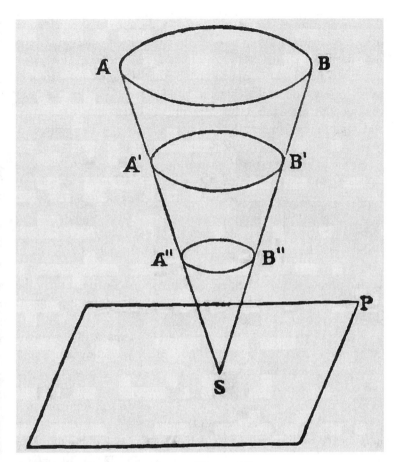

Figure 8.3. Taken from Bergson, *Matter and Memory*, 162.

a seer, a becomer."[30] Thus, these fabulations are more related to visions and becomings—that is, to the endless potentialities of the virtual—than, however subjective, to an individual memory. "Memory is not in us; it is we who move in a Being-memory, a world-memory,"[31] and here, I argue the Lynchian topology of the Möbius strip, with its conflation of inside and outside, makes particular sense with regard to the interplay of memory as passing present, the individual memory (inside), and the memory of the virtual, the ontological past that is not in us and in which we move.

In the one-sided topology of Lynch's Möbius memory, then, both the actualization of the passing present and the counteractualization of the ontological past run through the virtual itself—the twist in the Möbius strip, the actual locus of the fold. Indeed, the two memory narratives run back to back, but without a sense of mutual (or even one-sided) explanation or illumination: no memory is more real and can thus function as a stable reference point. This coexistence of contraries and oppositions defines the virtual and forces thought into being:

> We run in fact into a principle of indeterminability, of indiscernibility: we no longer know what is imaginary or real, physical or mental, in the situation, not because they are confused, but because we do not have to know and there is no longer even a place from which to ask. It is as if the real and the imaginary were running after each other, as if each was being reflected in the other, around a point of indiscernibility.[32]

Such a counteractualization "replaces and supersedes the form of the true, because it poses the simultaneity of incompossible presents, or the coexistence of not-necessarily true pasts."[33]

The topology of the Möbius strip has both a spatial and a temporal component—one might say it translates a spatial dynamics into a temporal process and vice versa. What works in the spatial register as a coexistence of opposites, as a simultaneity of two sides that are in effect one, in a temporal sequence or process still functions as a succession—that is, a succession of the two sides, of two narratives, in sequence, such that one narrative, which actually runs simultaneously with the other, follows only in the second run over the surface of the Möbius strip.[34]

This difference and duplicity of spatial and temporal registers (and of sequence and simultaneity, continuities and false continuities, or, even, movement-image and time-image) is played out by Lynch in his idiosyncratic fusion of both strategies. The false continuities and irrational cuts of the time-image delink the (carefully sutured and "logical") continuity of the movement-image—such that, according to Lynch, some people will have a problem following the narrative: "For those people, the intellect has blocked the little area between nerves, the synapse. And the spark does not jump across."[35] In order to make the spark jump, Lynch carefully uses (and deconstructs) well-known strategies of the movement-image (montage strategies, shot/

countershot, genre structures, etc.) for other means: he employs these tactics and expectations in the service of the time-image,[36] merging them to more specific time-image strategies such as optical and sound situations, cuts to the plane of the immanence of light (what Paul Harris calls the "plane of luminance"; for example, see Pete and Alice's sex scene in the desert), and so on.

In addition, Lynch inserts some structural shortcuts that pierce through the surface of the strip itself: centered around the mysterious reference to "that night," two scenes occur more than once in *Lost Highway*. These two scenes, of Fred in a dark hallway (with Renee calling, "Fred!") and of Pete in front of his parents' house (with Sheila calling, "Pete!"), when viewed in parallel, function like a wormhole that traverses the different virtual/actual event levels of the movie—I would even argue that if you mirrored these two scenes on two adjacent screens, the effect would be of one character changing over to the realm/screen of the other.

So what happens to Fred in the end? The last shot shows him in the process of transformation again. Lynch used almost the same scene in his second movie, *The Elephant Man*, where it denoted the effect of a traumatic experience on the process of giving birth to a "new subject." What will be the result of Fred's transformation? Yet another persona? Or will he retransform into Pete, thus adding another temporal twist to the narrative? Remember that Pete had been imprisoned once, not for murder but for car theft, and what the police will eventually find after Fred has transformed into Pete again will simply be Pete in a stolen car . . . only that now, since the cops had found Pete's fingerprints all over Andy's place, Pete will be charged for murder . . . but does that explain things? Do we now understand? In the U.S. remake of the thriller *Nightwatch*, the police inspector turned serial killer, played by Nick Nolte, philosophizes: "Explanations are just fictions to make us feel safe. Otherwise, we would have to admit the unexplained, and that would leave us prey to the chaos around us. Which is exactly how it is."

Now, is this just about schizophrenia? Fantasy? Pathology? In our attempt at mental sense making, at creating a coherent, linear, cause-and-effect narrative, we ultimately fail. Several scenes in *Lost Highway* willfully blur the separation between reality and fantasy or memory—in fact, the time-and-space scheme proposed by the film's

Möbius-like structure suggests otherwise. In Fred/Pete's perception, reality/fact and dream/fantasy cannot be separated; they interpenetrate each other: "I like to remember things my own way. . . . How I remembered them. Not necessarily the way they happened." We should take this seriously: we cannot do anything *but* remember things our own way; we cannot even perceive things *but* in our own way. Recent findings in neuroscience support this view—perception is always filtered through and tainted by memory and desire: the past is tainted by the present; the present is tainted by the past.

Thus, *Lost Highway* can either be taken as something that does not add up, that does not make sense (if we adopt the linear sense-making strategy), or tell us something profound about temporal structures of reality, desire, and memory, as well as the fact that reality, desire, and memory always interpenetrate each other, such that there simply *is* no truth or final meaning that adds up. When Alice, in the love scene in the desert, whispers, "You'll never have me," this tells us as much about the never-ending loop of desire (that creates this intersection of reality and fantasy) as it does about the mystery of *Lost Highway*. It treats its topic performatively and affectively, not just representationally, and denies its audience a cozy, objective perspective from without.

End Credits:
> Because the just ideas are always those that conform to accepted meanings or established precepts. . . . While "just ideas" is a becoming-present, a stammering of ideas, and can only be expressed in the form of questions that tend to confound any answers.[37]

NOTES

This essay has had a previous life as "On the *Lost Highway*: Lynch and Lacan, Cinema and Cultural Pathology," *Other Voices* 1, no. 3 (January 1999), republished with kind permission. However, it has undergone a significant (some would even go as far as calling it a sex) change: it started as a Lacanian analysis and then morphed into a Deleuzian one.

1. There is a plethora of books on Deleuze and film. For example, see Rodowick, *Gilles Deleuze's Time Machine*; Bogue, *Deleuze on Cinema*; and Pisters, *The Matrix of Visual Culture*.

2. The English translation of the epigraph states "images" instead of "thoughts," but of course, "thoughts" is correct. See the original: "Il n'y a pas des pensées abstraites qui se réaliseraient indifféremment dans telle ou telle image, mais des pensées concrètes qui n'existent que par ces images-là et leurs moyens." Deleuze, interviewed by Serge Daney, *Libération*, November 6, 1995.

3. Deleuze, *Cinema 2*, 156.

4. Deleuze, *Difference and Repetition*, 139.

5. Deleuze, *Cinema 1*, 7.

6. Deleuze, "The Brain Is the Screen," 366–67.

7. Marey, *La méthode graphique dans les sciences expérimentales*, xi.

8. Bergson, *Creative Evolution*, 332, 331.

9. Ibid., 18.

10. Deleuze, *Cinema 1*, 197, 155.

11. See Deleuze, *Cinema 2*, xi.

12. Ibid.

13. Ibid.

14. Ibid., 1–24.

15. Bergson, *Mind-Energy*, 159–60.

16. Deleuze, *Cinema 2*, 271.

17. Deleuze, *Negotiations*, 123.

18. A few books deal with the Lynch–Deleuze connection. For example, see Sinnerbrink, *New Philosophies of Film*, esp. the ch. on *Inland Empire*; and Glaser, *Provisorische Gegenwart*.

19. Gilmore, "The Lost Boys."

20. Corliss, "Mild at Heart," 77.

21. Szebin and Biodrowski, "The Making of *Lost Highway*."

22. Ibid.

23. Silverman, *The Subject of Semiotics*, 194–236.

24. Deleuze, *Cinema 2*, 277. The difference between "suture" and "desuturing" also parallels Richard Rushton's distinction between the modes of immersion and absorption: with immersion (the "default version" of how an affective relation between spectator and film is understood), "the film is there for me; not to offer the possibility of my becoming something or someone else, but to offer only the affirmation of the me that is me." "Deleuzian Spectatorship," 51. With the mode of absorption, however, images do not affect the spectator by coming from the outside, as it were—absorption works in the opposite direction: "One can have the sensation of bodily occupying that space in another world, the sensation of occupying the space of another being. To put it bluntly, one of the possibilities which absorption holds forth is the possibility of being another being." "Deleuzian Spectatorship," 50.

25. Celeste, "*Lost Highway*."

26. October Films, press kit.

27. Celeste, "*Lost Highway*."

28. Deleuze, *Negotiations,* 123.
29. Deleuze, *Cinema 2,* 82–83.
30. Deleuze, *Difference and Repetition,* 171.
31. Deleuze, *Cinema 2,* 98.
32. Ibid., 7.
33. Ibid., 131.
34. For an illustration, see the various Möbius strip GIFs and animations on YouTube. Lynch captures this duplicity in a short shot of the highway's middle line that appears a couple of times in *Lost Highway* in two variations: one shows two parallel, straight lines (simultaneity), and the other, a ruptured line (sequence). Note that in the latter the middle line looks almost like a seam—perhaps, a hint at the workings of suture in the realm of the movement image.
35. Kermode 1997.
36. For example, see Neofetou, *Good Day Today.*
37. Deleuze, *Negotiations,*38–39.

BIBLIOGRAPHY

Bergson, Henri. *Creative Evolution.* New York: The Modern Library, 1944.
———. *The Creative Mind: An Introduction to Metaphysics.* New York: Citadel Press, 1992.
———. *Matter and Memory.* Translated by Nancy M. Paul and W. Scott Palmer. New York: Zone Books, 1991.
———. *Mind-Energy: Lectures and Essays.* New York: Henry Holt and Company, 1920.
Bogue, Ronald. *Deleuze on Cinema.* New York: Routledge, 2003.
Bornedal, Ole. *Nightwatch.* Dimension Films, 1997.
Celeste, Reni. "*Lost Highway*: Unveiling Cinema's Yellow Brick Road." *Cineaction,* no. 43 (Summer 1997).
Corliss, Richard. "Mild at Heart." *Time,* April 7, 1997, 77.
Currie, Gregory. "Cognitivism." in *A Companion to Film Theory,* edited by Toby Miller and Robert Stam. Malden, Mass.: Blackwell, 1999.
Damasio, Antonio. *The Feeling of What Happens: Body and Emotion in the Making of Consciousness.* New York: Harcourt, 1999.
———. *Looking for Spinoza: Joy, Sorrow, and the Feeling Brain.* New York: Hartcourt, 2003.
Deleuze, Gilles. "The Brain Is the Screen: An Interview with Gilles Deleuze." In *The Brain Is the Screen: Deleuze and the Philosophy of Cinema,* edited by Gregory Flaxman, 365–73. Minneapolis: University of Minnesota Press, 2000.
———. *Cinema 1: The Movement-Image.* Translated by Hugh Tomlinson and Barbara Habberjam. Minneapolis: University of Minnesota Press, 1986.
———. "Cinema-1, Premiere." In *Two Regimes of Madness: Texts and Interviews,*

1975–1995, edited by David Lapoujade and translated by Ames Hodges and Mike Taormina, 210–12. New York: Semiotext(e), 2006.

———. *Cinema 2: The Time-Image*. Translated by Hugh Tomlinson and Roberta Galeta. London: Athlone 2000 Press, 1989.

———. *Difference and Repetition*. New York: Columbia University Press, 1994.

———. "Image mouvement image temps." Cours vincennes, St. Denis, February 11, 1983. Transcript at www.webdeleuze.com.

———. *Negotiations, 1972–1990*. Translated by Martin Joughin. New York: Columbia University Press, 1995.

Deleuze, Gilles, and Félix Guattari. *A Thousand Plateaus: Capitalism and Schizophrenia*. Translated by Brian Massumi. Minneapolis: University of Minnesota Press, 1993.

———. *What Is Philosophy?* Translated by Hugh Tomlinson and Graham Burchell. New York: Columbia University Press, 1994.

Gifford, Barry. Interview by Ron Wells. *Film Threat,* February 1997.

Gilmore, Mikal. "The Lost Boys." *Rolling Stone,* March 6, 1997.

Glaser, Tina. *Provisorische gegenwart: Reflexionen zu David Lynchs film "Lost Highway."* Vienna: Wiener Verlag, 2013.

Harris, Paul A. "Deleuze's Cinematic Universe of Light: A Cosmic Plane of Luminance." *SubStance* 39, no. 1 (2010): 115–24.

Hitchcock, Alfred. *Vertigo*. Paramount Pictures, 1958.

Kermode, Mark. Interview with David Lynch. *Q Magazine,* September 1997.

Lynch, David. *Lost Highway*. October Films, 1997.

Marey, Etienne-Jules. *La méthode graphique dans les sciences expérimentales*. Paris: Masson, 1885.

McGehee, Scott, and David Siegel. *Suture*. MGM, 1993.

Neofetou, Daniel. *Good Day Today. David Lynch Destabilises "The Spectator."* Washington, D.C.: Zero Books, 2012.

October Films. *Lost Highway* press kit. www.lynchnet.com.

Pisters, Patricia. *The Matrix of Visual Culture: Working with Deleuze in Film Theory*. Stanford, Calif.: Stanford University Press, 2003.

Rodowick, D. N. *Gilles Deleuze's Time Machine*. Durham, N.C.: Duke University Press, 1997.

Rushton, Richard. "Deleuzian Spectatorship." *Screen* 50, no. 1 (Spring 2009): 45–53.

Silverman, Kaja. *The Subject of Semiotics*. New York: Oxford University Press, 1983.

Sinnerbrink, Robert. *New Philosophies of Film: Thinking Images*. London: Continuum, 2011.

Szebin, Frederick C., and Steve Biodrowski. "The Making of *Lost Highway*: A Surreal Meditation on Love, Jealousy, Identity, and Reality." *Cinefantastique* 28, no. 10 (1997).

Woo, John. *Face/Off*. Paramount Pictures, 1997.

Hurray for Hollywood

PHILOSOPHY AND CINEMA ACCORDING TO
STANLEY CAVELL

Elisabeth Bronfen

In his essay "The Thought of Movies," seeking to explain how he, as a philosopher, came to start thinking about Hollywood films, Stanley Cavell turns the question around to ask instead: "How is it that someone whose education was as formed by going to the movies as by reading books, gets to thinking about philosophy professionally?"[1] Taking his own autobiography as point of departure, he explains that for his father, an uneducated immigrant from eastern Europe, and his mother, who was a prominent pianist in Atlanta, the movies they went to weekly with their son were the most reliable source for common pleasure for them as a family. Two aspects of this childhood experience subsequently drew Cavell back to Hollywood's classic period. In these films he not only found inspiration for philosophical questions he was concerned with as a professor of aesthetics and the general theory of value at Harvard. Throughout his career he also chose to explore the interface between moral philosophy and Hollywood so as to make a claim for a specifically American way of engaging philosophically with the world.

The first of his books on the specific possibilities open to film as an aesthetic medium, *The World Viewed,* is programmatically dedicated to his mother and father. As he notes in the introduction:

> Memories of movies are strand over strand with memories of my life.
> During the quarter of a century (roughly from 1935 to 1960) in which
> going to the movies was a normal part of my week, it would no more
> have occurred to me to write a study of movies than to write my auto-

biography. Having completed the pages that follow, I feel that I have been composing a kind of metaphysical memoir—not the story of a period of my life but an account of the conditions it has satisfied.[2]

His discussion is, in part, inscribed by a certain nostalgia for the cinematic world that came to be lost with the collapse of the classic Hollywood studio system. At the same time, at issue is the way an experience of film changes the way we view the world. Taking his cue from Emerson's turn to the ordinary as an answer to a sense of the loss of world, Cavell understands film as a reflection of the fact that we, as modern subjects, live and understand the world primarily by taking views of it. The cinematic experience, he suggests, allows us to understand the conditions by which the world reveals itself to us. Specific about the film image, in turn, is that it is projected onto a screen where we see things that are not actually present. What is produced is an image of the world, not the sight, look, or appearance of the world itself. The projected film image sustains the presence of a world predicated on the absence of the viewer. The reality of the film image is present to me while I am not in its presence. Yet a world of projected images that I know and see but in which I am not myself present is a world held at a spatial and temporal distance. The screen represents a boundary, screening me from the world it depicts and making me invisible. As a viewer, sitting in the movie theater, I am neither visible nor audible to the actor on screen, even while his image takes on presence for me.

Given this play with visibility and invisibility, with presence and absence, the projected world we view on screen offers an explanation for our inability to know others, as well as our own unknowability. By aesthetically reproducing our sense of being distanced from the everyday world, film, however, turns this limit on knowledge into a productive fantasy. Film invites us to understand the reality it projects on screen as a theatricalization of our own reality. The ease with which we identify with the world on screen corresponds to the fact that we have long since come to experience the everyday reality we are distanced from as theatrical. If, with the onset of modernity, self-explanations have always needed an element of drama to be fully convincing, at the historic moment when society has become fully dramatic, cinema rehabilitates our sense of reality in that the film image makes a claim for the theatrical power of reality. Cinema, Cavell insists, has not so much changed our ways of looking at the world as it has "entered a world whose ways of looking at itself—its *Weltanschauung*—had already changed, as if in preparation for the screening and viewing of film."[3]

The Comedy of Remarriage: A Meet and Happy Conversation

While *The World Viewed* invokes a broad spectrum of films, Cavell's subsequent books turn to the way classic Hollywood can be conceived along the lines of a conceptual space for American culture to think about itself. Two genres emerge as seminal to this project. *Pursuits of Happiness* isolates seven sophisticated comedies of the 1930s and 1940s under the rubric of what Cavell calls the comedy of remarriage, while *Contesting Tears* treats four melodramas of the same period as films about the unknown woman. If Cavell entitles the introduction to the first of these two books "Words for a Conversation," he does so to signal that the ability (or inability) of the hero and heroine to speak with each other is not only what distinguishes these two genres from each other. Conversation is also his own methodological concern. On the one hand, this concept refers to the personal experience as a moviegoer that he brings to bear on his discussion of Hollywood films. As he explains, because his discussion is based on his own experience of these films, they are themselves investigations of "ideas of conversation, and investigations of what it is to have an interest in your own experience."[4] On the other hand, the Hollywood films of the golden years exist in a state of philosophy because they engage with the question of moral perfectionism. Cavell's discussion of those films that mean something to him, because they have affected his experience as a scholar and a moviegoer, thus renders visible a conversation between philosophy and film studies.

The theme common to both the comedy and the melodrama genre concerns the creation of a new woman who stands in for moral perfectibility, in the sense of a recovery of humanity in all its fragility. The difference, in turn, consists in whether this moral transformation occurs with or against the gaze of the men determining such self-knowledge. Both genres address the conditions as well as the limits of mutual recognition, with the concept of marriage serving as the trope for the possibility of a shared recognition in the former and its impossibility in the latter. Reconciliation is predicated on the fact that a marriage promise can be broken, while a reassertion of this bond is achievable only through a metamorphosis that is also tantamount to a new view of the world. If in the course of the film narrative the legitimacy of marriage comes to be renegotiated, this results either in a reaffirmation of a shared life or in a radical repudiation of the possibility of a shared conversation.

The Philadelphia Story (1940), my example for Cavell's take on the remarriage comedy, is driven by a desire to bring a couple back together again. Though the romantic couple is intimately familiar, a discrepancy between the sexual and the social conception of marriage has come to threaten their alliance. The witty conversation they still share revolves around the question of what happiness means and the degree to which one is willing to change in order to achieve this. The decisive transformation of their attitude toward each other, in turn, involves a logic of repetition. To achieve happiness in marriage requires that two people, who once found each other, must do so a second time, because only then will they discover why they had been made for each other all along. In this act of recovery as rediscovery, Cavell locates a refiguration of the Emersonian worry that one may have missed the opportunity for moral perfectibility. The pursuit of happiness on which the comedy of remarriage is predicated thus emerges as a pursuit for the right degree of separateness, as this, in turn, determines the right degree of mutual acknowledgment. Cavell foregrounds the issue of the heroine's re-creation because it is primarily her transformation that signals the change Emerson calls for—namely, to become the person one always was, only doing so consciously. By coming together again, the couple, having first lost each other, gradually becomes aware that they are the same yet also changed in such a way that the promise of shared happiness can be reaffirmed.

Philadelphia Story famously ends in a second marriage ceremony after Tracy Lord (Katherine Hepburn) refuses both the journalist Mike (James Stewart) and the businessman George (John Howard) and instead returns to her estranged husband C. K. Dexter Haven (Cary Grant). As Cavell notes, "Having grown up together, or anyway having in some way created a childhood past together, remains a law for the happiness of the pair in the universe of remarriage comedies."⁵ Dexter succeeds in reclaiming his bride from his two rivals because Tracy has suddenly realized that she had merely deluded herself into thinking that George and she viewed the world in the same way. Yet she must also relinquish Mike, even though he was the one who, at the height of her inebriation the night before the wedding, had recognized the erotic allure her first husband was impervious to. Given that for Cavell the tentative quality of any recuperated self-knowledge is significant, he underscores that the remarriage between Tracy and Dexter leaves open the consequences of this choice. The film ends after Tracy and Dexter, together with his best man, Mike, have reached the altar, where the priest has begun to perform the wedding rites. Suddenly, however, the ceremony is disrupted by a spurt of light from the flashbulb of the publisher of *Spy* magazine, who has clandestinely slipped into this exclusive gathering. Astonished, all three characters look into his camera, which is to say they look directly at us.

Cavell reads this closure as an implicit reference to Shakespeare's *Midsummer Night's Dream,* based as this comedy is on "the idea that the public world of day cannot resolve its conflicts apart from resolutions in the private forces of the night." This therapy, leading to a resumption of wedding vows, he adds, occurs "by way of remembering something, awakening to something, and by forgetting something, awakening from something."⁶ Yet if Tracy herself admits that in light of what happened the night before her wedding, her eyes have been opened, the happy end of *Philadelphia Story* is predicated on a nocturnal awakening that Cavell only gestures toward. That evening, both Dexter and the bride's father had attacked her for her austere moral behavior, comparing her to an aloof goddess. To become a first-class human being, however, thus their claim, she would need to be able to not only forgive the fallibility of others but also recognize such frailty within herself. Astonished at these accusations, Tracy had gotten drunk on champagne, and once she is alone with Mike in the moonlit garden behind her villa, she suddenly discovers an erotic desire previously unknown to her. Mike unexpectedly declares his unconditional admiration for her while the lighting Cukor uses to illuminate his heroine corresponds to the erotic fire his words inspire in her. By asking her whether she sees how magnificent she is, he draws her attention to something she had always known about herself but that she can only now begin to acknowledge. After a passionate kiss, the two run off to take a dip in the pool, from where they return with Mike carrying Tracy in his arms, barely clad in her bathrobe and singing happily. They are met by Dexter and George, the other two men vying for her love. While the former is sure that Tracy will refuse to remember this excess once she has woken from her drunken state, the latter is filled with disgust at the inappropriateness of his bride's behavior.

The wedding that takes place the next day transforms precisely this transgressive sexuality into a socially sanctioned bond. With her eyes now opened to her own fallibility, Tracy does not repudiate the erotic intemperance of the previous night. She also does not, however, choose the man who had called forth this repressed self-knowledge but rather the man who is already sexually familiar to her. Yet the photograph that interrupts her wedding ceremony shows all three standing in front of the altar. Remarriage thus requires two aspects of self-knowledge. The heroine must accept symbolic codes that curtail the blithe narcissism she had enjoyed in her illicit encounter with Mike, even while it is this nocturnal experience that has transformed her into the first-class human being the remarriage comedy requires. Furthermore, when in the light of a new morning she once more takes the man with whom she has always shared an intimate conversation as her husband, Tracy preserves a piece of this nocturnal narcissism. As Cavell confesses, his notion of remarriage speaks to the fact that "you are enabled to remain with the one to whom you have been bound, by discharging your hostility on a past life with that one, or with a past version of that one."[7]

As the statue-like Tracy transforms into a first-class human being, able to both acknowledge her own fallibility and forgive her husband for the alcoholism that had been the cause of their divorce, a second thematic concern comes into play. Cavell reads this rebirth of the heroine also as a comment on the film's understanding of American democracy. If within Puritan doctrine the marriage covenant represents a miniature of the covenant of the commonwealth, then the wedding that takes place at the end of *Philadelphia Story*, in the city that gave birth to the U.S. Constitution, is also of national concern.

As an example of the manner in which Hollywood offers a cognitive space for cultural self-reflection, this film comedy raises the question of "whether America has achieved its new human being, its more perfect union and its domestic tranquility, its new birth of freedom, whether it has been successful in securing the pursuit of happiness, whether it is earning the conversation it demands."[8] The recuperated conversation between Tracy and Dexter thus mirrors a philosophical conversation about the conditions of the social contract that *The Philadelphia Story* implicitly entertains with the founding fathers of the Constitution: in particular, their claim that this newly founded nation sought to bring forth a natural aristocracy,

> not inherently superior to others, possessing qualities inaccessible to others, but one which is more advanced than others, further along a spiritual path anyone might take and everyone can appreciate.[9]

Cavell's reading of this film comedy is paradigmatic of his argument about the philosophical nature of cinema in yet a further sense. With it he unfolds a panoply of critical tropes that illustrate the way his hermeneutic process consists in using a discussion of cinema so as to bring literary and philosophical texts into conversation with each other as well. Cavell locates traces of Shakespeare's dramatic imagination in Cukor's comedy by first noting a correspondence to *Othello*. The three males of *The Philadelphia Story* may be construed as dividing up Othello's qualities—Dexter taking up his capacity of authority, Mike his powers of poetry and passion, and George "his openness to suspicion and jealousy."[10]

Yet it is above all *A Midsummer Night's Dream* that Cavell finds refigured, given that both the play and the film explore how nocturnal spaces help to work through conflicts posed in and by the ordinary everyday. Indeed, what for Cavell connects Cukor's comedy of remarriage most pointedly to *A Midsummer Night's Story* is that both unfold a passage leading from the "private forces of the night" into "the public world of consequences."[11] Correspondences between the two texts include the juice of the magic flower that resurfaces as the champagne Tracy Lord imbues to excess, falling in love, like Shakespeare's fairy queen, with a man socially beneath her class. The jealous yet dexterous Oberon, in turn, returns as her former husband, cleverly turning a complex love plot based on confusion and blindness in his favor in order to win back his wife. For the conversation between cinema, literature, and philosophy that Cavell seeks to uncover, what is seminal, however, is not the discovery of solid evidence attesting to a relation between these two texts. Instead, he emphasizes:

> I might rather describe my interest as one of discovering, given the thought of this relation, what the consequences of it might be. This is a matter not so much of assigning significance to certain events of the drama as it is of isolating and relating the events for which significance needs to be assigned.[12]

A further implicit intertext that Cavell uncovers for the witty sparring between Tracy and Dexter is Milton's description of a successful marriage as a meet and happy conversation. Although he concedes that Milton had in view "an entire mode of association, a form of life, he does also mean a capacity, say a thirst, for talk."[13] In his tract on divorce, Milton, after all, notes that "no effect of tyranny can sit more heavy on the commonwealth than this household unhappiness on the family."[14] If, then, the covenant of marriage is to be taken as a cypher for the covenant the American subject enters into with democracy, Cavell understands Hollywood film comedies to be "participating in such a conversation with their culture."[15] Part of this conversation is with the historical implications of certain key concepts of the Constitution, which the founding fathers wrestled over in Philadelphia some two hundred years before Cukor filmed *The Philadelphia Story*.

Cavell relates a discussion between Tracy and her detractors that ranges from what it means to be a first-class human being to the arguments philosophers have had since the signing of the Constitution about the implications and effects of this social contract. In his writings, De Tocqueville, for example, discovers a sympathy for eccentricity as well as a valorization of a freedom of thinking, both of which serve as an antidote to the tyranny of the masses that the French aristocrat had worried about during his travels through the newly founded democracy. Taken together with the notion of a natural aristocracy as it can be found in the correspondence between John Adams and Thomas Jefferson, Cavell sees here a conversation emerging about human perfectibility that Cukor picks up again when, in the course of his film comedy, he has his heroine transform into a first-class human being, conceived as the best self within any given person, independent of class and race. At the same time, Cavell also brings the notion of natural aristocracy as an expression of the humanity of the American subject to bear on the specific features of cinema as a medium. He discovers in the photogenic charisma of the star a visual correspondence to self-betterment, given that the camera (along with makeup and lighting) renders visible the best self in any given actress or actor and, as such, a potential for perfectibility that would remain invisible to the ordinary eye.

The conversation Cavell sees *Philadelphia Story* having with a set of philosophical concepts (natural aristocracy, best self, moral perfectibility) allows him to assign a very specific significance to the closure sequence. As already mentioned, Sidney Kidd, publisher of *Spy,* interrupts the marriage vows by capturing not only the bride and bridegroom but also his best man in photographs he is taking of this marriage ceremony because it is of national importance. In the closing moments of the film, we first see a frozen image of all three staring into his camera as if having been woken up by his flashlight, which is to say, as if woken from the dream that was the film's narrative. Seamlessly, this image transforms into an image in a photo album whose pages are being turned by an invisible hand, offering us a final image of Tracy in the arms of her recovered husband. Their lips are about to touch but are not yet touching. The film's closing sequence thus interprets the rebirth of its heroine as an act of creation shared by two married people, mutually dependent yet also with a margin of separation between them. The effect, however, hinges on precisely the self-reflexivity Cavell perceives as the point of connection between cinema and philosophy. The closing photographs can be taken as an official testimony

> that a certain public event has taken place, and that the event is essentially bound up with the achievement of a certain form of public comprehension, of the culture's comprehension of itself, or meet conversation with itself, the achievement, in short, of a form of film comedy.[16]

One further touch of transformation, however, needs to be taken notice of. At the end of *Philadelphia Story,* the heroine, who loses her statue-like aloofness by experiencing and then acknowledging her own fallibility as a woman, turns into the star Katherine Hepburn. The frozen photographs look like film stills from this film comedy, drawing our attention to the fact that we have been watching a Hollywood celebrity. Cavell's insistence that Hollywood entertains a conversation with American culture compels him to assign yet another significance to the shift from moving image to film still that marks the end of and our waking from this remarriage comedy. It is important to remember that, historically, *The Philadelphia Story* was also seminal for the rebirth of Katherine Hepburn as a new type of Hollywood star, which proved to be of national interest. After the success of this film, she came to embody American values such as sincerity, seriousness, and human sympathy for the rest of her career. Hepburn had bought the rights to the script, hoping to break with the image of the arrogant and headstrong actress who by the end of the 1930s was considered box-office poison. As though taking her cue from Emerson, she turned self-reliance to her favor, changed her public persona to fit the times even while remaining true to what the American audience adored in its female stars—a woman who self-consciously works to perfect herself even while remaining staunchly free in making her own choices.

Because the final moments of *Philadelphia Story* freeze the wedding scene into photographs, we too are able to awake from this projected world and our illusion of having partaken of it. And yet the status of the three people standing in front of the alter remains ambivalent, which is why the utopian gesture the comedy of remarriage makes a claim to is, for Cavell, compromised. Does the film end with the kiss that is about to occur and that would seal the promise of happiness? Or mustn't we say instead that the film ends with the photograph of an embrace predicated on uncertainty? The meet and happy conversation this film genre celebrates is shown to be limited to a play of light and shadow projected on a screen. The final image, reducing three players to a couple, inscribes yet a further disturbance. Even though Grant is now holding Hepburn in his arms as a sign that he has successfully won her from his rival Stewart, the lips of the two stars are either not yet or no longer touching. The kiss meant to seal this marriage covenant is one we do not partake of. The visual gap, so pointedly staged, instead calls up a memory of the only kiss Cukor has presented to us—namely, the one between Tracy and Mike during their nocturnal intoxication in the garden behind her villa. The remarriage—between Tracy and Dexter, between Hepburn and her fans—stands for a covenant of nation importance, predicated on the transformation of an unencumbered erotic liberty into moral responsibility. The Constitution does not declare happiness to be the right of every citizen, only its pursuit, so that like moral perfectibility, which the American project also seeks, happiness—and, thus, Hollywood's reflection of the state of the nation—remains achievable but not yet achieved.

Moving from Mourning to Morning: The Melodrama

In *Contesting Tears,* written some fifteen years later, Cavell reads a set of melodramas of the 1930s and 1940s (also called "women's weepies") as the dark inversion of the comedy of remarriage. If in comedy the heroine ultimately returns to a former husband after having gained insight into her desire, in melodrama she discovers the man she had initially chosen to wed is incapable of accepting her desire is separate from his. While both genres culminate in the rebirth of the heroine, melodrama negates precisely the couple's ability to partake in a meet and happy conversation on which the resolution of comedy is predicated. If the remarriage comedy, furthermore, stages a contest for recognition, the heartbreaking pathos in melodrama is based on the husband's refusal to acknowledge his wife, with her coming to accept why their conversation has failed. The metamorphosis she undergoes so as to forge for herself an independent life worth living lies beyond anything her husband could offer her. She thus comes to privilege solitude over a marriage based on discord and silent disregard. To accept the responsibility not only for her own romantic dreams of marriage but also for the disappointment of this aspiration means acting in such a manner that by renouncing her dream of marital bliss she will find a happiness adequate to the knowledge of herself she has gained.

While, according to Cavell, the remarriage comedy makes the heroine's desire known to those who have misjudged her, melodrama revolves around those aspects of her desire that cannot be transmitted to others. At issue is the ability of the heroine to acknowledge herself in her distinct separateness from the man to whom, because he reduces her to a projection of himself, she remains unknown and unknowable. In contrast to the heroine in comedy, her longing for independence cannot be subsumed under the meet and happy conversation of marriage because what the heroine in melodrama is instead forced to acknowledge is that she no longer shares with her husband the set of values necessary for such a conversation to be sustainable. For Cavell the solitude she is compelled to choose is not, however, an expression of self-sacrifice but rather a form of self-empowerment. If melodrama stages to excess the heroine's inability to make herself intelligible to her husband, this experience ultimately brings about her self-certainty. By speaking for herself, turning from her husband, and insisting on her own separateness, she overcomes self-doubt. She has found her singular voice and can now turn toward a freedom that, for the first time in her life, is tantamount to laying claim to her existence on her own terms. While marriage had stifled her voice because her husband could or would not esteem the value of her words, her discovery of a voice independent of him is tantamount to acknowledging her capacity to count. If she is re-created at the end of the film, then it is not in light of how those around her see her but rather by insisting on her right to remain unknowable to those who do not share the conceptual criteria by which she could be known.

For Cavell at issue is thus the question of a self-revelation to which only we, as the audience, can be privy. He once more makes use of the troubled interface between film character and star, claiming that what distinguishes the heroine of melodrama from her counterpart in the remarriage comedy is her ability to render herself (and her unknowability) visible in front of the camera. From Emerson's writings, in turn, he takes the claim that most people don't exist but rather haunt the world as ghosts of themselves. The philosophical aim of the melodrama of the unknown woman thus for him consists in the way it stages how such ghostliness can be overcome both individually and collectively. "The price of Emerson's proof of human existence, our exposure to the consciousness of otherness," he explains, "is that our relation to ourselves is theatricalized, publicized." This self-display is also of national importance given that American film, at its best, participates in Emerson's claim for self-thought and self-invention: "It has the space, and the cultural pressure, to satisfy the craving for thought, the ambition of a talented culture to examine itself publicly."[17]

At the beginning of King Vidor's *Stella Dallas* (1937), the eponymous heroine (Barbara Stanwyck) stands in front of her garden fence with a book in hand, seeking to draw the attention of Stephen Dallas onto herself. She may only be the daughter of one of the workers in his factory, but she dreams of a marriage to this elegant man and the upward mobility this would bring with it. He, in turn, welcomes the fact that she is romantically interested in him because his childhood sweetheart, Helen, has recently left him to marry someone else. One evening, they go to the movies together, and we see the tears in Stella's eyes as she watches the kiss that seals a marriage proposal on screen. As she walks home with Stephen, she explains to him that she yearns to be as cultivated and witty as the movie stars she adores and assures him that she could learn to speak and behave the way he does. The kiss with which he interrupts her flow of words leads seamlessly to marriage, and yet, one year later, Stella is forced to recognize how she has failed to adapt to the propriety her husband's affluent lifestyle dictates because it is, in fact, not to her taste after all. She now forbids her husband to curtail her allegedly improper self-expression. Insisting instead on the discrepancy between her taste and his, she refuses the meet and happy conversation on which marital success is based.

Even the birth of her daughter Laurel cannot hold their marriage together, and after Stephen has moved to New York without his family, he once more seeks solace with Helen. She is now a widow and invites him into the home she has built for her two sons, so familiar to him because they come from the same class. Stella, in turn, accepts her estrangement from her husband because she has transferred her dream of upward mobility to her daughter, whom she educates to fit into the very society to which, owing to her own eccentric taste, she can never belong. At the turning point of the film narrative, Stella selflessly stages a quarrel with Laurel, forcefully bringing about a separation from the daughter who unconditionally adores her, and then proceeds to agree to a divorce so that Laurel can live with her father and Helen, whom he subsequently marries. To fulfill the dream she has for Laurel, she refuses all further contact, hoping thus to ensure her daughter's unencumbered entrance into a world she had initially imagined for herself. Put in terms of the logic of melodrama,

Stella reaches self-knowledge precisely because she is willing to relinquish the very maternal happiness toward which her entire existence seemed to be oriented. Purposely turning away from the world of affluent propriety into which she has propelled her daughter in her stead, she can move into a new day, albeit one far more tarnished than the one available to the heroine of the remarriage comedy.

Cavell's reading of *Stella Dallas* hinges on the scene that sets up this break in a way such that the audience can experience it only as emotionally wrenching. The scene in the luxury hotel, in which Stella's flamboyant attire turns her into an object of public ridicule, draws its melodramatic power not from any catastrophic misunderstanding of how she should behave. Emotionally distressing about this scene, Cavell argues, is that Stella, who has sewn all of Laurel's tasteful wardrobe herself, knows precisely what shocking effect she will have on the elegant society she wants her daughter to be part of. Her vulgar self-presentation is a conscious strategy aimed at separating herself from Laurel precisely because she has come to know herself, which is to say, because she has come to acknowledge that she can never plausibly inhabit the world for which she has been grooming her daughter. If she does everything to appear distasteful to Laurel's cultivated friends, then it is not because she embraces vulgarity but rather because she now consciously seeks the repudiation of the society into which she knows she will never fit. Significant in Cavell's reading of Stella's choice is, thus, his insistence that we do not see her as a victim of her circumstances and instead empathize with the agency this choice entails. Not an emotional struggle is at issue, in the course of which a mother renounces her daughter, but rather the manner in which we are compelled to watch and, thus, affectively partake in the outrageous appearance with which Stella fulfills this sacrifice.

If, at the beginning of the film, she identified with the elegance of the silent movie star she saw projected on screen, seeking to emulate her, she now herself plays a movie scene, only the genre is no longer that of romantic comedy. Instead, we are confronted with a scene of assignation in which Stella shows herself ready to abdicate from her maternal role, forcing a daughter overidentified with her in filial love into acknowledging the need for separation. The dramaturgic formula Cavell offers for the melodrama of the unknown woman is as follows: Stella's ability to become the self that she always was (albeit unknown to both herself and others) is predicated on an acknowledgment of separateness on the part of the daughter. This entails recognizing herself as a woman over and beyond those very cinematic images she had initially sought to emulate. Given that an abdication from cinema's illusory dreams is, thus, the linchpin of his reading, Cavell makes much of the parallel between the scene in the movie theater at the beginning of *Stella Dallas* and the closing sequence. Stella now stands in front of the window of Stephen Dallas's town house as though this, too, were a second film screen. She is as absorbed by viewing her daughter's wedding ceremony taking place inside this home in the final sequence of the Vidor's melodrama as she was by the kiss between the two screen lovers at the beginning.

Laurel's marriage stages (and is staged) as a repetition of the film world that had prompted Stella's own unhappy marriage. As Cavell notes, she looks at her daughter as though Laurel were the unapproachable star of the romantic film narrative that proved not to be available to her. Standing in the rain in front of the iron gate to this house and, thus, irrevocably excluded from the festivities within, she is, however, explicitly marked as the star of a different genre, the melodrama. Helen, who throughout the film narrative alone understood Stella's generosity, has insisted on keeping the curtains to her magnificent living room open, sensing (and hoping) that there would be a clandestine viewer. Even though a crowd has formed around Stella, she alone is illuminated by the three-pointed lighting typical of the way Hollywood gave visual glamour to its stars during its golden years. Stella is thus staged as the privileged audience of a scene of marriage that, in turn, is shown at a distance because it is shot through the windowpane. What she views seems not only to shed light on her but also to serve as a scene of moral illumination. Given the way the actual star, Barbara Stanwyck, is lit, we are, furthermore, meant to recognize that Laurel is not the star of the happy-ending marriage promises. Instead, Stella is confirmed as the sole star in a melodrama, whose narrative acme celebrates her as a woman unknown to all except us.

A policeman asks Stella to move on, yet she begs him to let her remain a moment longer because she wants to see the bride's face after she has been kissed by the bridegroom. As in *Philadelphia Story,* this visual cypher for the completion of the wedding vow is disturbed, only in this case not because the light of a flashbulb causes the couple to look directly at us but because we get no close-up at all of the bride and groom. Instead, the final close-up the film offers us is of the mother, invisible to the person who, throughout the film, has meant the most to her. If the tears on Stella's face speak to the fact that she is enjoying the consummation of her daughter's romantic dream by proxy, they also signify that the transference of her fantasies onto Laurel is tantamount to her having overcoming these. Stella ecstatically turns away from the window qua film screen and proceeds to walk into the dark open space of a New York night while the camera captures her once more in a close-up, walking directly toward us as her tears turn into a radiant smile.

What has she seen in her daughter's face that the camera will not show us? Cavell surmises:

> May we imagine that we have here some Emersonian/Thoreauvian image of what Nietzsche will call the pain of individuation, of the passion Thoreau builds Walden to find, expressed as his scandalous pun on Mo(u)rning, the transfiguration of mourning as grief into morning as dawning and ecstasy?[18]

By turning her back to the window behind which her daughter's marriage is being performed, Stella affirms her freedom to leave behind not only her family but also the consequences of a marriage she thought would transform her into a better person. At issue is less what her new life will look like than the fact that by turning away she proves she has an open future. The rebirth of Stella is tantamount to the birth of a woman who insists on her idiosyncratic taste, who self-reliantly takes on self-knowledge yet who is also present on the screen in such an illusive manner that we are left merely with an intimation of her inner vision.

At the same time, this final turn toward the camera is also the creation of a new star, Barbara Stanwyck. At the beginning of *Stella Dallas,* she still reminds us of the savvy female lover of silent cinema, using her youthful charms to inveigle a wealthy man. In the hotel scene, in turn, she parodies the erotic flamboyance for which pre-Code Hollywood had become so notorious. Walking past us in the last moments of the film with little makeup and seemingly no elegance, she has, as Cavell notes, a future not only because we know she is about to return to the silver screen as the star of *Union Pacific* (Cecil B. DeMille), *Lady Eve* (Preston Sturges), *Double Indemnity* (Billy Wilder), und *Ball of Fire* (Howard Hawks). We also recognize her stardom because the camera makes her present to us as a star by remaining focused to the end both on her walk and her facial expression. *Stella Dallas,* like *Philadelphia Story,* thus hinges on precisely the self-reflexivity that for Cavell is the trademark of the conversation between philosophy and Hollywood for which he is making a claim. The promise of Stanwyck's return, of her reincarnation in future films, is also the one promise with which the film releases us.

The fact that this birth of Barbara Stanwyck as a new type of Hollywood star should be predicated on abdicating from the elegant romantic comedy that had inspired her dream of perfectibility is significant for two reasons. On the one hand, it corresponds historically to the self-censorship introduced by the Hays Production Code in 1933, censoring such sexually exploitative roles as she had played in *Baby Face,* in which she successfully sleeps her way to the top of a company, ending up as the wife of the boss. On the other hand, her transformation corresponds to the moral perfectionism Cavell finds repeatedly relayed in classic Hollywood. "The Emersonianism of the films I have written about as genres depict human beings as on a kind of journey," he explains "from what he means by conformity to what he means by self-reliance . . . from haunting the world to existing in it." Cavell takes the unknown woman's final choice of turning away to be a version of asserting one's *cogito ergo sum,* as "the power to think for oneself, to judge the world, to acquire . . . one's own experience of the world."[19] Stella's demand for a voice, for an adequate mode of self-expression and her insistence on drawing attention to her own subjectivity, emerges as a modern reappraisal of Emerson's demand for thinking.

For Cavell the philosophical question emblematically posed by the final scene of Vidor's melodrama involves the status of the renunciation of maternal love it celebrates. By turning away from the window, Stella sacrifices not herself but a dream of perfectibility she has recognized as being wrong for her: "Stella's gift of and for her daughter, painful as the challenge is, is not precisely, or is precisely not, self-sacrifice."[20] At the beginning of the film, hers was a ghostly existence, her visibility contingent on inscribing herself into the world of her husband. When in this closing scene Stella/Stanwyck not only turns her back on a world that has always had the quality of cinema (for her and for us) but in so doing passes by us, she stages for us that we can never know her, that she will remain separate from us. Having disclosed for the camera the intensity of her pain, Stanwyck performs the limit of such exposure. Rather than turning from us, she forces us to acknowledge that a kernel of unknowability remains of the woman—the heroine and the star—whose projection on screen had held our attention. She has finally gained her singular relation to the world, and this is one she will not (and cannot) share with us.

Cavell's love for the melodrama genre is, however, predicated on an additional autobiographical anecdote. If *The World Viewed* sets in with his description of his family's weekly visits to the movies, *Contesting Tears* ends with his recollection of the migraines his mother used to suffer from, suggesting this was her way of expressing a demand to be noticed. Her therapy for this mood was to play the piano in a darkened room, alone. Yet this is not the only maternal expression Cavell relates to his own preference for King Vidor's melodrama. Whenever this prominent Atlanta pianist wanted to get an opinion from her husband or her son regarding a new garment or ornament she was wearing, she would often ask, "Too Stella Dallas?" This scene most frequently occurred when they were about to leave their apartment for the Friday night movies. Cavell recalls that even then he knew his mother's reference to Stella Dallas was not aimed at dissociating herself from this film character. Rather, her question "was concerned to ward off a certain obviousness of display, not to deny the demand to be noticed."[21]

Based on the ambivalent response his mother entertained toward the American culture into which she, like so many Jewish immigrants from Europe in the first part of the twentieth century, placed her hope, Cavell discovers a final aporia in the melodramatic conflict played out between Laurel and her mother. This emotional conflict is concerned as much with the cultural experience of second-generation Americans as with the psychological separation between mother and daughter so necessary for individuation. As part of their constitutional right to a pursuit of happiness, the children of immigrants were able to become part of proper American society, even if this possibility was predicated on a demand to correct their speech, their clothes, and their demeanor according to its codes. Cavell calls this right a risk because no one can say for certain what is considered proper in America, nor how important such proper behavior might be, given that it corresponds to precisely the conformity Emerson argues against. "Such a child—I speak from experience—recognizes subjection to the familiar double bind," Cavell explains. "If I am not different from them (my parents) and do not enter into a society to which they cannot belong, thus justifying their sacrifices, how can they love me? If I am different from them and do enter where they cannot belong, how can they love me?"[22]

The final theoretical point one might make regarding the philosophical stance of the Hollywood melodrama is that there is no solution for the aporia of immigration into America. With her walk into an open, as yet undetermined future, Barbara Stanwyck, born Ruby Catherine Stevens in Brooklyn in 1907, embodies not only the emotional ambivalence of a working-class mother who can never properly arrive in the proper society to which her husband belongs. She also embodies the immigrant daughter who comes to fulfill her American dream as a Hollywood celebrity. The fact that King Vidor presents her double impersonation as a melodramatic enmeshment between self-sacrifice and self-determination offers one final proof for the significance of the conversation that cinema, according to Cavell, entertains with the culture from which it emerges, which it reflects and which it effects. This conversation is as absolute and as versatile as America's democratic notion of what it means to take part in a cultural project that remains achievable but not yet achieved.

NOTES

1. Cavell, "The Thought of Movies," 88.
2. Cavell, *The World Viewed*, xix.
3. Ibid., 226.
4. Cavell, *Pursuits of Happiness*, 7.
5. Ibid., 136.
6. Ibid., 142.
7. Ibid., 149.

8. Ibid., 152–53.
9. Ibid., 156.
10. Ibid., 142.
11. Ibid., 143.
12. Ibid., 144–45.
13. Ibid., 146.
14. Ibid., 150.
15. Ibid., 151.
16. Ibid., 160.
17. Cavell, *Contesting Tears,* 72.
18. Ibid., 212.
19. Ibid., 220.
20. Ibid., 184.
21. Ibid., 200.
22. Ibid., 213.

BIBLIOGRAPHY

Cavell, Stanley. *Contesting Tears: The Hollywood Melodrama of the Unknown Woman.* Chicago: University of Chicago Press, 1996.
———. *Pursuits of Happiness: The Hollywood Comedy of Remarriage.* Cambridge, Mass.: Harvard University Press, 1981.
———. "The Thought of Movies." In *Cavell on Film,* edited with an introduction by William Rothman, 87–106. Albany: State University of New York Press, 2005.
———. *The World Viewed.* Enlarged ed. Cambridge, Mass.: Harvard University Press, 1979.

Thinking Cinema with Alain Badiou

Alex Ling

Alain Badiou is, by any measure, one of the most original and exciting voices in continental philosophy today. His ambitious project (which involves not only a wholesale rethinking of ontology and phenomenology but also a radical reconfiguring of the place of philosophy itself) has moreover gained considerable currency in Anglophone academia in recent years. While the inaugural English translation of one of his books only appeared comparatively recently, in 1999, the uptake of his philosophy since then has been swift indeed, and today, a very respectable (and ever-increasing) number of Badiou's works are available in English, together with numerous collections of his writings, critical responses to his works, introductions to his philosophy, and so on.[1]

The sudden upsurge of interest in his thought is due in no small part to the fact that, positioning himself squarely against postmodern orthodoxy, Badiou holds that we are in no way condemned to a world ruled by the principle of repetition—where novelty is reduced to so many extensions, recyclings, and superficial transformations of forms of knowledge that are already operating in the situation—but rather are eminently capable of radical invention. Indeed, Badiou's philosophy is, in the final analysis, nothing short of a rigorous attempt to think novelty itself: a thinking, at one end, of how something new—and, crucially, universal—arrives in a world and, at the other, of how real global change can come about.[2] Which is equally to say that Badiou's principal concerns lie with the possibility of *thought* per se: of thought as divorced from the perambulations of knowledge, of thought as that which cuts through or "interrupts repetition" and delivers to us something *truly new*.[3] Needless to say, such original thought is fundamentally rare and doesn't occur just anywhere. In fact, Badiou holds there to be but four generic fields in which real thinking might take place—namely, art, politics, science, and love. Moreover, by virtue of this fact, these four fields also constitute the sole "conditions" of his philosophy—its sine qua non as much as its raison d'être—insofar as the single (and singular) objective of philosophy, as Badiou defines it, is that of bringing together or "rethinking" these disparate thoughts. Put simply, philosophy, for Badiou, is nothing less—and, it must be said, nothing more—than "the thinking of thought."[4]

This absolute need on the part of philosophy to investigate its own conditions has naturally proven to be the driving force behind much of the secondary scholarship surrounding Badiou's work, not least concerning his engagement with politics (specifically communism) and science (in particular, mathematics). Given this clear philosophical imperative, it is interesting that Badiou's many writings on cinema have to date received comparatively scant attention.[5] This critical oversight is perhaps unsurprising given that Badiou's best known musings on film appear (at least at first glance) to suggest that far from serving to condition his philosophy, cinema is in fact of little consequence to Badiou (a suspicion only further confirmed when we place these works alongside his more exuberant writings on poetry, theater, music, and the like). For one thing, Badiou's liberal use of terms like "contaminated," "impure," "parasitic," and "inconsistent" when discussing film would appear less than inspiring.[6] As with the cinema itself, however, appearances can be deceiving. In point of fact, Badiou's philosophical engagement with cinema stretches back at least as far as 1957, with the publication of his first paper on film, "La culture cinématographique," in the journal *Vin nouveau*.[7] Since then, Badiou has written well over thirty articles on cinema, founded and regularly contributed to two separate cinema journals (*La feuille foudre* and *L'art du cinéma*), appeared (in one way or another) in two of Jean-Luc Godard's films,[8] and even (supposedly) begun work on his own "big feature film," entitled *The Life of Plato*.

Moreover, when we look closely, we can discern a noticeable evolution in Badiou's thoughts on film. While previously content to define cinema alternatively as a "bastard art" and a "Saturday night art," we now find him saying that "cinema is today the only art that is cut to the measure of the world"[9] and that "in publishing the final synthesis of my philosophy . . . I will try to turn philosophy toward filmic expression."[10] Indeed, the gradual unraveling of a theory of appearing in *Logics of Worlds* arguably follows a decidedly cinematic logic, which is why it comes as little surprise that in his recent *Second Manifesto for Philosophy* Badiou argues that cinema's "advent of virtual images or images without any referent undoubtedly opens a new stage of questions of representation."[11] At the same time, however, we can isolate a number of constant themes present in Badiou's cinematographic writings: for example, the way cinema functions as a peculiarly pedagogical medium—one that introduces its audience "to something having to do with their orientation in the contemporary world, the world and its exaltation, its vitality, but also its difficulty, its complexity"[12]—as well as how, contrary to the other arts, cinematic thought is primarily conceived negatively, through a process of purification.[13]

In any case, as Badiou sees it, philosophy is obliged to engage with film for the very simple reason that "cinema is a philosophical situation."[14] The aim of this chapter is accordingly to consider Badiou's understanding of cinema itself—taken in the generic sense as an art almost entirely defined by its relation to other arts (and nonart)—and draw out some of the more interesting artistic and philosophical consequences of his position.[15] Following a brief examination of Badiou's "inaesthetic" conception of art and its relation to truth and philosophy, we will move on to discuss cinema's peculiar position among the arts before finally addressing some of the paradoxes Badiou's understanding of cinema gives rise to, as well as some of the challenges it presents his philosophical system as a whole.

Art before Philosophy: Inaesthetics

Central to Badiou's writings on art is his contention that art is not an object for philosophy but rather one of its fundamental conditions.[16] Needless to say, proclaiming art's "conditional" status is in no way to suggest that art serves, or is somehow subordinate to, philosophy. To the contrary, art is most assuredly its own master. In fact, the relationship is, if anything, the other way around, for while philosophy has a definite need for art, art can happily make do without philosophy. This one-sided relationship is one of the main reasons behind Badiou's rejection of traditional aesthetics—which he holds has little to add outside of establishing various rules and hierarchies of "liking"—in favor of an approach to art that limits its interest to the manner by which art effectively *thinks for itself* and, thus, might come to affect philosophy. Briefly, he calls this properly philosophical approach to art "inaesthetics" and defines it as "a relation of philosophy to art that, maintaining that art is itself a producer of truths, makes no claim to turn art into an object for philosophy. Against aesthetic speculation, inaesthetics describes the strictly intraphilosophical effects produced by the independent existence of some works of art."[17]

Of this definition we will suffice ourselves for the moment by saying that, as a philosopher, one of Badiou's foremost concerns is to examine art—or rather, particular arts (most notably, poetry)[18]—as constitutive of what he calls "universal truths" and, as such, as having something essential to offer philosophy. Indeed, anybody with so much as a passing interest in Badiou's thought will know that art constitutes one of the four Platonic conditions of his philosophy (alongside politics, science, and love) and that philosophy, as Badiou defines it, operates only inasmuch as it seizes these independent truths and places them in an immanent relation to one another. In point of fact, philosophy as Badiou defines it is itself fundamentally truthless, being rather the unique discipline tasked with thinking the compossibility of the various (artistic, political, amorous, and scientific) truths that litter the world (and that are themselves ultimately forms of *thought*). Or again, Badiou tells us there are truths that exist *out there,* prior to and wholly independent of philosophy, and that the latter's job is precisely that of grasping these diverse truths and "rethinking" (or rearticulating) them in such a way that they can be brought together to cohere in a single system, which is finally what he calls a *philosophy.* Thus, the relationship between art and philosophy (or indeed, between philosophy and any of its conditions) is for Badiou ultimately a "thoughtful" one, where philosophy is charged with rethinking the thoughts that art thinks.[19]

To come full circle, it is of course philosophy's structurally secondary nature—its forever coming *after* truths—that leads Badiou to write off aesthetics in favor of inaesthetics, which, as we have already seen, restricts itself to "the intraphilosophical effects produced by the existence of some works of art."[20] In a word, truths are what prescribe philosophy, and philosophy does not condescend to its conditions.

Returning then to Badiou's definition of inaesthetics, it is important to highlight how this term designates moreover the philosophical recapitulation of a relation between art and truth that is at once *singular* and *immanent*. This relationship is absolutely crucial for Badiou, and as such it is worth pausing to consider in some detail.

First, the relationship between art and truth is *singular* inasmuch as *every artistic truth is peculiar to the art in question*. So for example, a truth of painting won't be found in poetry, just as architecture or photography are highly unlikely to produce any authentic sculptural-Idea. This is in part a consequence of, on the one hand, Badiou's firm belief that the arts constitute fundamentally closed systems—Badiou explicitly holding that "no painting will ever become music, no dance will ever turn into poem" and that "all attempts of this sort are in vain"[21]—and, on the other, the fact that *every truth*, while universal in address as much as import, *is always the truth of a particular situation*, and in art this situation is generally (though not necessarily) the situation of a *particular* art. Or as Badiou puts it, every artistic truth is "in a rigorous immanence to the art in question": it is always a truth of *this* art, in *this* situation (and not another).[22]

Parenthetically, it is at this point that newcomers to Badiou's thought may be tempted to write him off as a "high modernist," insofar as it can at times appear as though he is recycling an (ostensibly discredited) line of thought generally associated with the modernist project, namely, the idea that the exclusive commitment of each art to its proper medium will finally allow them to lay bare their "pure form" (or, as Badiou would have it, their "generic truth"). While it is safe to say that Badiou is indeed at times arguing something not entirely dissimilar to this, we would be far off the mark were we to reduce his thought to this kind of Greenbergian "autonomizing" framework.[23] Indeed, while it is clear that for Badiou each art is entirely differentiated from the other arts (possessing its own form, possibilities, particular content and modes of expression, and so on), it is important to remember that for Badiou an artistic truth is always the truth of a particular artistic situation, and a "situation," so far as Badiou conceives it, is an incredibly plastic concept, inasmuch as it basically means *any grouping whatsoever.* Indeed, an artistic situation is in no way necessarily medium specific: obviously, there are plenty of examples of mixed artistic situations. So while Badiou, for example, praises someone like Malevich or Picasso for getting to the nub of painting by "exhibiting what in painting is the gesture of all painting" and in this manner "rendering the generic truth of painting's singular situation,"[24] he can equally celebrate someone like Duchamp, whose work—most notably, his infamous readymades—arguably explodes the very idea of medium specificity and exposes something vital in the artistic situation at large.[25]

Badiou however holds that the inaesthetic knot tying together art, truth, and philosophy is not only singular but also *immanent,* insofar as *artistic works are wholly present to the truths they fabricate.* This is a slightly more delicate point and results from Badiou's materialist conception of truths, the general idea being that an artistic truth (or any truth for that matter), despite its infinite nature, isn't simply the truth of a situation but is moreover itself situated. That is to say, it takes place *within* a given world. To summarize brutally: Badiou holds that an artistic truth is always embodied in an identifiable artistic configuration, whose origins lie in a vanished event—this being in general "a singular multiple of works"[26] that suddenly (and inexplicably) give form to what was previously formless[27]—and whose entire body is composed of the manifold artworks belonging to this configuration, which means each individual artwork serves as the fabric from which its truth is gradually woven. Needless to say, this "weaving" can, in principle, go on forever.[28] Hence, the infinity of a truth is in no way confined to a single finite work but rather comprises a virtually infinite sequence of works.[29] As such, the entire "being" of an artistic truth is located in its works, works that are, for complex reasons, *outside* artistic knowledge (or the "state of art") and, as such, proceed solely by chance. Thus, each individual work figures something like an investigation or an "inquiry" into the truth that it actualizes, piece by piece.

So in sum, Badiou defines an artistic truth as a material configuration that, issuing from an event and unfolding by chance alone, comprises an in principle infinite complex of works. Or again, to think art as both singular and immanent to truth is for Badiou one and the same as to think an artistic configuration.

An Inessential Art?

Badiou's peculiar take on cinema, however, throws something of a spanner in the works of his inaesthetic program, particularly with regard to these crucial concepts of singularity and immanence. This complication is ultimately a consequence of Badiou's thesis—which is, it must be said, latent in his own cinematographic writings—that cinema is, in the final analysis, an "inessential" art.

Needless to say, declaring cinema an inessential art isn't simply to say that cinema is unimportant artistically (although given Badiou's aforementioned tendency to use pejorative terms like "contaminated" and "parasitic" when discussing cinema, one could be forgiven for thinking so). Rather, cinema is, according to Badiou, inessential—or, alternatively, "baseless"—insofar as it is an art that is fundamentally devoid of essence, being in the final analysis "nothing but takes and montage."[30] As always, Badiou needs to be read here *to the letter*, inasmuch as a "take" must be understood first in its literal sense—as something that is "taken," wrested from its proper place—while "montage" is for Badiou (as it was for Deleuze) nothing other than a film's final arrangement, the ultimate coupling and uncoupling of all of these "taken takes." This means that cinema is, for Badiou, ultimately a "purloined" art, being first and foremost *the art of taking*. Or again, what is "proper" to cinema is, paradoxically, precisely its *impropriety*, its *inessentialness*, its figuring as an empty site of appropriation.

Crucially, however, Badiou holds that cinema's pilfering extends beyond its apparent relation to the visible and the audible to include the other arts. Indeed, at the very core of Badiou's cinematographic writings—and proceeding directly from his implicit contention that cinema is an inessential art—is his thesis that cinema is a fundamentally *impure* art form, in the sense that it "takes" all that it needs from the other arts (without, for all that, actually giving anything back).[31] In his own words, "cinema is the seventh art in a very particular sense. It does not add itself to the other six while remaining on the same level as them. Rather, it implies them—cinema is the 'plus-one' of arts. It operates on the other arts, using them as its starting point, in a movement that subtracts them from themselves."[32] Needless to say, seeing cinema as an inherently "impure" art form is not in itself anything especially new. To the contrary, this is a thesis that has been bandied about in various ways throughout the short history of cinema, most notably in the pioneering works of Ricciotto Canudo and André Bazin.[33] What Badiou brings to the mix is the way in which he resituates these well-established arguments in relation to his own concepts of art and truth and, of course, philosophy (whose relationship is, as we have seen, at once singular and immanent).

So taking cinema's impurity into account, Badiou's fundamental contention regarding film as an art form—and therefore not simply as a medium but as a form of *art* (and thus an agent of truth)—is that whenever an Idea visits us cinematically—whenever we encounter an effective "cinema-Idea"—it is always brought forth by way of a kind of intrafilmic "complication" with the other arts. An ostensibly original cinematic Idea may for example be indebted to a certain musical evocation, or an actor's peculiar theatricality, a balletic movement or a poetic phrase, and so on. As Badiou puts it, what cinema in effect does is "take from the other arts all that is popular, all that *could,* once isolated, filtered, separated from their aristocratic requirements, destine them to the masses."[34] As such, cinema at once "democratizes" the other arts—this being one of the principal reasons Badiou regards cinema somewhat ambiguously as a "democratic emblem"— while simultaneously figuring as "painting without painting, music without music, novel without subjects, theatre reduced to the charm of actors," and so forth.[35] The point being that in Badiou's theory of cinema each and every "cinema-Idea" is first taken—*stolen*—from other arts. Badiou is absolutely adamant about this: as he puts it in his paper on "The False Movements of Cinema," "Whenever a film really does organize the visitation of an Idea . . . it is *always* in a subtractive (or defective) relation to one or several among the other arts."[36] Or again, cinema's inessential nature means that its own Ideas—its truths—must in fact be first drawn from elsewhere, meaning even a truly original cinematic release is, in a very real sense, already a rerun.

The paradox is that this seemingly disreputable impurity is finally what Badiou holds to be the great power of cinema, inasmuch as its truly *artistic* role is ultimately that of "impurifying" Ideas that have first been given in the other arts, so as to create from this impurity altogether new Ideas (and thereby "bring to light" new facets of old Ideas). In Badiou's words, cinema's "force as a contemporary art lies precisely in turning—for the duration of a passage—the impurity of an idea into an idea in its own right."[37] In contradistinction to the other arts, cinema figures as the "great impurifier," procuring and amplifying Ideas that do not in truth belong to it.

Placing momentarily to one side this "idealization" of cinema, it is important to emphasize another aspect of cinema's impurity, namely, its *nonartistic* side, which relates to its peculiar status as a "place of intrinsic indiscernibility between art and non-art."[38] Basically, cinema figures for Badiou as an art that is in some sense *beneath* art. Indeed, Badiou explicitly holds that "no film strictly speaking is controlled by artistic thinking from beginning to end. It always bears absolutely impure elements within it, drawn from ambient imagery, from the detritus of other arts, and from conventions with a limited shelf life."[39] What this of course means is that—at least in the case of cinema—nonart is immanent to art *as a rule*.[40] Not only is every film, in the final analysis, a commodity circulating in a global market (which is produced by a certain number of laborers and manufactured within a specific system of economic and ideological relations),[41] but the voracious relation of the camera to the real means that no film can truly shield itself from the vulgar or stock images of the time.[42] It is with this in mind that Badiou highlights cinema's sewage plant–like properties, proclaiming how "with only slight exaggeration cinema could be compared to the treatment of waste."[43] Indeed, insofar as cinema figures for Badiou as something of a grey area between art and nonart, he contends that any properly artistic activity in cinema—that is, the effective passage of a cinema-Idea—can only be discerned as a "process of purification of its own immanent non-artistic character."[44] Which is to say that, for a film to be truly artistic, an (effectively interminable) process of purging must first take place. But, Badiou concedes, such an absolutely purificatory process can never be actually achieved. At best, such a "pure" cinematic ideal might only be approached asymptotically. To this effect Badiou concludes that "cinema's artistic operations are incompletable purification operations, bearing on current non-artistic forms or indistinct imagery."[45]

Now while it might seem that cinema's necessary nonartistry forecloses from the start any possibility of its attaining true (or "pure") artistic status, again, the paradox is that it is, according to Badiou, precisely in *maintaining* a degree of nonartistic content that cinema is guaranteed a certain artistic capacity. As Badiou sees it, an absolute purification of cinema's nonartistic content would actually work to *suppress* its artistic capacity, inasmuch as it is precisely through its inherent nonartistry that a film finds its "mass" address. Indeed, Badiou actually holds a film to be contemporary—and thus, at least potentially, "universal"—if and only if "the material whose purification it guarantees is identifiable as belonging to the non-art of its times."[46] Which, incidentally, is also why cinema is, for Badiou, *intrinsically* a mass art. For a film is truly contemporary, he says, only inasmuch as its principal internal referent is a "common imagery" and "not the artistic past of forms."[47] Thus, Badiou effectively posits a second impure movement at play in film, inasmuch as cinema "gathers around identifiably non-artistic materials, which are ideological indicators of the times . . . [and] *transmits* their artistic purification, within the medium of an apparent indiscernibility between art and non-art."[48] In this way cinema "democratises the movement by which art drags itself from non-art by drawing from this movement a border, by making from impurity the thing itself."[49] Which is to say, film also serves a kind of "filtering" function, "purifying" nonart and bringing it into art (in a kind of symmetry with its "impurifying" the other arts).

In sum, Badiou sees cinema as an inessential art, in the sense that it has no "essence" to speak of, no base material that is its and its alone. One of the consequences of this is that cinema figures as an inherently impure art form, inasmuch as it draws its material from, on the one hand, the other arts and, on the other, nonart. Thus, Badiou holds that whenever we encounter a true cinema-Idea, it is always brought forth by way of a kind of intrafilmic complication with the other arts. Yet at the same time, Badiou sees this as cinema's proper artistic role, insofar as film's principal task is that of impurifying Ideas that have first been given in the other arts (and thereby create from this impurity altogether new Ideas). Moreover, even truly "artistic" cinema is hopelessly complicated with nonart—being a "place of intrinsic indiscernibility between art and non-art"[50]—yet at the same time, it is precisely its inherent nonartistry that assures a film's *universality*, its "mass" address.

Cinema as Philosophy

Clearly, cinema introduces a number of problems into Badiou's understanding of the inaesthetic knot tying together art, philosophy, and truth, perhaps the most obvious being that cinema's impurity with regard to the other arts would seem to render the truths it elicits far from singular. Indeed, much like the medium itself, these truths are themselves fundamentally repetitious (being first drawn from elsewhere). It is moreover questionable whether he is able to surmount this problem through recourse to a kind of resingularization, that is, by holding that cinema "impurifies" Ideas belonging to the other arts and turns these impure ideas into new cinema-Ideas in their own right. Arguably, if cinema is to have any true artistic status, it needs to present something radically singular, something "pure" to cinema, something no other art can offer. So too is it questionable whether we can discern any singular "power" to cinema (in the sense that poetry, for example, "makes truth out of the multiple, conceived as a presence that has come to the limits of language,"[51] or dance "[provides] the metaphor for the fact that every genuine thought depends on an event," and so on).[52] Because, when it comes down to it, cinema's "democratic" power is inextricably entangled with the other arts, lying as it does in its ability to "popularize" these arts by "weakening their aristocratic, complex and composite quality"[53] and thereby destining them to the masses.

One might even go so far as to suggest that, at least structurally, cinema in fact shares a greater affinity with philosophy itself than it does with the other arts. For cinema's artistic imperative according to Badiou—namely, that of impurifying or "idealizing" Ideas, making of them new "cinema-Ideas"—is clearly analogous to philosophy's own concerted task to "rethink thought." Moreover, like cinema, philosophy (again, as Badiou conceives it) is basically an empty site of appropriation, whose role is to "compossibilize" truths. These truths, taken—or as Badiou puts it, "seized"—from outside itself, are themselves wholly indifferent to the "Truth" that philosophy finally constructs. Which is to say, philosophy, like cinema, does not remunerate its conditions. The congruence is difficult to ignore: cinema's "impurification" clearly corresponds to philosophy's "compossibilization," while film's "taking" neatly translates into philosophy's "seizure." Indeed, from its primordial connection to Plato's cave (which allegorically charts the journey of the philosopher, not the artist)[54] through its inessential and impure being (cinema figuring an empty site of appropriation) up to its "unique" artistic imperative (impurifying or idealizing Ideas that are first taken from elsewhere), it would seem that cinema has from the start been hopelessly entangled with philosophy.

Badiou himself registers this fact, concluding his paper on "Cinema as a Democratic Emblem" by observing not only that there is today "a clear requisitioning of philosophy by cinema—or of cinema by philosophy," but also that "after the philosophy of cinema must come—is already coming—philosophy *as* cinema, which consequently has the opportunity of being a mass philosophy."[55] Yet cinema can of course never *be* philosophy; rather, it can only *reproduce* it (much in the manner it reproduces the other arts). Moreover, if cinema bears something of a family resemblance to philosophy—or, for that matter, to antiphilosophy or sophistry, each of which in some sense mimic philosophy[56]—it must nevertheless maintain its proper distance. For regardless of its impure nature, cinema is foremost an art (albeit a singularly *complicated* art), which is to say a condition of philosophy, and the absolute separation of philosophy from its conditions is crucial lest philosophy succumb to the disaster of "suture."[57]

Where exactly this leaves cinema as an art form is difficult to answer, and one suspects it is this, rather than any inherent distaste for the medium itself, that causes Badiou still today to waver in his granting cinema a definite "artistic" status. Because in the final analysis, cinema, as Badiou conceives it, is torn between two heterogeneous (and fundamentally, repetitious) procedures: being at once the reproduction of art and the reproduction of philosophy itself.

NOTES

1. Since Norman Maderasz's translation of *Manifesto for Philosophy* in 1999, over thirty of Badiou's books have appeared in English, including his magnum opi: *Theory of the Subject, Being and Event,* and *Logics of Worlds.*

2. In his own words, "My unique philosophical question, I would say, is the following: can we think that there is something new in the situation, not outside the situation nor the new somewhere else, but can we really think through

novelty and treat it in the situation? The system of philosophical answers that I elaborate, whatever its complexity may be, is subordinated to that question and none other." Badiou and Bosteels, "Can Change Be Thought," 252–53.

3. In opposing authentic instances of novel thought—what he calls "truth-procedures"—to the calculable machinations of constituted knowledges, Badiou closely follows the work of Jacques Lacan, who understood thought (qua truth) as what punches a hole through knowledge and thereby "hollows out its way into the real." Lacan, *The Seminar of Jacques Lacan*, 228.

4. Badiou, *Deleuze*, 21.

5. It must be said that Badiou's work on cinema has in fact all too frequently been sidelined or simply written-off in secondary scholarship. To take a single example, Peter Hallward—in whom Badiou recognizes his "most well-versed and ardent interpreter and critic" (Alain Badiou, *Logics of Worlds*, 543)—contends in his seminal work on Badiou that, unlike the other arts, "Badiou is not entirely convinced of the artistic potential of film" and accordingly grants cinema only a single-page entry in his nigh on five-hundred-page tome. Hallward, *Badiou*, 206. Aside from a smattering of papers that critically engage with Badiou's work on cinema, the only sustained response to Badiou's work on film remains my own *Badiou and Cinema* (2011), although this may soon change now that Badiou's own various writings on film have recently been brought together by Antoine de Baecque in the collection *Cinema* (2013).

6. To take but a single example, in his best known essay on cinema, "The False Movements of Cinema" from *Handbook of Inaesthetics*, Badiou contends that cinema is an art that is "both parasitic and inconsistent" and that it is "internally and integrally contaminated by its situation as the 'plus-one' of arts." Badiou, *Handbook of Inaesthetics*, 83, 86. See also Badiou, *Infinite Thought*, 110; and Badiou, "Cinema as a Democratic Emblem," 4.

7. It is moreover worth noting that, prior even to this, Badiou had the distinction of running "that organization which was so invaluable back then, the high school cinema club." Badiou, *Cinema*, 1.

8. Excerpts of Badiou's 1966 paper "L'autonomie du processus esthétique" were quoted in Godard's *La Chinoise* (1967), while Badiou appeared as himself in Godard's recent *Film socialisme* (2010).

9. Badiou, "Le plus-de-voir," 90.

10. Badiou and During, "Le 21e siècle n'a pas commencé," 58.

11. Badiou, *Second Manifesto for Philosophy*, 122.

12. Badiou, *Cinema*, 18. Cinema, Badiou contends, is the art "that has formally captured more parts of the real—the real of the contemporary world—than the other arts," and as such is "the art that, still today, seems to me the most alive, the most active." Badiou and Tarby, *Philosophy and the Event*, 84.

13. Compare, for example, Badiou's 1957 "Cinematic Culture," in which he notes that the predominant signs of cinema's "conversion" into art are "essentially negative ones" (Badiou, *Cinema*, 28)—as we see for example in the familiar pro-

cess whereby ostensibly necessary filmic elements (actors, action, plot, continuity, etc.) are systematically excised in the hope of attaining to something "pure"— with his later assertions that "cinema is a negative art because it proceeds from too many things to a sort of reconstituted simplicity." Badiou, *Cinema*, 227.

14. Badiou, *Cinema*, 202.

15. Space constraints obviously preclude a complete overview of Badiou's entire cinematic oeuvre. For a more detailed account, the reader would do well to consult the collection *Cinema* (Badiou is, as always, his own best exegete) or alternatively my own *Badiou and Cinema*.

16. As we have seen, Badiou holds that, far from being an autonomous discipline, philosophy's singular role is rather that of organizing the structural compatibility (what he calls the "compossibility") of various thoughts that are drawn from four external sources or "conditions," namely, art, politics, science, and love. The conditioning of philosophy thus involves something of an inversion of the common conception of philosophical thought (wherein philosophy would be brought to bear on its conditions) to contrarily contend that philosophy can only be thought—in fact, constructed from scratch—by way of its conditions.

17. Badiou, *Handbook of Inaesthetics*, xiv.

18. While poetry certainly figures as the paradigmatic artistic example in Badiou's philosophy, his focus has arguably shifted somewhat toward cinema and cinematic form in recent years (notably with his recent elaboration of an objective or "nonphenomenal" phenomenology in *Logics of Worlds*). For example, while in establishing his mathematical ontology in the late 1980s in *Being and Event* and *Manifesto for Philosophy*, Badiou was perfectly content to substitute (following Plato) the word "poem" for the word "art"—referring to the four generic conditions in the latter work simply as "the poem, the matheme, the political and love. Badiou, *Manifesto for Philosophy*, 61. By the time of his *Second Manifesto for Philosophy*, we find Badiou arguing that what is imperative today with regard to art is that we "show how, following on the heels of cinema (the greatest artistic invention of the past century), new possibilities are springing up, without their exploration having, as yet, produced a decisive shift towards a fundamental reorganization of the classification and hierarchy of artistic activities." Badiou, *Second Manifesto for Philosophy*, 121–22.

19. In Badiou's words, "We must above all not conclude that it is philosophy's task to think art. Instead, *a configuration thinks itself in the works that compose it.*" Badiou, *Handbook of Inaesthetics*, 14.

20. Badiou, *Handbook of Inaesthetics*, xiv.

21. Ibid., 82.

22. Ibid., 13.

23. Cf. Clement Greenberg's famous declaration that "the essence of Modernism lies . . . in the use of the characteristic methods of a discipline to criticize the discipline itself—not in order to subvert it, but to enrich it more firmly in its area of competence." Greenberg, "Modernist Painting," 193. Jacques Rancière

most convincingly pursues this line of thought (with regard to Badiou) in his "Aesthetics, Inaesthetics, Anti-Aesthetics," 218–31.

24. Badiou and Sedofsky, "Being by Numbers," 124.

25. On the importance of Duchamp's readymades to Badiou's philosophy, see Formis, "Event and Readymade," 247–61; and Badiou, "Some Remarks concerning Marcel Duchamp." Another reason Badiou finds himself tarred with the modernist brush is of course his philosophical celebration of abstraction in art. Indeed, it is crucial for Badiou that every true artwork be on some level abstract. This necessary abstraction arises however not from any modernist sympathies (although Badiou's tastes certainly do run in this direction) but rather from the fact that art is, according to Badiou, a generic procedure and, as such, "it is abstracted from all particularity and it formalizes this act of abstraction." Badiou, *Polemics*, 146. After all, true art, in its fundamental *novelty*, can but appear at first as something wholly abstract (or unknown) to the world in which it appears.

26. Badiou, *Handbook of Inaesthetics*, 12.

27. Badiou holds every truth (or every instance of real thought) to originate in an event, which, roughly speaking, is a localized and entirely unpredictable rupture with the order of things, involving the sudden arrival on the scene of a radically new element (an element whose address is, for complex reasons, immediately universal). A single spark that ignites a political revolution, a new scientific theory compelling us to change our understanding of the world, an amorous encounter that turns your life upside down, a formal innovation that forces us to reassess the limitations as much as the possibilities of art: suddenly and unpredictably, something *happens* in the world and ruptures with its prevailing logic by pointing to a previously unimaginable *possibility*, something that had hitherto been impossible or unthinkable (as opposed to simply unconsidered).

28. While an artistic sequence can indeed become saturated (when the resources of the situation have dried up to the point that new works cease to be properly inventive), this in no way spells a truth's *finitude*. To the contrary, a truth is that which "ignores every internal maximum, every apex, and every peroration." Badiou, *Handbook of Inaesthetics*, 14. As Badiou puts it in *Logics of Worlds*, if an artistic configuration finds itself saturated, "this is not because it failed; it is because every subject, albeit internally infinite, constitutes a sequence whose temporal limits can be fixed after the fact." Badiou, *Logics of Worlds*, 81.

29. As Badiou puts it elsewhere, "Truth . . . compounds itself to infinity. It is thus never presented integrally." Badiou, "What Is Love?," 49.

30. Badiou, *Handbook of Inaesthetics*, 86 (trans. modified).

31. Badiou has more recently ameliorated this claim somewhat, conceding that while it thrives "parasitically" off the other arts, cinema at the same time thereby ensures their popularity by "opening" them up and "[weakening] their aristocratic, complex and composite quality." Badiou, "Cinema as a Democratic Emblem," 5. Cinema thus presents the "active democratization" of the arts: it is the seventh art that democratizes the other six, bringing them into the mass

sphere. Elsewhere, Badiou adds that cinema "doesn't just use [the other arts] or intermingle with them; it defies them and presents them with challenges that are hard to meet: to achieve by themselves, on their own, what cinema is able to do with them." Badiou, *Cinema*, 7.

32. Badiou, *Handbook of Inaesthetics*, 79.

33. Ricciotto Canudo for example firmly believed that cinema would come to constitute a kind of *Gesamtkunstwerk*, whereby cinema would "increasingly serve as Art's powerful coadjutor," arguing that "when the painter and the musician truly wed the poet's dream, and when their triple expression of a single subject is achieved in living light by the *écraniste* . . . films will reach us with a supreme clarity of ideas and visual emotions. We will recognize cinema as the synthesis of all the arts and of the profound impulse underlying them." Canudo, "Reflections on the Seventh Art," 293. Likewise, André Bazin spent much time defending cinema's impure status, proclaiming that films provide "an open sesame for the masses to the treasures of the world of art" (Bazin, *What Is Cinema?*, 167) and that far from being in competition with the other arts, cinema in fact involves "the adding of a new dimension that the arts had gradually lost from the time of the Reformation on: namely a public. Who will complain of that?" Bazin, *What Is Cinema?*, 175.

34. Badiou, "Cinema as a Democratic Emblem," 3.

35. Ibid., 4.

36. Badiou, *Handbook of Inaesthetics*, 86 (italics mine).

37. Badiou, *Handbook of Inaesthetics*, 83. In later writings, Badiou extends this to argue that "cinema transforms philosophy" insofar as it "transforms the very notion of idea. Cinema basically consists in creating new ideas about what an idea is." Badiou, *Cinema*, 202.

38. Badiou, *Infinite Thought*, 111.

39. Badiou, *Infinite Thought*, 111. As Badiou puts it elsewhere (in relation to Plato's theory of Forms), "If cinema is . . . the chance visitation of the Idea, this is in the sense in which the old Parmenides, in Plato, requires the young Socrates to accept, together with the Good, the Just, the True, and the Beautiful, some equally abstract if less respectable ideas: the ideas of Hair, or of Mud." Badiou, "Le plus-de-voir," 90.

40. In point of fact, while cinema is doubtless an absolutely impure art, this in no way means that the other arts are by contrast necessarily "pure." To the contrary, impurity is a fundamental law of art, inasmuch as art, *real* art, always involves the formalization of what was previously formless, the radical becoming-art of what was heretofore considered nonart or what, according to the artistic world in question, did not previously exist (again, this is especially obvious in the case of Duchamp, in particular his readymades). "Purification" is thus as much a subtractive gesture (eliminating apparent impurities) as it is a creative movement (formalizing or *bringing into form* what was previously formless, or pure-ifying what was impure). Indeed, it is precisely this movement that Badiou

holds cinema "democratizes"—namely, "the movement by which art drags itself from non-art by drawing from this movement a border, by making from impurity the thing itself." Badiou, "Cinema as a Democratic Emblem," 5.

41. As Badiou readily points out, "The cinema is *first and foremost* an industry," and it "requires money, a lot of money." Badiou, *Cinema*, 226.

42. As we will see, however, cinema's omnivorous nature can also paradoxically be seen to raise it "above" the other arts, Badiou conceding that "of all the arts, [cinema] is certainly the one that has the ability to think, to produce the most absolute, undeniable truth," due to the simple fact that it is "steeped in the infinite of the real." Badiou, *Cinema*, 18.

43. Badiou, *Cinema*, 226.

44. Badiou, *Infinite Thought*, 111.

45. Badiou, *Infinite Thought*, 111. Cf. Badiou, *Cinema*, 227: "My own hypothesis is that it has become impossible to master [cinema's] sensible infinity. This impossibility is the real of cinema, which is a struggle with the infinite, a struggle to purify the infinite."

46. Badiou, *Infinite Thought*, 113.

47. Ibid.

48. Ibid., 113–14.

49. Badiou, "Cinema as a Democratic Emblem," 5.

50. Badiou, *Infinite Thought*, 111.

51. Badiou, *Handbook of Inaesthetics*, 22.

52. Badiou, *Handbook of Inaesthetics*, 61. It is worth noting that Badiou's own treatment of dance here is itself a kind of creative repetition (à la cinema) of Mallarmé's own writings on ballet as constituting a "visual embodiment of thought." Mallarmé, *Mallarmé in Prose*, 112.

53. Badiou, "Cinema as a Democratic Emblem," 5.

54. As Jean-Louis Baudry (along with countless others) has observed, "The allegory of the cave . . . haunts the invention of cinema and the history of its invention." Baudry, "The Apparatus," 307.

55. Badiou, "Cinema as a Democratic Emblem," 5.

56. When Badiou notes for example that the "democratic art" of cinema is "the supreme witness to the resources of the present" (Badiou cited in Boyer, "Présents du pays," 11) it is hard not to register the underlying ambivalence of his words, his assessment clearly chiming with his description of "Great Modern Sophistry, linguistic, aestheticizing and democratic [that] exercises its dissolving function, examines impasses and draws the picture of what is contemporary to us. It is just as essential for us as the libertine was to Blaise Pascal: it *alerts* us to the singularities of the time." Badiou, *Manifesto for Philosophy*, 98.

57. A suture occurs when "instead of constructing a space of compossibility through which the thinking of time is practiced, philosophy *delegates* its functions to one or other of its conditions, handing over the whole of thought to *one* generic procedure." Badiou, *Manifesto for Philosophy*, 61.

BIBLIOGRAPHY

Badiou, Alain. *Being and Event.* Translated by Oliver Feltham. London: Continuum, 2005.

———. *Cinema.* Edited by Antoine de Baecque. Translated by Susan Spitzer. Cambridge: Polity Press, 2013.

———. "Cinema as a Democratic Emblem." Translated by Alex Ling and Aurélien Mondon. *Parrhesia* 6 (2009): 1–6.

———. *Deleuze: The Clamor of Being.* Translated by Louise Burchill. Minneapolis: University of Minnesota Press, 2000.

———. *Handbook of Inaesthetics.* Translated by Alberto Toscano. Stanford, Calif.: Stanford University Press, 2005.

———. *Infinite Thought: Truth and the Return to Philosophy.* Edited and translated by Justin Clemens and Oliver Feltham. London: Continuum, 2003.

———. "La culture cinématographique." *Vin nouveau* 5 (1957): 3–22.

———. "L'autonomie du processus esthétique." *Cahiers Marxistes-Léninistes,* nos. 12–13 (1966): 77–89.

———. "Le plus-de-voir." *Art press,* hors série (1998): 86–90.

———. *Logics of Worlds: Being and Event II.* Translated by Alberto Toscano. London: Continuum, 2009.

———. *Manifesto for Philosophy.* Translated by Norman Maderasz. Albany: SUNY Press, 1999.

———. *Polemics.* Edited and translated by Steve Corcoran. London: Verso, 2006.

———. *Second Manifesto for Philosophy.* Translated by Louise Burchill. Cambridge: Polity Press, 2011.

———. "Some Remarks Concerning Marcel Duchamp." *Symptom* 9 (June 2008). www.lacan.com.

———. "What Is Love?" Translated by Justin Clemens. *Umbr(a)* 1 (1996): 37–53.

Badiou, Alain, and Bruno Bosteels. "Can Change Be Thought: A Dialogue with Alain Badiou." In *Alain Badiou: Philosophy and its Conditions,* edited by Gabriel Riera, 237–61. New York: SUNY Press, 2005.

Badiou, Alain, and Eli During. "Le 21e siècle n'a pas commencé: Entretien avec Elie During." *Art Press,* no. 310 (2005): 56–58.

Badiou, Alain, and Lauren Sedofsky. "Being by Numbers." *Artforum* 33, no. 2 (1994): 84–87, 118, 123–24.

Badiou, Alain, and Fabien Tarby. *Philosophy and the Event.* Translated by Louise Burchill. Cambridge: Polity Press, 2013.

Baudry, Jean-Louis. "The Apparatus: Metapsychological Approaches to the Impression of Reality in Cinema." In *Narrative, Apparatus, Ideology: A Film Theory Reader,* edited by Philip Rosen and translated by Jean Andrews and Bertrand Augst, 299–318. New York: Columbia University Press, 1986.

Bazin, André. *What Is Cinema?* Vol. 1. Edited and translated by Hugh Gray. Berkeley: University of California Press, 1967.

Boyer, Elisabeth. "Présents du pays." *L'art du cinéma* 46–49 (2005): 5–12.

Canudo, Ricciotto. "Reflections on the Seventh Art." In *French Film Theory and Criticism: A History/Anthology 1907–1939.* Vol. 1, *1907–1929,* edited by Richard Abel and translated by Claudia Gorbman, 291–303. Princeton, N.J.: Princeton University Press, 1988.

Formis, Barbara. "Event and Readymade: Delayed Sabotage." *Communication and Cognition* 37, nos. 3–4 (2004): 247–61.

Hallward, Peter. *Badiou: A Subject to Truth.* Minneapolis: University of Minnesota Press, 2003.

Greenberg, Clement. "Modernist Painting." *Art and Literature* 4 (1965): 193–201.

Lacan, Jacques. *The Seminar of Jacques Lacan.* Vol. 1, *Freud's Papers on Technique, 1953–1954.* Edited by Jacques-Alain Miller. Translated by John Forrester. New York: Norton, 1991.

Ling, Alex. *Badiou and Cinema.* Edinburgh: Edinburgh University Press, 2011.

Mallarmé, Stéphane. *Mallarmé in Prose.* Edited by Mary Ann Caws. Translated by Rosemary Lloyd and Mary Ann Caws. New York: New Directions, 2001.

Rancière, Jacques. "Aesthetics, Inaesthetics, Anti-aesthetics" In *Think Again: Alain Badiou and the Future of Philosophy,* edited by Peter Hallward, 218–31. London: Continuum, 2004.

Thinking as Feast

RAYMONDE CARASCO

Nicole Brenez

> For me, your text is, I would say, of the order of the feast.
> Roland Barthes on Raymonde Carasco's postgraduate thesis in "L'essai en fête,"
> October 1975
>
> One enters the thought of Tarahumara one day, one beautiful day:
> this is inevitably a morning of feast.
> Raymonde Carasco, Spring 2005

The literary and cinematic work of the French philosopher and film-maker Raymonde Carasco-Hébraud (1939–2009) comprises a thorough analysis of the theoretical and practical circulations, intersections, and interrelations between verbal and audiovisual thinking. Author of sixty articles and three books, two published during her lifetime and one posthumously; editor of two collected volumes; and codirector, with her husband, Régis Hébraud, of sixteen films in both 16 mm and 35 mm, Carasco is perhaps the only professional philosopher to have created such an extensive literary and cinematic body of work. Some overlap between filmmakers and philosophers does exist. Jean-François Lyotard made three short films. Terrence Malick, Bruno Dumont, and Florent Marcie studied philosophy but left it for the cinema. Jean-Paul Sartre and René Schérer wrote screenplays. King Vidor's final film, *Truth and Illusion: An Introduction to Metaphysics* (1965), is an essay in philosophical-narrative form. In "Letters on the Blind" in *Tourner les mots,* Jacques Derrida analyzes *Derrida's*

Elsewhere, a film by Safaa Fathy about his life and work. The philosopher Daniel Ross, along with David Barison, directed *The Ister* (2004), a film about European philosophy narrated by French thinkers Philippe Lacoue-Labarthe, Jean-Luc Nancy, and Bernard Stiegler and by the German filmmaker Hans-Jürgen Syberberg. There are numerous other collaborations between filmmakers and philosophers: Robert Ménégoz and Simone de Beauvoir, André Delvaux and Jacques Sojcher, Jean Rouch and Edgar Morin, Yolande of Luart and Angela Davis, Lionel Soukaz and Guy Hocquenghem, Benoît Jacquot and Jacques Lacan, Claire Denis and Jean-Luc Nancy, Franssou Prenant and René Schérer, Olivier Azam and Noam Chomsky, Michel Gondry and Noam Chomsky, and, in a slightly different way, Gilles Deleuze and Claire Parnet. There is no lack of professional interactions between philosophy and film.

Nevertheless, Carasco offers a rare example of this interaction, perhaps comparable only to that of Alexander Kluge. Carasco was a creator who, as a philosopher and a filmmaker, freed herself from interdisciplinary divisions so that she could combine her speculative resources in the service of a larger poetic project. How can one define such an endeavor? And how are the respective dynamics of philosophy and film intertwined? To clarify, Carasco's project is to invent descriptive forms faithful to the event of encountering the world while considering, at every moment, the unheard and infinite richness of its multiple physical and mental movements. Although this encounter usually involves a human being, either singularly or as part of a community, for Carasco, through the prism of ethical and aesthetic requirements, it also involves a landscape, a light, a vibration, any sign of nature or culture. This encounter does not, however, belong to the traditional conceptions of otherness that face an affected ego; instead, the carasquian encounter requires a recasting of identities. Being true to life means having an experimental ethos. Carasco perhaps best expressed this idea in June 2004 during a get-together with filmmakers Philippe Grandrieux, Marcel Hanoun, F. J. Ossang, and Mounir Fatmi:

> I have filmed the Tarahumara people and their rites for twenty years,
> and in the course of my work, several Tarahumara gave me their friendship. Now a gift requires a countergift, that is to say a greater gift. For

a filmmaker, the one who is making the countergift is the audience, the people. There are always people around, "there are always people," it is almost a song title. We meet the other in the desire of the other and at the end realize that he is the same, "he" and "I" do not exist, there are no singularities, only flows of intensities, [to Philippe Grandrieux] intensities, more than energy, because energy is only physical. When you shoot, the one you shoot first gives you the immensity of difference, the irreducible difference, and you, you have to bring something to him, it is a necessity, it is an exchange and for me that's the politics. This is the city, which means belonging to a community, a community that is not a small clan. *The generosity of the creation, the generosity of life, is completely beyond us as individuals, let's say determinable ones; it is not even about individuality.* It is not about the meeting between two people, the flows of life are beyond us, they belong to the community itself. If I had not been a stranger in France, I certainly would not have gone to the Tarahumara, I would never have done films.[1]

With her husband, Régis Hébraud (a mathematics teacher), Carasco worked apart from the social and professional circles of recognition and commercialization, which reveals the ethical integrity of her relationship to the world and explains the delay of her critical reception. Carasco's work thus developed of its own necessity in a serene independence not connected, in any way, to autarky. Her work was readily available to anyone who wanted it, especially during her fertile dialogues with Jean Rouch at the Ethnographic Film Committee, but Carasco remained focused on its production rather than on its release—which makes it even more precious, since its very existence constitutes a model of freedom.

Biographical Details

Born June 19, 1939, in Carcassonne, France, Raymonde Carasco, the granddaughter of Spanish immigrants, met Régis Hébraud in October 1955 and married him in 1960. They had three children: Anne (1961), Emmanuelle (1966), and Jean-Baptiste (1972). From 1960 to 1964, Carasco studied the history of philosophy at the École normale supérieure (Fontenay-aux-Roses). In 1963 she obtained a diploma of higher studies (DES) at the Sorbonne. Supervised by Ferdinand

Alquié (a philosopher and a specialist in both surrealism and René Descartes, which qualified him to be a consultant on Roberto Rossellini's *Cartesius* in 1974), her research thesis was titled "Finalité morale et finalité naturelle dans la philosophie de Kant" (Moral finality and natural finality in Kant's philosophy). In 1964 Carasco received the highest teaching diploma in philosophy, which she taught, from 1964 to 1970, in the high schools of Bayonne, Chateauroux, and Toulouse. Appointed assistant professor of philosophy and aesthetics of cinema at the University of Toulouse–Le Mirail, she returned to Paris on a weekly basis to follow the seminars of Gilles Deleuze at the Centre universitaire de Vincennes and those of Roland Barthes at the École des hautes études en sciences sociales. In 1973, as part of Group 101, she organized a one-week conference in Toulouse, hosting André Téchiné, Jacques Bontemps, and Marcel Hanoun. On October 30, 1975, she defended her doctoral thesis, "La fantastique des philosophes," at the University of Toulouse–Le Mirail in front of a jury consisting of Roland Barthes, Gérard Granel, and Supervisor Mikel Dufrenne.[2]

After completing her thesis, in the summer of 1976 Carasco transformed her speculative research into a cinematic journey. Inspired by Eisenstein's and Antonin Artaud's creative travels, in 1931 and 1936, respectively, she began a series of journeys through Mexico with her husband. The result was a series of films about the Tarahumara, shot entirely in 16 mm from 1977 to 2003. In Pompeii, early in the summer of 1977, Carasco shot her first film, following in the footsteps of the Gradiva, a fictional character who blurred fantasy and reality and who would shape her creative path. In her homeland of France, she focused her work on her family. There, she shot three film essays devoted to her father, Julien, a mason who discovered the need to write as the result of an accident at work (1981–83), and a feature film inspired by the tragic life of her actress sister, *Rupture* (1989), featuring Bulle Ogier, Mireille Perrier, and Pascal Greggory. At the same time, she wrote scripts; travel notebooks; articles and books of literary, philosophical, and film analysis; correspondence; and diaries. Only a part of these many writings have been published.

In 1981 Carasco applied for a state doctorate under the supervision of Gilles Deleuze—primarily, to conduct a research project simply yet ambitiously titled "La cinématographie." But state doctorates were repealed in 1984, and thus, her endeavor would not be completed, at least in its strict, academic form. In 1984 she was appointed as a lecturer in film aesthetics in the Department of Philosophy at the University of Toulouse–Le Mirail. In January 1992, at the University of Paris VIII, she defended her habilitation, "L'idée de montage et l'expérience de l'écriture" (The idea of editing and the experience of writing), in front of a jury comprising Chairperson Jacques Rancière, Jean-Louis Leutrat, Jean-Claude Mathieu, Dominique Noguez, and Marie-Claire Ropars-Wuilleumier (her adviser). In 2000 Carasco was appointed professor of film studies at the University of Lille III. Starting in 1984, she led and codirected seminars at the Collège international de philosophie in Paris, including "Thought-Action (Film)" in 1984, "The Thought-Cinema" in 1998, and "Film-Body-Thought" in 2000.[3] These titles exemplify the core of her extensive thought.

Suffering from Alzheimer's disease, Carasco died on March 2, 2009. Since then, Régis Hébraud has devoted himself to ordering and scanning their considerable archive of films, photographs, and manuscripts. He is the editor of the series Poems for Raymonde, which includes *Filmer ce désert* (Shooting this desert, 2009) and *Los Matachines* (The Matachines, 2010).

Corpus

Carasco's available works can be divided into the following six categories:

1. Three of her books have been published: (1) *Hors Cadre Eisenstein* (Out of frame Eisenstein; Paris: Macula, 1979), an excerpt from her thesis, of which the larger part remains unpublished; (2) *Le portrait ovale* (The Oval Portrait; Chambéry: Éditions comp'act, 1996); and (3) *Dans le bleu du ciel: Au pays des Tarahumaras, 1976–2001* (In the blue sky: In the land of the Tarahumara; Paris: François Bourin, 2014), her diaries from her time in Tarahumara country.

2. She is the editor of two collected volumes: (1) *Contribution à une théorie du cinéma* (Contributions to film theory; Toulouse: University of Toulouse–Le Mirail, 1973) depicts the research activities of Group 101 during 1972—particularly, their involvement

with André Téchiné, Jacques Bontemps, and Marcel Hanoun. Though the book is labeled volume 1, no volume 2 was created. The material that would have comprised volume 2 found its way into her films. (2) "Henri Langlois" is a special issue of the journal *Loess* (January 13, 1987). To commemorate the tenth anniversary of Henri Langlois's death, Carasco collected documents and testimonies from several filmmakers. Far from being traditional interviews, her procedure demonstrated her love for the plurality of forms of both speech and listening:

All the contributions here . . . were initially aimless remarks, conversations at a cafe table during a first encounter, dialogues, or even some kinds of monologues. Done at once ("Manet's blacks are so beautiful, done at once," said Cézanne): the text, as if inspired by a foreign spirit, by Jean Rouch; the step by step, yet adamant meditation by Philippe Garrel; the continuous blast of Joris Ivens, torn from asthma and from *the Wind*, just before he left for China. All speech acts, oral things, words offered in the openness and freedom of a saying: Friendship, the word one must venture to utter.[4]

3. She published numerous, scattered articles in journals that were sometimes general interest and sometimes specialized in aesthetics, philosophy, literature, and film. Among the most recurrent of Carasco's topics are the body, the fragment, the event, the Tarahumara, Sergei Eisenstein, Antonin Artaud, Jean-Luc Godard, Joë Bousquet, Pier Paolo Pasolini, Michel Foucault, and eroticism.

4. Twenty films of various lengths were shot and edited in 16 mm (with three exceptions) between 1977 and 2003. The following is a full list in chronological order and is approved by Régis Hébraud: *Gradiva Sketch 1* (1978, 25 mins.), *Tarahumara 78* (1979, 30 mins.), *Tutuguri: Tarahumara 79* (1980, 25 mins.), *Julien: Portrait of a Visionary* (1981, 75 mins.), *Los Pintos: Tarahumara 82* (1982, 58 mins.), *Julien* (1983, 50 mins.), *The Yellow Rays* (1983, 15 mins.), *Yumari: Tarahumara 84* (1985, 50 mins.), *Rupture* (1989, 85 mins., 35 mm), *Passages* (1992, 16 mins., video), *Los Pascoleros: Tarahumara 85* (1996, 27 mins.), *Ciguri 96* (1996, 42 mins.), *Artaud and the Tarahumara* (1996, 50 mins., video),

Ciguri 98: Dance of Peyote (1998, 42 mins.), *Ciguri 99: The Last Shaman* (1999, 65 mins.), *Tarahumara 2003: The Crack of Time: The Before—The Apaches* (2003, 38 mins.), *Tarahumara 2003: The Crack of Time: Childhood* (2003, 44 mins.), *Tarahumara 2003: The Crack of Time: Initiation—Gloria* (2003, 48 mins.), *Tarahumara 2003: The Crack of Time: Raspador—The Sueño* (2003, 42 mins.), *Tarahumara 2003: The Crack of Time: La Despedida* (2003, 50 mins.).[5] Based on this list, we can see Carasco worked via a deepening dynamic dedicated to the unfolding of four figurative projects: human movement (passim); Tarahumara civilization (a cycle performed across three decades, a very rare case in the history of cinema); the figure of her father; and the figure of her sister.

5. A series of lost unfinished films and reels of rushes from the archives have been completed by Régis Hébraud and are available in a digital format. *Divisadero 77 or Gradiva Western* (36 mins.) was shot and edited in 1977 and then forgotten and later found in 2009. *Los Matachines: Tarahumara 87* (34 mins.) and *Portrait of Erasmo Palma: Tarahumara 87* (34 mins.) were shot in 1987 and edited in 2011. *Shooting This Desert* (2010, 7 mins.) has been edited from tails and claps in which one can see and hear Carasco, as well as from her sound recording of the eponymous poem. This series is ongoing.

6. A sound recording of Carasco is also available. In 2008 she lent her voice to the French version of *Divine Horsemen: The Living Gods of Haiti* (Re:Voir), on voodoo rituals, shot by Maya Deren between 1947 and 1954 and completed by her husband, Teiji Io, in 1981. The similarities between the paths taken by Maya Deren and Carasco are remarkable and worth further study: both filmmakers began with an experimental masterpiece devoted to the question of phantasm (*Meshes of the Afternoon* and *Gradiva Sketch 1,* respectively) and then later undertook a major ethnological investigation.

Background and Foci

In its foci, contents, and dynamics, the work of Carasco reflects a transcendental energy ("transcendental" in the Kantian sense)[6]—that is to say, a systematic returning to its determinations: the modalities for the perception of the world; the relationship between words and phenomena; and regarding film specifically, the relationship between "seeing and the real," irreducible to its appearances, between recording and understanding. From these Kantian foundations (the subject of her first research paper) and without having been affiliated with any group or movement, Carasco clearly belongs to the second structuralist generation.[7] The methodological framework in which her scriptural as well as filmic work is explicitly included comes from structuralism, Russian formalism of the 1920s, and their reinvestments made by Roland Barthes and Gilles Deleuze. This second generation transformed the structural approach to critical force, not only describing and explaining phenomena but also reconfiguring, thinking about it by other means. The respective and combined influences of Louis Althusser, Michel Foucault, Félix Guattari, and Jean-François Lyotard caused this generation to develop the work of thinking less as a process of clarification than as a gesture of rupture and invention.

In 1970 Carasco began publishing the following materials, which would later become elements of her PhD thesis: "Myth and Utopia: Approaching Rousseau I," "Myth and Utopia: Approaching Rousseau II," "Notes on *Letter to d'Alembert*," "Effractures/Fantastic," and "Editing Sheets for a Fantastic Approach to the Question of the (A) Form."[8]

In 1973, as part of Group 101, Carasco reflected on the concept of "third meaning" developed by Roland Barthes in *Cahiers du cinéma* (issue 222, July 1970). Her passion for gestures found repercussions from *Gradiva Sketch 1* onward, as shown by her ending statement to her essay in the collected volume *Contribution à une théorie du cinema*:

> The gesture of R. Barthes remains resolutely ON THE MARGIN of an attitude of reenactment, when sometimes the singular focus of a gesture differs from the attitude that carries it, when sometimes the precision of a wrist liberates the delicacy of a hand from a greater massiveness, indicating SOMETHING ELSE in the indubitable connection to the referred body.[9]

Herein lies the beginning of a work on the redistribution of those phenomena that link Carasco to Heinrich von Kleist's *Über das Marionettentheater* (1810), whose analysis of the sculpture *Boy with Thorn* and reflections about grace may be the secret backdrop to investigations of depiction yet to come.

Beyond themes and motifs such as disconnection and fracture, Carasco's path ran through two great gestures of liberation, which date from the summer of 1977. The first concerns the relationship between theory and film. Far from considering her first film essay as an opportunity to apply the propositions she had just formulated in her thesis, Carasco raised her first film to the level of a theoretical model. *Gradiva Sketch I* explores fundamental dialectics such as mobile and immobile, continuous and suspensive, body and phantasm, sketch and completion, and description and argumentation. This experimental and theoretical element later became a protocol for perceiving "the real" and for structuring a documentary endeavor. The second gesture concerns disciplinary liberation. "I do not want to become an anthropologist. This is one of my resistances. I love these people. They are political questions: these people are in the process of dying, no one says anything, they will die dancing," says Carasco during a dialogue with Jean Rouch in 1999.[10] By refusing to conform her quest to scientific models, she is not elaborating knowledge but creating an experiment or, maybe, a celebration, a sharing, or an entrance to the dream of the other—a process that in the end may create the more profound understanding. Comparing the Mexican diaries and studies written by Carl Lumholtz between 1894 and 1898 with Carasco's films (she of course had read Lumholtz and all available articles on the Tarahumara in Spanish and French, as her personal library testifies),[11] we see by the use of reverse shots everything her filmic oeuvre is not about: institutions, justice, and rituals of birth and burial—in short, the traditional ethnological subjects. Instead, it is a powerful exploration of running, dancing, singing, myths, speech, and the imaginary. As an expert observer, Lumholtz works to develop and objectively categorize phenomena; as an experimental philosopher, Carasco works to create intensity and depth and to invent a possible ethnography of the power of thought.

La Fantastique

The main concept by which Carasco invites us into her work is La Fantastique. In *Ciguri: Tarahumara 98,* Jean Rouch reads "The Rite of Peyote among the Tarahumara" by Antonin Artaud: "The Fantasy is from a noble quality, its disorder remains only apparent, it actually obeys an order that develops into a mystery and on a level which the normal consciousness does not reach but which Ciguri allows us to reach and that is the very mystery of all poetry."[12] Carasco starts by feminizing Fantastique (by changing the word's article from the masculine *le* to the feminine *la*), which directs the concept toward an act, practice, and mobility. What must be thus understood by La Fantastique?

In a first sense, that of her 1975 thesis, La Fantastique means "a materialist theory of the imagination" that favors the movement of rupture, break, exit—in a word, what Eisenstein considers as "ecstasy." Movements "off cinema," "off psychology," "off economy," "off aesthetics," "off topic":[13] La Fantastique intensely pinpoints the multiple standards bordering the cinema and separates them in order to give the filmic back to its ingenuity—that is, the specific properties of visual thinking in motion.

In a second and broader sense, developed in her Tarahumara notebooks, La Fantastique refers to creation (literary and cinematic). La Fantastique designates the movement by which phenomena overcome their fixations in order to reach that from which they are separated, like an unknown and magical double: for example, when a granddaughter of Spanish Republican resisters decides the Tarahumara—themselves resisters, because they run to escape from the Spanish conquerors—are "her people" and that she belongs to them.[14]

In his report on Carasco's thesis, Barthes explains how her thought is primarily concerned not with definition or explanation but rather with deployment and variation:

> The off-frame, for example, returns, but basically it is never unfolded, it is never analyzed, ana-lyzed, it is not defined, it is not described, simply, it comes back, each time in a different light. And thus you do not give yourself the task of demonstrating to convince, to win support, to subdue—which is very important—but I will say, to dangle, to insist, and I would say, because this is a word I will come back to because it's full of meaning for me, to fascinate: hypnosis is, typically, what happens thanks to the shiny circular return of a point before one's eyes. But the fascination is perhaps ultimately what moves most surely the subject.[15]

And indeed, Carasco's reflection proceeds by successive adjustments and enhancements, like a river that takes on marsh: concepts are organized not in chains that narrow them down but in rhizomatic constellations that are refined when approaching real-world phenomena.

In its uniqueness, simplicity, and splendor, *Gradiva Sketch 1*, Carasco's first film, crystallizes all of these sources, influences, propositions, and speculative processes.

Gradiva: A Visual Objection to a Theory

Let us retrace four steps in the rich and complex journey made by one of the figures who most inspired writers and visual artists throughout the twentieth century, Gradiva.

In 1903 the German novelist Wilhelm Jensen published *Gradiva: A Pompeian Fantasy*. In it Norbert Hanold, a young archaeologist, falls in love with the pose adopted by the bas-relief of a young woman in a collection of antiques. He names this sculpture Gradiva, "she who walks," because of the way her feet are pointing to the ground. Obsessed with this bas-relief, he finds himself in Pompeii, where at noon Gradiva suddenly appears and speaks to him. Through Jensen, Gradiva becomes the symbol of the undecidability between reality and dream.

In 1907 Sigmund Freud immortalized Jensen's novel in the study *Delusions and Dream in Jensen's Gradiva*. Through this study Gradiva becomes the emblem of fantasy, and according to Freud, Jensen's tale conveys the analytical power of a "psychiatric study."[16]

In 1976 Carasco published "Sheets of Editing for a Filmic Gradiva," wishing to make an adaptation of Jensen's *Gradiva* that contrasted the interpretation that made the novel unforgettable—i.e., Freud's.[17] By having Gradiva follow Dziga Vertov's theory of film as interval, she wants to free the young woman from the "black box of analysis":

> Let Gradiva go with the same firmness of her step to escape the black
> box of analysis, the machine that cuts the block of the dream, to
> dissociate conscious/unconscious twilight states, in short, to only read
> in the Pompeian *fantasy* so that the fantasm of a back-reproduction of a
> childhood memory is already there.[18]

In 1977, together with cinematographer Bruno Nuytten and assisted by Dominique Le Rigoleur, Carasco made several attempts to portray the motive fetishized by Norbert Hanold: the effect of the suspended movement of a woman's foot passing over a stone in Pompeii. While filming this scene, six different speeds were tested, from five hundred to fifty frames per second. And in the end, instead of presenting the entire forty-five-page script, the film merges gracefully with this preparatory work and becomes a lesson on adapting a literary and theoretical thinking to film: Why reproduce an entire fictional environment when a simple series of distinct slow-motion shots decomposing the movement can prove the inadequacy of Freud's interpretation? One can indeed understand the carasquian version of Gradiva as such: to elect a motive, to let it return, and to vary its descriptive modalities in terms of kinetic scrolling, of light, and of sound (an excerpt from the original score by Paul Méfano and an extract of Irene Jarsky's blows) does not belong at all to a psychological pathology. For it does not simulate a resurrection (Gradiva *rediviva,* the girl of Pompeii as a mythical justification of the young real woman, Zoe Bertgang, "the life that walks," Hanold's childhood sweetheart) but demonstrates the interminable nature of things.

Carasco's descriptive study honors the deep vibration that occurs with every living phenomenon, as simple and fleeting as it is, and considers it with the attention it requires when passing into the world. *Gradiva Sketch 1* spreads the vibration in several ways: through the monumental series of slow-motion shots; through the supernatural stir born of the heat of the stones, which seems to twist the film itself; by the sound of the flute; through the current surge of a little girl running into the dark ruins; and through (what we discover at the end of the credits) the brilliant fact that the character of Gradiva is played by two girls instead of one (Anne and Emmanuelle, the two daughters of the filmmaker). The visual fetish, the theoretical emblem is neither obsession nor delirium; it is reinterpreted as a laboratory of cinematic movements: the concrete intermittency between mobile and immobile (the frames); the psychic dialectic between fragment and infinite (frame and off-frame); and the gaps between the endless prodigality of the real and a relentless, descriptive assiduity and persistence. Thus, the line of a step becomes the site of a treaty on the descriptive components of film, a visual poem about the vibration of the phenomena (body and site), a kinetic demonstration of the possibility of challenging a theoretical analysis with simple plastic resources (visual and sound). Connecting the inaugural experiments of Étienne-Jules Marey and Lucien Bull with Deleuze and Guattari's criticism about Freud's reduction of the imaginary to a family romance, *Gradiva* describes cinema as the native landscape of the interval.[19] But the focus of this reflection is not on a strict materiology of film, as had the international structural cinema devoted itself since the 1960s. *Gradiva* does share formal traits with such movies: to begin with, seriality and the focus on a pattern. Starting with the form of a draft, the energy of the march, the complexity of the appearance, "it above all seeks to avoid to quickly pass by the side of life itself," as Jensen writes in a phrase Carasco chose as the epigraph to her "Editing Sheets."[20] Not quickly transitioning and thereby inscribing the film into the flow of life, it is not about accepting cinema as a recording tool, as a light touch, but about conceiving it from the editing, from the work of a formal composition. After the Pompeian laboratory, Mexico became the area of kinetic encounters held in the real:

> When we arrived in this month of August 77 in a place called the Divisadero, summer storms stole the evening light, women and children were collecting some seed necklaces and wooden dolls sold on the floor of this tourist place and fled hastily in a clutch: they were, not a Gradiva, but a multiplicity of Gradiva, light, incredibly stylish in their panic fallback move, fearing to expose their small sales, picking up young children. . . . I was looking for a Gradiva. And yet Gradiva was multiple, and she was becoming a people, men and women light-footed, winged.[21]

The Writing of Seeing

Here, I must emphasize an event that was repeated eighteen times between 1976 and 2001: a free spirit voluntarily went away, mandated by no institution, funded by her own resources, and moved only by her desire to follow in the footsteps of Eisenstein and Artaud. In other words, while undertaking her travels, Carasco was not accountable to anyone or anything: to no discipline, neither ethnography nor visual ethnology nor cinema, and to no institution, neither the university nor a production house. The only thing that moved her was her inner strength, which she calls "passion" in her notebooks. But what is this passion? Her notebooks give us better insight into this concept: a passion for "the writing of seeing," a common source of Carasco's both literary and filmic endeavors. The writing of seeing is the subject of multiple investigations, and its various dimensions follow each other and combine themselves with cross-fades. First was a historical investigation: seeing with one's own eyes what two modern visionaries, Eisenstein (Carasco's journey of 1976) and Artaud (all her others journeys), saw and adapted. She then engaged in an ethical investigation, experimenting with the approaches of others, to the point of challenging the identity of traditional carvings; an artistic investigation, bringing writing to the intensity and diversity of our sensory experience; and a philosophical investigation, rebuilding our belief regarding the real through the prism of the worship rituals and daily practices offered by the Tarahumara country. As such, the notebooks are autonomous; they are not preparatory material either for other texts or for movies that were being shot while Carasco was writing. Régis Hébraud specifies:

> We never used the notebooks for editing. And I'll never know why Raymonde did not use her Journal 87 when we had hard times editing *Los Matachines* and *Portrait of Erasmo Palma*. It was not until 2010, when I was using her notebooks, that I managed to finish these two edits.[22]

Carasco's notebooks are intended not to identify the characteristics of a people but to forge writing in light of individual encounters and psychic events (reasoned, emotional, intuitive, irrational, etc.) that will be born from them. "The diary flows in the course of the events. It expects the event. In which it is not written down. The writing itself is its own event. Write," intimates Carasco for herself on August 10, 1984.[23] Just as, before being able to join Mexico, one had to cross the Western speculative strata from Kantian criticism to Joë Bousquet's erotic books, through Giambattista Vico's *The New Science* (1725),[24] the notebooks turn her journeys into descriptive forms at the service of "seeing." Accounts, dream narratives, dialogues, fiction, legends, theoretical reflections, combinations of assumptions, summaries, syntheses, poems, notes, inquiries, diary theory, and conferences we see here springing from the ground, writing resources are adjacent and conjoined in a perfect formal freedom, which owes as much to the desire of reality as it does to the emancipatory examples of Ezra Pound's *Cantos* and Eisenstein's *Memoirs*. Her scriptural descriptive research, which must be compared with her cinematic descriptive research, led Carasco to what has become for us a literary oeuvre: the distinct or tentative dynamic that questions the precise and delicate rendering of a moment of color, a light, a body, a race, a pose, etc. Worshipping movement, the carasquian writing is measured continuously with beauty, elegance, the kinetic, and ephemeral phenomena in an equanimity that refers to the advice of the formalist essayist, screenwriter, and novelist Victor Shklovsky (who was one of Eisenstein's biographers): "We must look at everything as if we did not know if it is the navel of the world or a simple bump or hollow."[25] The power of attention and hospitality for singular phenomena (human, earthly, carnal, or imaginary) requires a supply of new words in order to reshape them from the inside—where theoretical reflection before the Mexican years, under the influence of Barthes and Lacan, led Carasco to the increased invention of neologisms, like "the (a) form," the "polEtique." For example, we can read, from March 13, 1997, in the notebooks: "These forces of creation we call Art, life itself, this intensive ordination we call the World, Earth and World."

The Warrior of "Dream"

Among said phenomena, Carasco keeps coming back to a mysterious and complex dimension that cannot be shared: one of mental activity, in turns relative and simultaneous to images, to dreams, to *Sueño*, to visions, to the work of thought and of "thought-image." Her notebooks invent an ethnology of mental experiences, both interrogative when Carasco directly draws from interlocutors of her Rarámuri[26] sources—starting with the shaman Ceverico—and affirmative when she incorporates their answers and assumptions in her own reality:

> You have the power of creation. *Fight for your own strength.* . . .
> *Conquer your own strength. Become a warrior.* Lead your fight. Forget
> the imaginary debt. The fake debt.[27] Do not take in the toils of the law.

> *Outside-power.* Autonomous combat, away from the war of men and
> women, the war against the power of men. Do not give your signature,
> your body, your little ear to another, even if it were another woman.
> Ghosts, nothing but ghosts. Like this, I started "the work of sueño,"
> perhaps as a warrior.[28]

As much as in the extraordinary journey she made alone in 1994,
discovering that Artaud had reproduced the words of Tarahumara
verbatim, as well as in her immediate feeling of belonging to a people
who had resisted the Spanish colonizers for centuries and of which
she collected as many signs as possible before its extinction (by poverty and acculturation), as well as in her deep friendship with shamans and musicians, it is probably here, in this war of mental liberation, that Carasco's path becomes Artaudian. Why, asks Jean-Louis
Brau (who met Artaud in 1947 and participated in the posthumous
publication of some of his Mexican writings), did Artaud feel the
need to leave for the Tarahumara country?

> He does not mean to find the traces of an ancient civilization, to delve
> into a mythological bath, but it is rather a revolutionary act in the
> Artaudian meaning: liberating the energy of the soul, as there is the
> liberation of energy from the atom.[29]

Carasco's notebooks explode with this loving and multifaceted energy, which belongs to the "positive powers of life."[30]

Accuracy of Seeing: The Tarahumaras with Spinoza

Filmic research is not a standard investigation (clarify, reveal, and dis-
tribute) but a sensitive alliance: enjoying the privilege of being there,
agreeing to not see everything, accepting the slow raising of some
traces, sampling some movements, some signs of harmless beauty,
before claiming the understanding of things, not sharing the secret
but the cult of secrecy, mystery, and trance—waiting, if necessary, for
years and relying only on affective certainties to capture what needs
to be filmed.

Initially focused on the movement of running and walking, as if
the Lumière cinematographers had been instructed by Étienne-Jules

Marey to preserve, from the body, only the kinetics (*Divisadero 77 or Gradiva Western* and, then, *Tarahumara 78* translate the figurative options elaborated by *Gradiva Sketch 1* onto the Mexican land), the vision leaves the motives of walking and running and widens from the magnificent Tutuguri to progressively describing the ritual as cultural specificities of the Rarámuri people, thanks to encounters increasingly fertile with great shamans, musicians, dancers. The Tarahumara oeuvre shows that each human movement results less from the singular nature of the actual individual body than from an overall relationship of man to the world—every gesture is a mythography and, of what Carasco describes about the Tarahumaras, as Jean Rouch did about the Dogon, shows us how we too are turbulent puppets, but pulled by less magical strings.

From *Los Pintos,* explains Régis Hébraud, film editing does not build an interpretation of Tarahumara movements: it describes "the Tarahumara's own staging of their rituals and dances."[31] *Yumari, Los Pascoleros, Ciguri 96, Ciguri 98: Dance of Peyote, Ciguri 99: The Last Shaman,* and the five episodes of *Tarahumara 2003: The Crack of Time* prove a double movement of growing proximity to the Rarámuri people of Nararachi, Norogachi, and Guachochi, examples of resistance to the Spanish colonizers and Christians imposing modern ways of acculturation, and fulfillment of the vision, facing the splendor of the rites (sublime Matachines, the King-Magi seen by Artaud), mountains, colors, and lights in the "land of the sorcerers." The composition of the film becomes simpler, shots increasingly long, the fields larger. The Tarahumara oeuvre proves a conquest of the powers of continuity, as the shamanic seeing reveals itself. Carasco explains:

What is this power of "seeing," which is particularly susceptible to dreams? . . . Suddenly, I realized that the question of "seeing," as I was formulating it until then, was the most naive. When I asked the shaman about the content and form of his vision, the presence of color, the appearance of being Ciguri, and the way he conversed with them, he would say that the colors were the same, the people do not appear more beautiful, or more immaterial. The world of Ciguri is not bigger or brighter, it is like ours, the Ciguri are someone like you and me who speak to the wizard as I can talk to him. . . . The work of thought, I think I understand, allows seeing in a standby mode. The wizard does not sleep when he "sees," he remains lucid, and this corresponds to Castaneda, as I read later, but equally to texts by Antonin Artaud: another level of consciousness is within reach, another plane of vision simultaneous to consciousness. I imagine how this work can be exhausting, as it always requires being in shape: If you are tired, numb and cold, you switch into sleep but the work is not done. This is so different from anything we could imagine, it is not based on hallucinations but on a work of thought that begins from the moment you are initiated and must be pursued relentlessly. F. [The Shaman] defines it as "a day and night work, the work of a lifetime." My belief is that this work of thought joined the philosophical work, that Spinoza called Bliss, the third kind of knowledge. What is at stake, are the infinite speeds of thought. I am thinking of the drawings Michaux did under the influence of mescaline, to Antonin Artaud at the end of his life: simultaneously head, eye, and hand that writes and draws. Such experiments require without end as much force as rigor. The rigor was the most striking quality of my shaman. In him, there was not an ounce of illumination, and that was fantastic.[32]

There is no other world; the work of "seeing" is to discover "the real" in its most radiant, sharpest, most active accuracy.

Conquered Editing: The Event of a Copresence

The clarification of the shaman's "seeing" and the discovery that Artaud's writings on Tarahumara rituals were documentary in nature, esteem, and friendship of their interlocutors, resided with the shaman himself, allowed for an event in *Tarahumara 2003: The Crack of Time: The Before—The Apaches.* In it Carasco admits to appearing in the same frame as the shaman Ceverico. It took twenty-six years for such a copresence to become ethically possible. In 1996 Carasco had appeared in a shot of *Los Pascoleros,* but she considered it a deplorable technical mistake. In 2003 she admitted her presence might no longer be seen as an intrusion, which confirmed the transformation of the "desiring machine" into a love territory.[33]

In "Writing and the Question of the Event," Carasco proposes a portrait of Michel Foucault as a filmmaker because his writing constantly changes and interchanges points of view on history. In the same way, Carasco's Tarahumara oeuvre becomes in its demonstration of continuously greater breadth and transparency subject to the terms in which Foucault commented on Nietzsche (cited in the same article):

> The world as we know it is not this figure, simple, where all events are cleared to accuse gradually essential features, the final sense, the first and last value; it is rather a myriad of tangled events; it seems today "wonderfully colorful, deep, full of meaning"; because a "host of errors and fantasies" has given birth to it and still populates it secretly.[34]

Does this mean that Carasco's trajectory offers reversibility between cinema and philosophy? As always, Carasco is much more accurate: "Philosophy is a tool, the cinema is a weapon."[35] If the kinship of copresence has become possible, it is because of the body of the film-maker, which comes to shield those that are endangered. The poem "Filming This Desert," written in April 2004, ends with the melancholic and sublime fusion of politics in mythology.

The Tarahumara are fading.
Away from themselves.
Everything will fade
the Tarahumara know
since always
pillars of the world
supporting the sky
the flat circle of the earth
even axes of the *Sueño*.
The gods had it declared,
before the beginning and the end of all worlds.
All disappears, all be revived
differently.
At this limit dies
el poder del sueño
Asi es. ¿No?
No hay otro camino.
It is therefore, is it not?
There is no other way.

—*Dialogue with the Shaman.*[36]

NOTES

I warmly thank Régis Hébraud, Bernd Herzogenrath, and Frédéric Sojcher.

1. Arnoldy and Brenez, "Raymonde Carasco," 79 (italics mine).

2. Gérard Granel is the author of books on Kant and Husserl and the French translator of Ludwig Wittgenstein, Antonio Gramsci, and Martin Heidegger; Mikel Dufrenne, specialist in phenomenology and aesthetics, is the author of the *Aesthetics and Philosophy* trilogy and coauthor of a book on Karl Jaspers with Paul Ricœur, *Karl Jaspers and the Philosophy of Existence.*

3. In the original French, the titles are "Pensée-Action (Cinéma)," "La Pensée-Cinéma," and "Cinéma-Corps-Pensée."

4. Carasco, "Le premier à parler cinema," 1 (italics in original).

5. The original French titles are as follows: *Gradiva Esquisse 1, Tarahumaras 78, Tutuguri—Tarahumaras 79, Julien—Portrait d'un voyant, Los Pintos—Tarahumaras 82, Julien, Les Rayons jaunes, Yumari—Tarahumaras 84, Rupture, Passages, Los Pascoleros—Tarahumaras 85, Ciguri 96, Artaud et les Tarahumaras, Ciguri 98— La danse du peyotl, Ciguri 99—Le dernier chaman, Tarahumaras 2003, la fêlure du temps: L'avant—les Apaches, Tarahumaras 2003, la fêlure du temps: Enfance, Tara- humaras 2003, la fêlure du temps: Initiation—Gloria, Tarahumaras 2003, la fêlure du temps: Raspador—le Sueño, Tarahumaras 2003, la fêlure du temps: La Despedida.*

6. "Being transcendental is everything in relation to the condition of a pos- sible experience, of what is presupposable via experience, and what is logically prior to it." Eisler, *Kant Lexicon,* 1034.

7. *The Course in General Linguistics* by Ferdinand de Saussure was published in 1916.

8. Respectively, in the *Annals of the Faculty of Arts and Social Sciences of Toulouse,* 1970; *Homo X,* 1971; *Annals of the Faculty of Arts and Social Sciences of Toulouse,* 1972; *Annals of the Faculty of Arts and Social Sciences of Toulouse,* 1974.

9. Carasco, "Marges," 23.

10. Raymonde Carasco, interview by Laury Granier, recorded at the Cinémathèque française, 1999, Archives Hébraud-Carasco.

11. Lumholtz, *Unknown Mexico*; see also Lumholtz, *A Nation of Shamans.*

12. Artaud, "Le rite du peyotl chez les Tarahumaras," 28.

13. Carasco, "La fantastique des philosophes"; the referenced concepts ap- pear in the table of contents.

14. A meaning of Tarahumara is "man who runs."

15. Barthes, "L'essai en fête," op. cit., 91.

16. Freud, *Le délire et les rêves dans la Gradiva de W. Jensen,* 172.

17. See Carasco, "Feuilles de montage pour une Gradiva cinématographique."

18. Ibid., 328 (italics in original).

19. "Its native place, the interval." Carasco, "Gradiva."

20. Carasco, "Feuilles de montage pour une Gradiva cinématographique," 324.

21. See Carasco, "Gradiva."

22. Régis Hébraud, message to the author, January, 21, 2014.

23. Carasco, "Carnets tarahumaras."

24. Some of the objects in Carasco's thesis.

25. Chklovski, *Technique du métier d'écrivain*, 29.

26. Rarámuri is the original name of the Tarahumaras. Raymonde Carasco keeps the word Tarahumara because of Antonin Artaud.

27. The symbolic and insolvable debt is a relationship between parents and children, the latter not being able to pay back the gift of life. In 1956–57, Jacques Lacan devoted a seminar to the Symbolic and the Real, including a study of the symbolic debt. *Le séminaire, Livre IV: La relation d'objet et les structures freudiennes*. Carasco's "imaginary debt" refers to that concept.

28. Carasco, "Carnets tarahumaras," March 13, 1997 (italics in original).

29. Brau, *Antonin Artaud*, 169–70.

30. "So being-animal is better than the man in the Tarahumara ethics. The Plant is itself perhaps better than the animal and closest to the positive powers of life." Carasco, "Carnets tarahumaras," August 9, 1984.

31. Régis Hébraud, Master Class, March 23, 2014, Cinéma du réel, Centre Pompidou, unpublished manuscript.

32. Carasco, "Les vitesses infinies de la pensée (modes d'accès)," 445–46.

33. To name their practice of shooting, Carasco-Hébraud uses a famous concept from Deleuze and Guattari (analyzing Artaud): "On site we learn to capture the event: we are creating what we may call the desiring machines, patience, luck and magic do the rest. A desiring machine is to be ready to turn some kind of event is to choose a point of view, a frame, a speed that is 'doing' light, and the point, and learn to wait." Hébraud, Master Class, March 23, 2014.

34. Michel Foucault, "Nietzsche, la généalogie, l'histoire," quoted in Carasco, "L'écriture et la question de l'événement," 15.

35. Jean Rouch, conversation, filmed at the French Cinémathèque by Laury Granier, 1999, Archives Hébraud-Carasco.

36. The French original reads: "Les Tarahumaras s'effacent. / D'eux-mêmes. / Tout s'effacera / les Tarahumaras / le savent / de tout temps / piliers du monde / ils supportent le ciel / le cercle plat de la terre / axes mêmes du Sueño. / Les dieux l'ont dit, / avant le commencement et la fin des mondes. / Tout disparaîtra, tout renaîtra / autrement. / À cette limite s'éteint / el poder del sueño / Asi es. ¿ No ? / No hay otro camino. / C'est ainsi, n'est-ce pas ? / Il n'y a pas d'autre chemin. / (Dialogue avec le Chaman)." Translation by Nicole Brenez and Julian Scherer.

BIBLIOGRAPHY

Arnoldy, Édouard, and Nicole Brenez. "Raymonde Carasco." In *Cinéma/politique: Trois tables Rondes*, 79. Brussels: Labor, 2005.

Artaud, Antonin. "Le rite du peyotl chez les Tarahumaras." In *Œuvres complètes,* vol. 9. Paris: Gallimard, 1971.

Barthes, Roland. "L'essai en fête." *Trafic,* no. 78 (June 2011): 88.

Brau, Jean-Louis. *Antonin Artaud.* Paris: La table ronde, 1971.

Carasco, Raymonde. "Feuilles de montage pour une Gradiva cinématographique." *Critique,* no. 346 (1976): 324–32.

———. "Gradiva." Unpublished screenplay, 1977. Archives Hébraud-Carasco.

———. "La fantastique des philosophes." Doctor's thesis, Université Toulouse–Le Mirail, Toulouse, 1975.

———. "L'écriture et la question de l'événement." *Kairos* 3 (1991).

———. "Le premier à parler cinema." In "Henri Langlois," special issue, *Loess,* January 13, 1987, 1.

———. "Les vitesses infinies de la pensée (modes d'accès)." In *Jeune, dure et pure: Une histoire du cinéma d'avant-garde et expérimental en France,* edited by Nicole Brenez and Christian Lebrat, 445–46. Paris: Cinémathèque française / Milan: Mazzotta, 2001.

———. "Marges." In *Contribution à une théorie du cinema.* Toulouse: Travaux de l'Université de Toulouse–Le Mirail, 1973.

Chklovski, Victor. *Technique du métier d'écrivain.* Translated by Paul Lequesne. 1927; Paris: L'esprit des péninsules, 1997.

Dufrenne, Mikel. *Aesthetics and Philosophy.* Vol. 1. Paris: Klincksieck, 1967.

———. *Aesthetics and Philosophy.* Vol. 2. Paris: Klincksieck, 1976.

———. *Aesthetics and Philosophy.* Vol. 3. Paris: Klincksieck, 1981.

Dufrenne, Mikel, and Paul Ricœur. *Karl Jaspers and the Philosophy of Existence.* Paris: Seuil, 1947.

Eisler, Rudolf. *Kant Lexicon.* Author's translation. Berlin: Oms, 1930.

Freud, Sigmund. *Le délire et les rêves dans la Gradiva de W. Jensen.* Translated by Marie Bonaparte and revised by Freud. 1907; Paris: Gallimard, 1971.

Lacan, Jacques. *Le séminaire.* Vol. 4, *La relation d'objet et les structures freudiennes.* Edited by Jacques-Alain Miller. Paris: Seuil, 1994.

Lumholtz, Carl. *Unknown Mexico: A Record of Five Years' Exploration among the Tribes of the Western Sierra Madre; in the Tierra Caliente of Tepic and Jalisco; and among the Tarascos of Michoacan.* 2 vols. New York: Scribner's Sons, 1902.

———. *A Nation of Shamans: The Huichols of the Sierra Madre.* 1900; Oakland, Calif.: Bruce Finson, 1990.

Rancière's Film Theory as Deviation

Tom Conley

If it existed in French, the word that follows might be called a portmanteau fashioned from *cartography* and *deviation*: *écartographies*. The neologism would designate a mix of theory and interpretive practice that could be described as a mapping of errant reflection. Steeped in Hegel and Marx and trained in dialectics, Jacques Rancière studies phenomena that an egalitarian ethic compels him to call into question or for which, in the interest of the ethics of investigation, he would wish that a critical distance or even dissentient position be taken. Disagreement, what he calls *dissensus,* prods the drive for equality: Where he locates convergence and divergence of politics and aesthetics in cinema, he studies contradictions, the very condition of their possibility, and he discerns inherent paradoxes that he qualifies as historically grounded. No sooner, from an egalitarian perspective and to better understand how and why given phenomena happen to be as they are, he moves about and away from them. His style of inquiry engages a process of *deviation*. It is no surprise Rancière examines the "fault lines" (*failles*) of films—whether traditional or experimental—where the images we see on the surface of a screen seem to be "deployed" and "dissipated" into the abstraction of the narratives that convey them.[1]

In Rancière's lexicon, *écart* is a privileged signifier. It can be seen and read in reverse to obtain the impression of a graphic *trace,* a mark of something that has disappeared, a line of inquiry that moves forward or, as will be discussed, forges ahead in the direction of things possible. For what follows a grounding hypothesis is that what Rancière says or observes about cinema is embedded in a historical geography, in which shards of autobiography inform his labors of interpretation and, at the same time, signal the elements of a political aesthetic. In a mode of discourse that has psychoanalytical resonance, he makes clear whence he speaks, where he "is coming from" and in what sense he wants to go. He clarifies what has led him to take note of the "subject-position" he assumes in charting a moving and evolving, ever-dialectical relation with film.[2]

Rancière has written of his "discovery" of the seventh art in at least two places. In *La méthode de l'égalité* (*The Method of Equality* [in French, a pun that equivocates on legality and equality], 2012), a series of interviews in which his interlocutors invite him to consider the evolution of his life and work, he recalls how cinema first captured his attention. As if coming "out of the past," cinema intervened in the political arena he recalls dominating the early and middle 1970s. He reaches back to the impact on French intelligentsia and a public that came with the 1972 publication of Gilles Deleuze and Félix Guattari's *L'anti-Œdipe*. Toppling the authority that Freudian psychiatry had held, theirs was a left-wing liquidation of the left. The "old" left that had militated in lockstep with Marx was bleeding into a newer social fabric, that of the middle class born after the end of World War II. The moment coincided with worker self-management of the Lip company (a manufacturer of watches), which signaled "the moment of the liquidation of the proletarian Left," and, too, with the emergence of *Les révoltes logiques,* the aptly named journal to which Rancière would adhere in seeking alternatives to Marxian (and fervently masculine) militancy.[3] In the context of debates over the *mode rétro* in then-current cinema, editors of the journal asked him to work on popular memory: which led him to compare left-wing militant films to John Douglas and Robert Kramer's *Milestones* (1975), an epic chronicle of disillusion in America in the "ashes of the 1960s" that he quickly associated with "an entire tradition of American cinema with its historical grounding and its typical fiction, *notably illustrated by the western* [in which] the history of the individual ends with adherence to a symbolic collective."[4] The Western residue stood in strong contrast to "French fiction, given its relation with an always pre-given people in its familiarity."[5] Rancière quickly strayed from this model in noting how, implicitly in its relation with the *mode rétro,* "popular memory" was pure ideology in its Althusserian sense (an imaginary relation to real modes of production), especially where the left, notably under socialist François Mitterrand, sanitized the history of its rise to power.

It was then that Rancière's own memory of popular cinema told him why he was taking a critical view of popular memory. Fifteen years earlier, a friend had told him that "real cinema was not Antonioni, Bergman, all that culturally legitimized stuff; no, you had to go and see *Esther and the King* [Raoul Walsh] or *Giant of Marathon* [Jacques Tourneur], and that was real cinema!"[6] Rancière flashed back to the early 1960s, to the MacMahon theater on the Right Bank and to *cinéclubs* such as the *Ciné qua non* and the *Nickelodéon,* where he had made his first contact with the seventh art. His "initiation" came when he was torn—in a strong sense, *écarté*—between the New Wave and the tradition of Hollywood cinema, perplexed or even upset over his attraction to "Minnelli, Walsh or Antony [*sic*] Mann and the trendy stuff among the highbrow bourgeois."[7] His work on politics, philosophy, and cinema would soon follow a broken path: "It's not that I stated one day that film and philosophy were two thoughts of the same type, but that's how territories, paths, investigations were constructed for me."[8]

A year before *La méthode de l'égalité,* in his prologue to *Les écarts du cinéma,* Rancière noted how cinephilia had linked the cult of art to the "democracy of pleasures [*divertissements*] and emotions" wherever it underscored how much the greatness of film lay not in the "metaphysical elevation of its subjects or the visibility of its plastic effects" but rather "in an imperceptible difference in the manner of putting traditional stories and emotions into images."[9] Cinephiles, as both he and many enthusiasts of *Cahiers du cinéma* and *Positif* remember, called it "mise en scène" without having a clear idea of what the term meant.[10] Cinephiles lacked an analytical discourse or a lexicon with which they could domesticate, regulate, or conceptualize their pleasures, much less turn them into scientific objects of study. Cinephilia, he avowed, was what offered access to a democratic sublime. Cinema had the possibility of becoming an *event*—most notably, where the pleasure of film called into question the categories of modernism. In the context of the "inventions of everyday life" it shared with those of its viewers, no matter what its provenance, cinema democratized aesthetics. Given what he felt was its opposition to higher orders of modern literature, it availed to him—and now, retrospectively, it avails to us—a means to discover in raw sensation the matter of both ephemeral and enduring *events.* In ordinary cinema he could return to a more intimate and more obscure binding of the marks of art, the emotions of the story and the discovery of the splendor that the most ordinary spectacle could take when projected on an illuminated screen in the middle of a dark room: a hand raising a curtain or that plays with a doorknob.[11]

It suffices to look at Rancière's recall of the contradiction he experienced in the pleasures of Hollywood through the lens of what, in two dense pages of *La méthode de l'égalité*, he calls a *cartographie des possibles*. Taken as a metaphor of social process, the formula reaches back to the early 1970s, where in his *Foucault* of 1986, writing on the heels of the philosopher's death in 1984, Deleuze distinguishes an archive from a diagram. The former is a "history of forms," a form being what "shapes [*forme*] or organizes given material"; it is what "forms [*forme*] or finalizes functions" and thus gives them an "objective function."[12] The latter

is no longer the auditory or visual archive, it's the map, cartography co-extensive with the entire social field. It's an abstract machine. Defined by informal [or unformed, *informelles*] functions and matters, it makes no *formal* distinction between a content and an expression, between a discursive and a non-discursive formation. It is an almost mute and blind machine at the same time it is a cause for sight and speech.[13]

The diagram does not represent a preexisting world but rather "produces a new type of reality, a new model of truth"[14] that brings forward "relations of force that constitute power"[15] and, hence, a "map of relations of force, a map of density, of intensity" that proceeds along primary links that can't be pinpointed and that are everywhere related to one another. He insists that the "archive, a history of forms," in doubled or passed by "a becoming of forces, a diagram" that resembles a stratigraphy of maps, the ones set upon the others, whence new formations can be drawn. In a poetic surge Deleuze famously relates the diagram to the oceanic line, a trace or tracing with neither beginning nor end, engaging a politics and an aesthetic of becoming that he associates with "1968, the line of a thousand aberrations," a line giving rise to a triadic definition of writing or tracing: to write is to struggle and to resist; to write is to become; to write is to make maps . . . .[16]

In his own mappings, Rancière deviates from the model: "I wasn't really enthusiastic . . . about this theme of the new cartographer."[17] Mantling a different set of terms, he remarks that what is "possible" (for Deleuze the *possible* being what would belong to the domain of the diagram) is opposed less to the impossible than to the category of the "necessary." "Put otherwise, the 'possible' does not define something yet to be actualized but rather a manner of thinking what is [*une manière de penser ce qui est*]."[18] It is a mode of writing, a "style" or manner of handling and of countenancing the world. In the spirit of an *écartographie,* in the mode of a broken analogy we can say, as with Deleuze, so then "not entirely" with Rancière:

> The necessary is the real that cannot fail to be [*ne peut ne pas être*].
> "Possible" is what might not be, what is not the consequence of a
> concatenation of preceding or predetermining circumstances. At the
> same time *it is what keeps space open* for another type of connections
> than that of the necessary. If we think in political terms, we can estab-
> lish a break [*clivage*] between what can be thought in the terms of the
> necessary and what can be thought in the terms of what exists as the
> emergence of a possible, the emergence of something that could not
> be. Which also means the emergence of a scene, of an actuality, of an
> *event* that can be thought as belonging to another distribution of the
> sensible to another system of coexistence than the normal system of
> the concatenation of reasons.[19]

For Rancière the formerly utopian turn in the cartography that Deleuze had extracted from Foucault ought better be understood as a *process* by which the possible is inserted in the real. In the new con-text the "real" appears to be mottling what Lacan and his adepts took to be, like the stone of *La nausée* that obsessed Sartre's well-named Roquentin, whatever resists being named or mediated by language. A spatial inflection in Rancière's distinction is salient. In his deviation from Deleuze and Foucault, Rancière is possibly keeping in mind the redistributions of space as they became imposed in nineteenth-and twentieth-century France, in the emergence of geographical in-stitutes, in the pedagogy of mapping, and in the birth of human geography, where in fact *quadrillage* and cartographic rhetoric, for the ends of power, reach unforeseen levels of effectiveness and social control.[20] Hence, through his dialogue he maps a model of deviation that perhaps "deterritorializes" what the philosopher is implied to have romanticized or reified in the ideology of popular memory. For Rancière cartography does not mean making a map that draws "contours of the territory and its divisions" but *opposing* or being at variance with "a model of distribution and of coexistence to models of exclusion borne by a certain vision of the time."[21] "Becoming" becomes an order of the possible, ostensibly more pragmatic than what its poetic innuendo had suggested, all the while remaining utopian. In setting May 1968 and the Arab Spring of 2010 on a same plane, Rancière argues that the two moments belong not to the idea of utopia but to that of "possibles" emerging from unlikely or unforeseen situations:

> Suddenly it appears that a world can exist without a hierarchy, of forms of popular presence, of gatherings that can deviate from dominant modes of logic [*en écart par rapport aux logiques dominantes*]. . . . The question, for example, is one of knowing if we think of what happened in 1968 is a stylish phenomenon tied to the behavior of youth, of the consumer society, to everything we're told about the *Trente Glorieuses* and company, which moreover weren't so glorious, or if we think that there is at stake a singular emergence that depicts [*dessine*] another history of these same years.[22]

From the relation he establishes with Deleuze and Foucault on cartography and the backward glance upon 1968, it appears that for Rancière deviation becomes a mean.

In what remains, it is worth examining how classical film figures in this process—notably, in what sometimes *elides* from his recall of the difficult pleasures—pleasures *mis à l'écart*—he felt in watching Westerns during the heyday of the *Trente glorieuses*. In the dark space of the postwar theater, cinephiles of the late 1950s, he recalls, possessed an uncommonly democratic virtue. They could appreciate the "most common spectacle" as a major event. But how and at what cost? Because the films America imposed on the French public belonged to the machinery of capital, it had to be asked how the viewer could enjoy them while taking exception, paradoxically, from within Hollywood's global operation. Rancière experienced difficulty in working through the relation between the reason of his emotion and that of an egalitarian ethic. Three films figure in a cavalcade of interrogative reflections:

> [In view of] the form of equality that in *Moonfleet* little John Mohun's smile and gaze accord with the designs plotted by his false friend Jeremie Fox, what relation could a student who was discovering Marxism at the beginning of the 1960s establish with the battle against social inequality? The justice the hero of *Winchester '73* pursues obsessively in regard to his evil brother, or in *Colorado Territory,* beneath the rock face where the forces of order were hunting them down, the joined hands of the outlaw Wes MacQueen and Colorado: what relation could be found in respect to the working world against the world of exploitation?[23]

The three films have become points of reference—wind roses, if one likes—in Rancière's historical geography. Within what André Bazin calls "the genius of the [Hollywood] system," the *events* to which Rancière refers, despite or even for reason of their origin, belong to a "method of equality," a line of thought that runs through all of his writing, which is especially salient in the two Westerns he recalls.

First is Anthony Mann. In a mosaic essay on the director, first appearing in *Trafic* (1992) and reprinted in *La fable cinématographique* (2001), Rancière cuts pieces from the director's Western cycle (eleven films, 1950–60) into a scintillating reflection on the auteur who deviates from the Aristotelian to which he adheres and on heroes driven to do what they must do for no reason of their own. *Winchester '73* stands as an implicit epigraph because the hero "does, obstinately, only one thing or, rather, two things in one."[24] He pursues and kills the man—his blood brother—who had shot their father and later pilfered from the hero the lever-action carbine he had won. The director strings together a narrative that goes from one commonplace to the next (strangers riding into a western town, a shooting match, an Indian attack, a disputed poker game, a bank robbery, a woman gone wayward . . .) and ends, in suspension, on another: "Some things a man has to do, so he does 'em."[25] A map of contradictions emerges from the obligations of the pursuant in the film and those of its director attending to his genre, the task of the latter being that of telling a story incarnated in the rifle: in short what, in the first shot following the credits, a throng of children might imagine when ogling the iconic gun mounted on a rack of antlers behind a storefront window. *Winchester '73* flickers into reflections on the hero who is and is not one, who comes from afar and happens to meet something or someone, whose actions ultimately meld with the film, at a point where he meets the "logic of the screenplay" and that of his encounters where, finally, "the success of the hero is nothing other than that of film."[26]

Rancière's coda about a hypothetical end (or a sequel) to *Winchester* is couched in irony. Everyone recalls how the battle between Lin McAdam (James Stewart) and enemy brother Dutch Henry Brown (Steve McNally) ends when, having caused Dutch to waste his ammunition, seeing Dutch Henry in full sight, Lin finally takes aim, shoots, and kills.[27] In disturbed perplexity he gathers himself after seeing his kin's lifeless body plummet earthward. High Spade (Milliard Mitchell) and an injured Lola Manners (Shelley Winters) await the fate of the pursuit that began after a botched holdup in the town of Tascosa. How can the film conclude? Will the hero bond with the woman? What will happen to High Spade? Where will they go where nothing or no one beckons? None of us, notes Rancière, "can imagine James Stewart, tasting the tranquility of his duty now accomplished, his Winchester mounted on a wall, between a Shelley Winters wearing an apron and two children graced with Stewart's blue eyes. Lin's companion vainly invites him to think of *what follows*. The "time after" will never come to distract the vigilance of the upholder of the law, or write his imaginary into the present moment of his gestures."[28] Rancière's irony, telling because the black-and-white gives no clue to the color of McAdam's eyes, touches on the force film acquires as it moves from story to myth.

Without aid of visual support, Rancière underscores the difficulties of give-and-take between the story and its Aristotelian underbelly. Lin has shot his prey: like a ragdoll, Dutch Henry's limp body falls by a dark rock beneath a great sky of vaporous clouds and above the tops of a few trees and the crown of a saguaro cactus (1:30:51–53).

Seen implicitly from McAdam's point of view (while he is in the field of view), the site on a ledge from where McAdam has shot his enemy shows Stewart and his shadow cast on the stone face. He hangs his head in what seems to be sadness over what he has done (1:30:53–59).

Figure 12.1. Dutch Henry's dead body falls from a precipice (*Winchester '73*, 1:30:52).

Figure 12.2. McAdam hangs in sadness after killing his brother (*Winchester '73*, 1:30:53).

Figure 12.3. Dissolve from McAdam, in sadness, to High Spade, with Lola (*Winchester '73*, 1:30:59).

Its effects displayed in an arresting tableau, the narrative takes pause just before the shot dissolves into a medium close-up (1:31:00) where, seated by a boardwalk, High Spade and Lola address each other.

For an instant (Figure 12.3) High Spade's face, under a black cowboy hat, emerges from Lin's dark silhouette underscored by the bright brim of his own hat. Lola's visage seems to emerge from the stone adjacent to Lin's shadow. This vital juncture—the lap dissolve being at once a visual oxymoron and a narrative device, even a "metaphor" or mode of transport carrying the viewer from the cliff back to Tascosa—sets the characters in an oneiric (call it mythic) space and time: High Spade is *in* and *of* Lin and vice versa, while Lola makes clear that the stone, in brilliant pathetic fallacy, lives and even looks at Lin. Melded in two landscapes, the three characters seem to be mourning an inexorable event whose import is beyond their ken. When the long dissolve gives way to the sight of the couple in dialogue, rolling a cigarette, licking the wrapper, and then putting it to his mouth, High Spade resumes the story:

Well . . . that's the way it was. The old man sired two sons. One was no good, never was any good . . . robbed a bank . . . and a stagecoach [his tongue continues to moisten the paper] . . . and when he came home and wanted to hide out [he gazes upon his cigarette] the old man wouldn't go for it . . . so Dutch shot him [now he puts it to his mouth and rears his head] in the *back*.

He scratches a match against a wooden case, lights the cigarette, and upon hearing a horse's whinny, looks away, behind Lola, toward what is *off* (1:31:00–1:31:26).

As the camera pans right to locate Lin in the distance, returning on horseback, the story that had begun with the repeating rifle transmutes into oedipal myth, arching its time and space (1876, near the Arizona–Mexico border) to another of a timeless nonspace. The couple runs into the depth of the visual field (High Spade in shadow, Lola in the light) to greet the hero coming "home from the hill." Another dissolve (1:31:38) blends them into the bodies of Lin and the horse from which he has just dismounted before the penultimate take sets the threesome in a two shot (Figure 12.5).

Figure 12.4. Licking a cigarette he has rolled, High Spade tells Lola of McAdam's early years (*Winchester '73*, 1:32:20)

Figure 12.5. High Spade and Lola meet McAdam upon return to Tascosa with his brother's cadaver (*Winchester '73*, 1:31:49).

In profile, to the left of the gleaming plaque on the stock of the Winchester just below, High Spade gazes upon Lin and Lola in each other's arms while Lin looks at his sidekick. Is High Spade "thinking" of a ludicrously "happy ending" that Rancière describes as if from the character's point of view? Does Lin's gaze tell his friend that he would now wish to be rid of him? And is Lola, liberated from a cowardly fiancé and the shackles of a sleazy bandit, dreaming of conjugal bliss? The camera eloquently refuses to resolve the matter by tracking in and tilting down to the carbine that (the film never shows) Lin had plucked off the cliffside after the murder. After the camera closes in and the characters turn their eyes toward the gun Lin holds in his right hand, "The End" comes forward, grafted onto a layered configuration where story, history, and myth are suddenly fused.

The attention Rancière draws to the *poetics* of the film can be seen in its displacement from its reception as a new kind of adult Western, to a Lacanian allegory of the gun-as-phallus that circulates in society as a signifier or as a summation of inherited conventions. Ostensibly born of a nagging sense of contradiction when he first saw the film (1960), his reflections of 1992 (or 2001) now imply that the film's proximity to myth, given its play of visibility and narrative in what Rancière calls a "thwarted fable" (*une fable contrariée*), makes it accessible to anyone and everyone. An object out of the past, it belongs to a collective, egalitarian public that can appreciate the work apart—*à l'écart*—from the consumerist industry in which it was born.

Second, and briefly, is Raoul Walsh. *Colorado Territory* (1949), a Western built upon the mythic design of the same director's *High Sierra* (1941), holds firm in Rancière's memory, no doubt for reason of a blazing conclusion that deviates from the earlier model. Building on the myth of Orpheus and Eurydice, *High Sierra* ends when, from a precipice high on the eastern slope of Mount Whitney, an agent of justice shoots outlaw hero Roy Earle (Humphrey Bogart) in the back. He plummets earthward (much like Dutch Henry) and strikes the ground with a thud, and in accord with classical theater, in a medium shot a chorus rushes forward to mourn the unlikely hero's demise. In *Colorado Territory* outlaw Wes McQueen (Joel McCrea), pursued by a sheriff and his posse, takes refuge in the ruins of a prehistorical community of troglodytes whose setting recalls the epic narrative shot in the same place in *The Vanishing American* (1925). In *Colorado Territory* a hired gunman, an Amerindian, climbs a steep ridge from where, high and above, he shoots McQueen. Wounded, the victim slides earthward just when his new partner, Colorado (Virginia Mayo), born of the territory itself, screams and runs to his rescue just before a host of lawmen arrive to riddle the fleeing couple with lead. In contrast to *High Sierra,* no time is afforded to weep.

Pushing aside the wounded McQueen, the wild woman fires two six-guns at the evil lawmen at the moment the couple succumbs to the rampage of gunfire.

They fall face downward; the camera closing on their coupled hands, their grasp becomes limp; and they die.

It cannot be said why Rancière has never written on the film or the director of *Esther and the Queen,* but in all events his fond recall of the finale brings him back to the quandary of not knowing how to "postulate a mysterious adequation between historical materialism on which workers' struggles are based and the materialism of the cinematographic relation of bodies to their space."[29] The unspoken element may be found in the film's deviation from its source. *High Sierra,* a masterpiece of "classical" film that makes no bones about

Figure 12.6. Colorado takes a revolver from Wes and readies to aim at the evil lawmen (*Colorado Territory,* 1:33:14).

Figure 12.7. Colorado shoots at the posse while Wes reaches to grab her left arm (*Colorado Territory* 1:33:25).

Figure 12.8. Riddled with bullets, Colorado and Wes fall to the ground where, hand in hand, they expire (*Colorado Territory* 1:33:28).

how the moment of its shooting (early 1941), prior to the United States' belated entry into World War II, blends into the Greek myth on which it is based, momentarily leaving spectators in a properly Aristotelian state of catharsis . . . before upbeat music accompanies the end credits that scroll upward in view of Mount Whitney.[30] The spectator is aroused in properly Aristotelian fashion before, during the moment of exit from the theater (when the film was first viewed), fear and trembling give way to a sense of tragedy that morphs into pure entertainment.[31] In *Colorado Territory* of eight years later, a final battle pits the good malfeasants against the loathsome order of law. Within the narrative (*muthos*), the spectacle (*opsis*) of gross injustice enacted on lovers set in a timeless and forbidding landscape leads the spectator less to catharsis than to unrequited anger over social contradiction. When the maddened heroine fires on the devious posse, she seeks justice. In the sequence as Rancière might have seen it in 1960, the law on which she fires was possibly tied to an economic complex aimed at repressing or even murdering the working class with which hero and heroine are affiliated. If the end of the film is read in view of

Rancière in Paris at the moment of his collaborations with Althusser, its grounding in myth gets transformed in the greater and deeper geological space of the Western and, in the postwar moment, acquires a sharpened political edge.[32] The heroine's failed action to right what is wrong raises consciousness about the forces—including Warner Brothers Studios, even with its affiliation with New Deal ideology— at the basis of the film's pleasure that foster social inequality.

Given that the end of *High Sierra* inspires *À bout de souffle* and that the end of *Colorado Territory* gives rise to avatars that include *Bonnie and Clyde*, Rancière's long-standing identification with Walsh's oater indicates why his theory argues for an ever-renewed and ever-renewing appreciation of classical cinema, if only because it is available to generations who have little idea of either its wealth or its renewed virtue when it is displaced into our moment. By way of conclusion, the *politique de l'auteur*, what had been the rallying cry of sanctioned specialists of mise-en-scène who may have brought Rancière to see *Winchester '73* and *Colorado Territory*, now turns into what, in the deviant drift of his words, becomes a *politique de l'amateur*. A movement toward and away from his preferred cinematic objects gets drawn into a slight but decisive turn:

> La politique de l'amateur affirme que le cinéma appartient à tous ceux qui ont, d'une manière ou d'une autre, voyagé à l'intérieur du système d'écarts que son nom dispose et que chacun peut s'autoriser à tracer, entre tel ou tel point de cette topographie, un itinéraire singulier qui ajoute au cinéma comme monde et à sa connaissance.[33]

> The politics of the amateur affirms that cinema belongs to all those, in one manner or another, who have traveled inside of the system of deviations that go with its name and that each and everyone can be authorized to trace between one point or another of this topography, a unique itinerary that adds to cinema both as world and as its knowledge. (my translation)

Rancière's discoveries about new and telling distributions of affect and sensibility took place in movie theaters over fifty years ago, in disquieting pleasures he felt amid the multiple ruptures among philosophy, cinema, and an egalitarian ideal. When Rancière, amateur of cinema, notes how he travels in one manner or another within a system of deviations, he engages an *écartographie*, which for his readers would be a mode of mapping productive conflict.

Given his cinephilia and now, a fairly broad body of work that includes Bela Tarr, consideration of what this volume of essays would wish to be his "philosophy" of cinema can only be speculative. If philosophy informs what he does with deviance and deviation, it would be dialectical, of Marxian orientation, bereft of any pregiven "method" (be it Cartesian or other) informing readings that range from Murnau to Godard and beyond. As the title of *La méthode de l'égalité* suggests, he builds on the context of social contradiction and a quasi-total social fact of class conflict to champion an egalitarian distribution of affect among spectators whose sensory virtues enable reflection on the unique experience of film. Affect is what spectators share through a complex—what Rancière would call a liberating— relation with the seventh art. It is what, early on in *Les écarts* and later, in its final pages on Pedro Costa, he signals as moments where sensation accrues almost unconsciously when we take note of some of the most common and often overlooked details of everyday life that film makes uniquely palpable. How and where they are viewed can be assumed less significant than the tension—hence, contradiction or variance—they crystallize in the politically charged aesthetic regime in which they are found. Thus, Godard is no different from Minnelli (although in *Le mépris,* the director cites *Some Came Running*); and Minnelli, by a short stretch of the imagination, from Bresson; or Bresson, from Tarr. The implied equality of films of different genres, styles, modes of composition, and historical moments owes to the commonality of a spectator's relation with cinema, which can happen to fall only within what, in almost all of his writings, he calls the "aesthetic regime" of art that follows the collapse of hierarchical orders in the arts that had held firm in monarchical orders.[34] After 1789 and with the advent of German romantic philosophy, affect could share and share alike in at once conscious and unconscious registers, in diurnal and nocturnal life, in the often minuscule differences we notice between things said and things seen, in the "mute speech" of writings that either inform or, *post facto,* are informed by cinema.[35]

As an implied or would-be philosopher of cinema, Rancière might qualify as a philosopher of the experience of film: experience, in other words (as in the etymon *experiential*, from *ex-periri*, what comes from essaying with the senses, from sifting, trying, or testing something in order to broaden or enrich knowledge), but also, by implication, to gain force from doubt, to engage an active relation with death and the unknown.[36] We "experience" life through cinema far more than we edify ourselves through what it represents—notably, we live with film through sublime details: a hand caressing a newel (in *Boudu sauvé des eaux*), a patch of light on a mountainside (in *Ride Lonesome*), or, for an instant, a child and a stranger peering at a display in a shop window (*M*). When sensed within the broader frame of perception, the details Rancière champions can be qualified, in a strong philosophical sense of the word, as *events*. An event can be "what happens" when viewers—and it is crucial they be within the "aesthetic regime" where sensation is equally parsed—have the impression that they share heightened *aesthesia* in what they behold. Deleuze, with whom Rancière shares a critical relation (given his *écarts,* how could it be otherwise?), calls this moment "a nexus of prehensions" (from *prehendere,* "to grasp" . . .). What touches gets touched, and what would be touched touches the toucher. What is below consciousness or prior to symbolic expression becomes "objectified," and equally, what would be of an objective quality (the cinematic image) gets internalized or "subjectified."[37] The pleasure Rancière obtains in viewing film owes to the details that touch. He often notes that in cinema "the devil is in the detail," and as such the detail is a crucial element the event that gives proof to the force of the devil, the *daïmon*, the force that splits, divides, or causes to deviate, or a "movement that turns round and round."[38]

By way of conclusion, we can ask if these reflections on classical cinema pertain to what Rancière does with contemporary work. An operative principle in *Les écarts* is built upon the changing relations of politics and aesthetics in classical film, in emerging cinemas, and, among established directors of the style of Straub/Huillet and Godard, in films constructed as philosophical essays. For Rancière, whose point is drawn from Gustave Flaubert in *L'éducation sentimentale* and other writings, the one can never be privileged at the cost of the other. In a brief and telling essay, *Béla Tarr, le temps d'après*, Rancière studies the œuvre of the Hungarian director capped by *The Turin*

Horse. The title of the monograph splits in two: Does it mean that Tarr's films deal with "the time after" the putative collapse of Communism in 1991? Or that, as a tourniquet, the title can be glossed as "Béla Tarr, time according to . . . ?" Rancière's summary on the back cover offers a first clue:

> D'*Almanach d'automne* (1984) au *Cheval de Turin* (2011), les films de Béla Tarr ont suivi la faillite de la promesse communiste. Mais le temps d'après n'est pas le temps uniforme et morose de ceux qui ne croient plus à rien. C'est le temps où l'on s'intéresse moins aux histoires, à leurs succés et à leurs échecs qu'à l'étoffe sensible du temps dans laquelle elle sont taillées.

> From *Almanac of Fall* (1984) to *The Turin Horse* (2011) Béla Tarr's films follow the failure of the promise of Communism. But the time after is not the uniform and morose time of those who no longer believe in anything. It's the time in which interest is less in stories [or histories], in their successes and failures, than in the sensitive fabric from which they are cut. (my translation)

Rancière cuts these words from the last paragraph of the first chapter. A minuscule shift or *écart* in the last sentence indicates how and why a philosophy of events informs his viewing and reading of cinema. The time after "is the time of *pure, material events,* against which belief will be measured for as long as life will sustain it."[39] Events are material; they are folded in perception of duration; and they tie subjects to milieus in which they live in order to allow them "to do what they have to do." They are allied with promise in both what they engage and what viewers make of the films themselves. Later, in the last chapter, Rancière iterates the same point in a reading of *The Turin Horse,* the feature whose idea came to Tarr from a major event in the annals of philosophy: during a sojourn in Turin, upon witnessing a horse martyred by humans, Friedrich Nietzsche fell irrecoverably into delirium.

At the beginning of the chapter, Rancière specifies the relation of the perception of time to that event. He reads Tarr directly against the grain of Flaubert. First is Tarr:

The time after is neither that of reason recovered, nor that of the
expected disaster. It is the time after all stories, the time when one
takes direct interest in the sensible stuff in which these stories cleaved
their shortcuts between projected and accomplished ends. It is not the
time in which we craft beautiful phrases or shots to make up for the
emptiness of all waiting. It is the time in which we take an interest in
the wait itself.[40]

The equivocation of *le temps d'après* comes forward at a point where
the English idiom cannot account for the sense of "according to":

Le temps d'après n'est ni celui de la raison retrouvée, ne celui du
désastre attendu. C'est le temps d'après [after + according to] stories
[+ histoires], le temps où l'on s'intéresse directement à l'étoffe sensible
dans laquelle elles taillent leurs raccourcis.[41]

Events take place when time is felt both after, on the heels of history—
be it the collapse of Communism, the sight of the Turin Horse, or a
person staring out of a window—and in accord with repetition that
underscores the difference between historical time and time as it is
experienced. Second is Flaubert. Appealing to *Madame Bovary*, describing an "event" (as if it were a long take in a filmed version of the
novel), Rancière writes (and Beranek translates elegantly):

Through the pane of a window, in a small town in Normandy or on the
Hungarian plain, the world slowly comes to be fixed in a gaze, to be
etched on a face, to weigh down upon a body's posture, to fashion its
gestures, and to produce that part of the body called soul: an intimate
divergence between two expectations: the expectation of the same,
habituation to repetition, and the expectation of the unknown, of the
way that leads toward another life. . . . A continuum at the heart of
which the events of the material world become affects, are enclosed in
silent face, or circulate in words.[42]

Nothing could be closer to the "event" as it is experienced in two
media at once different and of the same fabric, or *étoffe*.

What began with Rancière's cinephilia, the political aesthetic of
the "amateur" born of an impassioned relation with cinema in the late

1950s, gathers philosophical steam when the memories of what happened when he saw the films of Mann, Walsh, Rossellini, and others informs a political aesthetic giving rise to a "method of equality," available to one and all for common ends, based on the experience of *events* in literature, cinema, and life itself. Deviation is part of Rancière's *mode d'emploi*, or "user's guide," to the relation of film and experience.

NOTES

1. Rancière, *Les écarts du cinéma*, 25.

2. Subject-position is understood here in the way that analyst Joyce McDougall construes the "theaters of the mind," of the various poses a subject assumes in situations where contradictions are manifest, generally in constant mutation and differing intensities, in other words, everywhere and at all times in the lives we lead. In *Theaters of the Mind* (a translation of *Théâtres du je*), 13, McDougall notes the play of subjectivity when "our psyche seeks to know the illusion that we really know who we are when we say *I.*"

3. Rancière, *La méthode de l'égalité*, 81–82.

4. Rancière, *La méthode de l'égalité*, 84.

5. Ibid. (emphasis added).

6. Rancière, *La méthode de l'égalité*, 86.

7. Ibid.

8. Rancière, *La méthode de l'égalité*, 87.

9. Rancière, *Les écarts du cinéma*, 8.

10. Such is the effect in the retrospective turns in Jean-Louis Comolli's unfinished reflections that comprise, like an assemblage of ephemera of times past, in the twenty-one propositions that introduce the mass of *Corps et cadre: Cinéma, éthique, politique*, a work like Rancière's, arching back to the 1960s, takes pleasure in cinephilia, notably in the pages on the renewed encounters with early cinema (16–18).

11. Rancière, *Les écarts du cinéma*, 9. Here, it is as if allusion were being made to Michel de Certeau's *Invention du quotidien, 1: Arts de faire*, first appearing in 1980, roughly in the context of Rancière's first writings on film, for reason of the proximity of how its "spatial stories" (*récits d'espace*) (which amount to events) chime with the democratic ethic at work in Rancière. Schefer's *L'homme ordinaire du cinéma*, a work that Raymond Bellour called a Bible for theorists of the same moment, sought to discern how, fleetingly, cinema constituted unnamable *events* for its viewers. See Bellour, *Le corps du cinéma*, 16.

12. Deleuze, *Foucault*, 41. Visibly striking, in these paragraphs redundancy of *forme* and *former* indicates that the noun and the verb belong to a fairly personal idiolect, one in which reference may possibly be made to art historians

Henri Focillon (*Vie des formes*), Elie Faure (*L'esprit des formes*), Wilhelm Wör-ringer (his *Einfühlung*, or empathy, would be what emerges from the "con-tinuous" and "endless" line in *Form in Gothic*), and so on. The reader detects dialogue with Derrida, for whom *fors* and *force* were juxtaposed to what he took to be the inertia of *forme*, already in "Force et signification," a review of Jean Rousset's *Forme et signification*, later published as the first chapter of *L'écriture et la différence*.

    13. Deleuze, *Foucault*, 42 (emphasis added).

    14. Ibid., 43.

    15. Ibid., 44.

    16. The poetic thrust of the sentence is felt in the references to poet Henri Michaux, to musician Pierre Boulez, and to Herman Melville, author of "dia-grams" in his *Piazza Tales*. In the final sentence of the chapter, Deleuze quotes Foucault's remark of 1967—"I am a cartographer"—in a context that seems far more theoretical than its source, in which Foucault understood cartography to offer a practical means to reach a specific end. See Conley, *Cartographic Cinema*, 217n23.

    17. Rancière, *La Parole muette*, 259.

    18. Ibid., 256.

    19. Ibid., 257 (emphasis added).

    20. See Konvitz. *Cartography in France*; Christian Jacob. *The Sovereign Map*, especially pages on Ferdinand Buisson; Lacoste, *La géographie, ça sert à faire la guerre*. On human geography, see Guiomar. 'Le 'Tableau de la géographie de la France' de Vidal de la Blache."

    21. Rancière, *Bela Tarr, The Time After*, 9.

    22. Rancière, *La méthode de l'égalité*, 258.

    23. Rancière, *Les écarts du cinéma*, 10–11.

    24. Rancière, *La fable cinématographique*, 105.

    25. Rancière quoting James Stewart in Winchester '73, in *La fable cinémato-graphique*, 105.

    26. Rancière, *La fable cinématographique*, 121. Little mention is made of three of Mann's Westerns: he notes *Devil's Doorway* (1950) but not *The Furies* (1951) or *Cimarron* (1960). For the French reception of Mann's Western (exclud-ing the earlier noir cycle and the epics that end his career), see Bellour's entry in *Le western*, 276–80.

    27. See Deleuze, *Cinéma 1,*102.

    28. Rancière, *La fable cinématographique*, 107.

    29. Rancière, *Les écarts du cinema*, 10.

    30. In other words, W. R. Burnett, author of the pot-boiling novel on which *High Sierra* is based, uses the classical tradition to engineer this novel and many others he crafted in order to be turned into screenplays.

    31. In his chapter on Vincente Minelli's *Some Came Running* in *Les écarts du cinéma*, Rancière shows how "entertainment" in classical cinema becomes a

means and an end unto itself. The music accompanying the end credits of *High Sierra* attests to a slippage from Greek tragedy to the "industry" of pleasure.

32. On Rancière and Althusser, see Davis, "Althusser's Lesson."

33. Rancière, *Les écarts du cinéma*, 14.

34. Rancière develops the point at length in the introduction to *La fable cinématographique* (2001) and uses it as a blueprint for the composition of *Aesthesis* (2010), where the aesthetic regime is taken to replace that which, in an equally mosaic intellectual history of the representation of life itself, Erich Auerbach had launched at the end of World War II in *Mimesis*.

35. As Rancière makes clear throughout his aptly titled *La Parole muette*.

36. Rancière would be close to Montaigne, whose inaugural sentence of his final essay, "De l'experience" (*Essais*, vol. 3, ch. 13), translates that of Aristotle's *Physics*. Montaigne appears to exploit the partitive to fashion a tourniquet where desire can trope knowledge and where desire *as* knowledge attracts those who are drawn to it: "Il n'est desir plus naturel que le desir de connoissance" (No desire is more natural than the desire of knowledge). And then: "Quand la raison nous faut, nous y employons l'experience . . . , qui est un moyen plus foible et moins digne" (When reason fails us, we use experience . . . , which is a weaker and less dignified means). Of late, along a same line of thought, in a probing essay on how, today, cinema comes to us less in movie theaters than iPads or computer screens, referring to Michel de Certeau, Francesco Casetti notes how the changing character of the cinematic event attests to the mobility of its *experience*, in *The Lumière Galaxy*, 26–27.

37. Deleuze, "Qu'est-ce qu'un événement?" In his "ontology" of an event, Deleuze studies Leibniz through Whitehead, 102–4.

38. For Fletcher the *daïmon* drives allegory, the process that causes one thing to become another, in his classic *Allegory*. The devil's roundabout movement is taken up in Rancière, *Bela Tarr, le temps d'après*, 30.

39. Rranciére, *Béla Tarr, le temps d'après*, 9 (emphasis added).

40. Rancière, *Bela Tarr, the Time After*, 63–64.

41. Rancière, *Bela Tarr, le temps d'après*, 69–70.

42. Rancière, *Bela Tarr, the Time After*, 64.

BIBLIOGRAPHY

Bellour, Raymond. *Le corps du cinéma: Hypnoses, émotions, animalités*. Paris: P.O.L., 2009.
———. *Le western: Acteurs, auteurs, mythologies*, 276–80. Rev. ed. Paris: Éditions Gallimard, 1994.
Burnett, W. R. *High Sierra*. New York: Alfred A. Knopf, 1940.
Casetti, Francesco. *The Lumière Galaxy: Seven Key Words for the Cinema to Come*. New York: Columbia University Press, 2015.

Comolli, Jean-Louis. *Corps et cadre: Cinéma, éthique, politique.* Paris: Éditions Verdier, 2012.

Conley, Tom. *Cartographic Cinema.* Minneapolis: University of Minnesota Press, 2007.

———. "Reading Ordinary Viewing." *Diacritics* 15 (Spring 1985): 4–14.

———. "Screen Memories: From Jean Louis Schefer, *L'homme ordinaire du cinema.*" *New Review of Film and Television Studies* 8, no. 1 (March 2010): 12–21.

Davis, Oliver. "Althusser's Lesson." In *Jacques Rancière,* 2–15. London: Polity Press, 2010.

Deleuze, Gilles. *Cinéma 1: L'image-mouvement.* Paris: Éditions de Minuit, 1983.

———. *Foucault.* Paris: Éditions de Minuit, 1986.

———. "Qu'est-ce qu'un événement?" In *Le pli: Leibniz et le baroque,* 101–3. Paris: Éditions de Minuit, 1988.

Derrida, Jacques. *L'écriture et la différence.* Paris: Éditions du Seuil, 1967.

Fletcher, Angus. *Allegory: Theory of a Symbolic Mode.* Ithaca, N.Y.: Cornell University Press, 1980.

Guiomar, Jean-Yves. "Le 'Tableau de la géographie de la France' de Vidal de la Blache." In *Les lieux de mémoire,* edited by Pierre Nora, 1073–98. Paris: Éditions Gallimard, 1997.

Jacob, Christian. *The Sovereign Map.* Edited by Edward Dahl and translated by Tom Conley. Chicago: University of Chicago Press, 2006.

Konvitz, Josef. *Cartography in France, 1660–1848.* Chicago: University of Chicago Press, 1987.

Lacoste, Yves. *La géographie, ça sert, d'abord à faire la guerre.* Rev. ed. Paris: La Découverte, 2012.

McDougall, Joyce. *Theaters of the Mind: Illusion and Truth on the Psychoanalytical Stage.* New York: Brunner/Mazel, 1991.

Montaigne, Michel de. "De l'experience." In *Essais,* edited by Pierre Villey and Verdun-L. Saulnier. Paris: PUF/Quadrige, 1968.

Rancière, Jacques. *Bela Tarr, le temps d'après.* Paris: Capricci, 2011.

———. *Béla Tarr, the Time After.* Translated by Erik Beranek. Minneapolis: Univocal Press / University of Minnesota Press, 2013.

———. *La fable cinématographique.* Paris: Éditions du Seuil, 2001.

———. *La méthode de l'égalité.* Edited by Laurent Jeanpierre and Dork Zabunyan. Paris: Bayard, 2012.

———. *La parole muette: Essai sur les contradictions de la littérature.* Paris: Éditions Hachette, 1998.

———. *Les écarts du cinéma.* Paris: La Fabrique, 2011.

Schefer, Jean-Louis. *L'homme ordinaire du cinéma.* Paris: Éditions Gallimard, 1982.

13

Movie-Made Philosophy

Noël Carroll

Currently, the philosophy of the moving image is flourishing. It has already spawned a number of subfields. First, there is what might be thought of as "the philosophy *of* the moving image proper"—the domain of inquiry where the classic questions of philosophy, including those of ontology, epistemology, and ethics, are applied to the case of the moving image. Philosophers *of* the moving image proper, for example, ask, What is the moving image? Can documentary motion pictures be objective? and Can evil films, like *The Triumph of the Will,* nevertheless, at the same time, be aesthetically excellent?

However, coexisting with these more or less predictable philosophical interests in the moving image, there is also a thriving concern with what we may broadly label as "philosophy *in* the moving image" or "philosophy *in* cinema." This is a matter of identifying philosophical themes or theses in particular motion pictures—of for instance, finding philosophy *in* motion pictures—of finding the Myth of the Eternal Return in *Groundhog Day* or the question of the nature of personhood in *Blade Runner* or the issue of skepticism about the external world in *The Matrix.*

This enterprise, I speculate, by far dominates publication in the area of philosophy and the motion image. In the United States three different publishers have "Philosophy and ———" series, where the blank is frequently filled in by the name of a motion picture, such as a TV series. And most of the essays in those books are of the philosophy-in-cinema variety, as are the majority of articles in the American academic journal *Film and Philosophy.* In addition, Routledge has a series in which philosophers discourse on the philosophy found in individual motion pictures such as *Vertigo* and *The Thin Red Line.*

Of course, the reasons for the predominance of publication in the philosophy and cinema domain are not hard to come by. Integrating motion pictures into the philosophy curriculum makes philosophy more and more accessible to an ever increasingly screen-oriented student body. Showing movies that illustrate philosophical themes is the sugar that makes the abstract theory go down. So all of those titles like *Hitchcock and Philosophy* are potentially best-selling textbooks.

Furthermore, the pursuit of philosophy *in* cinema puts philosophers in the business of interpretation, thereby making themselves attractive to students in the neighboring departments of literary and cinema studies. Moreover, philosophical interpretation tends to be broadly humanistic, thus appealing to students sated by the "cultural turn" in adjacent branches of the humanities.

Of course, these material considerations are not meant to deny that many of the pertinent philosophers really enjoy finding their favorite philosophical themes in their favorite movie narratives. It is only to acknowledge that they could not indulge that pleasure if there were no pedagogical/institutional/economic base to support it.

At this point, it should be noted that there are at least two different kinds of activities that we may count as examples of the philosophy *in* cinema relation. In general, this approach regards the motion picture as an illustration of some or another philosophical tenet. But it may be an illustration of a tenet intended by the motion picture maker, or alternatively, the philosopher may use some film to illustrate the tenet in question which is unbeknownst, so to speak, to the creator of the motion picture. An example of the former case might be Bergman's relationship to the philosophical psychology of Eino Kaila in his *From the Lives of Marionettes*,[1] whereas an example of the latter case might be the use of Herzog's *Kaspar Hauser* as an illustration of Lacan's theory of language. In the Bergman case, the philosopher argues, plausibly, that Bergman intended to engage Kaila's views, whereas in the Herzog example, the commentator applies Lacan's theory of language to the film in the hope, perhaps, that the film will illuminate the theory as a metaphor might. Or one might say, in the Bergman case, the philosopher finds Kaila illustrated in the film, whereas in the Herzog case, the philosopher brings a theoretical grid to the film. This is how Žižek frequently appears to use movies.

Of course, in the case of discovering philosophy illustrated in a motion picture, the situation does not have to be as direct as it is in the relation of Bergman to Kaila. The motion picture creator may intend to be illustrating a more general, widely recognizable philosophical theme, like egoism. However, whether discovering philosophy in the motion picture or imposing it, both practices can count as examples of the philosophy *in* cinema approach, with the latter version being more liberal or tolerant than the other.

Furthermore, both variants of philosophy in cinema operate within a framework where the philosophy that is associated with the motion picture in question is not particularly original to the motion picture. The philosophy, so to speak, exists prior to the motion picture. It is an illustration of something else, where that *something else* is some specimen of literally already extant philosophy.

Yet if cinema can illustrate preexisting philosophy, the question naturally arises as to whether it might also be possible for cinema to produce philosophy. That is, can the moving image *do* philosophy? Do the creators of motion pictures possess the resources to make original philosophical contributions—can they propound philosophy *through* the moving image?

Clearly, motion pictures can possess philosophical themes, as Fritz Lang's *The Weary Dead* possesses the theme of fatalism. However, a motion picture may possess a certain theme without taking a specific position on it. *Blade Runner* raises the question of whether replicants are persons or could be, arguably, without answering it.

However, sometimes a motion picture will stake out or endorse a position on the theme it illustrates. And where a motion picture takes a stance on its theme, we can say that it has a thesis. For instance, King Vidor's *The Fountainhead* is *for* individualism of the Randian objectivist variety. Of course, this position quite literally antedated the film in the work of Ayn Rand, who also wrote its screenplay. Thus, the film merely illustrates a preexisting theory.

Nevertheless, insofar as it appears unobjectionable to suppose that movies possess theses, it is tempting to ask whether movies might be capable of producing original philosophical theses—that is, could a movie advance its own conception of individuality? What if Ayn Rand had first aired her philosophy in the movie *The Fountainhead* instead of her novel of the same name?

In the era of the art cinema, one often spoke of filmmakers like

Godard, Bresson, Bergson, and even Antonioni as philosophical. Thus, it does not sound strange to our ears to say that one can philosophize *through* the moving image. Yet in these cases, it was not always evident whether what was meant was that these filmmakers illustrated preexisting philosophical themes—as Antonioni was said to illustrate the theme of the meaninglessness of modern existence—or that these filmmakers developed original philosophical theses. Consequently, although the critical rhetoric surrounding the art cinema made the association of philosophy and movies sound very familiar, it did not settle the issue of whether movie makers could produce original philosophy by means of the moving image.

Indeed, formidable arguments have been marshaled in recent years attempting to demonstrate the impossibility or, at least, the implausibility of philosophizing through the moving image. In fact, these arguments are so powerful that one is tempted to say that such skepticism is the dominant perspective nowadays, at least among Anglophone philosophers.

It is to these skeptical arguments that I now turn. I shall try to show that they are not ultimately successful. There are, I contend, *some* cases of movie-made philosophy. And if some movie-made philosophy is actual, then movie-made philosophy is possible. Or so I shall attempt to demonstrate. Moreover, in defeating the leading skeptical arguments in this area of debate, I hope to vindicate the commonplace view that movie-made philosophy is conceptually feasible, thereby shifting the burden of proof in this matter back to the skeptics.

However, before embarking on that project, let me note parenthetically that although I am arguing about what is possible in the realm of philosophy *in* cinema, the debate itself belongs to the arena of the philosophy *of* the moving image proper, since it is a question concerning the epistemological limits of cinema.

On the Possibility of Movie-Made Philosophy

During the past decade and a half—undoubtedly prefigured and encouraged by the work of Stanley Cavell—Anglophone philosophers have become keenly interested in the philosophical potential of the moving image. Anthologies abound in which rank-and-file philosophers attempt to distill the philosophical message to be found in this or that movie.

Although many philosophers are interested in the relation between movies and philosophy, there is not a converging consensus about the nature of that relation. Some philosophers maintain that it is within the reach of the moving image to make contributions to philosophy that stand on all fours with the contributions made by card-carrying philosophers in journal articles and at academic conferences. Others argue that this is beyond the capability of the moving image.

Admittedly, this concern is more a worry in the analytic wing of contemporary philosophy than it is on the so-called continental side of things. After all, since Hegel, Schiller, and Schelling, continental philosophers have been comfortable with the idea that art could be philosophical. But the analytic tradition is more skeptical about these claims.

Such skeptics may concede that movies can illustrate philosophical ideas, motivate philosophical problems, suggest philosophical solutions, reframe problems, and possibly even present counter-examples to existing philosophical views. Nevertheless, the skeptics draw a line in the sand when it comes to the possibility of movies making philosophy—that is, of movies acting as a vehicle for the creation and substantiation of original, positive philosophical theses.

Three recent arguments against movie-made philosophy have been mounted by Paisley Livingston, Murray Smith, and Bruce Russell, respectively.[2]

Livingston's target is specifically fictional, narrative cinema; he challenges the notion that this kind of movie can make philosophy. Livingston begins by introducing two conditions that he maintains that proponents of movie-made philosophy allegedly believe must be met in order for any example to count as an instance of movie-made philosophy. He calls this "the bold thesis." Although Livingston identifies the bold thesis as a matter of requirements advanced by the friends of movie-made philosophy, I am less convinced of this and suspect that they represent Livingston's own standards, standards, indeed, more demanding than I believe that defending the possibility of movie-made philosophy requires.

But in any event, the first condition of the bold thesis à la Livingston asserts that X is a specimen of movie-made philosophy only if it is a historically innovative philosophical proposal rather than simply an illustration of a preexisting position. It must not be parasitic on previous philosophical discourse; it must be independent. Thus, Rossellini's *Socrates, Augustine, Pascal,* and *Descartes* do not count as movie-made philosophy, since the actors playing these philosophers are only prosaically repeating exactly what these original thinkers already said. Ditto Derek Jarman's *Wittgenstein.* This demand for innovative philosophy is called the *results condition.*

In addition to the independence requirement of the results condition, Livingston also requires that a candidate for the title of movie-made philosophy be articulated exclusively by cinematic means. Consequently, a cinematic recording of a contemporary philosopher, like the late Bob Solomon, sharing his thoughts with the camera on the philosophy of the emotions—as he does in one of the Great Courses produced by the Teaching Company—falls short of movie-made philosophy just because the mode of presentation does not really exploit features, like montage, that are putatively exclusive to the moving image. Rather, Solomon basically communicates his philosophy to listeners in the conventional way by lecturing. This exclusivity requirement is called the *means condition.*

With these two criteria in hand, Livingston presents the proponent of movie-made philosophy with what he regards as the dilemma of paraphrase. It goes like this: either the motion picture articulates a philosophical thesis that can be put into words—that can be paraphrased—or it doesn't. If it doesn't, then there is no call to suppose that it has propounded philosophy, either innovative or otherwise; the possibility of movie-made philosophy cannot be based upon something ineffable. It is on these grounds that Livingston rejects the influential project of filmosophy as defended by Daniel Frampton.[3]

If it can be put into words, however, Livingston maintains that this will run afoul of both the independence requirement and the demand for cinematic exclusivity. It will conflict with the cinematic exclusivity condition because if it requires a paraphrase in order to be identified as a piece of philosophy, then this particular piece of philosophy has not been forged exclusively by cinematic means alone. It needs language to finish the job inasmuch, as it supposedly depends upon the paraphrase.

Moreover, if the case in question requires a paraphrase that, as it undoubtedly will, must make reference to existing philosophical debates, then the candidate will not be altogether epistemically innovative. Thus, it will violate the independence requirement, thereby offending the results condition.

Murray Smith does not argue that there are things that philosophy can do, but that movies can't. Both can, for instance, concoct fictional thought experiments. However, the two practices fashion their thought experiments for different purposes. The philosopher hatches his in order to motivate a distinction or to pose a counterexample. He aims at truth. The movie maker presents her thought experiments, first and foremost, for the sake of art. These differing purposes—which we might call, roughly and only provisionally, the cognitive and the artistic—shape the design of the thought experiments as they are issued from these very different institutions. Ostensibly, the philosophical thought experiment will aspire to clarity, whereas the artistic thought experiment will aim for ambiguity, insofar as ambiguity is a value of art. Moreover, this commitment to ambiguity will cashier the movie candidate from the order of philosophy, since however virtuous ambiguity is in the realm of art, it is allegedly a disqualifying factor when it comes to philosophy.

Bruce Russell unabashedly identifies doing philosophy with explicit argumentation and explanation. Like Livingston, he would deny that a motion picture that contained literal, verbal argumentation and explanation would count as *movie-made* philosophy, since, he surmises, that if a movie has a philosopher or actor-playing-a-philosopher merely reciting an argument or an explanation outright, then it is not the movie that is making the philosophy but the monologue. For example, Roark's speech in *The Fountainhead* is not movie-made philosophy. It is language and not cinema that gets the credit here.

The intuition that underlies Russell's position is probably the thought that it is not enough to count as philosophy to simply signal a commitment to this or that philosophical notion. For example, merely indicating faith in determinism does not make one a philosopher. To warrant the label "philosophy" requires something more. Given his analytic background, Russell proposes that that something more is an argument.

Confronting the Skeptics

I do not find the metaphilosophical assumptions upon which the preceding skeptical arguments rest to be finally decisive. The requirement that movie-made philosophy be created solely through uniquely cinematic means is not ultimately compelling. Livingston attributes this criterion to proponents of movie-made philosophy, but I see no convincing reason to accept it, whether it originates with the friends of movie-made philosophy or, as I have suggested, with Livingston.

One problem with this requirement is isolating exclusively cinematic means. A feature of film, like the frequently mentioned example of montage, is shared with video, photography, perhaps fine art in general, poetry, and even the novel, as in the case of John Dos Passos. Recall, Sergei Eisenstein analogized cinematic montage with all of these. Nor have other candidates for the uniquely cinematic fared well either. But if there are no exclusive features of the cinematic medium or specific devices unique to the art form, then this demand is unrealistic.

Livingston seems to think that the lack of specificity here is a problem for the friends of movie-made philosophy. It will thwart their efforts to establish that the philosophy in question is really *movie*-made. But I suspect that it is Livingston who has set the bar too high in this matter. It is undoubtedly reasonable to demand that movie-made philosophy involve the deployment of devices typically associated with the art of cinema, but that requirement falls short of exclusivity and is easier to secure. In fact, I conjecture that what is really required here is nothing more than that the philosophy in question not simply be delivered by a prosaic audiovisual recording of someone baldly decanting the philosophy in question—even though, ironically enough, this capacity for recording would be an example of a feature of film often claimed by some to be specific to the medium!

Moreover, if the means condition can be met by cinematic structures characteristic of the motion picture that go beyond mere recording, as Livingston at least once, perhaps inadvertently, concedes, then it seems that movie-made philosophy is not as problematic as Livingston contends.

Aaron Smuts, for example, persuasively argues that the "Gods" sequence in Eisenstein's *October* presents a debunking genealogy of the

Christian god, unmasking via montage its origin in primitive beliefs.⁴ Montage may not be exclusively cinematic, but it is a typical structure of the art of cinema. So it should satisfy the requirement that movie-made philosophy should be recognizably cinematic, a reasonable expectation inflated beyond credibility by calling for exclusivity. Moreover, genealogy is a respectable form of philosophical debate, at least since Nietzsche.

In response to this example, Livingston says that it violates the results condition, since the meaning of the shot chain is too indeterminate; he maintains that it requires a paraphrase in order to be understood.

However, I am not persuaded that the Gods sequence is so indeterminate. What more compelling or even equally compelling alternative interpretations are there? What are the alternate interpretations that viewers are wavering between? Furthermore, although many viewers may require hearing Smuts's interpretation in order to make sense of the shot chain, that does not entail that the meaning of the sequence *depends* on the interpretation; Smuts did not require the interpretation to get the philosophical point of Eisenstein's montage. He saw what Eisenstein was up to, and then he interpreted it for others.

That is, the meaning of the shot chain does not depend ontologically upon the paraphrase/interpretation that some viewers may require to understand it; the meaning is carried by the montage and is recognized by astute viewers. Perhaps, Livingston is confusing Smuts's interpretation of the sequence with what it is an interpretation of, going on then to call the latter "a paraphrase." Yet what Livingston is calling a paraphrase is not a constituent of the meaning of the Gods sequence but is more akin to what we may very loosely and only metaphorically refer to as a "translation," a translation for the cinematically unsophisticated.

Thomas Wartenberg has interpreted the assembly line scene in Chaplin's *Modern Times* as an expansion upon Marx's view of the degradation of human labor under capitalism.⁵ Since Chaplin conveys this idea primarily by means of his comic mime of the way in which the repetitive work movement takes over the Tramp's body, perhaps Livingston might charge that it violates the means condition, since it could have been done on stage with equal effect. However, I think this is a more austere requirement than can be reasonably expected, since Chaplin gets his idea across without prosaically reciting it and since mime is a characteristic—though not an exclusive feature—of motion pictures, especially silent ones. Furthermore, if Livingston complains that Chaplin is only repeating, albeit gesturally, what Marx already wrote, Wartenberg can point out that the assembly line was invented after Marx was dead. So Chaplin, as Wartenberg argues, is not just parroting Marx but expanding upon him.

Perhaps, Livingston would attempt to reject Wartenberg's example of Chaplin by mobilizing his results condition and contending that this example still invokes preexisting Marxist ideas, even if it expands upon them. Yet does simply working within a Marxist framework, as G. A. Cohen did, discount his contribution as philosophy?

Livingston's results condition, if I understand it, claims that paraphrasing the view of a movie compromises its status as independent philosophy. But why? If I paraphrase a difficult passage from Kant for my students, does that compromise Kant's status as a philosopher? When one paraphrases a candidate of movie-made philosophy, one is interpreting the philosophy already cinematically advanced by the motion picture. It is not necessarily a matter of completing the philosophical idea in question. Livingston, it seems to me, may be confusing the interpretation of the motion picture for some audience to whom the filmmaker's idea is not obvious with the cinematic presentation of the ideas.

Sometimes, it appears that the problem of paraphrase for Livingston arises because the movie-made philosophy will presuppose some already existing philosophy. But doesn't all philosophizing require a preexisting discursive context? Presumably no philosophizing, at least since Thales (and probably not even then), emerges ex nihilo.

I suspect that Livingston would agree with this but then go on to explain that what he is getting at is that the philosophizing in question should be an original contribution. But what does Livingston mean by "original"? He can't mean that nothing quite like it has ever been seen or heard before. Little philosophy, if any, could survive a test like that.

Specifically, Livingston thinks that if something is paraphrased, it cannot be original. I have already challenged that view. But I think that the notion of an original contribution is exorbitant if that is understood as a totally original contribution. I think that Livingston appears to have made the criterion for original philosophizing way too demanding. He seems to think that if the paraphrase draws upon preexisting philosophical discussions, which it is indeed very apt to do, then that shows that the movie is not truly, epistemically independent. But I think that a standard this draconian would disallow most of what we are ordinarily ready to call philosophy. There aren't that many brand-new positions. There are generally new arguments, examples, refinements, and nuanced qualifications of already existing positions. Indeed, an absolutely independent philosophical thesis—one detached altogether from preexisting philosophical discourse—might just be too independent for any of us to grasp.

When Bernard Williams presented the counterexample to utilitarianism that imagined a man given the choice between killing one prisoner himself or all twenty prisoners being executed by their captors, he was contributing to the philosophical debate, though the position he was defending and the kind of thought experiment he contrived were not utterly unprecedented. Let us say, Williams's intervention here was "original enough." Perhaps, we can regard Wartenberg's example from *Modern Times* in a similar light.

Moreover, as long as the requirement of originality is not excessive, I think it can be met by certain motion pictures, especially within the realm of ethics and political philosophy. Godard's *A Married Woman,* for example, visually conveys a notion of objectification that will become important in feminist philosophy, especially with reference to pornography, in the decades after the film appeared. In the course of the film, Godard introduces advertising images of women's underclothing, notably bras, dissecting, in the manner of a pop artist, the ways in which the ads depersonalize and reduce the female models to sexual objects: they are their breasts.

These advertising images, of course, anchor the sequences in the film where the married woman has sex alternatively with her husband and her lover—where bodies are fragmented by the framing and editing in a way that suggests that the depersonalization, replaceability, and objectification that motivate the advertising imagery has taken over everyday life, a thought exemplified as well by the shot of the married woman walking under (as if dominated by) the enormous billboard of a woman—with outsized breasts—in a bra.

Likewise, the photo-negative images of the women being photographed in the swimming pool visually divest them of their individuality and reduce them to curvaceous bodies. This is not just a reflexive acknowledgment of the presence of the filmic medium, although it is that. It is also an acknowledgment of cinema's capacity to objectify, a concept that was arguably relatively original in its historical context.

In addition, it should be noted that Livingston's requirement of originality is biased in favor of some kinds of philosophy rather than others. For from certain points of view, one office of philosophy is to remind us of things known but forgotten or even repressed. Heidegger did not pretend to discover that human life was headed toward death. His task, among other things, was to remind us of this fact and of our tendency to deny it. Some movie-made philosophy may be similarly committed to recalling to mind certain essential truths about human life that, although well known, are easily, even willfully, forgotten. One might understand Billy Wilder's ingenious use of cinematic stardom in *Sunset Boulevard* in this way—as remindful of the fact of mortal aging and the costs exacted by the suppressing of this inevitable feature of human nature. Livingston's conception of originality would preclude—by fiat and without argument—this variety of movie-made philosophizing, although, in other respects, Wilder's film is a stunningly original and effective image of something many of us, particularly those of us of a certain age, need to remember on an almost daily basis.

Murray Smith's argument against movie-made philosophy on the basis of ambiguity is not conclusive, because at best he is dealing with tendencies. Perhaps much philosophy or, more accurately, most philosophy in a certain tradition goes in for clarity. But sometimes, a philosopher, especially one like Nietzsche, Kierkegaard or Philip Kapleau, from a nonanalytic tradition (or Wittgenstein from the analytic tradition), may have a motive for shrouding their thought experiments in ambiguity, while the thought experiments of some artists, like Charles Dickens in *Hard Times,* serve their artistic purposes by being blazingly clear. Ambiguity may be a primary literary value from certain critical perspectives, like the American new critics and, maybe, deconstructionists like Paul DeMan. But whether it is the ne plus ultra of artistic achievement is uncontroversially controversial. The philosophical thought experiment filmed by Pudovkin in his *Mechanics of the Brain,* for instance, exhibits not a smidgen of ambiguity, but it is no less artistic or cinematic for that.

Bruce Russell maintains that philosophy requires explicit argumentation and/or explanation. This demand, needless to say, will not be accepted by anyone who regards Nietzsche's aphorisms or genealogies or Wittgenstein's puzzles as philosophy. But even if we suppose Russell's criteria, for the purpose of argument, it is not clear that his skepticism about movie-made philosophy is conclusive.

A thought experiment is a form of philosophical argumentation. Russell allows this. But according to Russell, if a thought experiment is presented in the course of argumentation, its author has to accompany it with an explanation of how it works. This is something Russell finds lacking in motion pictures with philosophical pretensions, and indeed, if a movie did include such a verbal explanation literally, the philosophy would not be movie made for Russell for the same reasons it would not be for Livingston.

Yet I find it strange that Russell holds this position on thought experiments, since he agrees that motion pictures can provide counterexamples, where, of course, many counterexamples are thought experiments. Moreover, I am not convinced that movie-made thought experiments must always be attached to explicit self-explications, because I'm not persuaded that the thought experiments that union-certified philosophers bandy about always need to be explained. The context in which the counterexample is offered to informed listeners may be enough to drive the point home, as may happen in the discussion period after the presentation of a philosophical paper. The context, that is, may be so pregnant and the thought experiment so deft that everyone gets it on contact.

Moreover, there are cinematic contexts like this. In the avant-garde film world of the 1960s through the 1980s, there was an abiding commitment to isolating the nature of cinema by means of cinema. This was a metacinematic project dedicated to defining the cinema of the moving image cinematically. This commitment was overtly a concern of what was called structural film, which to my mind might have been more accurately labeled "minimalist cinema," since it was devoted to establishing the minimal ontological requirements for calling a candidate cinema. When one attended the screening of minimalist cinema, the informed viewer knew what was at stake—answering the question, What is cinema? by creating an exemplar of it.

Maybe the greatest work in this genre is Ernie Gehr's *Serene Velocity*,

279 •• NOËL CARROLL

a film of an empty, institutional hallway. By alternating the settings of his zoom lens, Gehr presents the viewer with static images that, with certain juxtapositions of shots, then burst into motion, thereby revealing the secret of animation aleatorically. This film has been so reduced in content that the only thing it is about is the appearance of motion. Yet insofar as we remain willing to call it a film, this implies that movement—or at least its technical possibility—is a minimal condition for cinema.[6]

A philosopher might have thought up an experiment like this. Gehr made it, thereby providing evidence for the hypothesis that movement—or at least its possibility—is a minimal condition for film status. Moreover, informed viewers of the avant-garde cinema recognized that this was the meaning or significance of *Serene Velocity* without being told, and they grasped the way in which *Serene Velocity* was evidence for this conjecture.

To Russell's objection that there is no argument here, we may reply that the argument is present in the mind of the informed viewer who, knowing the dialectical context in which the film is presented, works out how *Serene Velocity* answers the question, What is cinema? Just as Socrates maieutically elicits a geometrical proof from the slave in Plato's *Meno*, Gehr presents an experimental film to an audience primed to be on the lookout for an ontological claim about the nature of the motion picture, and then he, Gehr, guides them toward working out how *Serene Velocity* supplies evidence for a specific hypothesis regarding the nature of cinema. Moreover, even if Gehr's conjecture were false, that would not disqualify *Serene Velocity*'s philosophical ambitions. For if truth were required for something to qualify as philosophy, most professional philosophers would be out of business.

Russell may complain that Gehr's film itself does not explicitly announce to viewers what philosophical point it is evidence for. But that is unnecessary, since informed viewers understand the aims of minimalist cinema in the same way that professional philosophers usually do not need to be told how a given thought experiment does its work. The philosopher figures it out for herself. And even if it is explained to her, she must still think it through on her own, as does the viewer of *Serene Velocity*.

Moreover, recalling Livingston's criterion of originality, Gehr's emphasis on movement as the sine qua non of cinema was innovative during a period when photography was frequently, though wrongly, thought to be the best candidate for this title.

Contra Russell then, *Serene Velocity* demonstrates the possibility of movie-made philosophy, even in the face of his strictures. Although it does not sketch a step-by-step argument on the screen, it prompts and directs one in the mind of the viewer, the laboratory in which all thought experiments must be tested. It provides the evidence the audience needs to reach its solution, while the context of experimental cinema specifies the problem at issue. Furthermore, other experimental works have limned other features of cinema by deploying comparable strategies. Thus, Russell should not attempt to dismiss *Serene Velocity* as a one-off freak. There is more movie-made philosophy where that comes from.

Standing back, it seems that the preceding arguments against movie-made philosophy presuppose, either directly or indirectly, that the primary vehicle of philosophy must be language. But perhaps that presumption is up for grabs. Maybe audiences can be led to philosophical insights by having their experiences shaped and directed in certain ways. They may come to a philosophical conclusion on the basis of their acquaintance with the phenomenon in question through their own experience, as that experience has been molded in order to facilitate the recognition of the processes upon which the experience rests.

Call this appeal to the audience's experience of an artwork for the purposes of casting reflection upon how the artwork works on the audience a matter of *phenomenological address.* It is my contention that some films, like *Memento,* offer philosophical insight to reflective viewers by means of their phenomenological address to the audience. Specifically, for example, by means of its reverse narration, *Memento* makes its viewers aware of the amount of constructive activity they must conscript in order to put the story together for themselves. That is, the film's structure forces them to self-consciously fill in the gaps, to formulate expectations and to test them, and to retrospect, in an effort of determining consistency, what is going on in the narrative on a scene-to-scene basis. Thus, the film focuses our attention upon the kind of constructive activities in which audiences need to engage in response to any cinematic narrative, although these processes usually fly beneath our radar screen. The film makes the attentive viewer aware of this process of construction experientially, disclosing how the narrative mind works in the process of putting it through its paces.[7] This may be stated in words; it is not irretrievably ineffable. Nevertheless, the demonstration of the mind's participation in the construction of cinematic meaning here is in the experience of the activity in real time.

Furthermore, since the structures of phenomenological address need not be strictly linguistic and may remain inexplicit, the movie-made philosophy that comes by way of phenomenological address may not be threatened by the kinds of skeptical concerns I have rehearsed.

On Thought Experiments

So far much of the argument has been based primarily upon the presupposition that at least some motion pictures can be construed as doing philosophy on the grounds that they function as thought experiments in such a way that they raise, clarify, reframe, and even advance philosophical positions. However, some philosophers are apt to reject this suggestion on the grounds that no motion picture, fictional or otherwise, can be regarded as a genuine thought experiment or, at least, the sort of thought experiments that one encounters in philosophical lectures and writings. Deborah Knight, for example, maintains that fictional thought experiments are so disanalogous to philosophical thought experiments that they should not even be considered to belong to the same species.[8]

To this end, she presents a series of disanalogies. These include that thought experiments often involve science fiction, whereas most artistic fictions are not science fictions; that philosophical thought experiments are short, whereas artistic fictions are much longer; that the story is indispensable to artistic fictions, whereas it is not necessary for philosophical thought experiments; that philosophical thought experiments do not arouse emotions, whereas artistic fictions do; that philosophical thought experiments are unresolved, whereas artistic fictions have resolutions; and finally, paralleling the previously discussed view of Murray Smith, that philosophical versus artistic thought experiments have different institutional aims.

However, none of these disanalogies strike me as very persuasive. Knight is wrong in her first assertion that all or, even, most thought experiments involve science fiction. Searle's Chinese room and Danto's nine identical red canvases are famous philosophical thought experiments that do not involve science fiction. For every brain-in-a-vat thought experiment, there is a refutation of act utilitarianism that imagines framing an innocent homeless person. For every Putnam-esque twin Earth, there is at least one Rawlsian veil of ignorance. The counterexamples here are indefinitely great in number.

Knight is right that most philosophical thought experiments are short and that the fictional-cinema ones are short. But so what? Some philosophical thought experiments are longer than some fictions. What is Plato's imagining of his republic but a thought experiment, one longer than most movies. Moreover, the same point can be made with regard to Voltaire's *Candide*.

Furthermore, one complaint regarding contemporary philosophical thought experiments is that they are too short. In this respect, perhaps many of the relevant motion picture thought experiments are improvements on standard philosophical practice. And in any event, maybe some artistic/cinematic thought experiments need the length they go to in order to make the insight they are promoting sink in. What principled reason, in examples like these, does Knight have for limiting the word count of thought experiments?

Knight's notion that the story is not necessary to philosophical thought experiments is a bit obscure. A thought experiment is an intuition pump.[9] It is a tool for thinking. It is true that it is under-taken to promote thinking or even to provoke a certain thought. And of course, the thought's the thing. But if the thought is reached by means of the story that embodies the thought experiment, why is it unnecessary? Because there is always another way, another thought experiment, sans story, available to get to the thought in question? But how would someone know that this is the way things stand in every instance?

Knight maintains that fictional thought experiments recruit the emotions but that philosophical thought experiments do not. This is flat-out false. Consider thought experiments in moral theory, such as the killing of the innocent homeless person counterexample rehearsed in every introduction to ethics class. Surely, the intuition it evokes depends on a gut reaction, as do a great many of the other thought experiments deployed in debates in ethics and political philosophy.

At the very least, the emotions these thought experiments evoke are germane to our reflection upon these thought experiments and, in some cases, may be arguably decisive.

That thought experiments engage the emotions should be clear from the fact that they evoke intuitions, which, of course, are often connected to the emotions in everyday life, particularly in regard to ethical phenomena. Moreover, the connection of thought experiments to the emotions may be relevant to answering two of Knight's other misgivings. That is, in order to secure deep emotional responses, a fictional, cinematic thought experiment may require greater detail and, therefore, greater length than a typical philosophical thought experiment, *and* this may be why stories are not dispensable in the case of many fictional, cinematic thought experiments.

The view that philosophical thought experiments leave matters open, merely facilitating debate, is also wrong. Some philosophical thought experiments open up a question. But some compel one conclusion to the exclusion of others. The aforementioned counter-example to act utilitarianism belongs to this class. Admittedly, it is also the case that some movie fictions may promote philosophical reflection without suggesting. *Blade Runner,* in its original-release version, arguably exemplifies this possibility. Yet this hardly pertains to *all* thought experiments, whether propounded in philosophical essays or motion pictures. If *Vertigo* is a thought experiment that interrogates the notion that genuine love is love of the properties of the beloved, can there be any way to avoid the conclusion that Hitchcock unequivocally rejects this perspective?

Lastly, like Smith, Knight suggests thought experiments have different functions in the institution of philosophy than they do in the art world, including the movie world. Knight does not specify these alternative functions, but as we have seen, Smith does. Art world thought experiments in general and movie world thought experiments in particular aim at ambiguity, whereas philosophical thought experiments aim at determinate truth. This distinction, needless to say, is somewhat in tension with Knight's (mistaken) contention that philosophical thought experiments never aspire to resolution. But in any event, the distinction does not hold. Some literary and cinematic thought experiments are anything but ambiguous—consider *Animal Farm* and *Clockwork Orange* and their adaptations for the screen.

However, there are philosophers whose thought experiments are ambiguous enough to require interpretation. Think again of Wittgenstein, for example.

Concluding Remarks

In discussing motion pictures, it has seemed unexceptionable to associate them with philosophy. Undoubtedly, the relationship of cinema to philosophy is multifarious. Herzog, for example, may be said to be philosophical insofar as he consistently defamiliarizes human life, examining it from a position detached and quizzical and, therefore, philosophical. And moreover, it is hard to deny that some motion pictures have illustrated philosophical themes. But the question has been broached of late of whether it is possible for cinema to do philosophy—to philosophize through the moving image. I have tried to defend that possibility, primarily by challenging the various skeptical objections abroad today. However, although I have rejected the strongest, universalizing versions of those objections, I think the skeptics have performed a useful service insofar as they have foregrounded what is involved in calling movies philosophical. And I think they have at least shown that there is probably not as much movie-made philosophy as the commentators often believe. Movie-made philosophy is possible, in my view, but probably rare. It can come in various forms; it need not be thought of exclusively in terms of argumentation. But even in its variety, it is not commonly available. And we have the skeptics to thank for making that clear.

NOTES

I would like to thank Thomas Wartenberg for his comments on this paper.

1. See Livingston, *Cinema, Philosophy, Bergman.*
2. See Livingston, "Theses on Cinema as Philosophy"; Livingston, *Cinema, Philosophy, Bergman*; Smith, "Film, Art, Argument, and Ambiguity"; Russell, "The Philosophical Limits of Film"; Russell, "The Limits of Film Again."
3. See Frampton, *Filmosophy.*
4. See Smuts, "Film as Philosophy."
5. See Wartenberg, *Thinking on Screen.* For Wartenberg's response to critics, see "On the Possibility of Cinematic Philosophy."
6. See Carroll, "Philosophizing through the Moving Image."

7. See Carroll, "Memento and the Phenomenology of Comprehending Motion Picture Narration."

8. See Knight, "The Third Man."

9. The notion that intuitions play a viable role in philosophy has been challenged by some proponents of experimental philosophy on the grounds that so-called intuition pumps, like thought experiments, do not track what actual nonphilosophers think, as evidenced by questionnaires. And this might seem to undermine my case for movie-made philosophy, since it rests so heavily on the idea of movie-made thought experiments. However, I question the premise that the intuitions elicited by thought experiments in philosophical discussions are supposed to track what everyone allegedly thinks. Rather, thought experiments engender thinking as we strive to find a reflective equilibrium between our beliefs, our emotional responses, and the solution we are drawn to with respect to the problem the thought experiment highlights. Thought experiments in philosophy don't aim at what everyone supposedly already believes—i.e., what the x-phi questionnaires may establish—but on the way a certain set of circumstances elicits and clarifies reflective reasoning as it strives for equilibrium, thereby laying it open to criticism. To that extent, I think that intuitions, as obtained through thought experiments, still have an acceptable role to play in philosophical debate.

BIBLIOGRAPHY

Carroll, Noël. "Memento and the Phenomenology of Comprehending Motion Picture Narration." In *Minerva's Night Out: Philosophy, Pop Culture, and Moving Pictures,* 203–20. Malden, Mass.: Wiley-Blackwell, 2013.

———. "Philosophizing through the Moving Image." *Journal of Aesthetics and Art Criticism* 64 (2006): 173–86.

Frampton, Daniel. *Filmosophy.* New York: Wallflower Press / Columbia University Press, 2006.

Knight, Deborah. "The Third Man: Ethics, Aesthetics, Irony." In *Ethics in the Cinema,* edited by Ward Jones and Samantha Vice, 288–90. Oxford: Oxford University Press, 2013.

Livingston, Paisley. *Cinema, Philosophy, Bergman.* Oxford: Oxford University Press, 2009.

———. "Theses on Cinema as Philosophy." *Journal of Aesthetics and Art Criticism* 64 (2006): 11–18.

Russell, Bruce. "The Limits of Film Again." Talk at the Pacific Division Meetings of the American Society for Aesthetics, Asilomar, California, April 15–17, 2009.

———. "The Philosophical Limits of Film." Special issue on Woody Allen, *Film and Philosophy,* July 2000, 163–67.

Smith, Murray, "Film, Art, Argument, and Ambiguity." *Journal of Aesthetics and Art Criticism* 64 (2006): 33–42.

Smuts, Aaron. "Film as Philosophy: In Defense of the Bold Thesis." *Journal of Aesthetics and Art Criticism* 67 (2009): 409–20.

Wartenberg, Thomas. "On the Possibility of Cinematic Philosophy." In *New Takes in Philosophy,* edited by Havi Carel and Greg Tuck, 9–24. New York: Palgrave MacMillan / St. Martin's Press, 2011.

———. *Thinking on Screen: Film as Philosophy.* London: Routledge, 2007.

"Not Time's Fool"

MARRIAGE AS AN ETHICAL RELATIONSHIP IN
MICHAEL HANEKE'S *AMOUR*

Thomas E. Wartenberg

Amour (2012) is the latest in a series of films made by the Austrian
director Michael Haneke that center on a couple whose partners are
Georges and Anne. The films are not in any sense sequels, since despite sharing the same names, the characters in the different films
are not different versions of the same people, a fact indicated, for
example, by the different actors playing them, the different profes-
sions they have, and the very different circumstances in which they
live. Nonetheless, it is fair to say that the films do exhibit a certain
unity, for each film focuses on a central anxiety that upper-middle-
class or bourgeois couples face in the modern world. In each of the
films, the narrative depicts what happens when these slightly paranoid fears turn out to be accurate anticipations of the couple's future.
So in *Funny Games* (1997) the threat is home invasion, while in *Cache*
(2005) it is surveillance. In both cases the fear that appeared slightly
paranoid turns out to have been fully justified, and it leads to the
devastation of the couple in both films.

Amour initially appears to fit squarely into this sequence of films
when, after Georges and Anne return from a concert given by Anne's
former piano student Alexandre (Alexandre Theraud), their aesthetic
pleasure at the beauty of the performance is shattered by the discovery that someone has attempted to break into their apartment. Their
vulnerability to such violence unnerves the two old people. Using our
knowledge of Haneke's concerns, we might think that this film will
focus on the devastation the attempted break-in will visit upon the
elderly couple. But we would be wrong.

The danger along with the concomitant anxiety this elderly couple will have to face in *Amour* might be termed internal rather than external. Disease, disability, and the approach of death are certainly deep existential concerns that plague not only the upper-middle classes. But they do plague them, and *Amour* is remarkable for the manner in which it faces these issues head on and without any sugarcoating.

The film's brutal honesty has led some viewers to find *Amour* troubling. Although *Amour* garnered many awards, among others the Oscar for Best Foreign Film and the Palme d'Or at Cannes and many critics hailed it as a masterpiece, there was an undercurrent of reluctance to advise people to see the film, a trend epitomized by Francine Prose's blog posting in the *New York Review of Books* "A Masterpiece You Might Not Want to See."[1] The first paragraph of her review ends with the following question:

> Can a movie make you think that an artist has done something extraordinary, original, extremely difficult—and yet you cannot imagine yourself uttering the words, "You've got to go see *Amour*"?

The reason for this ambivalence on the part of reviewers like Prose—as well as, in my experience, many ordinary viewers of the film—is that *Amour* depicts the slow physical decline and eventual death of an elderly woman who is being cared for by her loving and attentive husband. As one friend of mine remarked, "We are all going to go through this. Why watch it before we are forced to experience it?" Such scruples have led people to avoid the film for fear they will be too upset by watching a none-too-pleasant fate that awaits them.

Surprisingly, when I saw the film, my reaction was nearly the opposite of these negative remarks, for I experienced the film as one of the most sensitive and insightful depictions of a marriage I had ever seen on screen. I was completely captivated by the loving attention with which the husband in the film takes care of his wife as she suffers increasing debility. In addition, it seemed to me an important corrective to the cinematic near obsession with the formation of romantic couples, as if the only question for films to address about love and marriage was whether two people were ready to commit themselves to one another. To my mind, the film shows what the commitment of marriage is really about, a topic I believe films have paid scant attention to.

In this chapter, I will explore my reaction to the film and make a case for *Amour* being an important addition to cinematic depictions of love and marriage. In addition, I will examine the film's claims about death and dying, a topic that, despite receiving increasing attention, still is subject to significant taboos in many places. Although I see *Amour* as making contributions to our understanding of the ethics of the process of dying, I will argue that it does not present a general justification for euthanasia, as some have asserted.

Philosophical Underpinnings

Let me begin by giving a quick summary of our philosophical understanding of cinematic depictions of love and marriage. The philosopher who first gave an account of how films address the issue of love and marriage in a philosophically significant manner was Stanley Cavell. In three books—*Pursuits of Happiness* (1984), *Contesting Tears* (1997), and *Cities of Words* (2005)—Cavell argues that narrative films, mostly from the 1930s, specifically those in two genres he calls "the comedies of remarriage" and "the melodramas of the unknown woman," make a genuine contribution to philosophy. The two earlier books present these films as helping us understand the nature of skepticism and how marriage allows for its overcoming. The final book substitutes the notion of moral perfectionism for the earlier talk of skepticism. In Cavell's latter work, the philosophical content of the films is made specific: they depict a character who has to make a decision about what is of fundamental value in his or her life.

In Cavell's view the crucial threat to a marriage is divorce or dissolution. Even when two people are "right for each other," they are faced with the philosophical problem of *acknowledging* each other as human beings. This is how Cavell interprets the problem of skepticism in regard to other minds as being a topic addressed by many popular films—films that focus on the difficulties of two people entering into and remaining bound by that joint undertaking we call a marriage.

Cavell's focus on (re)marriage reflects a feature of popular films. When one turns to Hollywood films, one discovers a narrow focus on romantic love. A list of the one hundred greatest films about love at IMDb is almost entirely composed of romances, such as *Pretty*

Woman and *Titanic*.[2] Such films depict the difficulties two people have in forming and maintaining a romantic couple, a (re)marriage.

Part of my interest in *Amour* is that it pays no attention to that issue, for the threat to its principal pair does not come from skepticism. Instead, the film focuses on exploring what I call "marriage as an ethical institution," that is, the ethical duties a marriage requires of the partners to it. Such a cinematic exploration of marriage is a rarity, and that's part of why *Amour* is so important. It breaks ground in cinematic depictions of marriage and does that, I will argue, in a philosophically significant way.

The specific focus of the film is on the ethical obligations that a partner has to his spouse when she experiences a serious illness, one that puts her on a path toward death. *Amour* shows that a marriage involves a commitment to one's partner that has to be maintained throughout one's life, no matter the circumstances. Indeed, as the circumstances get more dire, the demands on the partners increase. As the traditional wedding vow says, one is a husband or a wife "for better, for worse, for richer, for poorer, in sickness and in health, until death do us part." *Amour* depicts how a husband keeps his vow in the face of his wife's terminal illness as, because of a number of strokes, she gradually descends into paralysis and ultimately toward death itself.

Let me make two quick comments on my own work on philosophy and film. In *Unlikely Couples Movie Romance as Social Criticism* (1990), I took issue with Cavell, but from a point of view different from that which I have just articulated. I was interested in a certain tendency in romantic films toward the depiction of socially transgressive couples and the extent to which these films had the potential to put forward critical views of society. Nonetheless, like Cavell, my account centered on the question of whether a couple could be formed (or not), though it focused on the social factors constituting obstacles to a couple's formation.

In my second book on film, written more than a decade later, *Thinking on Screen: Film as Philosophy* (2002), I explored a number of different paths films could go down in order to make a contribution to philosophy. The central ones I discussed were the following:

- A film illustrating a philosophical thesis or theory
- A film "screening" a philosophical thought experiment

- A film posing the question of the nature of film as an artistic
  medium by challenging viewers' notions of what a film had to be

For my purposes here, we can focus on how films philosophize by screening a philosophical thought experiment.

In *Thinking on Screen,* I used the idea of a thought experiment to explain how films could contribute to philosophy in the cases of both *Eternal Sunshine of the Spotless Mind* and *The Third Man. Eternal Sunshine* more or less fits the pattern of romantic film I mention earlier, although it supplements its focus on the formation of an extremely unlikely couple with attention to an ethically problematic practice of partial memory erasure.

The Third Man (1947), however, both illustrates a philosophical claim and supplements it with an original idea by means of an extended thought experiment. First of all, it illustrates that one of the benefits of friendship is the loyalty of one friend when a slander is made against the other. But the film goes beyond this claim, which can be found in the *Nicomachean Ethics,* by showing that in a case in which one's friend turns out to be a criminal and generally unreliable person, such loyalty can be misplaced and lead one to make disastrous ethical decisions.

I shall treat *Amour* as also presenting a detailed and extended thought experiment. Through it, the film gives us an in-depth understanding of why it might be morally required, in certain circumstances, for a spouse to kill his partner when she is suffering from a terminal illness.

Is Marriage Incompatible with Killing Your Spouse?

The greatest challenge to seeing this film as a love story is that the character I describe as a loving husband, Georges (Jean-Louis Trintignant), kills his ailing wife, Anne (Emmanuelle Riva). The immediate question this raises is, How can killing one's spouse be an act of love? This is the stark challenge with which I believe *Amour* confronts its viewers: making sense of a very brutal act as an ethical act prompted by love.

Before considering this brutal act, it will be helpful to have a context for this prima facie immoral action. Georges's wife, Anne, has

suffered a series of strokes that has gradually left her nearly completely paralyzed. By the time Georges kills her, she needs constant
care for all of her physical needs and can utter only monosyllabic
words, many of them apparently meaningless. Georges has taken care
of her throughout her decline and has come to the realization that he
will no longer be able to care for her as a result of her increasing debility and his diminishing strength. It is at this point that he kills her.

The scene of Anne's death begins with Georges telling her a story
about an experience he had at summer camp as a ten-year-old. He
had not wanted to go to camp, and he hated the experience, not
being good at or interested in the compulsory sports emphasized at
the camp. One day, the lunch consisted of rice pudding. The head
of the camp told him he had to stay at the table until he ate the
pudding, a dish Georges abhors. "After three hours," he tells her, "I
was allowed to leave the table," leaving it to us to interpret the isolation and misery that he experienced. He continues, "I went up to
my room, got into bed, and had a fever of forty-two degrees. It was
diphtheria. They took me to the nearest hospital where I was put in
an isolation ward, which meant that Mom, when she came to visit
me, could only wave at me through a window."

Why does Georges tell Anne this story? Although Georges's stories
are one of the central features of this marriage, this story is not simply
one he happens to tell her. Georges's story vividly conveys the terrible
isolation and loneliness he experienced as a child at camp, especially
when he couldn't even communicate directly with his mother at the
hospital. Georges here conveys his understanding of Anne's situation,
in which she, like the young Georges, is unable to communicate
with anyone, although it is her body and not a hospital window that
stands between her and the ability to speak.

This moment in the film shows us Georges exhibiting his deepest
empathetic connection to Anne and her horrific situation. He uses
his own experience of utter despair as a young child to enter empa-
thetically into what it must be like for her. And it is this understanding, together with his awareness of the horrific feelings he takes Anne
to be experiencing, that leads Georges to perform his brutal killing.

Pausing for a moment at the end of his story—he is sitting on her
bed as he tells it to her–Georges grabs a pillow and firmly places it
over Anne's head, smothering her. Killing Anne proves agonizingly

difficult for Georges. Haneke films her body struggling and legs jerking in ways that seem pretty remarkable for a woman who could barely move earlier. Georges has to use all of his strength, together with the weight of his body, to successfully smother her.

Even if we accept the idea that Georges is a loving husband who decides he has no option but to kill his terminally ill wife, whose sufferings he can no longer bear—something I will argue for in a moment—we still have to ask, given the brutality with which he kills her, why he chose that form of death and whether his choice is ethically acceptable. Why not give her an overdose of drugs or withhold food and water?

I think that Haneke chose to have Georges smother Anne because he did not want to short-circuit our moral quandary over Georges's actions by giving us the easy out of seeing the killing of another human being as something that can be accomplished easily and without any qualms. The moral significance of the decision to end someone else's life, even if undertaken for their welfare, should not be passed over, and I believe that Haneke has chosen a cinematically powerful means of showing us the difficulty Georges has with carrying through a morally complex course of action that he has arrived at with great difficulty. Withholding food or water would be easier for us to accept as a humane course of action. But Haneke does not want to provide us with a way to take this act to be moral without giving it a lot of thought. He wants us to be shocked by what Georges does and to have to reflect about its morality.

The final moment in the scene of Anne's death conveys an important point as the camera lingers on Georges after he has suffocated Anne: even if killing your spouse is the morally right thing to do, it is a difficult act to carry out both physically and emotionally. It's clear that Georges feels the moral weight of what he has done. Even if he thinks he has acted in a morally correct manner, he no doubt regrets that circumstances have compelled him to do so. The film asks us to acknowledge the complex moral and emotional situation that Georges faces.

What makes killing Anne the right thing for Georges to do is that her life has become one of nearly unremitting pain and suffering. The film has conveyed this slowly, mostly through Anne's repeated cries for help but also through her slow but ongoing physical decline. It is the repeated nature of Anne's cries that provides one of the factors that impels Georges toward his decision, for they bring home to him the horror and the loneliness she must be experiencing, which is, he believes, akin to the misery he experienced as a child at summer camp.

Dying with Dignity

Central to the film's "case" for seeing Anne's death as the result of Georges's love for her is its depiction of his realization that his marriage to Anne requires he ensure her a "death with dignity," to use the phrase employed by proeuthanasia activists.[3]

Dignity is an important ethical value, one some philosophers even think is the primary one. Kant is generally recognized as the philosopher who makes dignity central to morality. In the *Groundwork to the Metaphysics of Morals,* he states that "morality, and humanity in so far as it is capable of morality, are the only things that have dignity."[4] Kant's linkage of dignity to the capacity for moral action is not, I believe, central to the idea of dignity, and we can take dignity as simply something that every human being is entitled to simply by virtue of their humanity. In other words, we owe it to human beings to respect their dignity and to act in such a way that their dignity is maintained in all circumstances.

It is those closest to us—our spouses, parents, children, and friends—upon whom this duty of protecting our dignity centrally devolves. It is a serious moral failing for one's parents, spouse, children, or friends to treat one in a manner that does not respect his or her inherent dignity as a human being.

One stage of human life where this moral requirement—that people be treated in only ways that respect their dignity—becomes paramount is during the process of dying. For many people, dying is an extended process of gradual decline rather than a quick, short-term event that they may not even consciously experience. For these people the imperative that they be treated with dignity is especially important, for their physical and, perhaps, mental decline makes it more difficult to maintain an attitude that respects it.

Since *Amour* never explicitly raises the issue of Anne being treated with dignity, it may seem as if I am imposing this concept upon the film. I think this objection is not justified and have two independent reasons for this.

First, in an interview with the Australian Film Commission about

Amour, Haneke, despite his avowal that he won't interpret his own work, says the following: "People always fight to maintain their dignity, and the more difficult the situation you're in, the bigger the battle." Haneke's use of the term "dignity" here suggests he thinks the film portrays the couple's struggle to maintain Anne's dignity. The director's claim is one important factor that licenses my use of this concept to characterize the ethical concern of the film.

But even without Haneke's explicit mentioning of this concept, I think there is sufficient reason to employ it, for I believe Anne's *dignity* is threatened in a series of incidents depicted in the film. I can make sense of their narrative significance only by taking them to show Anne facing threats to a value fundamental to her life that her illness has placed in jeopardy. And I further suggest that Georges comes to see the importance of acting to protect Anne's dignity as he witnesses the events that jeopardize it.

Threats to Anne's Dignity

A first threat to Anne's dignity occurs because of the humiliation she feels as she loses control of her basic bodily functions. In our society, at least, our ability to control certain basic aspects of our lives forms a basis for our sense of self-worth and, hence, dignity. Although we tend to presuppose that, as able-bodied adults, these matters are within our control, illness forces us to recognize our own dependency on our bodies, which can become potential enemies in our attempt to control our own life circumstances. When the facticity of our bodies make it impossible for us to control even the most basic tasks of our lives—consuming food and drink, as well as evacuating their waste products; moving our own bodies and tending to its cleanliness—we feel humiliated, as if we were somehow less valuable as human beings for being returned to an infant-like state of total dependence on others for even our most basic bodily functions. Clearly, this infantilization is humiliating and frustrating, threatening the dignity we have as human beings.

Anne has returned home from a hospital stay during which she had an unsuccessful operation that resulted in the paralysis of her right side. In consequence, Anne has become much more dependent on Georges, who she needs to put her into and take her out of her wheelchair.

One morning, as the couple awake and Georges begins to move Anne into her wheelchair so she can go to the bathroom, he discovers that Anne has pissed herself. After making this discovery, Georges calmly makes preparations to take Anne into the bathroom so he can wash and change her, all the while trying to keep Anne from feeling humiliated.

Georges goes off to fetch a towel, and Anne remains sitting on the edge of the bed. When Georges returns, he puts the towel on the seat of the wheelchair to keep it from getting wet, and he says to Anne:

GEORGES: It's no big deal. Come on.

He lifts her out of the bed into the wheelchair and pushes her through the hallway into the bathroom. He lifts her out of the wheelchair, sits her on the stool, and takes off her wet nightgown, pulling it over her head. She starts to sob inconsolably. He caresses her face.

GEORGES: Come on, darling. It's nothing serious. Things like that happen.

ANNE (SOBBING): I can't . . . take it any more.

He holds her tightly against him, strokes her hair, feeling helpless.

GEORGES: My love. My darling.[5]

Although Haneke's filmmaking style eschews dialogue in which a character reflects on her situation, it's pretty clear that Anne is humiliated by her lack of control over her own bodily fluids. This is an infantilizing experience, one that threatens to shatter her sense of herself, and makes it hard for her to retain any sense of herself as a being with dignity. What's especially chilling, though, is how the revolt of Anne's body makes it nearly impossible for her to express her rage and her humiliation. Her motorized wheelchair is about all she can use to express those emotions, and she uses it by driving at breakneck speed to the bathroom.

Georges, however, acts as we would hope a loving husband would, telling Anne she is attributing too much significance to this event. He reassures her this really is not anything to be ashamed of but something that simply happens in circumstances like hers.

In making these claims, Georges indicates his awareness of how humiliating wetting herself is for Anne and the need for him to get her to see that she should not attribute any significance to such events. She is, after all, not less of a person because her ailment makes her body less subject to her own control. Even though she experiences these things as shameful, they really aren't when you understand what is happening to her. That's what Georges, the loving husband, tries to convey to her both by his equanimity and by the words he speaks to her.

Although Anne at one point says he is a brute, she quickly qualifies this by saying he can be very kind. He exhibits this kindness here. He does not want Anne to let her own growing disability affect her sense of herself as a worthy human being, one deserving of respect and possessing inherent dignity. His gentle kindness is an expression of what he experiences as the appropriate way for a husband to deal with a wife's sickness. Once again, I think it appropriate to recall the phrase from the traditional marriage vow: *In sickness and in health.* Although this vow is very familiar to us, I don't know if we have contemplated what it entails as deeply as the film forces us to. What is it to take someone as your lifelong partner, even in sickness? Well, I see Georges as experiencing this and the film as pushing us to acknowledge what it means.

The second factor threatening Anne's dignity is the way in which health care professionals treat her. Although Anne has had a lifelong aversion to them—an antipathy that prompts her to ask Georges to promise not to send her back to the hospital after she has returned partially paralyzed—this seems like a personal idiosyncrasy until we witness how the nurses Georges hires to help him with Anne's care wind up treating her.

I would like to focus on two aspects of the nurses' humiliating treatment of Anne. The first is how one of the nurses infantilizes Anne by talking to her as if her physical decline was paralleled by a mental one.

Roughly brushing Anne's hair, the nurse addresses her in a cheery voice:

> NURSE: "There we are . . . now we're all beautiful again . . . so everybody will admire us . . . there . . . you see . . . wait . . . ." She then shows Anne how she looks in a mirror, "Well? . . . What do we say to that? Aren't we a pretty sight?"

The screenplay describes Anne's reaction as follows: "Anne, sickened, averts her eyes. Emits a muffled SOUND. The nurse ignores it."

NURSE: "You'll see, Monsieur will be dazzled by you."[6]

This is a crucial scene, for it indicates the difficulty Georges faces when he employs others to help him care for Anne, as he has come to realize he must as her mobility has declined. This nurse's treatment of Anne is completely demeaning, as if Anne's physical disabilities were indicative of parallel mental ones. But that is not the case, and the humiliation Anne feels is horrible to witness, both for Georges and for us.

The nurse's failures extend even further than this, however. The physical manner in which the aide harshly combs Anne's hair ignores Anne's cries of distress. It is as if Anne has lost her status as a full-fledged moral subject for the aide as a result of her loss of physical abilities. We are appalled by how the nurse ignores what Anne says. Anne's cries of "Help!" go unacknowledged as the aide roughly combs her hair, as if making Anne look pretty is something that needs to be accomplished no matter the cost in pain and suffering—as if Georges would really care whether Anne appeared attractive, with well-coiffed hair, at this stage in her illness.

During this scene and an earlier one I will discuss in a moment, Georges realizes Anne's request not to be returned to the hospital comes, at least in part, from her desire not to be humiliated, to die with her sense of her own self-worth and dignity in tact. The phrase "death with dignity" takes on a new meaning as we, along with Georges, realize how important it is for a human being not to be demeaned during the process of dying.

An earlier scene with the first nurse Georges hired emphasizes this point even more. The film shows the nurse helping Anne shower. As she handles her with calm efficiency, Anne repeatedly cries out, "Help! Help! Help!" Unphased, the nurse continues her task efficiently, talking to Anne reassuringly.

The nurse has a task to accomplish, bathing Anne, and like her fellow health care professional, she doesn't let Anne's protests stop her from doing what she needs to. She objectifies Anne by treating Anne's body like a purely physical thing that needs to be moved in

certain ways so that she—the nurse—can complete the task of bathing Anne. There is no acknowledgment on the nurse's part that Anne
is a person who feels pain when she is handled roughly. In addition,
the nurse simply ignores Anne's verbal response to such treatment,
as if Anne were not really trying to get her to stop mistreating her.
Indeed, as the aide leaves the apartment, she tells Georges that Anne's
cries are meaningless, that he shouldn't accord the content of what
Anne is saying—"hurts" or "help"—any significance.

> NURSE: You mustn't take it too seriously. Usually they always say
> something. She might just as well say, "Mom, Mom, Mom." It's just
> mechanical.[7]

Just mechanical!

All of this is in stark contrast to how Georges himself experiences
Anne when he interacts with her with loving care and warm gentle-
ness. When Georges returns to Anne's side once the nurse has left,
because she has been yelling "help" for some time, he calmly strokes
her hand, and slowly, her screaming diminishes and then "stops altogether."[8] It is clear the aides are wrong. Anne does use her limited
linguistic capacity to respond to her treatment in a manner that has
meaning and significance. Their dehumanizing and objectifying assumptions about Anne are a form of humiliation, a taking of her
dignity from her in an unacceptable manner.

The Morality of Killing Anne

I see Georges's decision to kill Anne as a response to two contradictory realizations. First, he recognizes that he can no longer continue
to take care of Anne on his own. It is this that spawned his decision
to hire the two nurses to help him care for Anne in the first place.
He needed someone younger and stronger who could deal with the
physical tasks required to take care of her. Although Georges refuses
his own daughter's offer of assistance—a theme I do not have time
to develop is the film's portrait of Eva (Isabelle Huppert) as self-
absorbed and unable to act in a respectful manner to either Anne
or Georges—he realizes he does need some assistance in caring for
Anne, since sending her back to the hospital has been ruled out.

At the same time, Georges also comes to see the only way to spare Anne humiliation and afford her a death with dignity is to eschew any contact with medical professionals. The two nurses symbolize the dehumanizing way in which medical professionals treat terminally ill and handicapped patients. After all, the jobs these people need to do leads them to act in ways determined by their sense of their own professional competence. But in so doing, or at least so the film claims, they act in ways that dehumanize their patients and rob them of the opportunity of dying with dignity.

My suggestion is that the only way open to Georges to resolve this contradiction is to kill Anne. But his doing so is the outcome of his love and devotion to her, for he takes her desires and needs to be primary. Georges sacrifices himself for Anne.

In fact, I think the film subtly suggests that Georges decides he needs to kill himself as well, although you may not agree with me. None of the reviews I have read raise the possibility that *Amour* ends with a suicide as well as a murder, although Georges's absence is duly noted. It's true Haneke proceeds here with a typical withholding of crucial evidence that makes it difficult for us to determine with certainty features of the fictional world he has created. Once again, this introduces a tentativeness with which one must present one's conclusions, for as in life, there is no certainty to be had.

"Burying" Anne

Georges's final act of love is his careful arrangement of Anne's corpse upon her deathbed. Despite his own decline, he leaves the apartment to buy flowers whose stems we see him painstakingly cut off. We see the results of Georges's actions in the first scene of the film, which Haneke's screenplay describes as follows:

THE PLAIN-CLOTHES DETECTIVE turns toward the big double bed placed against the back wall of the bedroom. On the right-hand bed, there's only the bare mattress. On the left-hand bed lies the partly decomposed body of an old woman. Where there once were eyes, now there are gaping holes. The corpse has been neatly dressed and is adorned with flowers that have already dried out a little. On her chest is a crucifix.[9]

Even the description of this scene, with the "gaping holes" where "there once were eyes," is horrific. When we see it so early in the film and with no understanding of the events that have led up to the display of Anne's corpse, we are horrified, puzzled, and intrigued. When we consider it in light of our experience of the film as a whole, we see it with increased comprehension. Georges's display of Anne's body in a manner similar to that in which bodies of famous people are laid in state is his final testament to her and the dignity that her manner of dying has conferred on her. And the contrast between the aesthetic display of the flowers around her corpse and the decay that has already begun to destroy it is striking.

To understand this scene, we need to see that there is a dramatic precedent for it in Antigone's burying of her brother in Sophocles's eponymously titled play. As Hegel points out in his *Phenomenology of Spirit*, burial rights are a means whereby human beings assert they are not merely physical beings but also, and perhaps more significantly, spiritual ones, if you permit me to use Hegel's terminology. For this reason Antigone cannot accede to Creon's ban on Polyneices's burial. By symbolically according her brother burial rights, Antigone affirms he is a spiritual being, one to whom dignity should be accorded. Hegel writes the following about the ethical significance of burial rites:

> The family keeps away from the dead this dishonouring of him by the desires of unconscious organic agencies and by abstract elements, puts its own action in place of theirs, and weds the relative to the bosom of the earth, the elemental individuality that passes not away. Thereby the family makes the dead a member of a community—which prevails over and holds under control the powers of the particular material elements and the lower living creatures, which sought to have their way with the dead and destroy him.[10]

Hegel is here both explaining the point of burial rites and making a connection to Antigone's need to bury her brother, Polyneices. Human beings need to assert their existence as, what Hegel calls, "spiritual beings" in order to show they are more than physical entities whose bodies will decay and pass again into the material world. Through a burial the family and the community of which it is a part assert their own power, their ability to transcend the merely physical.

An act that many find puzzling—Antigone's need to symbolically bury her brother against the orders of Creon, the head of the state— gains meaning through Hegel's explication of its rationale.

Hegel's account of the significance of burial helps us see what motivates Georges. By displaying Anne as she might be at a funeral, he has given her the only appropriate burial he can. And in so doing, he has presented a testimony of his love for her and how his taking her life is a manifestation of that love, despite what people might think. Her carefully arranged and displayed body is emblematic of a loving marriage that has come to an end with her and her husband's deaths. In it he accords her the dignity in death that he strove to maintain throughout her illness.

The Morality of Euthanasia

In order to accurately assess the philosophical significance of *Amour,* we need to do more than interpret the film. We need to assess the validity and generalizability of its claim that Georges's killing of Anne was a moral act.

There are a variety of possible positions in relation to the question of whether it is ever morally acceptable to kill someone who wants to die. Some people think there are no circumstances in which such a killing is morally acceptable. They would accept the following principle:

(PN) It is never morally acceptable to kill a person no matter what state they are in and what they want.

A different moral position would acknowledge there are certain circumstances in which it is morally permissible and perhaps even morally required to kill someone. For example, some people hold that, when a person no longer has any prospect of experiencing pleasure, being in a state of, say, unremitting intense pain, it is morally permissible to kill them, especially if they ask one to. Such people would accept the following:

(PK) When a person with a terminal illness is no longer able to take any pleasure in life and wants to die, it is morally permissible to kill her.

But *Amour* is a detailed and extended thought experiment that presents a new and quite compelling justification for a different moral principle. Instead of focusing on pleasure, as a utilitarian justification of euthanasia must, its focus is on a person's dignity. I take this principle to assert the following:

(PD) When the only way to preserve the dignity of a person with a terminal illness is to kill them, then it is morally required that one do so.

The rationale for this principle follows from the idea that a person's dignity is the most important thing that they possess. If this is true—and I acknowledge that many would reject it—then one must do what one can to enhance and protect that dignity. *Amour* shows us there are circumstances in which this concern will lead a person to kill someone else to preserve that person's dignity.

Earlier, I stressed Georges's actions spring from his recognition that being Anne's husband requires him to act as he does, that his killing her stems from the love he bears for her. This is because being her husband creates the obligation to care for her, in sickness and in health. And his love for her lets him see how precarious a hold she has on her own dignity in the face of her degeneration.

My suggestion, then, is that *Amour* provides a thought experiment whose intent is to support (PD) the obligation to kill someone to preserve her dignity. It provides a context in which Georges's actions, which under one description seem immoral and cruel, are seen as the reasonable outcome of a difficult and painful situation in which his wife's illness has placed him. The film enriches our ethical understanding by presenting us with an imaginary case that supports (PD).

But can we take *Amour*, then, to provide a general justification of euthanasia as an acceptable ethical practice in regard to the terminally ill? As you will recall, my claim was that Georges acts morally in killing Anne because her dignity is threatened and (PD) requires that Georges do whatever is necessary, including killing her, in order to protect her from the loss of dignity. What we now have to ask is how generalizable this result is.

Although I have argued we should accept (PD), we also need to recognize that only in rare circumstances would anyone need to act on this moral principle. This is because most people would rarely be in a situation in which the dignity of their spouse, child, or friend could be maintained only by their death. Normally, we are able to preserve a dying spouse's dignity by relying, for example, on our friends, children, and medical professionals. Only because Georges is unable to rely on these others can he justifiably kill Anne.

Of course, the film attempts to legitimate Georges's action by showing both that he is too physically infirm to care for Anne on his own and that there are no other people he can turn to who can assist in Anne's care while maintaining her dignity. Their daughter, Eva, has been shown to be so narcissistic that Anne does not want her to even visit. The two nurses are meant to show that medical professionals are concerned merely with the elongation of Anne's life, not with maintaining her dignity. Indeed, the two nurses are portrayed as significant threats to Anne's dignity. Although the building's superintendent and his wife do help Georges with shopping, their assistance is too minimal given the wide range of tasks with which Georges needs assistance.

But even if we admit that Georges faces a dire situation in trying to care for Anne and that this justifies his killing of her in accord with (PD), we also have to point out that this does not mean the film has shown euthanasia to be justified in more than extreme cases. Although the film has legitimately pointed out the danger that the modern medical profession poses to the dying, the film's portrayal of health care professionals is quite biased. Many people in the health field are not ruled by the objectifying and demeaning assumptions the film depicts the two nurses as accepting. In fact, many of them would be concerned with helping a dying person die with dignity. The film's case for the necessity of Anne's killing relies on specific features of her situation that I do not believe generally hold.

So despite its courageous and unflinching examination of the ethical obligations we owe to the dying, *Amour* cannot be taken to provide a general justification of euthanasia. Only in the special case of its isolated couple does (PD) apply. So even though we can judge Georges's killing of his dying spouse to be ethical, we cannot generalize from his situation to a more general acceptance of euthanasia as an ethically justified practice in the face of death.

Few viewers, for example, would have thought in detail about what it is like to care for a spouse with a degenerative disease and what one's ethical responsibilities are in such a situation. Although some viewers would already have taken euthanasia to be morally permissible in certain circumstances by embracing, say, (PK), I wonder how many of them would have also understood a different rationale exists according to which such an act is morally required.

But that's precisely what *Amour* confronts us with through its vivid and unflinching portrait of Anne's physical decline and Georges's response to it. It shows us that if we take a person's right to a dignified death seriously and see it as being as important as their right to be treated with dignity during their lives, then there may come a time when that right will convey upon a person's spouse the obligation to bring about her death. Difficult as his killing Anne is for him both physically and mentally, Georges acts from a sense of his marriage as an ethical relationship that requires him to perform an action he previously rejected out of hand as inappropriate.

I do not, however, think we should see *Amour* as providing an ethical justification for euthanasia in general. For as I argue, only in unique circumstances, such as those of this couple, would it make sense to judge euthanasia the only available means to maintain the dignity of the dying. So even as *Amour* enlarges our sympathetic understanding of what a marriage is, what sorts of obligations it imposes on its partners, and why it makes sense to view marriage as a paradigmatic ethical relationship, it does not offer a general defense of euthanasia as an ethical practice.

NOTES

Earlier versions of this paper were read to the Reel Deal film group in Detroit and the Cinematic Thinking Network Workshop on Ethics and/as Film. It has benefitted from comments received on both those occasions. Thanks go to Bruce Russell, Robert Sinnerbrink, and Damien Cox for their insightful comments and suggestions.

1. Prose, "A Masterpiece You Might Not Want to See."
2. Paneral, "Greatest Films about Love," IMDb, last updated September 2013, http://www.imdb.com/list/I6-psMCYFWE.
3. For example, see the Death with Dignity website, http://www.deathwithdignity.org.
4. Kant, *The Groundwork to the Metaphysics of Morals*, 33.
5. Hanneke, 41.

6. Haneke, 51.
7. Haneke, 47.
8. Haneke, 48.
9. Haneke, 2.
10. Hegel, *The Phenomenology of Spirit,* 452.

BIBLIOGRAPHY

Haneke, Michael. *Amour.* http://www.sonyclassics.com/awards-information/amour_screenplay.pdf, 2012.
Hegel, G. W. F. *The Phenomenology of Spirit.* Translated by A. V. Miller. New York: Oxford University Press, 1976.
Kant, Immanuel. *The Groundwork to the Metaphysics of Morals.* Translated by Jonathan Bennett. Early Modern Texts, last updated September 2008. www.earlymoderntexts.com.
Prose, Francine. "A Masterpiece You Might Not Want to See." *New York Review of Books,* January 7, 2013.
Sophocles. *Antigone.* Translated by Paul Woodruff. Indianapolis, Ind.: Hackett Publishing, 2001.
Wartenberg, Thomas E. *Thinking on Screen.* Abingdon, U.K.: Routledge, 2007.

Experience and Explanation in the Cinema

Murray Smith

All over Again, What Is Cinema?

From the beginning, cinema has been held up as a unique medium partly by virtue of the kind of attention it seems to demand. Appreciating a film involves a special combination of perception, cognition, imagination, and emotion. Cinema engages us across a wider range of our embodied mental capacities than any other medium of representation, extending from low-level reflexes to abstract reflection. Cinema engages not only our visual and auditory senses, in a direct fashion, but also our senses of touch and balance and, perhaps, even those of taste and smell, in an indirect fashion. Films can physically startle and cognitively stimulate us in equal measure and in concert; these aspects of our experience, moreover, should not be thought of as necessarily in tension with one another.

Most basically, cinema affords us a perceptual experience of depth seen in a flat surface, and—as the word *cinema* itself implies, from the Ancient Greek κίνημα, "movement"—an impression of movement upon that surface, where no actual movement occurs. Not only can cinema give us perceptual experience of spatially or temporally remote actual events—sitting here in Frankfurt,[1] in 2014, we could witness an opera being performed now in Berlin or the Rumble in the Jungle in Kinshasa in 1974—it can even give us a perceptual experience of "merely" imagined events. And a favorite trope of cinema has been the enfolding of the actual within the imagined, the non-fictional within the fictional, or the fictional rendering of cinema's ability to depict actual events. The canonical example and, perhaps, the prototype is *Citizen Kane* (Orson Welles, 1941) (Figure 15.1). A recent example is *District 9* (Neill Blomkamp, 2009), which presents us

Figure 15.1. The fictional newscast in *Citizen Kane*.

with three distinct threads of fictional nonfiction footage: newscasts, surveillance camera footage, and investigative documentary material (Figure 15.2). With the advent of CGI, the twin capacities of cinema to afford a perceptual experience of both actual and fictional events have never been more closely entwined (Figure 15.3).

Here, then, I want to revisit these basic facts about cinema and the nature of the experience that it affords us. In effect, I want to ask afresh the question posed by Noël Carroll in an essay from 1985: What is the source of "the power of cinema"?[2] How do we *explain* the distinctive *experience* it creates? And just as important, what theoretical resources do we need to draw upon in order to furnish such an explanation? My answers to these questions will take us through a discussion of method in the study of film and art more generally and then onto a discussion of cinematic spectatorship, concluding by saying something more about the sketch of cinematic spectatorship I've presented in opening this essay.

Philosophical Naturalism

Just as my subject matter here is central and familiar, so my approach will be orthodox. But with a twist. The approach I take to the question, What is cinema? has become a central approach in contemporary analytic philosophy, described by one commentator as "the current orthodoxy within Anglo-American philosophy, an outlook that shapes the way philosophers understand the mission and problems of philosophy,"[3] and by another (in still stronger terms) as the "most forceful metaphilosophical trend of the twentieth century."[4] And yet it is at best a minority approach in film theory (which at root is nothing other than the philosophy of film, in reality if not in name). The approach I refer to is *naturalism*. And let me stress at the outset that it is *philosophical naturalism*—naturalism as a philosophical stance—that I have in mind. If "naturalism" brings to mind Émile Zola or Gerhart Hauptmann or the Dardenne brothers or nineteenth-century geologists digging for fossils or naked sunbathing or "naturalization" à la Roland Barthes, you have the wrong concept in mind (even if there are interesting things to say about why we use the same or similar words to refer to these distinct phenomena).

Figure 15.2. Newscast, surveillance camera, and investigative documentary material in *District 9*.

Figure 15.3 Perceiving the fictional embedded within the actual in *District 9*.

As early as 1922, the American philosopher Roy Wood Sellars could declare, "We are all naturalists now!"[5] As this pronouncement suggests, the idea of naturalism as a philosophical stance has been debated for a century or more.[6] Broadly speaking, philosophical naturalism may be defined as a commitment to the pursuit of philosophical questions in the light of the knowledge and methods of the sciences or, more particularly, as the name suggests, the natural sciences (though how one defines and decides what is to count as a natural science turns out to be a surprisingly complex matter). Sellars himself described naturalism as "less a philosophical system than a recognition of the impressive implications of the physical and biological sciences."[7] Typically, naturalism in this sense is held to have two aspects: a substantive commitment to the study of all phenomena, including human behavior, as a part of the physically constituted, biologically evolved world, and a methodological commitment to the methods and standards of the natural sciences. (Sometimes, these principles are said to be detachable.)

A decisive moment in the history of philosophical naturalism came in 1951 with the publication of W. V. O. Quine's "Two Dogmas of Empiricism," followed almost two decades later by his "Epistemology Naturalized" in 1969. In these papers, Quine argued in favor of the continuity of philosophy with science and against the notion of "first philosophy"—philosophy as a practice standing prior to and in some sense above or wholly separate from empirical investigation. Note that notwithstanding the emphasis here on the Anglo-American context, the larger set of debates into which Quine was intervening were recognized beyond that context. Siegfried Kracauer, for example, was well aware of the debates concerning the nature of historical method and the extent to which history could be modeled as a science—another manifestation of naturalism—as they played out in the Anglo-American as well as the German context, commenting on them in his *History: The Last Things before the First* (posthumously published in 1969).[8] Kracauer himself argued for a middle path similar in spirit to the position I defend in this essay. Acknowledging the arguments of Wilhelm Dilthey, Kracauer recognizes the importance of "understanding" particular agents and events in history but nonetheless concludes that "since 'the freedom of history rises on the ground of nature-necessity,' historical reality contains uniformities and, indeed, causal relationships which call for the historian's attention also. A historian confining himself to 'understanding' in Dilthey's sense would miss a good deal of the 'components, factors, aspects' that lay claim to his understanding."[9]

In the succeeding decades, as a naturalized approach to epistemology became well established, so a naturalistic approach was taken to other domains of philosophy, including ethics, mathematics, reasoning and cognition, and even, eventually, aesthetics. The psychologist Gerd Gigerenzer and his associates, for example, are well known for their research on "fast and frugal heuristics"—that is, shortcuts, rules of thumb, and other informal reasoning routines characteristic of human cognition. One such cognitive shortcut identified by Gigerenzer and Daniel Goldstein is the *recognition heuristic,* according to which recognition of an object biases our assessment of it relative to another object in the same class that we do not recognize.[10] For example, when asked to say whether San Diego or San Antonio has a bigger population, subjects who had heard of the former but not the latter were much more likely to guess that San Diego had the bigger population. The mere fact of recognition nudges our assessment in favor of the recognized example. Another well-established phenomenon is the *primacy effect,* whereby we give more weight to the first feature that we encounter in relation to a person, object, or event than to subsequent features. Drawing on earlier work by David

Bordwell and Torben Grodal, Dan Barratt has applied this principle to *The Sixth Sense* (1999), arguing that our belief that Malcolm Crowe (Bruce Willis) is alive persists through almost the entire film, in spite of evidence to the contrary being waved in front of us, in part because of the weight carried by the depiction of Crowe at the film's beginning as alive and apparently surviving the gunshot wound in the film's opening scene.[11]

This example brings us to *cognitive film theory*—the main locus for the development of a naturalistic approach to film aesthetics. Originating in the work of Joe Anderson, David Bordwell, and other researchers at or associated with the University of Wisconsin–Madison in the 1970s and 1980s, cognitive film theory has become a recognized interdisciplinary field, institutionalized through a journal (*Projections*), a professional organization (SCSMI [Society for Cognitive Studies of the Moving Image]), and the annual SCSMI conference. Beginning with the emphasis in Bordwell's early work on the problem solving skills involved in comprehending narrative films, the field has developed in ways that broadly mirror the manner in which cognitive science itself has expanded, to encompass emotion, embodiment, and the extension of cognition through the physical and social environment.[12] Over the same period, evolutionary psychology and neuroscience have both become more prominent, with some arguing that the field should properly be conceived as *cognitive neuroscience.*[13]

It is important to recognize that the appeals to and the uses made of science in cognitive film theory and the naturalistic tradition of research more generally are quite diverse; naturalism comes in different varieties and strengths. Thus, for example, one can distinguish between "replacement" naturalism and "cooperative" or integrative naturalism, the former labeling the view that (natural) scientific methods will and should replace methods characteristic of the humanities, the latter designating the view that what is necessary is the joining of humanistic and scientific methods. (Note, though, how both positions contrast with cherry-picking from science—the practice of selective and ad hoc appeals to science, all too widespread in the humanities and in public debate in general.) Another important distinction to note is one I have already touched on in passing: that between scientific *knowledge* and *method.*[14] In pursuing a naturalistic approach to some phenomenon, the first job to be done is "simply" to make explicit and synthesize the scientific knowledge that is already, if provisionally, out there. The contribution of a naturalistic philosopher of mind like Daniel Dennett, for example, consists to a considerable degree in bringing together hitherto distinct research programs, teasing out their assumptions, figuring out how they fit or fail to fit, and working out the implications arising from this process of sifting, sorting, and integration.[15]

Adopting the scientific *method*—or scientific *methods*—in our pursuit of knowledge involves a much bigger (or at least, very different kind of) step, one relatively few researchers working in these interdisciplinary domains take. Most researchers end up sticking with the methods—the practical routines—they learned as young practitioners in a particular discipline. But there are examples where individuals and groups of researchers have embraced scientific method, as well as scientific knowledge, in aiming to answer questions traditionally posed within the humanities. Within cognitive theory, eye tracking and fMRI brain scanning have both been explored by teams involving researchers from the humanities as well as psychologists and neuroscientists. Film historian Richard Neupert, for example, has collaborated on eye tracking studies that reveal how viewers of abstract and stylized animated films still seek anthropomorphic features. An experimental study of Pixar's *Luxo Jr.* (John Lasseter, 1986), for example, showed that spectators focused their attention on the "heads" and "bodies" of the angle-poise lamps featured in the film (Figures 15.4a and 15.4b): "Even without faces, the lamps prompt spectators to center their gaze on the two lamp shades and their key gestures."[16] Viewers' attention is most likely captured, in such cases, by the distinctive "biological motion" mimicked by the animated figures. The exploitation of biological motion in animation is so pervasive that it stands in importance to the world of animated films as motion itself does for movies in general.[17]

Elsewhere, XPhi—experimental philosophy, or the application of experimental methods to philosophical questions in metaphysics, ethics, and aesthetics—has flourished over the past decade. Drawing on a variety of behavioral and neuroscientific methods, experimental philosophers have investigated the nature and content of moral and metaphysical intuitions, testing in particular their uniformity or variability across different groups, as well as the stability of character traits and personal dispositions.[18] And these research programs have both immediate precursors and more distant ancestors: empirical aesthetics was initiated by Gustav Fechner in the 1870s and continues to this day, while the "natural philosophers" working before the emergence of the institutionalized scientific disciplines of the modern era saw no sharp divide between empirical and philosophical investigation.[19]

In the Realm of the Subpersonal

All three of these areas of naturalistic investigation (cognitive film theory, XPhi, empirical aesthetics) focus on aspects of mind—on the intuitions and attitudes of various types of person and on the visual and other capacities of film viewers and art appreciators. Similarly, my opening characterization of the problem area under investigation emphasizes mental matters; what we are after, I say, is an explanation of our characteristic *experience* of cinema. A naturalistic perspective in this way leads us to the spectator and to ask the question, Just what kind of an entity is a "spectator"?

The pretheoretical answer is that a spectator is a *person*—that is to say, a more or less coherent, goal-oriented, conscious individual human agent, possessed of certain capacities, in Locke's words, a "thinking intelligent being that has reason and reflection and can consider itself as itself, the same thinking thing, in different times and places."[20] A spectator is such a being engaged in a certain kind of activity. That activity is at once a cognitive activity (it involves making sense of and experiencing films) and a social activity (we watch and discuss films with others). These two dimensions come together in what psychologists term "joint attention," the shared focus of two or more individuals on a single object. Joint attention emerges early in development, and in its mature form—most infants mastering the skill to this level by the age of fourteen months—involves not merely shared gazing at a single object of attention but mutual awareness of shared gaze. Agents jointly attending to an object are, in effect, attending to both the object and to each other's attention to the object, as is manifest in the glances of the agents alternating between the object itself and the other agents with whom they share their gaze (another behaviour mimicked by the desk lamps in *Luxo Jr.*; see Figure 15.4).[21]

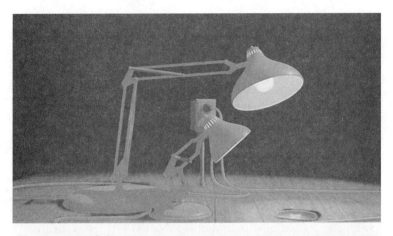

Figure 15.4. Biological motion and joint attention in *Luxo Jr.*

In contrast to the case of joint attention, much of the perceptual and cognitive work that we undertake when we make sense of a film happens at the level of the "cognitive unconscious"—rapidly and automatically, beneath the level of conscious intention, with little reflection or self-consciousness, or what Jenefer Robinson terms "secondary appraisal."[22] When we see spaces and characters in the two-dimensional surface of the screen and when we see figures in motion, we have little or no control over the processes that give rise to such experiences. In these cases, we see (or have the experience of seeing) things—volumetric figures in motion—that are not literally there.

In the same cognitively unconscious fashion, we also sometimes *fail* to see certain features that are present in the cinematic visual array, including some types of cut and camera movement, as suggested in the notion of "invisible editing." And moving up a level from such basic perception, when we recognize a character—that is, when we work out how to discriminate a character as an individual—or when we attribute thoughts and emotions to characters, we usually just do it, so to speak.[23] Getting an explanatory grip on how all this happens involves a journey into the realm of the *subpersonal*.[24]

Our personhood—our capacity to act as a conscious, goal-oriented intentional being and the capacity that enables us to become film spectators—supervenes upon a host of *subpersonal* capacities, that is, lower-level processing capacities that allow us to represent, deliberate on, and act in and on the world. Let us take the human "body clock" (circadian clock, to use the technical terminology) as an example of a subpersonal mechanism. The body clock regulates the cycle of waking and sleeping, and it does so beneath conscious intention. That is, we find ourselves getting tired or wakeful, but we can't simply decide to be wakeful or tired, as insomniacs especially know all too well. You can intervene—act intentionally—on your body by taking drugs or by undertaking certain activities or by setting up your environment in particular ways that are likely to make you feel tired or wakeful. But you can't just will or intend to be wakeful or tired.

The phenomenon of jet lag is particularly instructive in this regard. When we suffer jet leg, our body clock falls out of alignment with the temporal calibration of our location. In such a context, while at the level of conscious intention we know full well where we are within the cycle of the day, our body clock tells us something very different. So the example of the body clock shows how subpersonal mechanisms, while normally acting in concert to enable coherent agency, can function with some degree of autonomy and pull in different directions. Taken individually, these mechanisms are relatively "dumb" or, at least, limited in function; they are "subpersonal" precisely in the sense that in isolation none of them instantiate personhood. In unison, however, they afford the kind of reflective and flexible agency that falls within the scope of fully fledged personhood.

With this notion of the subpersonal in mind, let me return to the four ubiquitous features of our experience of cinema to which

I have alluded: seeing depth, seeing motion, failing to see edits and camera movement, and last, recognizing characters and attributing emotions to them. Each of these can be illuminated and explained by considering the subpersonal mechanisms that make them possible. For example, we know our perception of depth in a two-dimensional array depends on the fact that magno cells within the human visual system will respond to converging lines as indicative of a space receding in depth, while our perception of motion in the cinema arises due to the processing limitations of our visual systems. Above a certain frequency, "the visual system simply fails to detect the real difference between the successive changes in the static frames of a motion picture and the continuous changes of natural motion."[25] Our perception of motion in movies in this way depends on "a glitch in our visual system."[26] Our failure to perceive certain cuts and camera movements, however, can be attributed to the phenomena of *inattentional* and *change blindness.*[27] Our visual systems are much more selective than we take them to be, in terms of the amount of visual detail to which we are able to attend and that we can hold in mind at any moment. By drawing our attention to the action traversing a cut within a sequence and making the progress of the action across the cut as smooth and continuous as possible, our attention is taken away from the cut itself. We are unlikely to be aware of the cut, just as the subjects in the well-known "invisible gorilla" experiments were unlikely to spot the gorilla-suited individual strolling through the basketball players. In the same way that the attention of the subjects in these experiments had been directed toward the basketball players (and away from the gorilla), so in the case of films employing continuity conventions, the attention of spectators is directed toward the action (and away from the edits).[28]

Sympathizing with the Alien

So far, I've focused on how the subpersonal level is necessary to explain certain generic features of our experience of cinema (the perception of motion, depth, and the fluid, sometimes invisible, continuity across cuts). I want now to return to *District 9* to explore the phenomena of character recognition and attribution in the same light. *District 9* will also enable us to take a look at some subpersonal

318 •• MURRAY SMITH

phenomena characteristic of certain genres, as well as other features peculiar to this film. In this way I hope to scotch an oft-expressed worry about naturalized approaches to aesthetics, namely, that they can illuminate only very general phenomena and cannot accommodate the cultural or local features of works of art; for example, they can illuminate how we see motion on the screen but cannot enrich our understanding of motion in specific traditions or in particular works. To the contrary, I seek to show here that naturalism is no impediment to acknowledging and illuminating the particularity of the individual work.

District 9 is a blend of science fiction and horror but also a work of satirical commentary. The film narrates the story of a colony of aliens whose spaceship, as we've seen, breaks down over Johannesburg. The alien community then becomes the object of various, mostly unsavory, social dynamics and political agendas (all too) familiar to us. The story works as an allegory of South African apartheid, the aliens being segregated, exploited for their resources, and treated as primitive organisms not worthy of personal status.

The story focuses on three central characters: Wikus van de Merwe (Sharlto Copley), a none-too-bright bureaucrat working as the spokesman for the private corporation Multi-National United (MNU), enlisted by the government to evict the aliens from the township community that forms under the spaceship and to relocate them to what is effectively a prison camp; the alien assigned the name "Christopher Johnson" (Jason Cope), who is secretly working to repair the spaceship; and Christopher Johnson's son. Wikus becomes infected by an alien substance that gradually transforms him into an alien (Figure 15.5). In the course of this physical transformation, Wikus comes to understand from the inside how the aliens are being abused and exploited. He switches his allegiance and assists Christopher Johnson and his son in their efforts to repair the spaceship; in reciprocation Christopher Johnson holds out the hope to Wikus that his physical transformation can be reversed.

District 9 sets itself an interesting challenge in the way it combines horror with satire. Initially, the aliens are presented as an object of horror—an undifferentiated mass of ugly, insect or crab-like organisms (Figure 15.6) (humans refer to them with the "racist" epithet "prawn"; a journalist describes them as "bottom feeders"). But as the film progresses, the aliens become the object of sympathy, as a minority group abused by the political elite. The aesthetic challenge the film sets for itself is thus: How is it possible to make a character type, expressly designed in the first instance to revolt and literally "alienate" us, one that we can recognize, understand, and eventually root for? Let's take each of these three levels of response in turn.

The first of these levels is *recognition*—the differentiation of one individual from another in perception. Humans have a remarkable

Figure 15.5. Wikus van der Merwe's transformation from human to alien.

Figure 15.6. The aliens as objects of horror.

capacity for discriminating between and remembering individual faces—individual human faces, that is.[29] Our ability to process the individuating facial features and emotional expressions of species other than humans is much more limited (Figure 15.7). Our perception of the faces of other creatures is, so to speak, biased toward general "type" rather than individual "token." And while I'm stressing facial particularity here, the same may hold for our perception of bodily attributes: we may be much more sensitive to individual differences

Figure 15.7. In *District 9* our ability to read the facial expressions of the alien figures is limited, while our perceptual recognition of the emotional states of human figures is direct and immediate.

among our conspecifics than we are in relation to other species. It is not surprising, then, that *District 9* uses some bold bodily markers to help us pick out Christopher Johnson—above all his orange jacket (Figure 15.8). The only other major alien character in the film, Christopher Johnson's son, does not pose such a severe problem for recognition as he is virtually the only juvenile alien we encounter and stands out due to his distinctive size, posture, and gait (Figure 15.9).

How about our *understanding* of the alien characters—that is, our

Figure 15.8. Bodily markers of recognition in *District 9*: Christopher Johnson's orange jacket.

Figure 15.9: Christopher Johnson's child.

ability to recognize their emotions and other states of mind from their physiognomy? Here again, by creating an alien physiognomy blending the features of crustaceans and robots, the film limits the palette of emotional expression that is normally available to us through the human face. We haven't evolved to be able to perceive, in a fine-grained way, the emotional states of other creatures in their facial and bodily movements, and the further removed from us they are in evolutionary terms, the less attuned we are to these states. But of course, these are fictional aliens, not an actual species. So it is no surprise we find the filmmakers helping themselves to a few aspects of human facial expression, above all through the eyes (Figure 15.10), and many expressive human bodily postures and gestures, counterbalancing the alien otherness of their facial features. For example, when Christopher Johnson's main comrade is killed early in the film, Johnson strikes out in frustration, smashing the doorframe of his shack with his hand; later in the film, when he discovers his fellow aliens have been subjected to grotesque medical experiments, his bodily slump clearly conveys extreme distress (and the score works here to reinforce Johnson's grief-stricken state). In short, the "gross anatomy" of the aliens is much more anthropomorphic than is its facial topography.

The emotional "transparency" of Christopher Johnson, established by these techniques, lays the ground for the sympathetic attachment or *allegiance* with him and his son that the film fosters.[30] Because his thoughts, goals, and above all, suffering can be both perceived and felt by us—at the level of the cognitively unconscious—it is not hard for us to root for him. But our emotional understanding of and sympathy for Christopher Johnson and his son are not enabled only by these facial and bodily features. Another mechanism at work here is *situational understanding,* a process whereby we attribute thoughts and emotions to one or more agents on the basis of relations among them and the situation that they collectively constitute. Thus, when Christopher Johnson is first served with an eviction notice, our limited access to his emotions via familiar expressive routes is little impediment to our understanding his state of mind; we can readily *infer* his state of mind by understanding the situation and his position within it.[31] And once again, such understanding prepares the ground for our imaginative empathy and sympathetic allegiance with him.

Figure 15.10. Christopher Johnson's eyes widen in a familiar expression of alarm as his comrade is executed.

From Reflex to Reflection

My emphasis so far has been on rapid, low-level responses that must form the bedrock of any narrative film experience: perceiving depth and motion in a flat, still screen; individuating characters; attributing states of mind and traits to them; and responding emotionally to them. But I have alluded to the more abstract, social reflection the film is designed to prompt in us, in terms of its satirical commentary on apartheid, institutionalized racism, and capitalist exploitation. So how we do we get from the fast, low-level cognitive activity that a focus on the subpersonal helps to illuminate to the higher-order, more deliberative and reflective types of cognition that are just as much a part of our experience of films? How does my emphasis on the subpersonal square with my earlier claim that spectators are persons capable of high-level reflection?

It might be objected that the Lockean conditions for personhood I allude to earlier—continuity of consciousness and memory—are far in excess of what is necessary for spectatorship.[32] In one sense this is true: frogs, spiders, and a great many other species are capable of perceiving depth and motion in two-dimensional motion picture arrays.[33] But it seems that humans alone can see such representations for what they are; the frogs and spiders are not merely subject to the perceptual illusion of seeing moving, three-dimensional objects on a two-dimensional screen but thoroughly duped. There is nothing odd, for the naturalist, about the fact that humans share with other species many perceptual capacities and limitations; the "continuity of species" is one of the lessons that Darwin taught us. But it is a mistake to think naturalism only looks "downward" toward our distant evolutionary past and most basic perceptual capacities. Naturalism must give equal sway to those aspects of human mentation that separate *Homo sapiens* from other species. So we need something like those higher-order, Lockean conditions of personhood to make sense of human movie spectators. We need a naturalistic account not only of our ability to see depth and motion on movie screens but also of our ability to investigate and theorize perception, to invent the technology of cinema, and to reflect on the nature of animal agency, personhood, and the kinds of society that humans create.

Providing such an account would require attention to the role of so-called top-down cognition. Understanding *District 9* involves drawing on our existing stock of knowledge about apartheid and other aspects of the world the film evokes, as well as our skills of narrative understanding and preconceptions about genre. Such top-down cognition works in a dynamic interplay with the kind of bottom-up perception of the film I've stressed in this essay.

Nonetheless, three phenomena I have mentioned begin to move

us from the subpersonal to the personal and interpersonal and from the concrete to the abstract. Situational cognition is one bridge between these levels; joint attention is another. A third is our powerful and finely tuned capacity for facial perception, a capacity tied to the intensely social character of human existence. Joint attention, situational cognition, and facial perception all point to the fact that human cognition is intrinsically interpersonal—to be human or, at least, to be a fully flourishing human is to be part of a community of minds. In the fictional world of *District 9*, to be an alien of Christopher Johnson's species is to be part of a community of another kind of mind, but one not too distantly related to our own. The impoverished and depersonalized aliens gorge themselves on cat food just as impoverished communities around the actual human world console themselves with crack and meth and other such drugs. At one level, this is simply to spell out in further detail the terms of the allegorical satire articulated by *District 9* and the parallels it forges between actual apartheid and the treatment of the aliens.

But the film also implies a critique of *species chauvinism.* The aliens are not merely an allegorical representation of black South Africans under apartheid; the film complicates that reading by showing black South Africans becoming caught up in the xenophobia that the arrival of the aliens generates. Thus, the film suggests a more general thesis about the human propensity toward xenophobia. And serendipitously, the film also resonates with the naturalistic methodology I have been advocating, in two ways. On the one hand, the film is replete with what the psychologist Paul Rozin describes as "animal reminder" horror—disgust and horror elicited by reminders of our physical constitution, reminders that whatever else we are, we are biochemical organisms.[34] On the other hand, *District 9* implies that the kinds of cognitive sophistication, sensitivity of feeling, and complexity of value characteristic of human existence might very well hold for other species, too, even if we do not happen to cohabit with any other such species on this earth. In short, the film dramatizes the idea that the concept of a person is not identical with the concept of an individual human agent. While human individuals are our typical model of what a person is, individual members of other species in principle might come to warrant that description.

Conclusion

Nelson Goodman once mocked what he dubbed the "Tingle-Immersion" theory of art—credited to Immanuel Tingle and Joseph Immersion—according to which we must "submerge ourselves completely" in a work of art and then "gauge the aesthetic potency of the work by the intensity and duration of the resulting tingle."[35] In pursuing a naturalistic approach to cinema and its spectatorship and in emphasizing a subpersonal analysis of our engagement with films, I hope it is clear I have not intended to portray cinematic spectatorship as nothing more than a succession of tingles and sensations of varying intensity. Rather, my intention has been twofold. My first goal has been to demonstrate how our understanding of cinema may be enriched by reference to pertinent aspects of scientific method and knowledge, in this case concerning visual perception and our emotional engagement or "attunement" with members of our own species. My argument is not that we have *no* understanding of film spectatorship without these tools but that with them we have access to what I think of as *thick explanations*—explanations that seek to be as complete, multileveled, and unified as possible.[36]

My second goal has been to explore the relationship between two significant features of cinema: on the one hand, its basis in *perception* and, on the other hand, its capacity to prompt and sustain, if not quite philosophy, then certainly abstract, reflective *thought* (on the nature of racism, apartheid, and personhood, in the case at hand). Our appreciation of any film is founded on our perception of it and involves a variety of low-level mechanisms and effects that taken individually might be pretty "dumb." Nonetheless, such phenomena are, or at least can be, genuinely thrilling on their own terms, while at the same time acting as the building blocks for the more reflective, higher-order cognition cinema is certainly capable of sustaining.

NOTES

1. An earlier version of this essay was delivered as a Kracauer Lecture at Goethe-University Frankfurt on November 11, 2014, available for download at http://www.kracauer-lectures.de/en/winter-2014–2015/murray-smith. My thanks go to my hosts, Vinzenz Hediger, Martin Seel, and Marc Siegel, for their generous invitation and insightful feedback.

2. See Carroll, "The Power of Movies"; reprinted in Carroll, *Theorizing the Moving Image*.

3. Ritchie, review of David Macarthur, *Understanding Naturalism*.

4. Keil, "Naturalism," 254.

5. Sellars, *Evolutionary Naturalism*, i.

6. Keil indicates that the term was already in widespread use by the end of the nineteenth century; G. E. Moore developed his notion of the "naturalistic fallacy" in *Principia Ethica*, published in 1903; consider also the theme and title of C. D. Broad, *The Mind and Its Place in Nature* (1925).

7. Sellars, *Evolutionary Naturalism*, i.

8. See Kracauer, *History*. The text was completed after Kracauer's death by Paul Oskar Kristeller.

9. Kracauer, *History*, 44. The embedded phrases are from Reinhold Niebuhr and Isaiah Berlin, respectively.

10. Goldstein et al., "Group Report," 178.

11. See Bordwell, *Narration in the Fiction Film*, 38; Grodal, *Moving Pictures*; Barratt. "'Twist Blindness.'"

12. For example, see Bordwell, *Narration in the Fiction Film*; Branigan, *Narrative Comprehension and Film*; Carroll, *Theorizing the Moving Image*; Smith, *Engaging Characters*; Tan, *Emotion and the Structure of Narrative Film*; Grodal, *Moving Pictures*; Anderson, *The Reality of Illusion*; and Plantinga, *Moving Viewers*. For a recent overview and collection of papers, see Nannicelli and Taberham, *Cognitive Media Theory*.

13. This is the position taken by John Searle, for example, who argues that consciousness and intentionality are properties of the brain and that the study of (human) cognition must be neuroscientific. See Searle, "Putting Consciousness Back in the Brain."

14. A distinction parallel but not reducible to the distinction between metaphysical and methodological naturalism.

15. For example, see Dennett, *Consciousness Explained*.

16. Neupert, *John Lasseter*, 58.

17. See Johansson, "Visual Perception of Biological Motion."

18. See Appiah, *Experiments in Ethics*; Alexander, *Experimental Philosophy*; and Greene, *Moral Tribes*. In the domain of aesthetics, see Meskin et al., "Mere Exposure to Bad Art"http://philpapers.org/rec/MESMET; and Liao, Strohminger, and Sripada, "Empirically Investigating Imaginative Resistance." On the relationship between early modern and contemporary experimental philosophy, see "Experimental Philosophy: Old and New," University of Otago website, http://www.otago.ac.nz/library/exhibitions/experimental_philosophy.

19. The International Association of Empirical Aesthetics is the main academic society representing empirical aesthetics, founded by Daniel Berlyne and others in 1965. The tradition, represented in the work of Fechner, Berlyne, Colin

Martindale, and Anjan Chatterjee, is also continued by the recently founded
Max Planck Institute for Empirical Aesthetics in Frankfurt.

20. See Locke, *An Essay Concerning Human Understanding*, ch. 27, sec. 9.

21. Tomasello, *The Cultural Origins of Human Communication*, ch. 3.

22. Robinson, *Deeper than Reason*, 75–9. On the "cognitive unconscious,"
see Plantinga, *Moving Viewers*, 49–50.

23. Character recognition is the focus of my *Engaging Characters*, ch. 4.

24. For background to the paragraphs that follow, see Dennett, "Philosophy
as Naive Anthropology."

25. Anderson, *The Reality of Illusion*, 61–75; see also Bordwell, *Narration in
the Fiction Film*, 99–110.

26. See Bordwell, "You and Me and Every Frog We Know."

27. See Chabris and Simons, *The Invisible Gorilla*.

28. Ibid., ch. 1.

29. See Bruce and Young, *Face Perception*.

30. On allegiance, see my *Engaging Characters*, ch. 6.

31. The role and significance of such situational understanding was made
apparent by Heider and Simmel's classic study and accompanying animated
film on the attribution of states and traits to others: Heider and Simmel, "An
Experimental Study of Apparent Behavior."

32. My thanks to Paisley Livingston for this objection.

33. See Bordwell, "You and Me and Every Frog We Know."

34. See Rozin, Haidt, and McCauley, "Disgust."

35. Goodman, *Languages of Art*, 111–12.

36. On "thick explanation," see my *Film, Art, and the Third Culture*, ch. 1.

BIBLIOGRAPHY

Alexander, Joshua. *Experimental Philosophy: An Introduction.* Cambridge: Polity
Press, 2012.

Anderson, Joseph D. *The Reality of Illusion: An Ecological Approach to Cognitive
Film Theory.* Carbondale: Southern Illinois University Press, 1996.

Appiah, Kwame Anthony. *Experiments in Ethics.* Cambridge, Mass.: Harvard
University Press, 2008.

Barratt, Daniel. " 'Twist Blindness': The Role of Primacy, Priming, Schemas,
and Reconstructive Memory in a First-Time Viewing of *The Sixth Sense.*"
In *Puzzle Films: Complex Storytelling in Contemporary Cinema*, edited by
Warren Buckland, 62–68. New York: Wiley-Blackwell, 2009.

Bordwell, David. *Narration in the Fiction Film.* Madison: University of Wisconsin Press, 1985.

———. "You and Me and Every Frog We Know." David Bordwell's Observations on Film Art, September 20, 2015. http://www.davidbordwell.net.

Branigan, Edward. *Narrative Comprehension and Film.* New York: Routledge, 1992.

Bruce, Vicki, and Andy Young. *Face Perception.* Hove, U.K.: Psychology Press, 2011.

Carroll, Noël. "The Power of Movies." *Daedalus* 114, no. 4 (Fall 1985): 79–103.

———. *Theorizing the Moving Image.* Cambridge: Cambridge University Press, 1996.

Chabris, Christopher, and Daniel Simons. *The Invisible Gorilla: And Other Ways Our Intuition Deceives Us.* New York: Harper Collins, 2010.

Dennett, Daniel C. *Consciousness Explained.* London: Allen Lane, 1991.

———. "Philosophy as Naive Anthropology: Comment on Bennett and Hacker." In *Neuroscience and Philosophy: Brain, Mind, and Language,* edited by Maxwell Bennett, Daniel Dennett, Peter Hacker, John Searle, and Daniel Robinson, 73–95. New York: Columbia University Press, 2003.

Goldstein, Daniel G., et al. "Group Report: Why and When Do Simple Heuristics Work?" In *Bounded Rationality: The Adaptive Toolbox,* edited by Gerd Gigerenzer and Reinhard Selten, 178. Cambridge, Mass.: MIT Press, 2001.

Goodman, Nelson. *Languages of Art: An Approach to a Theory of Symbols.* 2nd ed. Indianapolis, Ind.: Hackett Publishing, 1976.

Greene, Joshua. *Moral Tribes: Emotion, Reason, and the Gap between Us and Them.* London: Penguin, 2013.

Grodal, Torben. *Moving Pictures: A New Theory of Film Genres, Feelings, and Cognition.* Oxford: Oxford University Press, 1968.

Heider, Fritz, and Marianne Simmel. "An Experimental Study of Apparent Behavior." *American Journal of Psychology* 57, no. 2 (April 1944): 243–59.

Johansson, Gunnar. "Visual Perception of Biological Motion and a Model for Its Analysis." *Perception and Psychophysics* 14, no. 2 (1973): 201–11.

Keil, Geert. "Naturalism." In *The Routledge Companion to Twentieth Century Philosophy,* edited by Dermot Moran, 254. London: Routledge, 2010.

Kracauer, Siegfried. *History: The Last Things before the Last.* New York: Oxford University Press, 1995.

Liao, Shen-yi, Nina Strohminger, and Chandra Sekhar Sripada. "Empirically Investigating Imaginative Resistance." *British Journal of Aesthetics* 54, no. 3 (2014): 339–55.

Locke, John. *An Essay Concerning Human Understanding.* London, 1689.

Meskin, Aaron, Mark Phelan, Margaret Moore, and Matthew Kieran. "Mere Exposure to Bad Art." *British Journal of Aesthetics* 53, no. 2 (2013): 139–64.

Nannicelli, Ted, and Paul Taberham, eds. *Cognitive Media Theory.* New York: Routledge, 2014.

Neupert, Richard. *John Lasseter.* Urbana: University of Illinois Press, 2016.

Plantinga, Carl. *Moving Viewers: American Cinema and the Spectator's Experience.* Berkeley: University of California Press, 2009.

Ritchie, Jack. Review of *Understanding Naturalism,* by David Macarthur. *Notre Dame Philosophical Reviews,* November 10, 2009. https://ndpr.nd.edu/news/24219-understanding-naturalism.

Robinson, Jenefer. *Deeper than Reason: Emotion and Its Role in Literature, Music, and Art.* Oxford: Clarendon Press, 2005.

Rozin, Paul, Jonathan Haidt, and Clark R. McCauley. "Disgust." In *Handbook of Emotions,* 3rd ed., edited by Michael Lewis, Jeannette M. Haviland-Jones, and Lisa Feldman Barrett, 761–62. New York: Guilford Press, 2008.

Searle, John. "Putting Consciousness Back in the Brain: Reply to Bennett and Hacker." *Neuroscience and Philosophy: Brain, Mind, and Language,* edited by Maxwell Bennett, Daniel Dennett, Peter Hacker, John Searle, and Daniel Robinson, 97–124. New York: Columbia University Press, 2003.

Sellars, Roy Wood. *Evolutionary Naturalism.* New York: Russell & Russell, 1922.

Smith, Murray. *Engaging Characters: Fiction, Emotion, and the Cinema.* Oxford: Clarendon Press, 1995.

———. *Film, Art, and the Third Culture.* Oxford: Oxford University Press, 2017.

Tan, Ed. *Emotion and the Structure of Narrative Film: Film as an Emotion Machine.* London: Routledge, 1995.

Tomasello, Michael. *The Cultural Origins of Human Communication.* Cambridge, Mass.: Harvard University Press, 1999.

Acknowledgments

I offer my gratitude to the University of Minnesota Press, in particular Danielle Kasprzak and Anne Carter, for giving us the opportunity to publish this book and to all the wonderful people who contributed to this volume—it has been a real pleasure.

Special thanks go to Yasmin Afshar for all of her work.

I dedicate this book to Janna and Claudia and to the memory of Frank.

Contributors

Nicole Brenez teaches cinema studies at University of Paris 3–Sorbonne nouvelle. She is a senior member of the Institut universitaire de France and curates the French Cinémathèque's avant-garde film series. She is author of *De la figure en général et du corps en particulier: L'invention figurative au cinéma; Abel Ferrara; Traitement du lumpenprolétariat par le cinéma d'avant-garde; Cinéma d'avant-garde mode d'emploi;* and *Jean-Luc Godard théoricien des images;* and editor of *Jeune, dure et pure: Une histoire du cinéma d'avant-garde et expérimental en France; La vie nouvelle/nouvelle vision, Jean-Luc Godard: Documents;* and *Le cinéma critique: De l'argentique au numérique, voies et formes de l'objection visuelle.*

Elisabeth Bronfen is professor of English and American studies at the University of Zurich and Global Distinguished Professor at New York University. She is author of *Over Her Dead Body: Death, Femininity, and the Aesthetic; The Knotted Subject: Hysteria and Its Discontents; Home in Hollywood: The Imaginary Geography of Cinema; Specters of War: Hollywood's Engagement with Military Conflict;* and *Night Passages: Literature, Philosophy, Film.*

Noël Carroll is Distinguished Professor of Philosophy at the Graduate Center, CUNY. He is author of *Living in an Artworld; Art in Three Dimensions; Minerva's Night Out: Philosophy, Pop Culture, and Motion Pictures;* and *Humour: A Very Short Introduction.*

Tom Conley teaches in the Department of Visual and Environmental Studies and the Department of Romance Languages at Harvard University. He is author of *An Errant Eye: Poetry and Topography in Early Modern France; The Self-Made Map: Cartographic Writing in Early Modern France; Film Hieroglyphs;* and *Cartographic Cinema,* all published by the University of Minnesota Press. With T. Jefferson Kline, he is coeditor of *The Wyle-Blackwell Companion to Jean-Luc Godard.*

Angela Dalle Vacche is professor of film studies at the Georgia Institute of Technology. She is author of *The Body in the Mirror: Shapes of History in Italian Cinema; Cinema and Painting: How Art Is Used in Film;* and *Diva: Defiance and Passion in Early Italian Cinema.* She is coeditor of *The Visual Turn: Art History and Classical Film Theory* and editor of *The Color Reader* and *Film, Art, Media: Museum without Walls.*

Gregory Flaxman is associate professor of English and comparative literature at the University of North Carolina–Chapel Hill. He is author of *Gilles Deleuze and the Fabulation of Philosophy* (Minnesota, 2011) and editor of *The Brain Is the Screen* (Minnesota, 2010). With Robert Sinnerbrink and Lisa Trahair, he is coauthor of the forthcoming *Understanding Cinematic Thinking: Film-Philosophy in Bresson, Von Trier, and Haneke.*

Bernd Herzogenrath is professor of American literature and culture at Goethe University Frankfurt. He is author of *An Art of Desire: Reading Paul Auster* and *An American Body/Politic: A Deleuzian Approach* and editor of *The Farthest Place: The Music of John Luther Adams; Time and History in Deleuze and Serres;* and *media/matter.* He is editor, with Patricia Pisters, of the media-philosophical book series thinking/media.

Alex Ling is research lecturer in communication and media studies at Western Sydney University. He is author of *Badiou Reframed* and *Badiou and Cinema.* He is coeditor and translator, with A. J. Bartlett, of Badiou's *Mathematics of the Transcendental.*

Adrian Martin is professor of film studies at Monash University, Melbourne. He is author of *Phantasms; Once Upon a Time in America; Raúl Ruiz: Magnificent Obsessions; The Mad Max Movies; Last Day Every Day; What Is Modern Cinema?* and *Mise en Scène and Film Style: From Classical Hollywood to New Media Art.* He is coeditor of the online film journals *LOLA* and *Screening the Past* and the books *Movie Mutations* and *Raúl Ruiz: Images of Passage.*

John Ó Maoilearca is professor of film and television studies at Kingston University, London. He is author of *Bergson and Philosophy, Post-Continental Philosophy: An Outline* and *Philosophy and the Moving Image: Refractions of Reality* and editor of *Bergson and the Art of Immanence* and *The Bloomsbury Companion to Continental Philosophy.* His most recent book is *All Thoughts Are Equal: Laruelle and Nonhuman Philosophy* (Minnesota, 2015).

Robert Sinnerbrink is Australian Research Council Future Fellow and senior lecturer in philosophy at Macquarie University, Sydney. He is author of *Cinematic Ethics: Exploring Ethical Experience through Film; New Philosophies of Film: Thinking Images;* and *Understanding Hegelianism* and coeditor of *Critique Today.* He is coauthor, with Lisa Trahair and Gregory Flaxman, of the forthcoming *Understanding Cinematic Thinking: Film-Philosophy in Bresson, Von Trier, and Haneke.*

Murray Smith is professor of film studies at the University of Kent, Canterbury, codirector of the Aesthetics Research Centre at Kent, and president of the Society for Cognitive Studies of the Moving Image. He is author of *Engaging Characters: Fiction, Emotion, and the Cinema; Trainspotting;* and *Film, Art, and the Third Culture.* He is coeditor of *Film Theory and Philosophy; Contemporary Hollywood Cinema;* and *Thinking through Cinema.*

Julia Vassilieva is lecturer in film and television studies at Monash University, Melbourne. She is coeditor of *After Taste: Cultural Value and the Moving Image.* Her *Life. Narrative. Event.* is forthcoming.

Christophe Wall-Romana is associate professor in the Department of French and Italian at the University of Minnesota and affiliated faculty in the graduate major for moving image studies. He is author of *Cinepoetry: Imaginary Cinemas in French Poetry* and *Jean Epstein: Corporeal Cinema and Film Philosophy.* He is translator of *The Intelligence of a Machine,* by Jean Epstein, and cotranslator of the forthcoming *Invention and Imagination,* by George Simondon.

Thomas E. Wartenberg is senior research fellow in philosophy at Mount Holyoke College. He is author of *Thinking on Screen: Film as Philosophy; Unlikely Couples: Movie Romance and Social Criticism;* and *Fight Club.* He is active in philosophy for children and author of *Big Ideas for Little Kids: Teaching Philosophy through Children's Literature* and *A Sneetch Is a Sneetch and Other Philosophical Discoveries: Finding Wisdom in Children's Literature.*

Index

actual, xiv, 1–2, 18–19, 42n41, 61, 93,
  106, 125, 127, 164–65, 169, 172,
  174–75, 205, 245, 268, 306, 308,
  310, 322, 325
affect, ix, xii–xiii, xvi–xviii, 14, 27–29,
  31–32, 39, 52, 54, 68, 70, 72, 76,
  80, 83, 91–94, 96–97, 100–101,
  167, 172, 176, 177n24, 193, 203,
  220, 234, 256–57, 260
Agamben, Giorgio, 8–9, 20nn20–23,
  122, 125, 129n34, 129n39
allegiance, with characters, 31, 322,
  328n30
Alquié, Ferdinand, 222
Aristotle, 81, 104, 247–48, 255,
  263n36; *Nicomachean Ethics,* 290
Artaud, Antonin, xvi, 30, 66,
  68–70, 72–79, 82, 84, 84nn2–8,
  84nn10–12, 85nn14–16, 85n18,
  85nn20–28, 85nn30–47,
  86nn49–70, 87n81, 222, 224,
  228, 231–32, 234–36, 238n5,
  238n12, 239n26, 239n29, 239n33;
  Le cinéma brut, 80; Theater of
  Cruelty, 66–67, 71, 84n9
atmosphere, 51, 53, 55, 80, 137
Azam, Olivier, 220

Bazin, André, viii, xvii–xviii, 10,
  45–46, 49, 57, 59, 84n9, 112, 117,
  128n5, 129n27, 132–38, 140–56,
  156n1, 156nn3–5, 156nn9–13,
  157n15, 157n17, 157n22, 157n24,
  157nn29–30, 157nn33–34,
  157n36, 157n38, 158n42, 207,
  215n33, 247
behaviorism, 8–9, 16

Benjamin, Walter, 40, 43n55, 45, 49,
  57, 77, 87n84
Bergson, Henri, viii, ix–x, xiv, xviii,
  xxiiin6, 1–7, 9–10, 14, 16–19,
  19nn2–3, 19nn5–8, 19nn11–12,
  20nn14–19, 20n24, 20nn41–44,
  43n52, 92, 94, 98–100, 103–4,
  106, 108n33, 132, 146–47, 150–51,
  153–55, 156n1, 157n41, 158n45,
  163–64, 172–73, 177nn8–9,
  177n15, 268
Blanchot, Maurice, 66, 84n1, 84n5
Blomkamp, Neill: *District 9* (2009),
  xxii, 306, 309–10, 317–18, 320–21,
  324–25
Bontemps, Jacques, 222, 224
Bordwell, David, viii, 59, 64n46,
  115, 128n15, 128n17, 129n52, 312,
  327nn11–12, 328nn25–26, 328n33
Bousquet, Joë, 224, 232
Brau, Jean-Louis, 234, 239n29
Bresson, Robert, 257, 268
Bull, Lucien, 231
Buñuel, Luis: *Le chien Andalou*
  (1929), 68

Carasco, Raymonde, xix–xx, 115,
  129n18, 219–37, 238n1, 238n4,
  238nn9–10, 238n13, 238nn17–20,
  239n21, 239nn23–24, 239nn26–28,
  239n30, 239nn32–35
Carroll, Noël, viii, xx, 24, 28, 35–38,
  41n4, 42n18, 42n43, 43n49, 43n51,
  53, 56, 63n25, 64n36, 283n6,
  284n7, 308, 327n2, 327n12
Cavell, Stanley, viii, xi, xviii, xix,
  38, 180–91, 193–98, 268, 288–89;

Contesting Tears (1996), 182, 190, 197, 288; *Pursuits of Happiness* (1981), 182, 198nn4–7, 199nn8–16, 288; *The World Viewed* (1979), 43n54, 197, 198nn2–3, 199nn17–22
Cezanne, Paul, 151–53, 155, 224
cinematic cartography, 241, 244–46, 262n16, 262n20
cinematic fable, 247, 253, 262nn24–26, 262n28, 263n34
cinephilia, 54, 79, 90–91, 133, 243, 246, 257, 260, 261n10
classic Hollywood cinema, xix, 181–82, 196
coenasthesis, xvii, 93–94
cognitive film theory, viii, ix, xxii, 312, 314
comedy of remarriage, xix, 182–86, 189–91, 193, 288
communism, 47–48, 51, 129n36, 139, 141–42, 201, 259–60
condition, xvi, xviii, xxi, 35–37, 47, 57–58, 61, 69, 100, 125, 140, 149, 169, 181–82, 186, 201–4, 210–11, 213n16, 213n18, 216n57, 238n6, 241, 269–74, 278, 324
Costa, Pedro, 257
Cukor, George: *The Philadelphia Story* (1940), 184, 186–87, 190

Deleuze, Gilles, viii, ix–xiv, xvii–xviii, xxiiin5, xxiiinn7–8, xxiiin11, xxiiinn13–15, xxiiin17, 1, 3, 18–19, 19n1, 19n3, 28, 30, 42n20, 42n28, 52, 54, 62, 63n28, 64n56, 70, 77, 82, 85n17, 85nn19–20, 86n44, 86n48, 87n76, 87nn79–80, 87n84, 90, 94, 99–100, 103, 105–6, 108n34, 108n36, 112, 128n7, 161–65, 176, 176n1, 177nn2–6, 177nn10–14, 177nn16–18, 177n24, 178nn28–33, 178n37, 206, 212n4, 220, 222, 226, 231, 239n33, 242,

244–46, 258, 261n12, 262nn13–16, 262n27, 263n37
Deren, Maya, 225n6
Descartes, René, 7, 69, 80, 86n71, 98, 222, 270; deviation (*écart*), xx, 241, 245–46, 253, 256–57, 261
diagram, 244–45, 262n16
dignity, xxi, 116–17, 293–304, 304n3
distribution, of space, 245–46
Dreyer, Carl Theodor, 67, 73–74
Dufrenne, Mikel, 222, 238n2
Duhamel, Georges, 83, 87n84
Dulac, Germaine, 84n7; *The Seashell and the Clergyman* (1928), 67–68
Du Luart, Yolande, 220

education, 6, 24, 38, 47, 144, 155, 180, 258
Einstein, Albert, 111, 153, 158n45
Eisenstein, Sergei, xvii–xviii, 46, 48, 52, 57, 77, 111–28, 128nn1–2, 128n4, 128nn10–12, 128nn15–17, 129nn18–19, 129n22, 129nn28–32, 129n35, 129nn37–38, 129nn43–46, 129n48, 129n52, 154, 161, 222–24, 228, 231–33, 272–73
ekstasis, 126–27
Emerson, Ralph Waldo, 181, 183, 189, 191, 195–96, 198
Epstein, Jean, xvi–xvii, 30, 42n28, 45–48, 54, 57, 76, 90–107, 107nn1–3, 107nn5–6, 108nn9–31, 108nn36–39, 108nn41–42, 109nn43–49
equality, as method, 241–42, 247, 257, 261
euthanasia, xxi, 288, 293, 301–4
event, vii, xx, 27, 29–30, 34, 42n41, 61, 82, 97, 112, 114, 116–17, 127, 138, 141, 148–49, 175, 187–88, 205, 210, 211n1, 212n12, 213n18, 214n25, 214n27, 220, 224, 232, 236–37,

239n33, 243, 245–47, 250, 253,
258–61, 261n11, 263nn36–37, 293,
306, 308, 311
exile, 47, 51
experience, xv, xvii, xx, xxii, 1–2,
11–12, 24–27, 30–40, 48, 50, 52,
56, 62, 70, 73, 77, 80–83, 90, 93,
99, 112, 145, 149, 151, 155, 162, 170,
175, 180–82, 185, 191, 193, 196–98,
223, 232–33, 238n6, 257–58,
260–61, 263n36, 279–80, 287,
289, 291, 293, 295–96, 298, 300,
306, 308, 314–17, 323–24

face, xiii, 15, 17, 28, 31, 37, 52–55, 60,
63n17, 93, 107, 119, 168, 194–96,
220, 247–48, 250, 260, 295, 313,
320, 322, 328n29
facial perception, xxii, 320–22, 325
fairy tale, 50–52, 55
Fatmi, Mounir, 220
fiction, 36, 46, 48, 50, 95–96, 138,
175, 222, 230, 232, 242, 269, 271,
280–82, 299, 306–8, 310, 318, 322,
325, 327nn11–12, 328n25

Gehr, Ernie: Serene Velocity (1970),
277–78
gesture, xiv, xxii, 1, 3, 5–9, 14–15,
17–19, 20nn21–23, 28–29, 31,
58–60, 62, 68, 82, 128, 136, 184,
189, 205, 215n40, 226–27, 235,
248, 260, 313, 322
Giacometti, Alberto, 152, 158n44
Grandrieux, Philippe, 220–21
Granel, Gérard, 222, 238n2
Greggory, Pascal, 222

Hanoun, Marcel, 220, 222, 224
Hébraud, Régis, xx, 219, 221, 223–25,
232, 235, 238, 239n22, 239n31,
239n33
Hegel, G. W. F., 53, 101, 241, 269;

Phenomenology of Spirit (1807),
300–301, 305n10
Heidegger, Martin, 85n19, 115, 238n2,
276
homosexuality, xvii, 92, 100–101,
108n39

immanent, xvii, xix, 1, 5, 13–14, 77,
81, 94, 99, 105, 138, 161, 175, 203–8
impure, 74–75, 132, 149, 157n18, 201,
206–11, 215n33, 215n40
inaesthetics, xix, 202–6, 210,
212n6, 213n17, 213nn19–23,
214n26, 214n28, 214n30, 215n32,
215nn36–37, 216nn51–52
inessential, xix, 206–7, 209, 211

Jensen, Wilhelm, 229, 231, 238n16
joint attention, 314–15, 325
journalism, 48–49, 133, 183, 318

Kant, Immanuel, xv, xxi, 5, 25–26,
32–34, 39–40, 41n8, 104, 137, 222,
225–26, 232, 238n2, 238n6, 274;
Groundwork to the Metaphysics of
Morals (1785), 293, 304n4
Kittler, Friedrich, xxiiin1, 85n29
Knight, Deborah, xxi, 280–82, 284n8

language, xvi–xvii, 14, 47, 55, 75,
86n44, 95–97, 101, 112, 118, 120,
138, 146, 150, 171, 210, 245, 266,
270–71, 279, 328n35
Lasseter, John, 327n16; Luxo Jr.
(1986), 313
Leibniz, G. W., xvi, 69–70, 80–81,
85n17, 87n75, 87nn77–78, 263n37
Le Rigoleur, Dominique, 230
Leth, Jørgen: The Five Obstructions
(2003), xiv, 3–4, 9–14, 16, 18
Livingston, Paisley, xxi, 13, 16, 20n33,
269–74, 276–78, 283nn1–2,
328n32

Lumholtz, Carl, 227, 238n11
Lynch, David, 168, 177n18; *Lost Highway* (1997), xviii, 161, 165–67, 170–76, 178n34
lyrosophy, xvi, 91–92, 99–100, 102, 106, 107n3

machine, ix, xvii, 17, 30, 50, 58, 73, 76, 84, 85n26, 85n29, 87n82, 93, 98, 100, 102–3, 105–6, 107n2, 147–48, 162, 176n1, 229, 236, 239n33, 244, 246
Mann, Anthony, 243, 247, 261, 262n26
Married Woman, A (Godard), 275
melodrama, xix, 61, 182, 190–94, 196–98, 288
Merleau-Ponty, Maurice, viii, xviii, 132–33, 147, 151–56, 156n5, 157n41, 158n47, 158n49
metempsychosis, 83–84
Milton, John, 187
Möbius strip, 170–74, 176, 178n34
modernity, xvi, 49, 57, 91–92, 94–95, 108n36, 138, 181
montage, 29, 36, 52, 76, 91, 93, 111, 113–15, 117–20, 126, 128nn10–11, 129n19, 129n45, 134, 150, 154, 163, 174, 206, 223, 238n17, 238n20, 270, 272, 273
moral perfectionism, xix, 182, 196, 288
Mounier, Emmanuel, xviii, 132, 142–44, 146, 153, 155–56, 157n26, 157n28, 157nn31–32, 158n45
movement-image, x, xvii, 76, 112, 162, 165, 167, 169, 174, 178n34
movie-made philosophy, xx, 268–74, 276–77, 279–80, 283, 284n9

Nancy, Jean-Luc, 115, 127, 128n3, 129n47, 129n53, 220
naturalism, philosophical, xvii,

xxi–xxii, 16, 101–2, 308, 310–14, 318, 324–26, 327nn3–7, 327n14
non-art, 208–9, 215n40
nonfiction, 46, 138, 306, 308
Nuytten, Bruno, 230

Ossang, F. J., 220

parallelism, 69, 81
Pascal, Blaise, xi, xviii, 17, 132, 147–50, 157nn39–40, 216n56, 270
Perrier, Mireille, 222
personhood, xxii, 265, 316, 324, 326
philosophy in film, xi
photogeny, xvi, 91–95, 99, 102, 107, 108n9, 188
plane, unified intellectual, xvii, 97–100
politics of the auteur/amateur, xx, 256–57
Prenant, Franssou, 220
primacy effect, 311
Prose, Francine, 287, 304n1

quantum physics, 151, 153, 158n45

recognition, of characters, xxii, 310–11, 317, 319–21, 328n23
recognition heuristic, 311
representation, xi–xii, xiv, 9, 14, 18, 34–35, 76–78, 86n47, 93, 99, 103, 114, 177, 124, 162, 167–68, 170, 176, 202, 263n34, 306, 324–25
Rouch, Jean, 84n9, 220–21, 224, 227, 235, 239n35
Russell, Bruce, xxi, 269, 271, 277–79, 283n2, 304

Sartre, Jean-Paul, xviii, 132–34, 136–44, 146–47, 152, 154, 156nn2–3, 156nn5–8, 157n14, 157n16, 157nn19–20, 157n23, 219, 245

Shakespeare, William, 61; *A Midsummer Night's Dream*, 184, 186; *Othello*, 186
Shklovsky, Viktor, 233
silent cinema, 46, 55, 195
singular, xiv, 3, 34, 62, 80, 92, 129n47, 191, 197, 201, 204–7, 210–11, 213n16, 216n56, 220, 226, 233, 235, 246
situational cognition, 325
skepticism, xix, 265, 268, 277, 288–89
Smith, Murray, viii, xxi, 11, 31, 269, 271, 276, 280, 326n1
Smuts, Aaron, 272–73, 283n4
species chauvinism, 325
Spinoza, Baruch, xvi, 69–70, 80–81, 85n17, 86–87nn71–74, 92, 94, 98–99, 234, 236
St. Augustine, xviii, 132, 147, 149, 157n37, 157n40, 270
subpersonal, xxii, 314, 316–17, 324–26

Téchiné, André, 222, 224
theater, xvi, 8, 15, 24, 26, 28–29, 31–32, 34–36, 48, 56, 61–62, 66–67, 71, 73, 75, 77, 84n3, 84n9, 85nn23–26, 87n83, 133–34, 137, 139–40, 148, 181, 194, 201, 207, 226, 243, 246, 253, 255–56, 261n2, 263n36

thick explanation, 326, 328n36
thought experiment, 47, 271, 275–83, 284n9, 289–90, 302
time-image, x, 162, 164–65, 169, 172, 174–75
topology, 161, 170, 173–74
truth, xvi, xix, 15, 17–18, 57, 67, 74, 80, 84, 176, 202–5, 207–8, 210, 212n3, 214nn27–29, 216n42, 219, 244, 271, 276, 278, 282

Vico, Giambattista, 232
Vidor, King, 219, 267; *Stella Dallas* (1937), 192, 194, 196–98
virtual, xiv, 1–3, 6, 15, 18–19, 19n3, 35, 47, 68, 76–77, 87n83, 93, 98, 106–7, 165, 169, 172–75, 202
Von Trier, Lars, xiv, 3–4, 9–10, 12–13, 16, 18, 32

Walsh, Raoul, 243, 253, 256, 261
Wartenberg, Thomas, viii, xxi, 273–75, 283; *Thinking on Screen: Film as Philosophy* (2007), 283n5; *Unlikely Couples: Movie Romance as Social Criticism* (1999), 289

Žižek, Slavoj, xi, 117, 129n26, 266